American Furniture

AMERICAN FURNITURE 1997

Edited by Luke Beckerdite

Published by the CHIPSTONE FOUNDATION

Distributed by University Press of New England

Hanover and London

Cover Illustration: Detail of the hood of a tall clock case attributed to Peter Raff with movement attributed to Peter Whipple, Pulaski County, Virginia, ca. 1815. (Courtesy, Colonial Williamsburg Foundation; photo, Gavin Ashworth.)

Design: Wynne Patterson, Pittsfield, Vermont
Photography: Gavin Ashworth, New York, New York

Published by the Chipstone Foundation, 7820 North Club Circle, Milwaukee, WI 53217
Distributed by University Press of New England, Hanover, NH 03755
© 1997 by the Chipstone Foundation
All rights reserved
Printed in the United States of America 5 4 3 2 1
ISSN 1069–4188
ISBN 0–87451–851–2

Contents

Editorial Statement

American Furniture is an interdisciplinary journal dedicated to advancing knowledge of furniture made or used in the Americas from the seventeenth century to the present. Authors are encouraged to submit articles on any aspect of furniture history, essays on conservation and historic technology, reproductions or transcripts of documents, such as account books and inventories, annotated photographs of new furniture discoveries, and book and exhibition reviews. References for compiling an annual bibliography also are welcome.

Manuscripts must be typed, double-spaced, illustrated with black-and-white prints or transparencies, and prepared in accordance with the *Chicago Manual of Style*. Computer disk copy is requested but not required. The Chipstone Foundation will offer significant honoraria for manuscripts accepted for publication and reimburse authors for all photography approved in writing by the editor.

Luke Beckerdite

Preface

The Chipstone Foundation was organized in 1965 by Stanley Stone and Polly Mariner Stone of Fox Point, Wisconsin. Representing the culmination of their shared experiences in collecting American furniture, American historical prints, and early English pottery, the foundation was created with the dual purpose of preserving and interpreting their collection and stimulating research and education in the decorative arts.

The Stones began collecting American decorative arts in 1946, and by 1964 it became apparent to them that provisions should be made to deal with their collection. With the counsel of their friend Charles Montgomery, the Stones decided that their collection should be published and exhibited.

Following Stanley Stone's death in 1987, the foundation was activated by an initial endowment provided by Mrs. Stone. This generous donation allowed the foundation to institute its research and grant programs, begin work on three collection catalogues, and launch an important new journal, *American Furniture*.

Allen M. Taylor

Introduction

Luke Beckerdite

The 1997 volume of *American Furniture* is comprised of papers presented at "A Region of Regions: Cultural Diversity and the Furniture Trade in the Early South," a symposium cosponsored by the Chipstone Foundation and the Colonial Williamsburg Foundation. In many respects, these essays continue a dialogue that began five years earlier at a symposium titled "Diversity and Innovation in American Regional Furniture," which examined furniture produced in the northern and middle Atlantic regions during the seventeenth, eighteenth, and early nineteenth centuries. Both symposiums explored a variety of topics central to the study of American material life, including the relationship between artisanry and ethnic identity; the cultural, economic, stylistic, and technological factors influencing diversity and choice; the effect of social relationships, expectations, and aspirations on patronage; and the development and diffusion of transatlantic and American regional styles.[1]

By the 1920s, a handful of scholars—primarily dealers such as Mr. and Mrs. J. L. Brockwell of Petersburg, Virginia, J. K. Beard of Richmond, Virginia, and Joe Kindig, Jr., of York, Pennsylvania—began to realize that southern decorative arts were regionally distinctive and different from those produced elsewhere in America. In the October 1923 issue of *Antiques*, Beard advertised "Virginia Gate-legged Tables" for $3,000 per dozen, a remarkable offering considering the scarcity of late seventeenth- and early eighteenth-century examples today. Many of these early attributions were based more on family or recovery histories than on stylistic or structural details; however, early antiquarians understood that certain woods used in furniture making were indigenous to the South.[2]

Esther Singleton's *The Furniture of Our Forefathers* (1901) was the first book to discuss furniture used in the South during the colonial and early Federal periods. Although most of her research was based on period correspondence, inventories, and other documentary sources, she illustrated several pieces of southern furniture and discussed the social and domestic contexts of similar forms. Paul H. Burroughs's *Southern Antiques* (1931) was the first monograph devoted solely to southern furniture and one of the earliest regional studies. Since the publication of Irving W. Lyon's *Colonial Furniture of New England* (1891), most of the books on American furniture had been large pictorial compendiums of objects from New England, New York, and Pennsylvania. Burroughs sought to dispel the myth that southerners imported virtually all of their furnishings from Britain and to prove that "many craftsmen came to the southern colonies and produced work . . . comparable with the best made in [other areas of] America."[3]

Despite the work of the aforementioned scholars and a newer generation of antiquarians such as E. Milby Burton, Henry Green, and Frank Horton, myths and prejudices toward southern decorative arts persisted. During his lecture on regional characteristics in American furniture at the first Antiques Forum in Williamsburg in 1949, Joseph Downs, curator of the American Wing at the Metropolitan Museum of Art, remarked that "little of artistic merit was made south of Baltimore." During the question and answer session that followed, an irate southern lady asked Downs if his statement had been made "out of prejudice or ignorance."[4]

The 1949 Antiques Forum served as a catalyst for new research on southern decorative arts. Three years later, "Furniture of the Old South 1640–1820" was the subject of the Antiques Forum, a landmark exhibition at the Virginia Museum, and a special issue of *Antiques*. More importantly, the events emanating from the first forum inspired Frank Horton and his mother, Theo. L. Taliferro, to begin laying the groundwork for the Museum of Early Southern Decorative Arts (MESDA), which opened in January 1965. A visionary from the outset, Horton intended the museum to be a resource for other scholars and students of southern history and material culture. With support from the National Endowment of the Humanities, MESDA launched an unprecedented field and documentary research program in 1972. To date, the museum has recorded detailed information on over 75,000 artisans working in 127 different trades, entered the information on a computerized database, and assembled photographic files on approximately 25,000 objects made in the South. To disseminate this information, MESDA began publishing the *Journal of Early Southern Decorative Arts* in 1975 and the Horton series of monographs in 1988. The first publication in the series, John Bivins's *The Furniture of Coastal North Carolina, 1700–1820*, set a standard for regional furniture studies that has yet to be surpassed. All of the articles presented in this volume of *American Furniture* and virtually every recent publication in the field of southern decorative arts owe a deep debt of gratitude to Frank Horton and MESDA's dedicated staff.[5]

Just as MESDA has led the way in documenting southern artisans and their work, the Colonial Williamsburg Foundation has led the way in interpreting American material culture. Prior to the 1970s, the buildings at Colonial Williamsburg were essentially "architectural settings for 'tasteful' assemblages of great collections." Since then, the foundation's curators, conservators, archaeologists, and historians have used inventories, pictorial sources, objects with local histories of use, and other forms of documentation to recreate the regional context of the town's buildings and furnishings. The redecoration and refurnishing of the Governor's Palace in 1980 revolutionized the way museums exhibit and interpret historic houses and their contents. It is a great credit to the foundation and its staff that this process of re-evaluation and refinement continues today. Colonial Williamsburg staff members have also made numerous contributions to southern furniture scholarship. Wallace Gusler's *Furniture of Williamsburg and Eastern Virginia, 1710–1790* (1979), Ronald Hurst and Jonathan Prown's *Southern Furniture, 1680–1830: The Colonial Williamsburg Collection* (1997), and articles by other members of the foundation's curatorial, conservation, and historic trades divisions are among the most significant works in the field.[6]

The Charleston Museum and Historic Charleston Foundation have been equally instrumental in focusing attention on the Low Country's history, architecture, and material culture. The Charleston Museum's extraordinary furniture collection, currently displayed in the museum and its historic houses, received national attention following the publication of E. Milby Burton's "The Furniture of Charleston" in the 1952 issue of *Antiques* and *Charleston Furniture, 1700–1825* in 1955. Subsequent scholars such as Chris Loeblein of the Charleston Museum and J. Thomas Savage, Robert Leath, and Jonathan Poston of the Historic Charleston Foundation are largely responsible for the recent renaissance of interest in the city and its culture. The Historic Charleston Foundation's staff deserves special credit for aggressively preserving important properties, for accurately restoring, furnishing, and interpreting the Nathaniel Russell House, Aiken-Rhett House, and Powder Magazine, and for publishing books and articles on Low Country material culture.[7]

The Baltimore Museum of Art and Maryland Historical Society's impact on southern furniture scholarship are revealed by a host of landmark exhibitions and publications including *Baltimore Furniture: The Work of Baltimore and Annapolis Cabinetmakers* (1947), William Voss Elder, III's *Maryland Queen Anne and Chippendale Furniture of the Eighteenth Century* (1968), *Baltimore Painted Furniture, 1800–1840* (1972), Elder and Lou Bartlett's *John Shaw, Cabinetmaker of Annapolis* (1983), Gregory R. Weidman's *Furniture in Maryland, 1740–1940: The Collection of the Maryland Historical Society* (1984), and *Classical Maryland, 1815–1845* (1993). Also contributing to the study of Maryland history and decorative arts are a number of historical commissions and trusts and county and town historical societies.

Historical societies and house museums such as Homewood, Mount Vernon, Gunston Hall, Kenmore, Monticello, and Hope Plantation have traditionally collected, preserved, and published objects with local and often site-specific histories. Because of their documentation, such objects serve as benchmarks for identifying the work of individual shops and schools and for understanding regional cultures, economies, and tastes. Much of the work on specific shop traditions is due to the efforts of independent scholars such as Sumpter Priddy, III, J. Roderick Moore, and Jim and Marilyn Melchor, whose research has appeared in catalogues, books, and articles in *Antiques*, the *Journal of Early Southern Decorative Arts*, and *American Furniture*.

Crediting all of the individuals and institutions responsible for the current state of southern furniture studies is beyond the scope of this introduction. As the aforementioned exhibitions and publications suggest, interest in the field is growing at an astonishing pace. If the Colonial Williamsburg Foundation's current exhibition *Furniture of the American South: The Colonial Williamsburg Collection*, Ronald Hurst and Jonathan Prown's *Southern Furniture, 1680–1830: The Colonial Williamsburg Collection*, and John Bivins and Bradford Rauschenberg's forthcoming monograph *Charleston Furniture, 1680-1820*, are any indication, an exciting future awaits us.

1. "Diversity and Innovation in American Regional Furniture" was sponsored by the Wadsworth Atheneum, Trinity College, and the Chipstone Foundation and held at Hartford, Connecticut, in 1993. The papers presented at this symposium appeared in Luke Beckerdite and William N. Hosley, eds., *American Furniture* (Hanover, N.H.: University Press of New England for the Chipstone Foundation, 1995).

2. Conversations with Frank L. Horton and Joe Kindig, III. *Antiques* 4, no. 4 (October 1923): 193.

3. Paul H. Burroughs, *Southern Antiques* (Richmond: Garrett & Massie, Inc., 1931), p. v.

4. Conversations with Frank L. Horton.

5. The author thanks Frank Horton, Martha Rowe, and Cornelia Wright of MESDA for information on MESDA's programs and artisan and photographic files.

6. *Colonial Williamsburg Today* 3, no. 2 (spring 1981). William N. Hosely, "Regional Furniture/Regional Life," in Beckerdite and Hosley, eds., *American Furniture*, p. 6.

7. See, for example, Maurie D. McInnis and Robert A. Leath, "Beautiful Specimens, Elegant Patterns: New York Furniture for the Charleston Market, 1810–1840," in *American Furniture,* edited by Luke Beckerdite (Hanover, N.H.: University Press of New England for the Chipstone Foundation, 1996), pp. 137–75.

American Furniture

Jonathan Prown

A "Preponderance
of Pineapples":
The Problem of
Southern Furniture

*For generous helpfulness in bringing the material together, [thanks] to Miss
Sophie Harrill, of Knoxville, who, having become resentful of Northern insinua-
tions as to the preponderance of pineapples among antiquities of the South, has
undertaken to furnish proof of the existence of far finer fruits of early craftsmanship below the Mason Dixon Line.*

Antiques, January 1927

▼ THIS VOLUME OF *American Furniture* is comprised of
essays presented at "A Region of Regions: Cultural Diversity and the Furniture Trade in the Early South," a 1997 symposium cosponsored by the
Chipstone Foundation and the Colonial Williamsburg Foundation.
Together with the publication of *Southern Furniture, 1680–1830: The Colonial
Williamsburg Collection* and its accompanying exhibition, these essays bring
much-needed attention to an American regional craft tradition that for the
most part has received only parochial notice. By revealing the unexpected
multicultural flavor of the region, these studies also point toward new direc-
tions in American furniture scholarship, notably in the areas of regionalism
and material culture methodology. On a more theoretical level, these publications challenge time-honored assumptions about American furniture
and, in doing so, subvert popular notions about American history and culture.

My essay will suggest a new interpretive framework upon which to
ground recent southern material culture scholarship. More specifically, it
will explore and critically reassess the "Idea of the South," which not only
shapes conventional American furniture analysis but also fundamentally
informs popular interpretation of American history. Two main themes will
be forwarded. The first suggests that southern furniture scholars need to
recognize and, when necessary, respond to cultural generalizations that are
poorly informed or deliberately fictive. New publications and exhibitions of
new studies will help counterbalance the narrow focus of conventional decorative arts literature. Quantity alone, however, will not reshape deeply entrenched cultural notions, notably, the common tendency to portray the
early North and, in particular, New England as normative and the early
South as deviant. American popular history traces the roots of national
identity to the Puritans who landed at Plymouth Rock in 1620, not to the
Virginians who founded Jamestown more than a decade earlier. Such interpretive imbalances, in turn, suggest a reconsideration of popular ideas
about the South that reflect "distorted cultural stereotypes and even exag-
gerated caricatures of the mythic entity that can mislead and misinform."[1]

Paradoxically, the second part of this essay proposes that significant insight can emerge from a closer inspection of certain lasting ideas about regional identity. This strategy entails looking not at what northerners and southerners were but rather at what residents of both regions *perceived* the North and South to be. Thus, while scholars need more thoughtfully to contextualize prejudicial characterizations of the South they also need to recognize the power of popular regional depictions to reveal hidden truths that can offer valuable insight into early American material culture.

The inferior status of southern furniture in the American decorative arts world has many causes. To be sure, much of the blame lies with early American collectors, dealers, and scholars who equated the South's agrarian character with an inability to engage in sophisticated or large-scale furniture production. Yet, their viewpoint represents less a cause than a symptom of the minimal consideration of southern furniture. Even more significant is a particular moment in time—one that is universally recognized by historians but rarely mentioned by decorative arts enthusiasts. On April 9, 1865, at Appomattox Courthouse in Virginia, General Robert E. Lee signed terms of surrender ending the four-year conflict between the Confederate States and the Union. More than just the end of the Civil War, this date marks the very instant when the cultural perspective of the white South was effectively rendered illegitimate (fig. 1). (The perspective of the black South never even

Figure 1 Charles Kimmel, *The End of the Rebellion in the United States*, New York, 1865. Lithograph printed in black and green olive on woven paper. (Courtesy, Library of Congress.)

attained widespread recognition.) Not content with the demographic, economic, and political gains that came with victory, northern leaders sought to fundamentally reconfigure the South. Expressing a typical view, Senator Thaddeus Stevens, a prominent reconstructionist, called for a total reform of the region: "The foundation of their institutions—political, municipal, and social—must be broken up. This can only be done by treating and holding them as a conquered people."[2]

Post–Civil War popular history plainly reflects the overwhelming success of the North's cultural triumph. Explained one staunch defender of the Old South, "The North defeated the South in war, crushed and humiliated it in peace, and waged against it a war of intellectual and spiritual conquest." The victors earned the right to redefine and reshape the American story, which ever since has been filtered through a northern lens and colored to satisfy northern sensibilities. As a consequence, general understanding of the American past is incomplete and, instead, mirrors Winston Churchill's war aphorism that "The victors forget, the vanquished remember."[3]

Even the most rudimentary historical assumptions reflect how the distinction between fact and fiction is blurred to create a morally palatable national narrative. We need only look at common attitudes about the Civil War. General Ulysses S. Grant and other northern military and political leaders are justly cited for their help in ending the atrocity of slavery. On the other hand, popular history conveniently forgets that some of these northern leaders, including Grant, were slave owners, while a number of key southern military leaders, including General Lee, publicly denounced the institution. Portrayals of President Abraham Lincoln are similarly skewed. Although widely hailed in historical lore as a progressive social reformer and

Figure 2   The Rail Candidate, attributed to Louis Maurer and published by Currier & Ives, New York, 1860. Lithograph on woven paper. (Courtesy, Library of Congerss.)

leader in the fight to end slavery, Lincoln was actually a staunch social conservative who in 1860 was elected president of a slaveholding republic and whose campaign platform unmistakably defended the individual rights of the slave states. Deleted from popular memory is Lincoln's profound discomfort with the idea of freeing slaves, whom he wanted to "return" to Africa; indeed, the author of the Emancipation Proclamation once informed a group of African-American leaders that "in this broad continent not a single man of your race is made the equal of a single man of ours . . . it is a fact . . . it is better for us both, therefore, to be separated" (fig. 2).[4]

Of course, historical revisionism of this sort resonates discordantly within our collective national consciousness and undermines traditional character-

Figure 3 David Hunter Strother, *The Horse Camp in Dismal Swamp*, North Carolina, 1865. Ink wash on beige paper. (Private collection; photo, Andre Lovinescu.)

Figure 4 Cupboard, Amherst County, Virginia, 1760–1840. Oak. H. 66¼", W. 25½", D. 11¼". (Courtesy, Colonial Williamsburg Foundation; photo, Hans Lorenz.)

izations about the progressive North and the backward South (fig. 3). These examples are not meant, however, to rekindle centuries-old interregional antagonisms nor to mitigate in any way the human tragedy of the South's "peculiar institution." Instead, these examples validate Churchill's adage that history is not a fair game. On April 9, 1865, the North earned the right to reconfigure the American story. In the decades that followed, northern scholars, dealers, collectors, and curators laid the conceptual foundations for an American *furniture* story, which fully realized de Toqueville's prophesy that "the civilization of the North appears to be the common standard, to which the whole nation will one day be assimilated." Still largely intact today, the American furniture story is centered around the same regional hierarchy that defines popular history. Here, regionalism acts as a metaphor for the construction of national identity, and the "Americanness" of a given furniture form is measured in terms of its allegiance to accepted, northern standards.[5]

For more than one hundred years, private and institutional collections, exhibitions, and publications have claimed to present the topic of "American furniture." Few, however, allude to southern craft traditions. When the South is included, the resulting analysis is based more on common myth than on demonstrable fact. Portrayals of the region, although of diverse flavor, inevitably lead back to one familiar theme: the South as a culturally impaired place (fig. 4). In the American furniture story, southern furniture exists less as an accepted regional craft tradition than as a chronic interpretive problem. Examples of this perspective range from Rachel Raymond's observation in the December 1922 issue of *Antiques* that no evidence survives to indicate any southern furnituremaking legacy; to Joseph Downs's infamous declaration at the 1949 Williamsburg Antiques Forum that little of artistic merit was made south of Baltimore; to Morrison Heckscher and Leslie Greene Bowman's undocumented hypothesis in *American Rococo* (1992) that early southern furniture primarily represents the "part-time work of farmers." Similarly shaded is an American furniture connoisseurship that describes a stylistically confused New England chair (fig. 5) as "harmonious" but refers to an important southern Masonic master's chair as lacking "total coherence" (fig. 6). Echoing a common assumption about southern furniture, the criticism of the master's chair alludes to "aesthetic shortcomings," including poorly conceived arm supports, oversized pilasters, and decorative motifs that "cling to the sides of the openwork back as if tossed into a magnetized box."[6]

Popular generalizations about the cultural illiteracy of the early South cumulatively have functioned as a kind of public anaesthetic, limiting inquiry into southern craft traditions. The authors of this volume of *American Furniture* seek to redress the interpretive imbalance by building upon the pioneering research of Paul Burroughs, E. Milby Burton, and Frank Horton, and the subsequent work of John Bivins, Wallace Gusler, Brad Rauschenberg, Sumpter Priddy, Gregory Weidman, Luke Beckerdite, and others. By focusing on the rarely acknowledged cultural diversity of the region, this scholarship reexamines and substantially redefines the tradi-

Figure 5 Side chair, Portsmouth, New Hampshire, 1725–1740. Maple. H. 40¹/₂", W. 18", D. 18". (Private collection; photo, Douglas Armsden.)

tional historical roles assigned to southern wares and artisans. Even so, significant obstacles remain in the form of certain lingering cultural assumptions. To move beyond these obstacles and overcome the perceived problem of southern furniture, we need to delve further into the "Idea of the South" and, specifically, to reconsider the historical and mythological character of the region. Such an approach promises to clear the way for more thoughtfully contextualized interpretations of the region's diverse material culture traditions.

What does it mean to say "the South" or to describe something as "southern"? In American popular history, these otherwise neutral regional terms are culturally charged. Unlike any other region, the South exists in a different realm and is subject to a different type of historical interpretation. As historian Larry Griffen notes, the South invariably is linked to chronic prob-

Figure 6 Benjamin Bucktrout, Masonic master's chair, Williamsburg, Virginia, 1766–1777. Mahogany with walnut; painted and gilded ornament, original leather. H. 65¹/₂", W. 31¹/₄", D. 29¹/₂". (Courtesy, Colonial Williamsburg Foundation; photo, Hans Lorenz.)

lems of economy, racism, and social difficulties. In other American regions, however, equally significant shortcomings—including the treatment of Native Americans, non-Anglo immigrants, and women, and issues surrounding child labor, urban blight, and ghettoization—are not similarly scrutinized. Only in the South are the problems equated with the region as a whole.[7]

Historian C. Van Woodward suggests that this skewed perspective is even more evident when the South is viewed through the lens of comparative history. America, despite select regional deficiencies, invariably is portrayed as a great success story. The South, on the other hand, is distinguished by a long litany of failures. Whereas America is depicted as a land of opportunity, progress, and prosperity, the South represents a land of poverty, frustration, and failure. The distinctive identity of the South additionally is grounded in the un-American experience of defeat and submission, not only in the military arena but also in the economic, social, political, and philosophical realms. Finally, even the region's self-conscious allegiance to premodern European cultural traditions digresses from the celebrated myth of American innocence, which idealizes the settlers' escape from the sinful Old World and subsequent creation of a productive New World.[8]

Woodward's reading of the South, while not complete, does hint at crucial regional differences not included in the telling of the American story, which casts the South in the shadow of northern cultural achievement. Fundamentally, the early South diverged from the North in its faithful adherence to a broad spectrum of Old World Christian and cultural traditions. The region's conservative social and political ideology and its adoption of a decentralized and minimally interventive governmental structure reflect this orientation; so, too, do the familiar Jeffersonian ideals of private virtue and individual liberty (fig. 7). Southern culture especially resembled premodern Europe in its fundamental reliance on the land—an orientation that provided a shared form of life and common language for white planters, and a tragically common American experience for slaves. Beyond the obvious demographic differences associated with the pervasive agrarian orientation, the South diverged from the North in many other ways as well. Historian Mechal Sobel argues that the essence of a culture is reflected in its sense of time. In the face of the emerging northern capitalist model, late eighteenth- and early nineteenth-century southerners differed in their ideas about time and time management. In the slave-powered agrarian South, time was regulated less by mechanical clocks than by the rhythms of nature, a pattern that subsequently inspired widespread northern mythologizing about the "leisurely" and "lazy" character of the South.[9]

After 1790, mounting regional differences in the form of industrialization, improved transportation networks, faster lines of interregional com-

Figure 7 Francis Blackwell Mayer, *Independence, Squire Jack Porter*, Frostburg, Maryland, 1858. Oil on millboard. (Courtesy, National Museum of Art.)

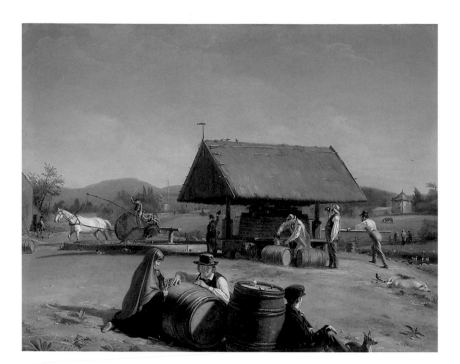

Figure 8 William Sidney Mount, *Cider Making*, Stony Brook, New York, 1841. Oil on canvas. (Courtesy, Metropolitan Museum of Art.)

munication, national educational reform, and, later, abolitionalism brought about a highly fertile period in the evolution of southern and northern mythic identities. In the eyes of outsiders, the South's conservative ways became equated with cultural backwardness and regarded as contrary to progressive national values. American character instead was linked to blossoming ingenuity, productivity, and industry—attributes invariably associated with northern culture and esteemed in opposition to southern social and economic conservatism (fig. 8).

Not surprisingly southern elites saw these national and regional developments from a different perspective. In the preface to *Swallow Barn*, a novel written as a rebuttal to the rising tide of abolitionist literature, John Pendleton Kennedy lamented:

> An observer cannot fail to note that the manners of our country have been tending towards a uniformity which is visibly effacing all local differences. The old states, especially, are losing their original distinctive habits and modes of life, and in the same degree, I fear, are losing their exclusive American character.

White southerners increasingly adopted a kind of fortress mentality and defended the full spectrum of the region's cultural traditions. Echoing the reactionary flavor of many southern newspapers and magazines, Kennedy wrote:

> [The southerner] thinks lightly of the mercantile interest, and, in fact, undervalues the manners of the large cities generally. He believes that those who live in them are hollow-hearted and insincere, and wanting in that substantial intelligence and virtue, which he affirms to be characteristic of the country.

Within the South's increasingly self-conscious definition of its own regional identity emerged the fully evolved southern "Cavalier," a mythic figure

Figure 9 Robert Brammer and Augustus A. Von Smith, *Oakland House and Race Course*, Louisville, Kentucky, 1840. Oil on canvas. (Courtesy, J. B. Speed Art Museum.)

steeped in honor and integrity, indifferent to money and business, and imbued with a high sense of social decorum and civic awareness. This image brings to mind Jefferson's "natural man"—part planter, part aristocrat, part hunter, and part horseman—whose benign yet self-indulgent lifestyle fueled characterizations of a South that "at its best is relaxed; at its worst is either asleep or frenzied" (fig. 9).[10]

Given the general exclusion of southern cultural perspectives, however, the South of American popular history ultimately must be understood as a kind of cultural fiction that, in many ways, would be unrecognizable to early American eyes. Defined less as an actual place with its own historical legacy than as a lingering idea or belief, the South is distinguished by its long-standing opposition to basic American values and exists as a blight on the cultural and political landscape. This mythic region assumes an exhaustive range of guises: the Savage South, the Plantation South, the Proslavery South, the Redneck South, the Demagogic South, the States Rights South, the Bucolic South, the Regressive South, the Intolerant South, the Evangelical South, the Aberrant South, and the Lazy South. Especially familiar is the "Old South," a term so frequently and carelessly applied that it now is largely devoid of any cultural or symbolic meaning.[11]

Each of these images of the South has some basis in reality, yet none alone tells the whole tale (fig. 10). Moreover, given the dominant northern cultural orientation of popular history, we also need to recognize the source of many of these persistant images. While southern apologists such as Kennedy, William Wirt, and John C. Calhoun contributed to our popular understanding of southern character, we must also finally acknowledge the enormous fictive contributions of northerners such as writers Harriet Beecher Stowe and William Lloyd Garrison, and musicians David Christy, Stephen Foster, and Dan Emmett, who penned the song "Dixie" in 1859. In his novel

Intruder in the Dust William Faulkner elaborated on the North's seemingly limitless fascination with the South, and in particular its "volitionless, almost helpless capacity and eagerness to believe anything about the South not even provided it be derogatory but merely bizarre and strange enough." The same gullibility has long guided conventional analysis of southern furniture and still informs the common assumption that southern wares are proportionally and decoratively abnormal—a perspective embodied in the descrip-

tion of a North Carolina demi-lune table as burdened by "unusual, heavy moldings" and "massive construction techniques" (fig. 11).[12]

Given their complex origins, popular ideas about American regional character need to be more closely scrutinized to evaluate their historical validity and interpretive usefulness. Toward this end, historian David Smiley argues for reconsideration of the "Idea of the South," a conceptual abstraction that nevertheless represents a crucial historical reality upon which people acted, risked, and even died. Historians Patrick Gerster and Nicholas Cords likewise claim that historical reality not only encompasses what can be directly proven but also what is *believed* to be true. The authors specify two dominant approaches to American mythology. The first perspective—one that is all too easily adopted by southern decorative arts scholars—stresses the negative aspect of myth. This attitude is epitomized in the words of Thomas Bailey, who concludes that "a historical myth is . . . an account or belief that is demonstrably untrue, in whole or substantial part." More informative, however, is a second perspective that centers around Henry Nash Smith's belief in the culturally unifying aspect of myth as "an intellectual construction that fuses concept and emotion into an image." Viewed in this light, popular generalizations about regional identity can hint at certain cultural truths about both the South and the North and offer a way to move past the time-worn debate about whether southerners are "racist baboons or the true heirs of Aristotle" toward the more important consideration of how such opinions came to be formed.[13]

The potential for popular history to inform material culture analysis remains an open area for investigation. For instance, intriguing parallels link the changing character of late nineteenth- and early twentieth-century ideas about the South to emerging attitudes about American decorative arts. Historian George Tindall notes that, after 1880 or so, Americans became captivated with the South. This change of heart largely reflected a sympathetic reaction to the perceived inequities of Reconstruction, as well as a rise in nostalgic southern romances and a recognition of the New South with its social and political emulation of northern norms. But, the 1920s saw the reemergence of a markedly different perspective, what Tindall calls a "kind of neoabolitionist myth of the Savage South." Placed back into the national spotlight were a wide range of southern problems, including lynching, child labor, the Scopes trial, poor education, and endemic health problems—a critical viewpoint that can be traced not only to the writings of unapologetic cultural observers such as H. L. Mencken but also to introspective southern literature such as William Faulkner's *Sanctuary*. The national criticism was so great that it fueled a coordinated and, as during the antebellum era, reactionary southern response, embodied in the widely read Agrarian manifesto *I'll Take My Stand* and the historical scholarship of Wilbur J. Cash and Ullrich B. Phillips.[14]

Parallel changes characterize decorative arts trends of the same period. In their eagerness to identify important early furnituremaking traditions, late nineteenth- and early twentieth-century furniture scholars were responsive to southern as well as to northern material culture. Although unmistakably

Figure 12 Advertisement by J. K. Beard of Richmond, Virginia, in *Antiques* 4, no. 4 (October 1923): 193.

Figure 13 G. Bridgman, *America*, London, ca. 1870. Colored lithograph on paper. (Courtesy, Amon Carter Museum.)

Figure 14 Clothespress, Williamsburg, Virginia, 1760–1770. Walnut with yellow pine. H. 56⅝", W. 49½", D. 23". (Courtesy, Colonial Williamsburg Foundation; photo, Hans Lorenz.)

inclined toward the superiority of northern traditions, authors nevertheless explored objects that crossed a wide range of regional and class lines. Wallace Nutting, a highly influential furniture scholar and entrepreneur, illustrated many southern furniture forms in his *Furniture Treasury* (1928). Likewise, early issues of *Antiques* (first published in 1922) reflect a decidedly democratic vision of early American artisanry, and many of the articles, queries, and advertisements center around southern themes (fig. 12). By the late 1920s, however, this egalitarian focus gave way to the formal creation of a northern-based American furniture canon. Popular understanding of the American furniture story was reshaped by a series of influential exhibitions and sales, for example the establishment and subsequent expansion of the American Wing at the Metropolitan Museum of Art during the mid-1920s, the sale of the Reifsnyder (1929) and Flayderman (1930) collections, and the growing dominance of northern antiques dealers.

A reconsideration of common assumptions about American regional identity reveals other new material culture perspectives. In opposition to the Cavalier we find the Yankee, a figure who in post–Civil War popular history frequently possesses the transcendent qualities of curiosity, asceticism, and single-mindedness. But this mythic incarnation, particularly conspicuous in the novels of Horatio Alger, was not universal, even among north-

Figure 15 Detail of the paneled back of the clothespress illustrated in fig. 14.

erners. In the face of rising urbanization and industrialization, nineteenth-century New Hampshire social critic and novelist Sarah Josepha Hale nostalgically longed for lost Puritan values. She argued that the founding ideals of spirituality, community, and the Protestant ethic were being subsumed by new liabilities of the northern character and by the growing tendency toward selfish acquisitiveness and predatory greed (fig. 13). Even more critical were non-northerners, whose observations rarely appear in the telling of the American story. A Scottish visitor to New England in 1833 noted:

> The whole race of Yankee peddlers, in particular, are proverbial for their dishonesty. They warrant broken watches to be the best time-keepers in the world; sell pinch-beck trinkets for gold; and have always a large assortment of wooden nutmegs and stagnant barometers.[15]

In this light, the Yankee character of New England furniture can be seen anew. Even a cursory consideration of eighteenth-century New England furniture, in particular urban wares, reveals a kinship with the parsimonious Yankee spirit. A penny-pinching mentality seems linked to the common regional craft practice of minimal and, at times, blatantly cheap case construction. Unlike many southern makers—who emulated sophisticated British construction in the use of structurally reinforcing dustboards, composite foot and drawer blocking, and floating-panel drawers and case backs (figs. 14, 15)—New England artisans often took a far less meticulous ap-

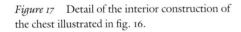
Figure 16   Chest of drawers, Boston, 1770–1780. Mahogany with white pine. H. 32¹/₈", W. 35³/₄", D. 21". (Courtesy, Colonial Williamsburg Foundation; photo, Hans Lorenz.)

Figure 17   Detail of the interior construction of the chest illustrated in fig. 16.

proach. On even the largest case furniture forms, drawers are often tenuously supported by thin, nailed-on runners, which have the additional flaw of restricting the normal seasonal expansion and contraction of the case (figs. 16, 17). Furthermore, the Yankee mindset is echoed in the carefully

Figure 18 Dressing table, Boston, 1735–1750. Walnut, walnut veneer, and birch with white pine. H. 32¹/₄", W. 33³/₈", D. 21¹/₂". (Courtesy, Colonial Williamsburg Foundation; photo, Hans Lorenz.)

veiled substitution of inexpensive materials. Although there may have been legitimate regional shortages of good timber, the insertion of stained-maple rear rails on mahogany and walnut chairs is an excessively frugal shortcut by any standard, as perhaps is the artful insertion of stained birch cabriole legs on some early walnut case pieces (fig. 18).[16]

At the same time, the mythic Yankee serves as a foundation upon which to compliment New England furniture. The blossoming, post-Revolutionary northern preoccupation with material gain and upward social mobility may well have worked alongside the conservative New England retention of local craft traditions to create that region's many wonderfully expressive furniture forms. For many prosperous New England merchants, shapely bombé, serpentine, and blockfront case pieces served as requisite symbols of wealth and social status (see fig. 16). Ultimately, the interpretive purview of American material culture analysis needs to recognize all sorts of evidence. In the case of early northern furniture we should pay attention to traveller John Kirke Paulding's observations about his own northern identity. In *Letters from the South, Written During an Excursion in the Summer of 1816*, Paulding commented:

> I have heard it often remarked in our part of the world, with great self complacency, by portly traders and brokers, who fancied themselves at the pinnacle of refinement, because they had a splendid equipage and fine furniture; "that the middle and eastern States were at least a century before the southern, in refinement and civilization." Upon inquiring into the grounds of this notion, I found it uniformly originated in the vulgar prac-

tice of confounding mere personal comforts, and little domestic knick-knackery with the qualities of the mind, or the exercise of the intellectual faculty. Thus, in the eyes of stupidity, the fine coat makes the gentleman, all over the world.

Perhaps eye-catching New England furniture worked as well as a "fine coat."[17]

Southern material culture, as with early southern culture in general, is usefully seen in opposition to northern precedent, but we first need to overcome the prevalent decorative arts tendency to mimic the biases of American popular history. At best, the stylistic simplicity of southern furniture is seen as evidence of the region's agrarian character and lack of large-scale urban centers; at worst, the austerity of southern furniture is cited as proof of cultural inferiority. Recent furniture scholarship counters these common assumptions by not only demonstrating the unparalleled structural sophis-

Figure 19 John Selden, clothespress, Norfolk, Virginia, 1775. Mahogany with yellow pine and mahogany. H. 74¼", W. 50⅛", D. 23¾". (Private collection; photo, Hans Lorenz.)

Figure 20 Design for a clothespress on plate 129 in the third edition of Thomas Chippendale's *Gentleman and Cabinet-Maker's Director* (1762). (Courtesy, Colonial Williamsburg Foundation.)

Figure 21 Alexander Spotswood Payne and his brother, John Dandridge Payne, with their Nurse, attributed to the Payne Limner, Goochland County, Virginia, 1790–1800. (Courtesy, Virginia Museum of Fine Arts; gift of Miss Dorothy Payne.)

tication of much southern furniture but also by revealing the urban British origins of many designs (figs. 19, 20). The essays in *American Furniture* further this new outlook by exposing the remarkable cultural diversity of the early South.

Still, many questions about southern furniture beg to be answered, even in the analysis of the widespread preference for neat-and-plain forms, which wealthy coastal patrons favored despite having access via transatlantic trade to much more ornate furniture. Southern scholars have documented that this style partly reflected concerns about the stability of intricately carved or veneered furniture in the inhospitable southern climate. To what extent however, was the neat-and-plain style also shaped by the distinctive cultural and demographic character of the coastal South and, in particular, by the hierarchical relationships in both the immediate and extended plantation family? Perhaps the style suitably reflected the material needs and beliefs of a people who were, according to Paulding, "brought up in habits of servility to those above them, and accustomed from their earliest youth to pay a deference to rank, riches, and stations, independently of merit and virtue." Although Paulding goes on to say that the same residents were not averse to climbing the social ladder aggressively, could the real and imagined plantation landscape have reduced or perhaps redefined how white southerners "kept up with the Joneses"? In comparison to their northern peers, southern planters not only had far fewer neighbors to impress, but also most visitors to their homes generally came from an identical domestic situation.[18]

Might the style, moreover, reflect the region's decision not to embrace the capitalist-industrial model? As early as 1688, William Fitzhugh of Virginia wrote to his London merchants asking them to send an assortment of silver plate that was "strong & plain, as being less subject to bruise, more serviceable, & less out for the fashion." Similarly, in 1699, a speaker at the College of William and Mary noted that the education of Virginia children in England taught more about luxury than learning, and countered the "simple and less costly way of living in Virginia." Could neat-and-plain furniture have functioned as a comfortable, old friend in a world that otherwise was becoming increasingly unfamiliar to the South?[19]

Southern furniture studies also need more thoughtfully to consider the legacy of slavery. If the basic tenet of material culture scholarship is that artifacts are shaped by the specific needs and beliefs of both the makers and users, then we certainly must ask how the material expressions of both planters and slaves were shaped by slavery, which, according to historian Eugene Genovese, is "the foundation upon which the South rose" (fig. 21). Mechal Sobel argues that African-American traditions influenced elite white southern culture in several significant ways. She not only notes the African origins of early southern ideas about time and work, but also attitudes about space, the natural world, spirituality, and the afterlife. Was southern furniture similarly influenced, even in subtle ways, by African Americans, many of whom worked in furnituremaking trades? For evidence we might well look to site-specific examples, including Jefferson's mountaintop slave community at Monticello. The furniture made there by African-American joiners needs to be evaluated not only in terms of its affinity to European craft traditions brought there by immigrant shopmasters but also in terms of potential ties to African-American customs. In the process, we should consider the specific shop contributions of Jefferson, who closely oversaw the operation and provided many of his own designs. Although professionally connected to elite white culture, Jefferson was raised by and spent much of his private life with African Americans. Equally important evidence survives in the furniture of Thomas Day, a free black artisan in antebellum North Carolina (fig. 22). While unmistakably aware of published urban designs, Day's work also is distinguished by a highly idiosyncratic and, perhaps, Afro-American-centric decorative vocabulary.[20]

Similar cultural questions surround the complex intermingling of British, Germanic, and Swiss traditions in the southern backcountry (fig. 23). For

Figure 22 Side chair attributed to Thomas Day, Milton, North Carolina, ca. 1850. Mahogany, walnut, rosewood, and mahogany veneer with tulip poplar. H. 35¹/₂", W. 17³/₄", D. 16". (Courtesy, North Carolina Museum of History.)

Figure 23 Chest of drawers, probably Shenandoah County, Virginia, 1794. Walnut with yellow pine. H. 67³/₄", W. 41¹/₄", D. 23". (Courtesy, Colonial Williamsburg Foundation; photo, Hans Lorenz.)

example, how did German and non-German perceptions about substantial construction inform the design of furniture and houses? Were these material manifestions tied to deeply rooted German ideas about the shaping of strong personal character? Indeed, were Germanic ideas about the proportion and construction of artifacts in any way informed by cultural notions about the preferred shape of the human form, as suggested by early allusions to the "sturdy, four-square German," to his "jolly portly" wife, and to his children who were described as chubby "rogues with legs shaped like little old fashioned mahogany bannisters"?[21]

Southern material culture scholarship is still in its infancy, and therefore less encumbered by the entrenched interpretive legacy that confronts northern scholars. This freedom from constraint, in turn, facilitates the implementation of innovative analyses of southern history and identity. In his reconsideration of the Puritan origins of American national identity, social historian Jack Greene cites the formative cultural contributions of the early South. Paralleling Greene's emphasis on American diversity, the essays in this volume of *American Furniture* counter the culturally monolithic orientation of conventional decorative arts interpretation and question the rules commonly used to measure "quality" and "value." By doing so, these new perspectives expand our understanding of the American story and, more specifically, the American furniture story.

In the end, the mansions, mockingbirds, and magnolias that characterize the South in American popular history are both real and unreal; so, too, are the region's sideboards, slab tables, and sugar chests. Thoughtful consideration of not only historical but also mythological evidence will promote a healthy rethinking of American cultural assumptions and a much-needed reevaluation of southern regional identity.

ACKNOWLEDGMENTS   The author thanks Dr. James Whittenburg, Ronald Hurst, and Luke Beckerdite for their editorial insights and Graham Hood, Betty Leviner, Martha Katz Hyman, Susan Shames, Wallace Gusler, Brock Jobe, and Jessie Poesch for their research assistance. Dr. Katherine Hemple Prown deserves special recognition for her substantial intellectual and editorial contributions to this essay.

1. *Antiques* 11, no. 1(January 1927): 27. Jack P. Greene, *Pursuits of Happiness: The Social Development of Early Modern British Colonies and the Formation of American Culture* (Chapel Hill: University of North Carolina Press, 1988), p. 5. Larry J. Griffen, "Why Was the South a Problem to America?" in *The South as an American Problem*, edited by Larry J. Griffen and Donald H. Doyle (Athens: University of Georgia Press, 1995), p. 19. Anne Norton, *Alternative Americas: A Reading of Antebellum Political Culture* (Chicago: University of Chicago Press, 1986), p. 8.

2. As cited in Griffen, "Why Was the South a Problem to America?" p. 25.

3. Richard B. Harwell, "The Stream of Self-Consciousness," in *The Idea of the South: Pursuit of a Central Theme*, edited by Frank E. Vandiver (Chicago: University of Chicago Press, 1964), p. 23. Frank L. Owlsley, "The Irrepressible Conflict," in *I'll Take My Stand: The South and the Agrarian Tradition* (1930; reprint ed., Baton Rouge: Louisiana State University Press, 1977), p. 66.

4. C. Vann Woodward, *The Burden of Southern History* (Baton Rouge: Louisiana State University Press, 1968), pp. 69–81.

5. As quoted in Richard N. Current, *Northernizing the South* (Athens: University of Georgia Press, 1983), p. 35. This idea paraphrases Toni Morrison's concept of race as a literary metaphor

for being American (see Toni Morrison, *Playing in the Dark: Whiteness in the Literary Imagination* [Cambridge, Mass.: Harvard University Press, 1992], p. 47).

6. Rachel Raymond, "Construction of Early American Furniture, II. Eighteenth Century Types," *Antiques* 2, no. 6 (December 1922): 255–56. Morrison H. Heckscher and Leslie Greene Bowman, *American Rococo, 1750–1775: Elegance in Ornament* (New York: Harry Abrams for the Metropolitan Museum of Art and the Los Angeles County Museum of Art, 1992), pp. 180–81, fig. 123. For more on the context of the master's chair and its relationship to Masonic symbolism and ritual, see F. Carey Howlett, "Admitted into the Mysteries: The Benjamin Bucktrout Masonic Master's Chair," in *American Furniture*, edited by Luke Beckerdite (Hanover, N.H.: University Press of New England for the Chipstone Foundation, 1996), pp. 195–232. Jonathan Fairbanks and Elizabeth Bidwell Bates, *American Furniture, 1620 to the Present* (New York: Richard Marek Publishers, 1982), pp. 89. Heckscher and Bowman, *American Rococo*, p. 166.

7. Griffen, "Why Was the South a Problem To America?" p. 14.

8. Woodward, *Burden of Southern History*, pp. 15–21, 190.

9. Although these differences have not been thoughtfully commented upon by decorative arts scholars, they have been the focus of considerable research by historians. Mechal Sobel, *The World They Made Together* (Princeton, N.J.: Princeton University Press, 1987), pp. 21–67.

10. John Pendleton Kennedy, *Swallow Barn* (1851; reprint ed., Baton Rouge: Louisiana State University Press, 1986), pp. 9, 35. William R. Taylor, *Cavalier and Yankee: The Old South and American National Character* (London: W. H. Allen, 1963), p. 133. James M. Dabbs, *The Southern Heritage* (New York: Alfred A. Knopf, 1959), p. 35.

11. Griffen and Doyle, eds., *The South as an American Problem*, p. 1. Also, it is important to recognize the "New South," a post-1880 political and economic faction dedicated to the emulation of the northern capitalist-industrial model. George Tindall, "Mythology: A New Frontier in Southern History," in *Myth and Southern History*, vol. 2, *The New South*, edited by Patrick Gerster and Nicholas Cords (Urbana and Chicago: University of Illinois Press, 1989), p. 10. Marshall Davidson, "The Old South," *Antiques* 61, no. 1 (January 1952): 40.

12. Patrick Gerster and Nicholas Cords, "The Northern Origins of Southern Mythology" in Gerster and Cords, eds., *Myth and Southern History*, pp. 46–47. As quoted in Griffen, "Why Was the South a Problem to America?" p. 11. Fairbanks and Bates, *American Furniture*, p. 328. To their credit Fairbanks and Bates are among the few northern decorative arts scholars to present many southern furniture forms in a complimentary light.

13. David L. Smiley, "Quest for a Central Theme," *Atlantic Quarterly* 71, no. 3 (summer 1972): 20. Gerster and Cords, eds., *Myth and Southern History*, pp. 1, xiv. Michael O'Brien, *The Idea of the American South, 1920–1941* (Baltimore, Md.: Johns Hopkins University Press, 1979), p. xi.

14. Tindall, "Mythology," pp. 5–6.

15. Taylor, *Cavalier and Yankee*, pp. 95–96, 133. Current, *Northernizing the South*, p. 29.

16. The author thanks Ronald L. Hurst for first suggesting this interpretation.

17. John Kirke Paulding, *Letters from the South, Written During an Excursion in the Summer of 1816*, 2 vols. (New York: James Eastburn & Co., 1817), 1:118–19.

18. Paulding, *Letters*, 1:126–30.

19. Carole Shammus, "English Born and Creole Elites in Turn-of-the-Century Virginia," in *The Chesapeake in the Seventeenth Century: Essays on Anglo-American Society*, edited by Thad W. Tate and David L. Ammerman (Chapel Hill: University of North Carolina Press, 1974), p. 288. As cited in Richard Beale Davis, ed., *William Fitzhugh and His Chesapeake World, 1671–1701* (Chapel Hill: University of North Carolina Press, 1963), p. 246.

20. Eugene D. Genovese, "The Shaping of a Unique Society," in *Major Problems in the History of the American South*, edited by Paul D. Escott and David R. Goldfield (Lexington, Mass.: D. C. Heath, 1990), pp. 277–79. Sobel, *The World They Made Together*, passim. For more on Day, see Rodney Barfield, "Thomas Day: Cabinetmaker," in *Nineteenth Century* 2, no. 3/4 (autumn 1976): pp. 23–32; and Laurel C. Sneed and Christine Westfall, "Uncovering the Hidden History of Thomas Day: Findings and Methodology" (private publication prepared for the North Carolina Humanities Council, 1995).

21. Paulding, *Letters from the South*, 2:93, 1: 142-43. The author thanks Wallace Gusler for this reference.

Robert A. Leath

Dutch Trade and Its Influence on Seventeenth-Century Chesapeake Furniture

▼ DURING THE 1930s, American furniture historians first began to speculate on the surprising "Continental" features found on seventeenth-century Chesapeake furniture. To the discriminating eye, this furniture appeared different from contemporary New England work, while displaying a closer affinity to furniture from the Dutch colonial regions of New York and New Jersey. Material culture and documentary evidence strongly suggest that Dutch traders and artisans were the principal source of Continental influences in the seventeenth-century Chesapeake. Archaeological evidence of extensive Dutch trade in tobacco has been found at Jamestown and Flowerdew Hundred Plantation in Virginia, St. Mary's City and Providence in Maryland, and other sites throughout the region. Dutch trade in the Chesapeake is also well documented in the historical record. By the third quarter of the seventeenth century, the term "Dutch" was applied to chairs, tables, chests, cupboards and other forms in Chesapeake inventories; however, it is extremely unlikely that all of these objects were imported from Holland. Given the extent of Dutch involvement in the region's early history, it was inevitable that their styles would influence furniture making in the Chesapeake.

The seventeenth century is universally considered the golden age of Dutch culture. After the ten northern provinces of the Habsburg Lowlands united in 1579 under the Union of Utrecht, a bloody war for independence against the Spanish ensued. By 1609, the Spanish had withdrawn from the Netherlands, and almost immediately the new nation—the "Lands of the United Netherlands"—became the preeminent maritime and commercial power of western Europe. The Dutch established colonies in South Africa, Indonesia, Formosa, Japan, North and South America, and the Carribean. In North America they controlled New York, New Jersey, and Delaware; in South America they controlled Surinam; and in the Carribean they controlled Curacao and St. Eustatius. With colonies to the north and the south of the Chesapeake, the Dutch were strategically positioned to exploit the market for Chesapeake tobacco.[1]

By the first quarter of the seventeenth century, Dutch traders had established a close relationship with the English settlers of Maryland and Virginia, who considered them former political and religious allies. During the Dutch wars for independence against Roman Catholic Spain, England and Holland had formed a powerful military alliance. By the 1580s, Queen Elizabeth I was allowing English troops to fight with the Dutch, and in 1595 she dispatched an army under the command of the Earl of Leicester. Many

Figure 1 Unknown artist, *Sir Thomas Dale*, England, ca. 1615. Oil on canvas. 80" × 45". (Courtesy, Virginia Museum of Fine Art, Adolph D. and Wilkins C. Williams Fund; photo, Ron Jennings.)

of the English soldiers who served in the Netherlands later became prominent leaders in Virginia. Sir Thomas Dale (fig. 1), for example, fought with the Dutch from 1588 to 1609, when he departed for Virginia under the auspices of the Virginia Company of London. He became the first marshal of the new colony and served as the deputy governor from 1611 to 1618. As a reward for his former service, the States General of the United Netherlands granted seven years back wages to Dale in 1618 and expressed their appreciation for his "service . . . in Virginia." In their grant, the Dutch authorities noted that Dale had "sailed . . . to Virginia . . . to establish a firm market there for the benefit and increase of trade [for the Dutch]." Other Virginia leaders who served in the Netherlands were Sir Thomas Gates, Sir George Yeardley, and Nathaniel Littleton. These men were part of a powerful pro-Dutch faction who influenced Virginia's political and commercial affairs.[2]

During the first three quarters of the seventeenth century, Dutch trading ships sailed regularly through the waters of the Chesapeake, exchanging household and luxury goods for tobacco. In 1619, these traders left an indelible mark on Virginia history when they sold "20 and odd Negroes"—the first African slaves brought to the colony. Thirty years later, a promotional pamphlet on Virginia's economy noted that there were twelve Dutch ships anchored in the Tidewater region on December 25, 1646. The most detailed account of Dutch trade in the Chesapeake is the journal of Captain David Peterson DeVries. Between 1633 and 1637, he made four voyages up the James River to purchase tobacco. In 1635, DeVries discovered four other Dutch ships, which "make a great trade here every year." On his voyage to Jamestown in 1633, DeVries visited the home of Governor John Harvey, who entertained him with "a Venice glass" of sherry. With Harvey's permission, DeVries traded openly for tobacco at Newport News, Kicotan, Flowerdew Hundred Plantation, and Jamestown. During his trips, DeVries made several important observations on the Dutch tobacco trade; in 1635, he wrote that for a Dutch trader to succeed in the Virginia tobacco market, "he must keep a house here, and continue all the year, that he may be prepared when the tobacco comes from the field, to seize it."[3]

With the support of the colonial governments of Virginia and Maryland, Dutch traders established permanent trading posts at strategic points along the Chesapeake waterways in order to maximize their access to the tobacco market. In 1641, merchants Derrick and Arent Corsen Stam built a trading post in Accomack County on Virginia's Eastern Shore. Their clients included Nathaniel Littleton, the former English soldier who had fought in the Netherlands. Littleton leased the Stams land, a sloop, and a barge. Six years later, Rotterdam merchant Simon Overzee settled in Lower Norfolk County, Virginia. After two financially advantageous marriages (the first to Sarah Thoroughgood and the second to Elizabeth Willoughby), he moved to St. Mary's City, Maryland, where he traded during the 1650s. In 1649, a group of Rotterdam merchants established a trading post at Kicotan, midway between Jamestown and Flowerdew Hundred Plantation on the James River. Other Dutch trading posts in Virginia during the 1640s and 1650s were William Moseley's in Lower Norfolk County and Derrick Derrickson's in York County. By 1660, there were at least five Dutch settlements established solely for the purpose of trading for Chesapeake tobacco.[4]

Chesapeake planters depended on Dutch traders for many of their household and luxury goods. In 1623, the governor and council of Virginia reported that the Dutch "take away much [of] our Tobacco . . . [b]ecause many of their commodities [such] as Sacke, sweete meates and strong Liquors are soe acceptable to the people." When Puritan leader Richard Ingle seized the Dutch ship *Speagle* at St. Inigoe's Creek in St. Mary's County, Maryland, in 1643, he found her holds laden with "strong waters," sugar, lemons, shirts, hats, stockings, frying pans, and other household goods. The "Goods brought from the Dutch Shipe" had a value equal to twelve hundred pounds of Maryland tobacco. Dutch cargoes typically included "all sorts of domestic manufactures, brewed beer, linen cloth, brandies, or other distilled liquors, duffels, coarse cloth, and other articles for food and raiment."[5]

During the English Revolution, Dutch trade in the Chesapeake expanded as commerce between Britain and her colonies deteriorated. In 1650, however, the emboldened English government under Cromwell passed the first Navigation Act to prohibit Dutch trade and to require that all Virginia tobacco be shipped directly to England aboard British ships. The colony's governor, Sir William Berkeley, attacked the new law and lamented its economic effect on the colonists:

> The Indians, God be blessed round about us are subdued; we can onely feare the *Londoners,* who would faine bring us to the same poverty, wherein the *Dutch* found and relieved us; would take away the liberty of our consciences, and tongues, and our right of giving and selling our goods to whom we please.

Between 1652 and 1674, England and the Netherlands fought three successive wars, largely over restrictions against Dutch trade in the colonies. In 1664, England took control of the Dutch colonies in New York, New Jersey, and Delaware. As trade restrictions in the Chesapeake increased, a pro-Dutch political faction consisting of Governor Berkeley and members of the Yeardley, Littleton, Thoroughgood, and Custis families intervened. Not only did trade continue, but a small number of Dutch families migrated to the Chesapeake from former Dutch colonies, perhaps seeking congenial ground among old friends and trading partners. Among these immigrants was Augustine Herrman, a merchant and surveyor who had been involved in the tobacco trade between New Netherland and the Chesapeake since the 1650s. Herrman moved to Cecil County, Maryland, in 1660 and later published one of the most important maps of Maryland and Virginia (fig. 2). The Dutch population in the Chesapeake remained small, however, and assimilated quickly into the English-speaking community.[6]

Numerous artifacts associated with the Dutch trade have been excavated at seventeenth-century archaeological sites throughout the Chesapeake region. Dutch pottery and other ceramics—German stoneware and Chinese export porcelain—bartered for tobacco are relatively commonplace. At Kicotan, over half of the tobacco pipes excavated were made in Holland.

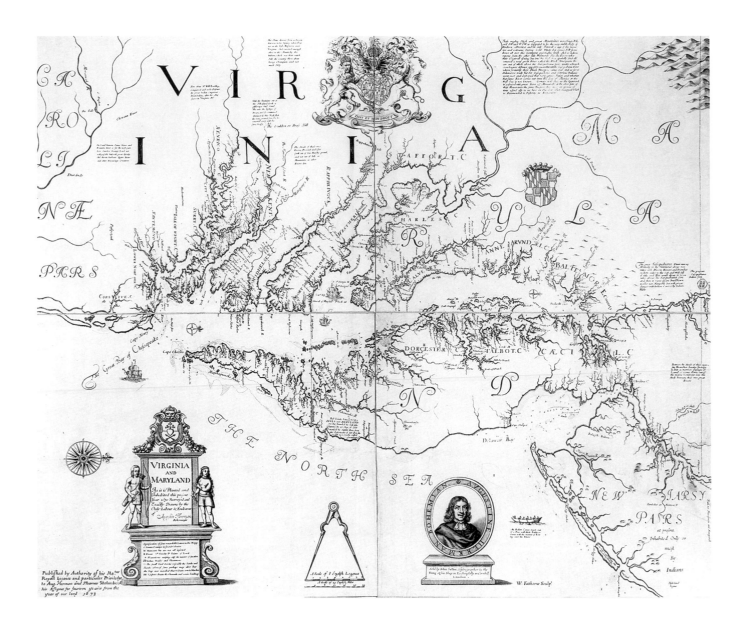

Figure 2 Augustine Herrman, *Virginia and Maryland*, 1670. Engraving on paper. 32" × 37". (Courtesy, John Carter Brown Library, Brown University.)

Similarly, large quantities of Dutch tin-glazed earthenware (including fireplace tiles), lead-glazed earthenware, and bricks (which arrived as ballast) were recovered at Jamestown. Excavations at Flowerdew Hundred Plantation have produced one of the most emblematic symbols of the Dutch presence—a cast brass medallion depicting Maurice, Prince of Orange, Count of Nassau, dated 1615 (fig. 3). The medal commemorates Maurice's induction into the English Order of the Garter in 1612, in honor of his service in the war against Spain. One of Maurice's soldiers in the Dutch war for independence was Sir George Yeardley, the founder of Flowerdew Hundred Plantation in 1619. After excavating the home site of Dutch merchant Simon Overzee at St. Mary's City, Maryland, archaeologist Henry Miller noted that "the evidence strongly implies that the Dutch, rather than the London merchants, dominated the tobacco trade during the first decades of settlement in Maryland." Miller's findings were amplified by archaeologist Al Luckenbach, whose recovery of Dutch trade materials at

Figure 3 Medallion of Prince Maurice of Orange, Holland, 1615. Cast brass. 1³/₄" × 1¹/₂". (Courtesy, Flowerdew Hundred Museum.)

Providence in Anne Arundel County, Maryland, revealed "an unsuspected connection of such strength that a reevaluation of this historic period is required."[7]

The inventory of Captain William Moseley (d. 1671) reveals a great deal about the impact of Dutch trade on the material culture of the early Chesapeake. Moseley lived in a large (by seventeenth-century Chesapeake standards), two-and-a-half-story house with an entry, a hall, and a master bedchamber on the first floor, three additional chambers on the second floor, and a study and storeroom in the garret (see appendix A). Furnishing "Mr. Moseley's Study in the garrett" were a little table, a small case of drawers, and "a parcell of Books some french dutch Latten & English." In the "hall chamber" on the second floor were eight chairs, a close stool, a small table, a looking glass, "a little frame to putt a bason on," and "one great dutch trunck & what linnen is in it" valued at 3,470 pounds of tobacco. Moseley's best furnishings were reserved for the "hall" on the first floor. The hall was generally the most elaborate room in seventeenth-century households, and it served a variety of social functions. Moseley's hall furniture included a bed, a couch and two cushions, six chairs, five stools, a "side Borde & Cloath," a table and carpet, six pictures, a looking glass, and "a greate dutch Cash," or *kast*, valued at 500 pounds of tobacco. This value was more than twice that of any other case piece in his house. Moseley's inventory also lists the contents of the kast, which were valued at 2,300 pounds of tobacco: "his woolen waring apparrell . . . 1300, a parcell of Linnen . . . 500, one old Cloaths Suite . . . 300, a small parcell of Buttons & thread a small Remnant of Sewing a Capp & a paire of topps . . . 200." Used for the storage of linens and other expensive household textiles, kasten were the most important furniture forms in seventeenth-century Dutch homes. The use of Moseley's kast differed significantly from the standard Dutch pattern, since it housed his personal clothing as well as linen and household textiles.[8]

Similar patterns of usage are revealed in a court case involving Simon Overzee. According to depositions taken in 1658, Overzee's plantation near St. Mary's City consisted of a kitchen, a dairy, a quarter for his indentured servants, and his main residence. Overzee's house contained a hall and a master bedchamber, with additional sleeping space for guests in the loft. In the Overzees's bedchamber was a closet for the storage of "meate & other necessaries of household" and a "Great Dutch Trunk" for Mrs. Overzee's wardrobe. Her dresses and larger garments were kept in the top compartment, and her bodices, aprons, neck pieces, and other small items were kept in "the Under Drawers."[9]

Seventeenth-century Chesapeake inventories are replete with references to a variety of furniture forms specifically identified as "Dutch" (see appendix B). The majority of these references are from areas where the Dutch tobacco trade flourished, such as Norfolk County, Virginia, and the Eastern Shores of Virginia and Maryland. In 1657, Edward Dowglas of Northampton County on Virginia's Eastern Shore bequeathed to his daughter "one Dutch cupboard," and in 1673, John Fawsett of neighboring Accomack County left his son a "great Dutch chest." Similarly, the 1676 inventory of

John Carr of Cecil County, Maryland, lists "6 turn'd dutch chairs" valued at 360 pounds of tobacco. Unfortunately, most of these inventories fail to specify whether the objects were imported from Holland or made by local tradesmen in a style perceived as being "Dutch." The August 18, 1696, inventory of Thomas Teackle of Accomack County, Virginia, appears to be an exception. Although it includes ambiguous references to a "Round Dutch Table" and "an old Dutch cupboard," his inventory also lists "a pokomoke wheele of the Dutch fashion." The term "pokomoke," which refers to the creek (Pocomoke) dividing Virginia's and Maryland's Eastern Shores, suggests that Teackle's spinning wheel was made by a local tradesman in what his appraisers considered "the Dutch fashion." Evidently, some early Chesapeake joiners were capable of replicating Dutch forms.[10]

Homer Eaton Keyes was one of the first American furniture historians to speculate on the Continental aspects of seventeenth-century Chesapeake furniture. In an article on American joined chairs, Keyes illustrated a rare

Figure 4 Armchair, probably Virginia, 1650–1690. Oak. (Courtesy, Wadsworth Atheneum; photo, Museum of Early Southern Decorative Arts.)

Figure 5 Court cupboard, possibly Virginia, 1620–1680. Oak. (Illustrated in *Antiques* 24, no. 9 [October 1938]: 216.)

example "discovered by Mr. Goodwin in Virginia" (fig. 4). The chair's fielded, molded back panel and sawn legs differed from the New England examples he illustrated, prompting him to write: "It is perhaps significant that these features occur in a chair . . . from a part of the country . . . [with] settlers from the Continent." Keyes reasserted the argument for Continental influences in seventeenth-century Chesapeake furniture when he published a photograph of an oak court cupboard found "amid squalid surroundings" in Virginia (fig. 5). Keyes wrote:

> There seems no reason to doubt that it hails from the 1600's. But what was the nationality of its author? On that point we can say only that the cupboard shows not a trace of English tradition. The backboard along the top, the rectangular posts and the central drop, the closed back of the lower compartment and the double fielding of the panels recall renaissance cupboards of the European continent . . . Was this massive article of furniture made somewhere in Virginia by a European immigrant, or was it brought from across the ocean? . . . If the cupboard may be given clear title to an American birthright, it will occupy an important place in the domain of our earliest furniture.[11]

Despite previous misconceptions, the Chesapeake's artisan community was never uniformly English (see appendix C). As early as 1608, the Virginia Company of London sent "eight Dutchmen and Poles" to work as glass

Figure 6 Clothes cupboard, Virginia, 1650–1690. Walnut with yellow pine. H. 61$\frac{1}{2}$", W. 61$\frac{3}{4}$", D. 20". (Collection of the Museum of Early Southern Decorative Arts.)

blowers at Jamestown, and recent archaeological excavations have uncovered numerous examples of their work. Four of the "Dutchmen" in this group were later dispatched to work as carpenters for the purpose of building a "castle" for the local Indian chief, Powhatan. In 1621, the Virginia Company instructed Governor Francis Wyatt to "take care of the Dutch sent to build saw mills" and to ship lumber down the James River for export to Europe. Six years later, the Council and General Court of James City County, Virginia, noted that "Derrick the Dutch Carpenter" had agreed to build a boat for a local Englishwoman. After the English conquest of New York, New Jersey, and Delaware, a small number of Dutch families moved to the southern colonies, particularly Maryland. Many of these emigrés were carpenters, such as Matthias Peterson, Peter Mills, and Thomas Turner, whose naturalization records specify their Dutch origins. Turner reported that his birthplace was "Middleborough, Province of Zealand" when he applied for naturalization in Anne Arundel County in 1671. Also among the carpenters who emigrated from New Netherland to Maryland were Remy Lefer, Nicholas Fontaine, and Joseph Deserne, whose names appear more French than Dutch. From the outset, New Netherland was an ethnic polyglot of Dutch, Swedes, Finns, Germans, Walloons, and French Huguenots. The 1681 inventory of Dutch carpenter Henricke Cloystockfish lists tools appropriate for his trade, including nine old chisels, ten caulking irons, seven old planes, three old hammers, one old axe, three old adzes, two old saws, "an old Chest with some old Tooles," and "a parcell of old Dutch Bookes."[12]

Less than two dozen pieces of seventeenth-century Chesapeake furniture are known, but nearly a quarter have stylistic and structural features more closely associated with the Dutch-influenced furniture of New York than with the predominantly British-influenced products of New England. The clothes cupboard illustrated in figure 6 provides the strongest evidence of Dutch influence on early Chesapeake joinery. Although its walnut primary wood, fielded panels, and dovetailed construction caused scholars to date the cupboard between 1690 and 1710, Dutch-trained joiners in the Chesapeake produced "close Cupboard" forms by the 1660s. Documentary and physical evidence strongly suggest that this piece was made in Virginia during the third quarter of the seventeenth century.[13]

Although the seventeenth century is generally considered the age of oak furniture, Virginia walnut was shipped to England for "waynscot, tables, cubbordes, chairs and stooles" during the 1630s. The joiner who made the clothes cupboard used walnut for the front, canted corners, sides, moldings, and spindles, and yellow pine for the top, bottom, and back. The top and bottom boards are dovetailed to the sides, and the backboards are nailed to the top and bottom and pinned to the sides (fig. 7). Joiners in the Netherlands began using dovetail construction during the early sixteenth century.

The design of the clothes cupboard is unique. Although other colonial case pieces such as Germanic *schranken* and French *armoires* were used for storing clothes and household textiles, the form most closely associated with the clothes cupboard is the kast from Dutch-settled areas of New York

Figure 7 Detail of the back of the clothes cupboard illustrated in fig. 6.

Figure 8 Kast, New York, 1650–1700. White and red oak. H. 70", W. 67", D. 25". (Courtesy, Metropolitan Museum of Art, gift of Millia Davenport, 1988.)

and New Jersey (see fig. 8). By extension, the Virginia cupboard may be interpreted as a vernacular version of the magnificent Amsterdam kast depicted in Pieter de Hooch's, *Portrait of a Family Making Music* (fig. 9). At first, this comparison may seem absurd; however, both pieces employ similar frame-and-panel construction (figs. 6, 9); both rest on separate turned feet (fig. 10); both have raised panel doors (fig. 11); and both have canted

Figure 9 Pieter de Hooch, *Portrait of a Family Making Music*, Holland, 1663. Oil on canvas. 39³/₄" × 46". (Courtesy, Cleveland Museum of Art, gift of the Hanna Fund.)

corners. The kast in de Hooch's painting has carved baroque pilasters at the corners, whereas the Virginia-made example has long, mannerist spindles.

The clothes cupboard has at least four structural details associated with Dutch or Dutch colonial kasten—fielded panels, moldings run directly on the frame, mitered mortise-and-tenon joints, and dovetails. The panels on the cupboard have distinctive, concave fields that were cut with a large hollow plane, whereas those on New York kasten (see fig. 8) were typically formed with a panel plane. The fielded panels on the Virginia piece, nevertheless, almost certainly emanate from a Continental tradition, since fielded panels rarely occur on English work before the 1660s or on New England work from the seventeenth century. Such panels do occur, however, on New York kasten by the middle of the seventeenth century.[14]

The panel-and-frame construction of the clothes cupboard also relates more closely to Dutch joinery practices than to English ones. As on many New York and Dutch kasten, the doors of the cupboard have directly

Figure 10   Detail of a turned foot on the clothes cupboard illustrated in fig. 6.

Figure 11   Detail of the mitered joinery and raised panels on the clothes cupboard illustrated in fig. 6.

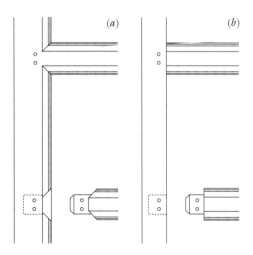

Figure 12   Drawing of a (*a*) mitered mortise-and-tenon joint and (*b*) flat-faced mortise-and-tenon joint. (Adapted from a drawing in Peter M. Kenny, Frances Gruber Safford, and Gilbert T. Vincent, *American Kasten: The Dutch-Style Cupboards of New York and New Jersey 1650–1800* [New York: The Metropolitan Museum of Art, 1991], p. 12; artwork, Wynne Patterson.)

molded stiles and rails and mitered mortise-and-tenon joints (see figs. 6, 8, 11, 12*a*). In English panel-and-frame construction, stile and rail moldings are typically applied, or they are planed on only one of the adjoining framing members (see fig. 12*b*). As might be expected, no seventeenth-century New England furniture displays mitered mortise-and-tenon joinery. Other northern European details on the clothes cupboard are the diamond-shaped pins used to secure the mortise-and-tenon joints and backboards and the splines between the backboards (figs. 7, 13).

Most importantly, the clothes cupboard is the earliest piece of southern furniture with dovetail construction (fig. 13). In the colonies, dovetail joinery first appears on furniture associated with a small group of London-trained artisans who arrived in Boston and New Haven during the 1630s and early 1640s. In their work, and in most New England furniture of the seventeenth century, dovetailing is limited to the drawers of joined case pieces. Furniture historian Robert Trent has shown how dovetail technology could have arrived in London as early as the 1540s through the importation of chests from Danzig, Prussia, the Netherlands, Cologne, France, Italy, and the Iberian Peninsula. These chests, which featured board and dovetail construction, were favored by merchants and lesser gentry in England's major ports. On the clothes cupboard, dovetails are used to attach the top and bottom boards to the sides. The early appearance of board and dovetail joinery on the Continent and its scarcity in Anglo-American furniture support the assertion that the clothes cupboard was made by a joiner trained in a northern European tradition.[15]

The clothes cupboard has a number of features that differentiate it from related Continental forms, such as the kast, schrank, and armoire. Its asymmetrical facade is the most obvious anomaly. The large compartment on the right is fitted on three sides with a pegboard for hanging clothes (fig. 14), and the smaller compartment on the left has two shelves for storing folded textiles (fig. 15). William Moseley's "great dutch Cash" may have been outfitted in a similar fashion, for it contained suits of clothes, "woolen war-

Figure 14 Detail of the pegboard in the clothes cupboard illustrated in fig. 6.

Figure 13 Detail of the dovetailed top and splined backboards on the clothes cupboard illustrated in fig. 6.

ing apparrell," and linens. No Continental precedent for this interior arrangement is known, although Moseley's inventory suggests that it could be a regional adaptation.

Like the clothes cupboard, many early Chesapeake chairs (figs. 16, 17) have features that differentiate them from contemporary New England work and also link them to New York examples (fig. 18). Virginia chairs typically have turned arms that project beyond the front post rather than being tenoned into them, as on most English and New England examples. Overpassing arms are relatively common on seventeenth- and eighteenth-cen-

Figure 15 Detail of the interior shelving on the clothes cupboard illustrated in fig. 6.

Figure 16 Armchair, southeastern Virginia, 1680–1700. Cherry. H. 41³/₄", W. 23¹/₂", D. 23¹/₂". (Collection of the Museum of Early Southern Decorative Arts.)

tury chairs from Holland and France. The Chesapeake had a small Dutch and French population during the seventeenth century, but between 1700 and 1710 the French population increased dramatically owing to the emigration of Huguenot refugees to southeast Virginia. The armchair illustrated in figure 17 has another detail found on chairs from the Netherlands and France—a row of small turned finials tenoned into the crest rail. Three other Chesapeake chairs share this distinctive feature.[16]

One of the clearest manifestations of Continental influence in the Chesapeake is the stretcher table illustrated in figure 19. The table was purchased earlier this century by dealer Bessie L. Brockwell of Petersburg, Virginia, who discovered many of the surviving examples of seventeenth-century Chesapeake furniture. Made of black walnut and cedrela, a tropical hardwood probably imported from the West Indies, the table has a dovetailed frame and legs that are braced into the corners and pinned. Although the braces wedging the legs have no known parallel, some early New York City draw-bar tables have exposed dovetail frames (see fig. 20). Furniture historian Peter Kenny has attributed these tables to Dutch joiners and

Figure 17 Armchair, Virginia, 1680–1700. Cherry, hickory, and white oak. H. 43½", W. 25", D. 22¾". (Collection of the Museum of Early Southern Decorative Arts.)

shown how their dovetail frames relate to the base construction of contemporary New York kasten. The Virginia table could have been made by a Dutch tradesman who immigrated to the Chesapeake region after the English conquest of New Amsterdam.[17]

The most compelling evidence that Dutch styles had a lasting influence on Chesapeake furniture centers around George Hack, a Dutch physician who died in Accomack County, Virginia, in 1665, and his indentured servant John Rickards. Hack's widow, Anna, subsequently moved to Maryland with her two sons and was granted citizenship by a special act of the colonial legislature. Maryland records describe her as "born in Amsterdam, Holland," and her sons, George and Peter, as "born at Accomacke, Virginia." The Hack family was granted citizenship on the same day as Augustine Herrman and his family.[18]

Although Rickards is referred to as a "carpenter" in Accomack records of 1668, the tools that were at his disposal during his indenture were more varied than that trade required. Hack's inventory listed "1 Crosscut Saw, 2 old whipsaws, 1 rest & a file, 1 old broad ax, 1 hatchet, 1 Pr. Iron compasses, 13

Figure 18 Armchair, New York or New Jersey, early eighteenth century. Maple, ash, and cherry; painted black. H. 50", W. 23", D. 18". (Courtesy, Albany Institute of Art and History.)

Figure 19 Stretcher table, eastern Virginia, 1690–1720. Walnut with cedrela. H. 26", W. 46¼", D. 32¼". (Courtesy, H. L. Chalfant Antiques.)

plaines small & great, 1 handsaw, 3 small saws, 2 percer Stocks & 5 percer bitts, 1 glue pott, 3 gowdges, 7 Chissells & 5 gimletts, 1 hamer, 1 pr. of pincers, 1 drawinge knife & 1 coopers adds, 1 howell, 5 turning tools, 2 broken holdfasts & 1 bench hook." The thirteen planes, turning implements, and glue pot suggest that Rickards was both a turner and a furniture joiner.[19]

In 1668, Rickards signed an indenture with Anne Boote of Accomack County, in which he agreed to make fifty-four pieces of furniture.

> These presents bindeth mee John Rickards . . . to pay or cause to be paid unto Mrs. Anne Boote . . . These followinge works, Eight bedsteads, Nine tables & ten formes, five close Cupboards, five Courth Cupboards, one Courth Cupboard very handsome according to Mrs. Boote her directions, one close Cupboard also, Six Spinne wheeles, five chaire Tables, four chests this worke is to bee done by me Jno. Rickards . . . or else to forfeit one thousand lb. of Tobacco.

Mrs. Boote undoubtedly intended to sell most of Rickards's work; however, the "very handsome" court cupboard and clothes cupboard made "according to Mrs. Boote" were probably for her personal use. The latter phrase shows how seventeenth-century patrons interacted with tradesmen and influenced the design of their household furnishings. Court cupboards and "close cupboards" like the example illustrated in figure 6 were obviously popular forms in Virginia during the third quarter of the seventeenth century.[20]

Indentures and apprenticeships clearly contributed to the persistence of Dutch furniture-making traditions in the Chesapeake. In 1673, Rickards took William Phillpott as an apprentice for the unusually short term of three years and nine months. Rickards agreed to teach Phillpott the "vocation of [the] Carpenters Trade" and furnish him with "such Carpenters Tooles as the Said Phillpott Worketh with in the time of his Servitude" at the end of his indenture. Since William Phillpott was undoubtedly a young man in 1673, it is possible that the shop tradition that began with Rickards's indenture to Hack extended into the early eighteenth century.[21]

Figure 20 Draw-bar table, New York City, 1690–1710. Red gum with tulip poplar and pine. H. 29³/₄", frame dimensions: 35⁷/₈" × 20³/₈". (Private collection; photo, Gavin Ashworth.)

Clearly no Continental Europeans were more involved in the commercial and political affairs of the Chesapeake region than the Dutch. During the first quarter of the seventeenth century, they sailed to the Chesapeake to barter for tobacco. Dutch traders established permanent settlements at strategic points along the region's waterways, and Dutch artisans immigrated to the region. Although the Dutch were gradually assimilated by the larger English population, documentary and material evidence indicates that they had a profound impact on the material life of the seventeenth-century Chesapeake region.

ACKNOWLEDGMENTS   For their assistance with this article, I thank Robert Trent, Luke Beckerdite, Peter Kenny, Martha Rowe, Ronald Hurst, Jay Gaynor, and especially Frank Horton.

1. Simon Schama, *The Embarrassment of Riches: An Interpretation of Dutch Culture in the Golden Age* (Berkeley: University of California Press, 1988), pp. 53–57. C. A. Weslager, *The Swedes and the Dutch at New Castle* (New York: Bart, 1987), pp. 1–24.

2. Charlotte Wilcoxen, *Dutch Trade and Ceramics in America in the Seventeenth Century* (Albany, N.Y.: Albany Institute of History and Art, 1987), pp. 13, 19–25. For the reference to Sir Thomas Dale, see p. 19.

3. John R. Pagan, "Dutch Maritime and Commercial Activity in Mid-Seventeenth-Century Virginia," *Virginia Magazine of History and Biography* 90, no. 4 (October 1982): 485–501. Wilcoxen, *Dutch Trade and Ceramics*, p. 20. David Peterson DeVries, "Voyages from Holland to America, A. D. 1632 to 1644," translated by Henry C. Murphy, *Collections of the New York Historical Society,* second series, vol. 3, part 1 (New York: D. Appleton and Company, 1857), pp. 32–37, 74–78, 123–27.

4. Pagan, "Dutch Maritime and Commercial Activity," pp. 485–501. See also, Jan Kupp, "Dutch Notarial Acts Relating to the Tobacco Trade in Virginia, 1608–1653," *William and Mary Quarterly* 30, no. 4 (October 1973): 653–55.

5. Wilcoxen, *Dutch Trade and Ceramics,* p. 20. "Richard Ingle in Maryland," *Maryland Historical Magazine* 1, no. 2 (June 1906): 131–33, 140. "Petition of certain Dutch Merchants to the States General," in *Documents Relative to the Colonial History of the State of New York; Procured in Holland, England and France,* edited by E. B. O'Callaghan (Albany, N.Y.: Weed, Parsons, and Company, 1856), pp. 436–37.

6. Pagan, "Dutch Maritime and Commercial Activity," pp. 493–501. Wilcoxen, *Dutch Trade and Ceramics,* p. 21. "Denization of Augustine Herman," *Maryland Historical Magazine* 3, no. 2 (June 1908): 170; Wilcoxen, *Dutch Trade and Ceramics,* p. 24.

7. For the connection between Dutch trade and Chinese export porcelain in Virginia, see Julia B. Curtis, "Chinese Ceramics and the Dutch Connection in Early Seventeenth-Century Virginia," in *Vereniging van Vrienden der Aziatische Kunst* (Amsterdam: Mededelingenblad, 1985), pp. 6–13; and Wilcoxen, *Dutch Trade and Ceramics,* pp. 73–80. Information on Kicotan is from personal communication with William Pittman, Department of Archaeological Research, Colonial Williamsburg Foundation. John L. Cotter, *Archaeological Excavations at Jamestown* (Washington, D.C.: U.S. Department of the Interior, Archeological Research Series Number Four, 1958), pp. 172, 185, 201–86. James Deetz, *Flowerdew Hundred: The Archaeology of a Virginia Plantation, 1614–1864* (Charlottesville: University Press of Virginia, 1993), pp. 43–44. Henry M. Miller, *A Search for the "Citty of Saint Maries"* (St. Mary's City, Md.: St. Mary's City Commission, 1983), p. 82. Al Luckenbach, *Providence 1649: The History and Archaeology of Anne Arundel County Maryland's First European Settlement* (Annapolis, Md.: Maryland State Archives and Maryland Historical Trust, 1995), p. 2.

8. Inventory of Captain William Moseley, October 16, 1671, Norfolk County, Va., Wills, Deeds, &c., bk. E, 1666–1675, folios 105–7. Unless otherwise noted, all primary sources cited in this article are from transcriptions in the artisan and personnel files at the Museum of Early Southern Decorative Arts (hereinafter cited as MESDA), Winston-Salem, North Carolina. For a discussion of the Dutch kast, see T. H. Lunsingh Scheurleer, "The Dutch and Their Homes in the Seventeenth Century," in *Arts of the Anglo-American Community in the Seventeenth Century,* edited by Ian M. G. Quimby (Charlottesville: University Press of Virginia for the Winterthur Museum, 1975), pp. 15–29; Reinier Baarsen, *Dutch Furniture 1600–1800* (Amsterdam: Rijksmuseum, 1993), pp. 8–9, 14–15, 24–25, 34–35; and Peter M. Kenny, Frances Gruber Safford, and Gilbert T. Vincent, *American Kasten: The Dutch-Style Cupboards of New York and New Jersey 1650–1800* (New York: Metropolitan Museum of Art, 1991), pp. 1–10.

9. Gary Wheeler Stone, "St. John's: Archaeological Questions and Answers," *Maryland Historical Magazine* 69, no. 2 (summer 1974): 157–58.

10. Will of Edward Dowglas, November 12, 1657, Northampton County, Va., Deeds, Wills, &c., nos. 7 and 8, 1655–1668, folio 77. Will of John Fawsett, October 16, 1673, Accomack County, Va., Wills, Deeds, Orders, &c., 1673–1676, folio 7. Inventory of John Carr, September 16, 1676, Maryland Prerogative Court, Inventories and Accounts, vol. 2, 1676, folio 281. Inventory of Thomas Teackle, August 18, 1696, Accomack County, Va., Wills &c., 1692–1715, folio 138a.

11. Homer Eaton Keyes, "Notes on American Wainscot Chairs," *Antiques* 16, no. 6 (June 1930): 523. Homer Eaton Keyes, "Riddles & Replies," *Antiques* 24, no. 9 (October 1938): 216.

12. John Smith, *The Complete Works of Captain John Smith,* edited by Philip L. Barbour, 3 vols. (Chapel Hill: University of North Carolina Press, 1950), 2:180–200. William W. Hening, *The Statutes at Large; being a Collection of all the Laws of Virginia* (New York, 1823), p. 115. Minutes of the Council and General Court, James City County, Va., July 2, 1627. Jeffrey A. Wyand and Florence L. Wyand, *Colonial Maryland Naturalizations* (Baltimore, Md.: Genealogical Publishing Co., 1986), pp. 2–6. For more on the ethnic origins of New York's artisan community, see Kenny, Safford, and Vincent, *American Kasten*, pp. 14–15; and Neil D. Kamil, "Hidden in Plain Sight: Disappearance and Material Life in Colonial New York," in *American Furniture*, edited by Luke Beckerdite (Hanover, N.H.: University Press of New England for

the Chipstone Foundation, 1995), passim. Inventory of Henricke Cloystockfish, May 17, 1681, Maryland Prerogative Court, Inventories and Accounts, vol. 7, 1680–1682, folio 11.

13. The clothes cupboard was discovered in eastern Virginia by Richmond dealer J. K. Beard. In 1940, Frank L. Horton purchased it from Beard's estate. For other interpretations of this clothes cupboard, see James R. and Marilyn S. Melchor, "Analysis of an Enigma," *Journal of Early Southern Decorative Arts* 12, no. 1 (May 1986): 1–18; and John Bivins and Forsyth Alexander, *The Regional Arts of the Early South: A Sampling from the Collection of the Museum of Early Southern Decorative Arts* (Chapel Hill: University of North Carolina Press for MESDA, 1991), p. 23.

14. Kenny, Safford, and Vincent, *American Kasten*, pp. 10–15.

15. The London joiners who immigrated to Boston included Ralph Mason (1635), John Davis (1635), and Henry Messinger (1640). The London joiners who immigrated to New Haven included William Russell and William Gibbons (1640). For more on these men and the origins of dovetail construction in London and New England, see Benno M. Forman, "The Chest of Drawers in America, 1635–1730: The Origins of the Joined Chest of Drawers," *Winterthur Portfolio* 20, no. 1 (spring 1985): 9–14; Robert F. Trent, "The Chest of Drawers in America, 1635–1730: A Postscript," *Winterthur Portfolio* 20, no. 1 (spring 1985): 31–48; Benno M. Forman, *American Seating Furniture, 1630–1730* (New York: W. W. Norton for the Winterthur Museum, 1988), p. 42; Benno M. Forman, "Urban Aspects of Massachusetts Furniture in the Late Seventeenth Century," in *Country Cabinetwork and Simple City Furniture*, edited by John D. Morse (Charlottesville: University Press of Virginia for Winterthur Museum, 1970), pp. 12–16; Robert F. Trent, "New England Joinery and Turning before 1700," in *New England Begins: The Seventeenth Century*, 3 vols. (Boston: the Museum of Fine Arts, Boston, 1982), pp. 501–9; 522–26, nos. 481, 482; and Robert F. Trent, "Recent Discoveries in Early New England Furniture," lecture at the 1997 Antiques Forum, Williamsburg, Virginia. The Savell shop of Braintree, Massachusetts, also used dovetails to join drawer sides to drawer fronts (Peter Follansbee and John D. Alexander, "Seventeenth-Century Joinery from Braintree, Massachusetts: The Savell Shop Tradition," in *American Furniture*, edited by Luke Beckerdite [Hanover, N.H.: University Press of New England for the Chipstone Foundation, 1996], pp. 94–96).

16. Bivins and Alexander, *Regional Arts of the Early South*, p. 21. Roderic H. Blackburn and Ruth Piwonka, *Remembrance of Patria: Dutch Arts and Culture in Colonial America 1609–1776* (Albany, N.Y.: Albany Institute of History and Art, 1988), p. 175. John T. Kirk, *American Furniture in the British Tradition to 1830* (New York: Alfred A. Knopf, 1982), p. 236, fig. 768. I am grateful to Ronald Hurst for bringing this illustration to my attention.

17. For the history of this table, see accession files, Colonial Williamsburg Foundation. Peter M. Kenny, "Flat Gates, Draw Bars, Twists, and Urns: New York's Distinctive, Early Baroque Oval Tables with Falling Leaves," in *American Furniture*, edited by Luke Beckerdite (Hanover, N.H.: University Press of New England for the Chipstone Foundation, 1994), pp. 113–14.

18. Inventory of George Hack, May 22, 1665, Accomack County, Va., Deeds and Wills, 1664–1671, folio 28a. Wyand, "Naturalizations Granted by Enactment of Private Laws," *Colonial Maryland Naturalizations*, p. 5.

19. Inventory of George Hack. For an excellent discussion of early woodworking tools, see Jay Gaynor, "'Tooles of all sorts to worke': A Brief Look at Trade Tools in 17th-Century Virginia," in *The Archaeology of 17th-Century Virginia*, edited by Theodore R. Reinhart and Dennis Pogue (Richmond, Va.: Archeological Society of Virginia, Special Publication no. 30, 1993), pp. 311–56.

20. Bond of John Rickards to Anne Boote, June 6, 1668, Accomack County, Va., Orders, Wills &c., 1671–1673, folio 231.

21. Articles of Agreement between William Phillpott and John Rickards, January 9, 1673/4, Accomack County, Va., Wills, Deeds, Orders, &c., 1673–1676, folio 32.

Appendix A

Inventory of Captain William Moseley, 1671

An Inventory & appraisement of the Estate of Capt. Wm. Moseley being taken and appraised the 10th day of November 1671 by the under written who were sumoned & sworne to that purpose by vertu of an order of Court the 16th October last past as following:

Vizt.

	lb. tob.
In Mr. Moseley's Study in the Garrett	
Impr. A parcell of Books Some french dutch Latten & English all att	3000
A Case of Small draws a little table & other small trifles	160
In the Garrett	
A Small parcell of tooles & Lumber	400
In the Chamber over her owne Roome	
one feather Bead and Boulster one Rugg & blankett one Sheete a matt bead stead & bead straws	1000
one Couch a feather boulster & pillow & blankett	200
7 Chayres, weights & scales a small looking glasse a towell frame and [illegible]	200
a little trunck and Box	100
In the Porch Chamber	
a feather bead & furniture as It Stands	2500
a table and foure Chayres & a little Cushion	300
2 truncks a Box a looking glasse a Brush & window Curtains and a few pipes	300
In the Hall Chamber	
8 Chayres a Close stoole a small table 3 small Chushions a Carpett & little Baskett	860
one greate dutch trunck & what linnen is In It	3470
one small trunck wth linnen a scarlett wascote & trifles holland dublett	2220
a payre of andirons a fire shovell one other small trunck one looking glasse one spoone a small parcell of Earthen things a little frame to putt a bason on a pocket knife & a little stoole	750
foure picktures 100; for what is in a little Closett 100	200

ROBERT A. LEATH

In the Hall

a feather bead & furniture as It Stands	1700
a Couch & Couch bead blankett & 2 Chushions	300
a side Borde & Cloath 2 Chushions a pewter bason & yoar and several saltes & a dish	250
a table & Carpett Six Chaires 5 Stooles	550
2 Chests 4 boxes a looking glasse and a Brush	550
a paire of Brasse andirons & Snuffers & a Brasse Branch of Candle Sticks [illegible]	560
Six picktures a frame & a parcell of Earthen things a partison & a Baskett 600; a greate dutch Cash 500	1100
his woolen waring aparrell	1300
a parcell of Linen	500
one old Cloaths Suite & [illegible]	300
a small parcell of Buttons & thread a small Remnant of Sewing a Capp & a paire of topps	200

Carried to the other side	22,870

lb. tob.

Brought from the other side	22, 870

In her owne Roome

a feather bead & furniture as It Stands	1200
a trundle bead and furniture	300
a Couch and Couch bead Chusion, blankett, Cradle and what's in It	300
a table two formes 8 Chayres & 3 stooles	650
a Chest of draws & 2 boxes	700
one pr. of Iron andirons, tongs, Slice Snuffers bellows warming pan, 2 picktures and a looking glasse Lanthorne & other trifling things	550

In the Entry

a Chest a box a table a Safe 2 Stocks Some knives & other Lumber	350

Under the Stayre Case

a Small parcell of tooles & other Lumber	200

In the milke house

a table some Caskes, a parcell of trays & bowls, panns Juggs and other Earthen things & wooden trenchers	400
204 lb. of pewter	2500

In the passage to the kitchen

a Shelfe of small brasse a lamp and a Lanthorne	700

In the kitchen

a parcell of Iron potts kittles Spitts and frying panns a Copper & a Brasse kettle	1100
an Iron Rack andirons pott Racks dripping panns and some Brasse things on a Shelfe an old Brasse Stewpan & an old still	700
three gunns & other Lumber	970

In a shead things there	80

Without doores

an old Cart & wheeles 2 ploughs and one sett of Irons	400
a parcell of old tooles and other Lumber	380
an old boate & Apurtenances & Canoe	500
Tables & other horse harnesse	300
about 60 head of Hoggs young & old	6000
about 18 head of Hoggs at the plantacon att lin haven bye	
Informacon about one year old one [illegible]	2000

In the Sider house

a parcell of Salt and an Iron Chayne	600
pestle and Sliceyards & Canhooke	300
one old negro man & woman	3000
one young negro man & woman	10,000
one mollatto woman 5000; one negro girle about 3 years 1800	6800
one negro boy about 1 _ yeares old	2000
a Boy about [illegible] yeares old sonne of the mollatto woman her mother being a negro woman	2600
an English man servant about 2 yeares to serve	1000
a Signett Ring and a small parcell of Riband	00
a little old Sash	20

Carried to the other side	lbs.	68,770
Brought from the other side		68,770

5 lbs. and an ounce of Silver being Exactly weighed wth. brasse weights & Scales a hatt and Silver hatband which Shee Informed us Shee had disposed of	00
Mrs. Moseleys Side Sadle & furniture	300

	lbs.	69,270

Wee the Subscribers being sumoned & sworne appraisors of the Estate of Capt. Wm. Moseley decd. have accordingly to the best of our Judgments appraised what was Brought unto us as upon this Inventory upwards which Amounts unto the Some of Sixty nyne thousand two hundred & seventy pounds of tob. & Caske besides the five lbs. & one ounce of Plate which wee did see weighed in with scales which wee have here unto Subscribed this 11th day of November 1671

> Tho: Bridges
> Tho: viz. Jun.
> Will Hancock
> Henry Spratt

debts due to the Estate

Impr. Capt. Carvers note	190
Tho: Cartwrites bill	383
James Jeslands bill	400
Wm. Boultons bill	84
Humphry Smiths bill	110
Capt. Jn. Custis debt	5000
	6167

Wm. Moseleys bill of gallaway
being a desperate debt   650

a list of the Horses Sheepe & Cattle belonging
to the Estate of Capt. Wm. Moseley decd. vizt.

One stone horse about 5 yeares old, two old mares one young mare
one blind mare about 2 yeares old, a yearling horse

Sheepe

five yewes, one Ram one weather

Cattle

18 young Cows, 5 very old, 5 hayfers 3 yeare old Each, two hayfers
2 yeare old, 6 yearling hayfers, somme Steeres 5 yeare old, 3 Steeres
foure yeare old, six steere 3 yeare old, one bull foure yeare old,
five yearling steers, two steers Calves of this years fall

Att Lin haven plantacon

foure Cows and a bull Calfe 5 yearling hayfers & one year
ling Steere

> Sworne to in open Court by Mrs. Mary Moseley
> to bee a true Inventory of Capt. Wm. Moseley's Estate
> the Crop, one Bead & her wearing Cloathes
> Excepted this 15th November 1671
>
> Wm. Porter Court Clerk

Source: Norfolk County, Va., Wills and Deeds, bk. E, 1666–1675, folios
105–7.

Appendix B

Dutch Objects in Seventeenth-Century Chesapeake Wills and Inventories

"one Dutch cupboard"	Northampton County, Va.	Will of Edward Dowglas, November 12, 1657
"greate Dutch Trunk [with] Under Drawers"	St. Mary's County, Md.	Case of Simon Overzee, *Maryland Archives,* 41, 1658
"High German and Dutch Books"	Accomack County, Va.	Inventory of George Hack, May 22, 1665
"One Round Dutch Table"	Unspecified county, Md.	Inventory of Hugh Stanley, October 1, 1669
"a parcell of Books some french, dutch, Latten & English . . . one greate dutch trunck . . . one greate Dutch Cash"	Norfolk County, Va.	Inventory of William Moseley, 1671
"my great Dutch chest"	Accomack County, Va.	Will of John Fawsett, August 15, 1673
"Parcell of Dutch earthen ware"	Anne Arundel County, Md.	Inventory of William Neale, March 13, 1675/6
"a map of Amsterdam . . . 1 dutch painted cupboard"	St. Mary's County, Md.	Inventory of Richard and Elizabeth Moy, February 14, 1675/6
"6 turn'd dutch chaires"	Cecil County, Md.	Inventory of John Carr, September 16, 1676
"parcell of old Dutch Bookes"	Unspecified county, Md.	Inventory of Henricke Cloystockfish, May 17, 1681
"one Dutch cubert & cloth"	Norfolk County, Va.	Inventory of Adam Keeling, March 19, 1683/4
"the greate Dutch presse . . . in the dineinge Roome"	Northampton County, Va.	Will of John Custis, March 18, 1691/2
"a Dutch Chest"	Accomack County, Va.	Will of Owen Collonie, September 19, 1693
"2 du[t]ch painted boxes"	Essex County, Va.	Inventory of Francis Marriner, February 22, 1693/4

"a Dutch chest . . . one Dutch case with twelve glass bottles . . . a Dutch table . . . foure leather Dutch chaires"	Northampton County, Va.	Will of Robert Fletcher, November 29, 1695
"One Du[t]ch Table"	Isle of Wight County, Va.	Inventory of Thomas Taberer, February 4, 1694/5
"Iron bound dutch box"	Isle of Wight County,. Va.	Inventory of Nicholas Smith, July 23, 1696
"a pokomoke wheel in the Dutch fashion . . . a Round Dutch table . . . an old Dutch cupboard"	Accomack County, Va.	Inventory of Thomas Teackle, August 18, 1696
"Parcell of Dutch Earthen Ware"	Isle of Wight County, Va.	Inventory of Capt. James Benn, May 1, 1697

Source: Artisan files, Museum of Early Southern Decorative Arts.

Appendix C

Dutch and Other Continental Tradesmen in the Seventeenth-Century Chesapeake Region

"eight Dutchmen and Poles"	glass makers	James City County, Va., 1608
"Derrick the Dutch Carpenter"	carpenter and shipwright	James City County, Va., 1627
Thomas Turner	carpenter	Anne Arundel County, Md., 1653
Bartholomew Engelbretson	carpenter and cooper	Lower Norfolk County, Va., 1659
Augustin Herrman	surveyor	Cecil County, Md., 1661
Nicholas Fountaine	carpenter and cooper	Calvert County, Md., 1665–1703
Peter Mills	carpenter	St. Mary's County, Md., 1667–1685
Matthias Peterson	carpenter	Talbot County, Md., 1671–1686
Cornelius Vorhoofe	carpenter and shipwright	Accomack County, Va., 1668
Hans DeRinge	carpenter	Baltimore County, Md., 1672
Michael Paulus Vanderford	carpenter	Talbot County, Md., 1672–1692
Joseph Diserne	carpenter	York County, Va., 1679–1704
Henricke Cloystockfish	carpenter and shipwright	Unspecified county, Md., 1681
Remy Lefer	carpenter	St. Mary's County, Md., 1688

Source: Artisan files, Museum of Early Southern Decorative Arts.

John Bivins

The Convergence and Divergence of Three Stylistic Traditions in Charleston Neoclassical Case Furniture, 1785–1800

▼ AS MUCH AS ANY OTHER cultural remnant, furniture from the shops of Charleston cabinetmakers reveals a sophisticated pattern of stylistic development throughout the eighteenth century. This pattern was nourished not only by the cosmopolitan disposition of the city's inhabitants but also by the complexity of design trends arriving from widespread sources. Charlestonians were ever eager to learn of styles that were both new and modish, as long as they were not excessively flamboyant. From the 1730s to the end of the colonial period, furniture made in the city reflected South Carolina's position as the diadem in the crown of British mercantilism. Charleston did not export finished goods, but her ships were filled with naval stores, rice, and indigo, all of which brought enormous fortunes to Low Country planters and merchants while handsomely lining the Crown purse. Due to the vast web of business affairs inexorably binding South Carolina planters and merchant houses to British factors, the transmission of British fashion to the city was not only rapid but almost monolithic—at least until the end of the 1760s. After that point, a growing community of Continental artisans began to have a signal effect on Charleston's furniture. Rapidly following that phenomenon was a host of further design stimuli sailing into Charleston harbor with the American coastal trade, which grew at an astonishing rate during the last decades of the century.

The transition that began in Charleston furniture during the 1770s espoused many ideals characteristic of the neoclassical style already current in London. Despite the well-entrenched British baroque and rococo modes that were so much a part of Charleston furniture before the 1770s, the end of the Revolution coincided in Charleston with a surprisingly abrupt and widespread housecleaning of the "old" styles, perhaps more so than in any other American city. Although the high standards of largely British shop practices did not diminish, they were often applied to new furniture forms. Familiar old forms such as double chests instantly vaporized in cabinet shops seeking to provide movables suitable for fashionable Charleston interiors in the "antique" style. Single houses remained the most common architectural unit, but they were equally transformed. Double and triple piazzas erupted on the long axis of these dwellings, and centrally oriented and more elegant private entrances off the street became the norm. Ceilings continued to rise, and chimneypieces formerly caparisoned with leafage and scrolls "conveyed," as Thomas Chippendale put it, "from the French Renaissance" were no longer tolerated with anything less ordered than carved paterae, reeding, and composition tableau ushered forth from the ruins of

Herculaneum. Political grievances aside, Britain remained the mother of taste, but it was not long before Charlestonians found it equally comfortable to cast an eye upon the fresh efforts of their own countrymen. This phenomenon was a mighty contrast to what had gone on for most of the five decades preceding the flight of the last royal governor out his back door and down Vanderhorst's Creek to the harbor. More of England left Charleston with William Campbell than just the presence of the Crown.

The interruption of Charleston's cabinet trade brought about by the Revolution was not especially protracted. Most cabinetmakers working late into the Revolutionary period found themselves short of supplies two years after the war began. Mahogany, fasteners, hardware, glass, varnish components, and glue were imported, and British control of the shipping lanes, as well as loss of British trade links, soon obliterated the availability of such necessities. The capture of the city by Sir Henry Clinton's troops in May 1780, perhaps one of the signal British victories in the American theater of war, enabled some cabinetmakers—particularly those of loyalist bent—to attain materials as usual. The British sailed out of Charleston's harbor in mid-December 1782, but although the war was over for South Carolina, time passed before old mercantile links were reestablished. Patterns of trade had been changed forever. Much of the Caribbean was now accessible to American shipping, as were the Continent and the Orient. South Carolina's place in the American maritime race for new foreign markets, as well as its ability to compete in the rapidly changing commerce between domestic ports, did not resolve itself for some years after the Revolution. Charleston's dominance among southern ports in its maritime trade eventually diminished somewhat, partially due to the gradual shift from rice and indigo production to cotton and to competition from other ports that had been of little significance during the colonial period.

In Charleston, shifts in both coastal and transatlantic trade naturally affected the bench trades. During the two decades following the war, however, the business of the city continued much as it had, buoyed initially by a postwar boom, only to be palliated for a time by an economic depression that persisted until the late 1780s. By 1790, when Charleston was again flush with fortune, her population had risen to over sixteen thousand, about five thousand more individuals than during the 1770s. In the new era, the nature of Low Country society remained essentially unchanged from the model that had been in place before the end of the seventeenth century. This societal pattern contrasted greatly with that of New England and the middle Atlantic states, and even with the aristocracy of the lower Chesapeake. Fiercely competitive and materialistic Barbadian planters, skilled in both tropical plantation management and political manipulation, had established a social model that suffused the Low Country from the earliest settlement and prevailed well into the nineteenth century. In contrast with Barbados, the Low Country was geographically vast. Whereas a sugar baron in Barbados might have worked no more than two hundred acres of cane, the succeeding generations of their progeny in South Carolina typically owned thousands of acres. Unlike the Chesapeake settlers, Carolina planters were less inclined to develop self-sufficient, isolated domains. They remained steadfastly tied to the business and cultural affairs of Charleston, much to the benefit of the city's large community of artisans who produced wares "suitable for the country" as well as more elaborate work for the sumptuous residences that scores of planters maintained in town.[1]

Through most of the colonial period, Charleston furniture styles were thoroughly wrapped in thick layers of British fashion. During the golden years following the Seven Years War, and particularly after 1765, the city seemed increasingly open to winds of change from whatever direction fashion wafted. Even before the end of the colonial period some of these stylistic breezes blew from unexpected quadrants, approaching gale force after the mid-1780s. The shift toward the "antique" style had begun in the city during the decade preceding the Revolution. Ironically, the earliest proprietors of the new taste were not staunch members of a British contingent in Charleston's cabinetmaking trade but were a band of immigrant Germans. By the early 1770s, these men had introduced Franco-German styles, albeit with a strong British twist.

Research by J. Thomas Savage has placed Martin Pfeninger (d. 1782) at the center of this transformation. Following in his stylistic footsteps, and without doubt previously associated with him, were other Germans such as Charles Desel, Henry Gesken, and Jacob Sass, all of whom were working during the 1770s and quickly rose to prominence following the Revolution. Other members of the "German school" who likely were in the city before the end of the Revolution were George Henry Warner and Nicholas Silberg, the latter a Swede. In contrast to earlier Germanic settlers in South Carolina who were primarily from the southwestern states—Baden, Württemberg, and the Rhenish Palatinate—a number of these later emigrés came from the northwestern states—Hesse and the Electorate of Hanover. The latter state developed wide-sweeping stylistic ties with London after the ascent of the "German Georges" to the English throne in 1714. The transmission of British style to north Germany by the House of Hanover at length made its way to Charleston. Henry Gesken was born at Hanover in 1748, and Jacob Sass was born at Schenstad in Hesse in 1750. Charles Desel, from the French spelling of his name, could have been either Alsatian or Swiss, but his Revolutionary War service alongside Sass and Gesken in Charleston's German Fusiliers as well as his membership in St. John's Lutheran Church establish his credentials in the city's German community. All of these men carried Anglo-German style in the cultural baggage they brought to Charleston.[2]

The influence of the north Germans upon Charleston furniture of the late colonial and early neoclassical periods proved to be profound. All senior members of this German school probably arrived in South Carolina during the 1760s as a result of the Bounty Act of 1761, a nefariously administered attempt to lure increasing numbers of Protestant settlers to the Low Country's hinterland. Between 1761 and 1768, the act led to the emigration of upwards of four thousand settlers, mostly Ulster Scots, Irish, and Germans, all of whom were sent sixty miles or more inland, largely to townships that had been erected in the 1730s. The townships that were either primarily or partially German were Saxe-Gotha, Orangeburg, New Windsor, Amelia, and Londonborough. Artisans such as Pfeninger, Sass, and Gesken, who possessed elevated urban skills, did not remain in these upcountry settlements but quickly joined the small but tightly knit German community in Charleston. Even amidst the complex social stratification of the city, this subculture, in usual Teutonic fashion, maintained a good deal of its cultural identity through and beyond the eighteenth century. The upcountry German townships, not surprisingly, were assimilated even later than the community in Charleston.[3]

While the cabinetmakers of Charleston's German school flourished, deaths, financial failures, retirements, and, most particularly, unpopular political alliances contributed to the decimation of Charleston's "old guard" of British-tradition cabinetmakers. John Fisher, Thomas Elfe's last trade partner, was a loyalist who escaped with the British fleet in 1782, thereby losing his substantial Charleston estate, including an unfinished, three-story brick house on Elliott Street. Thomas Hutchinson, an early partner of Elfe, died in 1782; Elfe had preceded him in 1775. Elfe's son, Thomas, inherited the business, but he was also a loyalist and quickly sought refuge in Savannah. Abraham Pearce, who had come to Charleston from London in 1763, was a successful carver and cabinetmaker who performed a considerable amount of work for Elfe during the 1770s. Like John Fisher, he returned to England at the end of the war. Richard Magrath, whose lengthy and rambling advertisements identified him as a major importer of British furniture during the 1770s, appears to have returned to London by 1777 after a brief stint at running a ferry across the Combahee River south of Charleston. John Packrow left Charleston for Georgetown in the late 1760s but returned to the city during the Revolution, finally giving up the cabinet trade in 1778 to run the same ferry that Magrath had abandoned. Stephen Townsend retired from the trade in the early 1770s for more genteel pursuits, but his former partner, William Axson, resumed the trade after the war. Axson became one of the most respected artisans in the city, for he led the cabinetmakers in Charleston's Federal Procession in 1788.

The British cabinetmakers who did manage to struggle through the decade between 1775 and 1785 included established shop masters such as Axson, Mungo Finlayson, John Gough (who was a very enterprising free mulatto), and John Ralph, who had done a good deal of contract work for Elfe. Another of these shop masters was one of Elfe's former subcontractors, William Luyten, who was a successful cabinetmaker on his own. In 1787 he advertised the sale of his stock-in-trade and appears to have become a merchant. Lesser-known cabinetmakers working during this troubled decade were John Howe, Thomas Snead, George Stewart, James Simmons, Eleazer Philips, and Thomas Cooke, another former Londoner. Philips, like Axson and several other fellow cabinetmakers, was a patriot. He was imprisoned by the British in 1780 but continued in the trade well into the nineteenth century.[4]

About fourteen cabinetmakers working in Charleston between 1775 and

1785 bridged the gap between the colonial period and the Federal era. Of the eight shop masters who headed establishments capable of significant production, three were Germans—Desel, Sass, and Gesken. Shortly thereafter, they were joined by two other cabinetmakers who emerged from the German community, Warner and Silberg. Also associated with one of the German shops was Charles M. S. Nauman, who died in Charleston in 1786 at the age of fifty-two, a seasoned journeyman. The presence of this German minority within the city's cabinetmaking establishment is evident in the earliest surviving examples of Charleston neoclassical furniture. These foreigners, in fact, formed the first cabinetmaking partnerships in post-war Charleston. Charles Desel and Englishman John Ralph appear to have been associated in 1783. By March 1784, Desel had formed a partnership with Henry Gesken. These men were in business together on Church Street at least until 1789 and possibly as late as 1794. Both were eminently successful as artisans and entrepreneurs. Neither the firm nor its principals ever advertised, probably because they had no need to do so. Gesken died in 1813, and his estate papers have not been found; however, Desel's 1808 inventory, which totaled almost $15,000, included twenty-six slaves, tools, benches, and unfinished furniture. Jacob Sass was one of the appraisers of the estate.[5]

Two other individuals who probably carried elements of German-school style and construction into the neoclassical period were George Henry Warner and Nicholas Silberg. Unfortunately, we do not know just when either of these men arrived in the city, but it seems likely that both may have been there during the Revolutionary period. Warner was in Charleston by April 1784, when he witnessed a will. Silberg, who was born in Sweden about 1750, does not appear in Charleston records before May 1786, when court records refer to the firm of Warner & Silberg. In February 1787, Silberg announced the termination of that partnership, and Warner disappeared from city records after August of the same year. Silberg formed a partnership with John Ralph in 1793, which lasted for three years. He died in 1801.[6]

Not working with a partner but destined to become the most prominent of the German contingent was Jacob Sass, who was the first cabinetmaker to announce his renewed trade in post-Revolutionary Charleston. A year after the British departed, Sass advertised that he had moved to "a large and commodious shop," where he carried on the "Cabinet and Upholsterer's Business . . . where the citizens and others who are unacquainted with the custom of this Country, may be supplied with every necessary for Funerals on the shortest notice."[7]

Linked with the pre-Revolutionary work of Pfeninger and his colleagues are four neoclassical pieces attributed to two shops: a library bookcase owned by William Alston (1756–1839) (see Thomas Savage's article in this volume, p. 123, fig. 29), a secretary-and-bookcase with a swelled pediment (fig. 1), a clothespress (fig. 4), and a secretary-and-bookcase on legs (fig. 6). Both secretaries and the press are attributed to the same anonymous shop. Alston, the scion of an enormously wealthy planter family, purchased the Miles Brewton house in 1791, a fitting complement to his numerous plan-

Figure 1 Secretary-and-bookcase, Charleston, 1785–1790. Mahogany and mahogany veneer with white cedar, red cedar, and white pine. H. 105³/₄", W. 48¹/₂", D. 24³/₈". (Courtesy, Charleston Museum; photo, Gavin Ashworth.)

tations. The secretary-and-bookcase illustrated in figure 1 was owned by John Bee Holmes, who inherited John Edwards's famed library bookcase (see Savage, pp. 106–7, fig. 1).[8]

The attenuated, Louis XV–style base and regional details of inlay and veneer tie the Alston library bookcase to one of the German-school shops whose master was associated with Pfeninger. The base of the Alston bookcase, in fact, is almost exactly the same size as the Edwards example and appears to have been constructed from the same standing patterns or geometric formulas. Whereas the magnificent Edwards piece has no details that are entirely neoclassical, the Alston library bookcase quietly slips into the new style with the form of its inlay (including quarter-fans) and the hardware on its lower drawers. Like the Alston piece, the Holmes secretary-and-bookcase retains a goodly smattering of vocabulary from the Pfeninger period, most particularly the Germanic, swelled pediment (fig. 1). On the secretary, this distinctive baroque feature contrasts with more modish, British details such as the delicate scroll moldings, "Chinese" door tracery, neoclassical writing compartment (fig. 2), and inlaid bracket feet. The leafy, incised inlay on the pediment (fig. 3) seems an attempt, albeit far less refined, to carry on a tradition established by Pfeninger a decade earlier (see Savage, pp. 106-7, fig. 1).[9]

The fine clothespress illustrated in figure 4 (an object often referred to as a "wardrobe" in post-Revolutionary Charleston) has a pediment with elliptical tympanum openings that rise in a tightly decreasing radius to the

Figure 2   Detail of the writing compartment of the secretary-and-bookcase illustrated in fig. 1. (Photo, Gavin Ashworth.)

Figure 3   Detail of the pediment of the secretary-and-bookcase illustrated in fig. 1. (Photo, Gavin Ashworth.)

Figure 4 Clothespress, Charleston, 1785–1790. Woods and dimensions unrecorded. (Courtesy, Charleston Museum.)

plinth, similar to those on German-school case pieces from the 1770s. The configuration of the plinth is a close match to that of the Holmes secretary-and-bookcase, and the entire tympanum is outlined in stringing, a typical Charleston feature during and after the 1770s (figs. 3, 5). The husk inlay on the plinth and frieze of the press appears to be the work of the artisan who

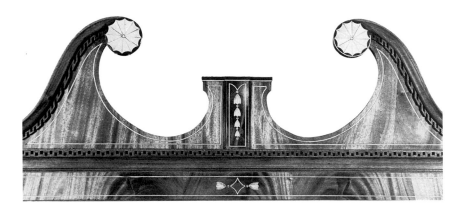

Figure 5 Detail of the pediment of the clothes-press illustrated in fig. 4.

made the leafy inlays on the Alston library bookcase. The husks (fig. 5) are somewhat fatter than those shown in figure 3, and the incising is different. Regardless of variations between the husks of the Holmes secretary and those on the clothespress and Alston library bookcase, all three pieces document the earliest use of neoclassical-style husks in the Low Country.[10]

Along with the pervasive style of Charleston's German school, both the press (fig. 4) and secretary-and-bookcase on legs (fig. 6) reveal the earliest influence from the northeast coast of America upon the city's neoclassical furniture. The composition of the frieze stringing of both pieces, with horizontal husks at each side and another pair reaching out from a central, hollow-sided lozenge of stringing, is a Charleston harbinger of the crossed-string friezes long considered a stylistic hallmark of cabinetmakers working in Salem, Massachusetts, by the 1790s. The same is true of the fanlike rosette inlays, as well as the narrow inlaid pilasters centering the plinths. The rosettes and finial of the Holmes secretary-and-bookcase (fig. 1) are twentieth-century replacements; the original rosettes were probably carved flowers, possibly the pomegranate-like blooms gracing the pediment of the Salem secretary-and-bookcase illustrated in figures 26 and 27. Crossed-string friezes not unlike those shown in figures 4 through 6 occur on British furniture, but they tend to be somewhat less exuberant than their American counterparts.[11]

The foot pattern used on the press and on the Holmes secretary-and-bookcase is essentially the same (figs. 1, 4), although the feet of the former have damaged responds. This style of foot occurred in Britain earlier and was in the Boston-Salem orbit by the 1780s. The Edwards library bookcase (see Savage, pp. 106–7, fig. 1) employs a less vertical version of the same design for its feet. Chippendale illustrated an embryonic version of this pattern in the third edition of *The Gentleman and Cabinet-Maker's Director* (1762), and commissions that he executed for Nostell Priory and Harewood House have feet identical to the Charleston/Massachusetts ones. Just how early such details, especially the crossed-string friezes, appear in the Massachusetts Bay area is a matter of conjecture. Most evidence of this style seems to occur on Salem furniture made after 1790, but the Charleston pieces illustrated here were probably made between 1785 and 1790. In any event, the rapid flowering of this style is more than evident in surviving Massachusetts

Figure 6 Secretary-and-bookcase on legs, Charleston, 1785–1790. Mahogany and mahogany veneer with cypress and yellow pine. H. 101³/₄", W. 49¹³/₁₆", D. 24⁷/₁₆". (Courtesy, Baltimore Museum of Art.) The pediment and frieze are constructed on a separate dovetail frame.

furniture made just after the 1780s. Charleston's adaptation of these and other Massachusetts details was both immediate and incredibly widespread, springing forth in the work of as many as two dozen shops operating between the late 1780s and 1810. Only a small sampling of this furniture is illustrated here.[12]

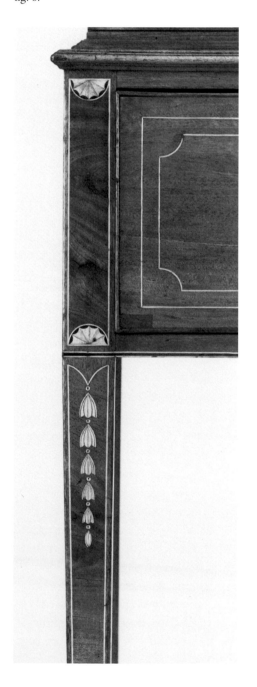

With a pediment essentially identical to that of the press (figs. 4, 5) and a sequence of medial moldings that match those on the Holmes secretary-and-bookcase (fig. 1), the secretary-and-bookcase on legs illustrated in figure 6 is a rare form in Charleston furniture. Few other single-drawer secretaries with legs have been recorded in South Carolina, although various renditions of such pieces are seen from New England south to the Cape Fear region of North Carolina. The Charleston example is nearly fifty inches wide, much larger than one might expect for a secretary on legs, usually a far daintier form. The lofty scale of the city's rooms undoubtedly had a great deal to do with the proportions of Charleston neoclassical furniture; however, the fat girth of some of these pieces also fits baroque proportional ideals, which Teutonic cabinetmakers grimly clung to despite all odds of fashion. The German-school shops responsible for most of the surviving Charleston furniture of the 1780s also may have meddled with their patrons' perception of fashion, touting the notion that pragmatism of size and relative squareness of mass, both near and dear to the German heart, carried more weight than design-book diatribes on dynamic proportion.

Like the other two pieces from the same shop and typical of the earliest of Charleston neoclassical furniture, the pediment of the secretary-and-bookcase on legs (fig. 6) retains the Doric dentil favored in the city during the colonial period. Also like the Holmes secretary-and-bookcase (figs. 1, 3) and the press illustrated in figures 4 and 5, the secretary-and-bookcase on legs has a removable pediment. In 1771, cabinetmaker Richard Magrath described this structure as "neat and light Pediment Heads, which take off and put on occasionally."[13]

The long, cross-grained panels of veneer on the legs of this secretary-and-bookcase (fig. 6) are a direct derivation of pre-Revolutionary, German-school work. These panels are complemented by similar ones on the leg stiles that are finished top and bottom with half-fans (fig. 7). The lack of inlaid cuffing below the leg panels is also an early feature. The face of the secretary drawer is veneered, but with relatively unfigured wood. The interior of this drawer is similar to that of the Holmes secretary-and-bookcase (fig. 2). Both pieces have square prospect doors with lunetted-corner inlay that echoes the stringing on their exterior drawers (figs. 1, 2, 6). The base of the secretary-and-bookcase on legs is essentially a large table. Its sides, back, and drawer rail are tenoned into the legs and secured with glue rather than wooden pins. Although not examined, the lock rail is probably dovetailed to the tops of the leg stiles.

The Holmes secretary-and-bookcase, Alston library bookcase, and secretary-and-bookcase on legs, along with six other case pieces and four tables that represent the work of three other Charleston shops, show how details introduced by Germanic shopmasters during the late 1760s and 1770s persisted after the Revolution. Not only are these pieces seminal examples of Charleston neoclassical furniture, but they document the early arrival of stylistic influences from other American coastal cities. Although these outside influences merged with and in some instances displaced local traditions, many of the distinctive characteristics of Charleston neoclassical furniture can be associated with the city's German-school shops: broad edge-banding on doors and drawers; contrasting panels of cross-grained, string-surrounded veneer on case stiles, rails, and foot facings; mitered and book-matched face veneers on door rails and stiles; and vastly simplified attempts at imitating the gloriously incised inlay attributed to Martin Pfeninger (see Savage, pp. 106–7, fig. 1). Similarly, the paneled backs and full-bottom dust-boards favored by British-tradition workmen and wholeheartedly adopted by the Germans are the norm rather than the exception.[14]

The retention of such details undoubtedly resulted from the growing size of the German cabinetmaking community in the city, most of which by the late eighteenth and early nineteenth centuries was largely comprised of South Carolina–born artisans. Joining the ranks of the senior cabinetmak-ers like Sass, Desel, and Gesken, all of whom worked well past 1800, were successful young artisans like Michael Muckinfuss, John Gros, who was apprenticed to Jacob Sass, Sass's own son, Edward George Sass, John Mich-ael Philips, Thomas Sigwald, George Henry Warner, and George Daniel Rou. Between the early 1770s when the first immigrant German cabinet-makers appeared in the city and 1820, over twenty-one cabinetmakers (excluding a number of joiners) of German extraction worked in Charles-ton. As the Germanic element in the trade expanded, however, so did the cabinetmaking business in general. Between 1780 and 1790, about forty arti-sans made up the trade in the city. During the following decade, almost two dozen journeymen and shopmasters were added to that number, and by the 1800–1810 period there were over a hundred cabinetmakers in Charleston, excluding workmen in ancillary trades such as carving, turning, and uphol-stery. Some non-Germans were unquestionably apprenticed to the German masters. Others were influenced by details employed by the German shop-masters, and still others, some of them recent emigrés from abroad, such as Robert Walker, introduced new details that added to the catalogue of Charleston furniture trends. These new styles included compositions famil-iar in Britain, New York, and, to a far lesser degree, Philadelphia. Although influence from the German school continued through the 1790s, the rapid growth of the city's cabinet trade and the considerable increase of furniture imported to Charleston in the coastal trade had an impressive effect on Charleston fashions after the 1780s. The result was a steady metamorphosis, albeit in an elegant way, of the stylistic statements that the German cabi-netmakers had made in Charleston for two decades.[15]

William Jones is one of the non-German cabinetmakers who clearly was a child of the German conclave yet dipped more than a toe into the waters of Massachusetts style. Based upon a labeled chest of drawers that de-scended in the DeSaussure family (fig. 8), four case pieces have been attrib-uted to his shop. These objects provide a clear window on the shifting sands of fashion in Charleston's cabinet trade at the end of the 1780s. Since he was not an orphan, nothing is known of Jones's apprenticeship, nor do we even know whether he was a South Carolina native. There is no question, how-ever, that he was either an apprentice or journeyman—or both—in one of the more prominent shops of the German school. He first appears in city

Figure 8 Chest of drawers labeled by William Jones, Charleston, 1788–1789. Mahogany and mahogany veneer with white pine, ash, tulip poplar, and mahogany. H. 34$^{1}/_{2}$", W. 42", D. 21$^{3}/_{4}$". (Collection of the Museum of Early Southern Decorative Arts.) The drawer-face veneers and stringing are replaced.

records in 1787, located at the corner of Church and Tradd Streets. In August 1788, Jones, who described himself as a "Cabinet maker and Under-taker," placed a notice that he had "Removed from No. 24, corner of Church and Tradd streets, to No. 54, Meeting street." A similar notice appeared in May 1789, indicating that Jones had moved from Meeting Street to 51 King Street. He was listed there in Milligan's city directory for 1790. Significantly, this property appears to be the same lot and building—evidently containing both a residence and a shop—that was purchased by Charles Desel in August 1790. At that time, Desel evidently was still in partnership with Henry Gesken on Church Street. Milligan's directory does not list Desel at 51 Broad until 1794, where he remained until his death in 1807.[16]

Jones obviously was a successful tradesman. His advertisements were largely placed to inform his patrons of address changes and to seek journeymen. He advertised for a journeyman in the summer of 1790, and the following November he sought "ONE or TWO Journeymen Cabinet–Makers." In both March and April of 1791 he again advertised for journeymen and noted that he had added upholstery to the services of his shop. Another notice in December 1791 announced a move to "No. 40 Tradd Street," where Jones intended to carry on the "CABINET & UPHOLSTERY BUSINESS in a more extensive manner than before." The same advertisement again sought two journeymen for the cabinet trade "and one to the upholsterers line." Jones became a member of the South Carolina Society in the spring of 1792 and died the following November. One of the appraisers who signed his inventory of February 1793 was Jacob Sass.[17]

Figure 9 Detail of the label on the chest illustrated in fig. 8.

Figure 10 Detail of a canted corner and foot on the chest illustrated in fig. 8.

The inventory, which described Jones as a "Cabinet Maker deceased late of Tradd Street," is both extensive and revealing. The "Stock in Trade" listed four "Mahogany Bedsteads" valued at £3.10 each, a "Pair Inlaid Tea Tables" valued at £5 apiece, 3 "Setts" of dining tables, an "inlaid Cellerett," an inlaid "Slabb" table, a "Comode," a "Beaureau" valued at £5, two easy chairs, an unfinished sofa, two unfinished "Wardrobes" valued at £10, ten pairs of "Mahogany Carved Bed Posts" valued at only 14 shilling a pair, and other unfinished work including a bookcase, desk, commode, tea table, and a "Chest of Drawers," the latter valued at £5. The shop contained "Sundry Mahogany Table Leggs & Rails . . . Cutt up Chair Stuff . . . 12 Turned Bed Posts," and other assorted furniture components along with a good deal of lumber, including mahogany, ash, pine, and "Sundry Drying Wood & Stringing." A "lot of hair," along with "22M Brass Nails" and "girth Webb," tacks, "Hair Seating," and mattress covers attest to the upholstery portion of the business. Besides furniture, coffin hardware, and "Sundry Tools," the shop contained seven "new & old" workbenches, together worth £3.10. Also on hand were seventeen pieces of finished furniture, but since they are interspersed in the inventory with eight unfinished pieces and parts for fourteen bedsteads, it is unlikely that the finished pieces were imported furniture warehoused by Jones.[18]

The most significant documentation of Jones's Charleston career is the fragment of a label pasted over a lock inside one of the drawers of the DeSaussure chest (figs. 8, 9). Most of the label was destroyed when the lock was removed, but it is possible to extrapolate the missing portion. Accompanying illustrations of tasseled drapery, an upholstered armchair, and a shield-back side chair stuffed over the rails was the text: "WILLIAM JONES,/Upholsterer & Cabinet Maker/N... Meeting Street/Charleston." The competently-engraved label is signed "Abernathie" in the lower right corner. Thomas Abernathie (d. 1796) first advertised his trade to the citizens of Charleston in June 1786. In January 1795, he was located at 42 Queen Street, where he advertised as an "Engraver in General" and offered to carry out "Copper Plate Printing . . . With accuracy and dispatch." In a notice published late in 1786 he indicated that he also conducted "the business of a Land Surveyor."[19]

The "N... Meeting Street" address on Jones's label suggests that he made the chest between August 1788, when he advertised that he had moved from the corner of Church and Broad to Meeting Street, and May 1789, when he informed his clients that he had "removed" to 51 Broad. When discovered, the chest was almost as shabby as its mutilated label. The rear feet and face veneers of the drawer fronts were missing, and the cockbeading had been cut flush with the altered drawer faces. Typical of Charleston case furniture of the 1780s and early 1790s, the drawers were not veneered on horizontally-laminated cores. To avoid excessive waste from sawing the serpentine facade from single, thick boards, Jones face-glued three pieces of thin, full-height mahogany scantling together, resulting in visible vertical joints inside several drawers. The veneer facings of the foot cants were also missing. They have been replaced with the inclusion of simple outline stringing to match the existing front faces of the feet (fig. 10). The single-line string on the feet suggested a similar treatment for the drawers, which, judging from other work attributed to Jones, probably had book-matched veneers originally. Following the usual treatment of the later phase of the German school, the case cants have horizontally grained panels of mahogany outlined with a single string. The base molding above the foot cants is cut integrally with the wedge-shaped pieces forming the cants themselves.

The case design of Jones's chest is similar to a pre-Revolutionary Charleston example attributed to Pfeninger and his associates in the German school (see Savage, p. 116, fig. 14). The serpentine front, canted corners, and sharp coves behind the cants are a subdued British response to the French style. Chests of this plan follow the design of a "Commode Cloths Press" that Chippendale illustrated in all three editions of the *Director* (pl. 130 in the 3d edition). Chests of drawers with the same plan occurred in Philadelphia at about the same time that the Pfeninger example was made, probably during the mid- to late 1770s. Brock Jobe has proposed that this form could have been brought to Charleston from New England; however, few Massachusetts-school examples can be dated before the 1780s. Two canted-corner chests from Salem (in the Diplomatic Reception Rooms, U.S. Department of State) certainly could date early in that decade, but a majority of the early examples appear to be from South Carolina and Pennsylvania shops. In Charleston, the canted-corner plan evidently originated in the German-school shops, since its earliest appearance is the base of the Edwards library bookcase, which probably dates no later than 1770 (see Savage, pp. 106–7, fig. 1). As on the chest attributed to Pfeninger, the case cants of the Jones chest, as well as the coves behind them, are formed from full-height vertical appliqués at the leading edges of the case sides; the joint at the front is covered by the veneer facings of the cants. Unlike the flat cants of the Jones chest, the cants on the Pfeninger piece are "swelld" at the feet, a detail much in tune with the baroque fugues of the German school. The Jones piece is virtually the same size as the Pfeninger example, and both have ungraduated drawers like a chest that descended in the Porcher family of Charleston. The latter chest, illustrated in figures 13 and 14 of E. Milby Burton's *Charleston Furniture, 1700–1825,* has veneer-paneled canted corners and replaced feet.[20]

With their dramatically scrolled returns, Jones's bracket feet (fig. 10) are considerably bolder than those used by Jacob Sass and his contemporaries. They demonstrate the importance of identifying the standing patterns used in early cabinet shops. Tracings verify that the same template was used to cut the feet of two considerably more important pieces—a dressing chest (fig. 11) and the secretary-press shown in figure 14. This pattern evidence conclusively links these pieces with Jones's shop, for no other Charleston cabinetmaker is known to have used this foot template. Also supporting an attribution to Jones are the construction of these objects and the style of their veneers and inlays. All have full-bottom dustboards (dustboards that are the full thickness of the drawer rails) and paneled backs (except for the labeled chest, which has a replaced back). The chest of drawers illustrated in

Figure 11 Dressing chest attributed to William Jones, Charleston, 1785–1790. Mahogany and mahogany veneer with white pine, mahogany, and red cedar. H. 37⁷/₁₆", W. 40¹³/₁₆", D. 23⁷/₁₆". (Courtesy, Winterthur Museum; gift of Commander and Mrs. Duncan I. Selfridge.)

Figure 12 Detail of the veneer and inlay on the drawers, feet, and cants of the dressing chest illustrated in fig. 11.

figure 13 of *Charleston Furniture* fits these parameters (with the exception of its replaced feet) and is also attributed to Jones's shop.

Charles Montgomery attributed the Jones dressing chest (fig. 11) to Rhode Island "largely on the basis of early ownership"; however, many wealthy Charlestonians summered in Newport to escape the "vapours" of the Low Country, and they undoubtedly brought furniture with them. Aside from Jones's foot design and the addition of quarter-fan inlays on the drawer fronts, this piece fits into the stylistic mainstream of German-school work of the 1780s. The characteristically wide banding of the drawer fronts is much like that of the serpentine press illustrated in figure 16, and the banding is the same material, which appears to be West Indian rosewood. On the dressing chest, however, the panels of mahogany veneer on the drawers are book-matched and outlined with herringbone stringing (fig. 12). The same banding and stringing surrounds the top of the chest (fig. 13). The cores of the drawer fronts consist of four horizontal laminates of white pine, one of the earliest occurrences of this structure in Charleston where solid cores—usually either mahogany or red cedar—were the norm through the 1780s. The insides of the drawer fronts are "pinked" (painted with a wash coat to resemble mahogany), a common practice in Charleston as it was in Britain and elsewhere in America. Full-height panels of satinwood, also outlined with herringbone stringing, adorn the faces of the case cants.[21]

The top drawer of the dressing chest is fitted for both writing and toilet accouterments (fig. 13). Flush-fitted to rabbets in the drawer sides is a slid-

Figure 13 Detail of the upper drawer of the dressing chest illustrated in fig. 11, with dressing glass deployed.

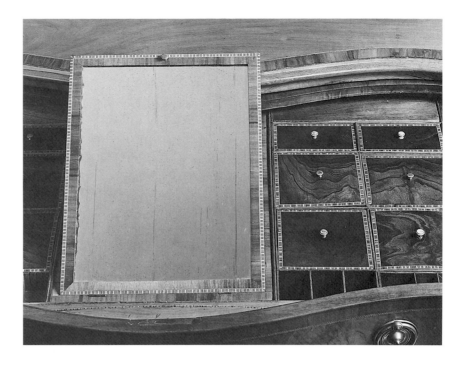

ing cover originally lined with baize or thin hide—sealskin was a favored covering in Charleston—that covered the inset surface. The lined area of the slide is surrounded with the same veneer used for the drawer banding. A similar writing slide, but made of solid mahogany, is fitted to the top drawer of the chest attributed to Jones and illustrated in figure 13 of *Charleston Furniture*. On the dressing chest (fig. 11), the frame of the upper drawer is mahogany, as are those of most dressing chests. When the slide is pushed to the rear, like the example illustrated in *Charleston Furniture*, it reveals complete fitments for toiletry (fig. 13), but in far more lavish fashion. This dressing drawer is surely one of the most sumptuously fitted examples made outside the British Isles. The ratchetted looking glass in the center has crossbanded veneer surrounded by geometric stringing in black, green, red, and yellow. Eight large, square, covered compartments have the same edging and are veneered with figured rosewood. Another covered area in front of the glass is veneered with a light-colored wood, and much of its surface is filled with a large, green-dyed, pointed ellipse. Open compartments on each side are partitioned, the smaller on the left with adjustable partitions. To gain access to the lidded rear compartments, the drawer must be pulled more than two-thirds out of the case, which required sliding supports flush-fitted into dadoes cut in the drawer sides. At the rear of the drawer, these slides have projecting, rectangular lugs that engage dadoes in the case sides to support the extended drawer. George Hepplewhite illustrated this system in plate 74 of *The Cabinet-Maker and Upholsterer's Guide* (1st ed., 1788).

The dramatic range of colorful veneers and stringing used on the dressing chest is carried to a pinnacle of visual display on a secretary-press attributed to Jones (fig. 14). With the exception of its linear facade and different drawer pulls, this secretary seems almost en suite with the dressing chest. The same drawer banding, herringbone stringing, and quarter-fans sur-

Figure 14 Secretary-press attributed to William Jones, Charleston, 1785–1790. Mahogany and mahogany veneer with white pine, red cedar, and tulip poplar. H. 99¼", W. 49⅜", D. 24⅝". (Courtesy, Diplomatic Reception Rooms, U.S. Department of State.) Both the upper and lower cases have paneled backs.

rounding brilliant, book-matched mahogany veneers are employed, and the herringbone stringing is carried to the feet like the previous example (fig. 12). The face of the secretary drawer is veneered and cockbeaded to simulate a pair of drawers when closed (fig. 14). The net result is much the same as the facade of the clothespress shown in figure 16, but without the serpentine plan and canted corners. The drawer proportions, banding (again probably West Indian rosewood), format of the door surfaces, and proportions of the door stiles and rails link this secretary-press with the serpentine

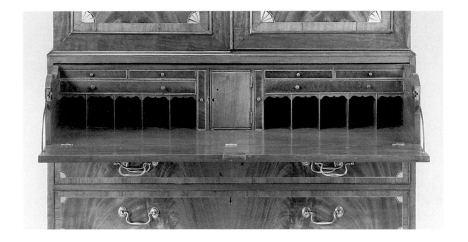

Figure 15 Detail of the writing compartment of the secretary-press illustrated in fig. 14.

Figure 15 Detail of the writing compartment of the secretary-press illustrated in fig. 14.

press illustrated in figure 16 and strongly suggest that Jones was a journeyman in the shop that made that magnificent piece.

The writing compartment of the secretary-press (fig. 15), including the proportions of the prospect, is very much like that of the Alston library bookcase (see Savage, p. 123, fig. 29), but with small drawers arranged at the tops of the side tiers rather than the reverse as on the Alston example. On the secretary-press, the interior drawers are outlined with the same geometric polychrome stringing used on the dressing chest (fig. 13). The three oak-leaf paterae in the frieze appear to be identical to the leg stile inlays of a neoclassical, German-school side table illustrated in figure 68 of *Charleston Furniture*, although this similarity is no proof of any association other than perhaps the same source for ornament. The most important aspect of this secretary-press is its close stylistic and structural tie with pieces that are the most representative of transitional, post-Revolutionary, German-school furniture such as the Alston library bookcase and the serpentine press illustrated in figure 16.[22]

The serpentine press and a related secretary-press (see Savage, p. 122, fig. 28) are particularly strong expressions of the neoclassical phase of Charleston's German school. Stylistic and structural details associate both pieces with a 1794 desk-and-bookcase (at the Winterthur Museum) signed by Jacob Sass and suggest that they could also be from his shop. Although the serpentine press is generically similar to one shown in plate 130 of the *Director,* it departs dramatically from the British norm with the compressed, five-drawer arrangement of its base—a peculiar feature of Charleston's German school, echoed in the facade of the secretary-press attributed to Jones. The bases of most British clothespresses are seldom more than three drawers in height, often less; however, German schranken frequently have taller bases with more drawers.

The edge-banded and quarter-fan-inlaid doors of the serpentine press are finished much in the same manner as the Alston library bookcase and, like that piece, display small, incised inlays at each miter of the wide, bookmatched veneers of the door stiles and rails. This feature is a very distinctive north German detail shared by the Edwards library bookcase, which has husks rather than leaves accenting its door miters (see Savage, pp. 106–7, fig.

Figure 16 Clothespress, Charleston, 1785–1790. Mahogany and mahogany veneer with white pine. H. 91", W. 53¼", D. 25¾". (Private collection; photo, Dirk Bakker.)

Figure 17 Detail of a foot and canted corner of the clothespress illustrated in fig. 16. (Photo, Museum of Early Southern Decorative Arts.)

1). The expense of making commode-front doors of this type must have been substantial. Each door is composed of a series of vertical laths set into rails at the top and bottom, a "coopering" technique common to north German commode-form schranken and bookcases and no doubt employed in Britain as well. Typical of the work of the German school, the serpentine press has string-surrounded, contrasting panels of veneer on the cants of both the lower case and the feet (fig. 17). Double stringing outlines all of the case stiles and rails in a simplified version of the heavy triple-string used in

Figure 18 Detail of the frieze of the clothespress illustrated in fig. 16. (Photo, Dirk Bakker.)

Figure 19 Tea caddy, Britain, 1780–1800. Woods and dimensions unrecorded. (Courtesy, Philip H. Bradley, Inc.; photo, John Bivins.)

the same positions on the Edwards library bookcase. The same double string is also used on the sides of both upper and lower cases.

Aside from the considerable expense of creating a serpentine-front case piece fitted with interior linen drawers of matching plan, the most compelling feature of this press is its frieze The latter is filled with a profusion of fine inlay that includes nine elliptical, figural inlays interspersed with eight inlays that simulate fluting (fig. 18). This decoration lends the appearance of a Doric frieze composed of metopes and triglyphs. The frieze is remarkable in the use of figural inlay with white backgrounds, the earliest known occurrence of such inlay in Charleston. On a dense ground cut from a material such as holly, box, or pear, the leaves and stems of the floral decoration are dyed green. There is no documentation to suggest that any inlays of this type were made in Charleston, although by the end of the eighteenth century they had become a hallmark of the neoclassical style there. The source almost certainly was Britain, where similar white-background inlay is common on tea caddies (fig. 19) and occurs sporadically on furniture, particularly on tables.[23]

The work of William Jones is one of the best, yet most subtle, examples of the intrusion of northern coastal influence upon the stylistic tradition of Charleston's German school. The regional similarities between the secretary-press attributed to him (fig. 14) and the serpentine press (fig. 16) are so apparent that Jones's departure from the German-school norm almost goes unnoticed. The maverick stylistic expression lies only in the pediment geometry of the secretary-press. The tympanum openings have an entirely different configuration from the elliptical profiles used by the German-school shops, descending in a broad curve from the plinth and then rising with a gently decreasing radius to the pediment crown. The curves of the pediment crown also deviate from German-school work of the 1780s. Rather than rising abruptly from the sides, as in the pediments of the pieces illustrated in figures 1, 4, and 6, the pediment of the secretary-press begins with a gentle upward sweep until it reaches the rosettes, where it makes an abrupt transition to a decreasing radius, thrusting the rosettes toward the plinth. This architecture, like the frieze stringing on the clothespress and secretary-and-bookcase on legs shown in figures 4 and 6, again marks the beginning overlay of Massachusetts Bay furniture styles upon Charleston's German-school work of the late 1780s and early 1790s. This effect is only slightly mitigated by Jones's insertion of dark-colored, string-surrounded spandrels in the tympanum, a dramatic feature more characteristic of Charleston.

Also typical of Charleston case furniture of the 1780s, but much in contrast to Massachusetts work, is Jones's use of full-bottom, full-depth dustboards. On the secretary-press (fig. 14), the drawer bottoms are divided by central muntins, which Jones did not employ in either of the previously illustrated chests of drawers. The secretary-press, however, is over forty-nine inches wide, so the addition of muntins was a practical solution to utility; the muntins better distribute weight across the considerable span of the drawer bottoms, preventing them from popping out of their front dadoes.

A British structural detail, center-muntin drawer bottoms occur frequently on large Charleston case pieces made during the colonial period and well into the 1820s. This structure usually appears in conjunction with dust-boards that extend at least three-quarters along the depth of the case.[24]

As the preceding furniture demonstrates, during the late 1780s and early 1790s, Charleston cabinet shops began responding to strong stylistic influences from the urban North. The first and most prevalent influence emanated from the Massachusetts Bay region—particularly Salem—and began to diminish before 1810. Regrettably, our understanding of this effect is somewhat limited by the lack of current research on neoclassical Bay furniture. One of the main problems in understanding the inception of Massachusetts influence in Charleston is in pinpointing exactly when the neoclassical style began to emerge in Boston and Salem. By the early 1790s, a distinctive Massachusetts Bay vocabulary in the new taste was maturing rapidly, despite the fact that many tradesmen and patrons in the Boston area still clung to old-fashioned rococo and baroque forms. Claw-and-ball feet and cabriole legs remained popular in Massachusetts cabinet shops through the 1780s, but if found behind a shop bench in Charleston they would have been cast over the seawall at the Battery.

The Massachusetts Bay was the center of an enormous surge in international trade after the Revolution, and its merchants could not avoid exposure to the new views of the Palmyrian world. Understanding the acceptance of this style is skewed by the very late publication of Hepplewhite's *Guide* (1788). This book presented some furniture designs that were popular during the 1760s, which prompted Thomas Sheraton to chide: "not withstanding the late date of Heppelwhite's book, if we compare some of the designs . . . with the newest taste, we shall find that this work has already caught the decline, and perhaps, in a little time, will suddenly die in the disorder." Unfortunately, furniture historians have inherited the disorder, since we have little more than books of architecture, manuscript sketches by various designers and artisans, and surviving furniture to determine what cabinetmakers knew of the neoclassical style in the years preceding the *Guide*. They certainly did know of it, for by the time Chippendale issued his revised *Director* in 1762, most of his commissions involved neoclassical compositions.[25]

Notwithstanding the relative paucity of knowledge compiled about the development of neoclassical modes in the Massachusetts Bay region just after the Revolution, elements of this highly identifiable style clearly had found their way to Charleston well before William Jones's death in 1792. Familiar Charleston details, particularly those associated with the German school, carried on into the nineteenth century and continued to evolve stylistically. Superimposed upon these styles were architectural form and ornament arriving in the city from far up the coast. As we have seen, this absorption did not necessarily cast aside everything that had gone before. The clothespress illustrated in figure 20 is a case in point. With a history of descent from Henry Strobel of Charleston, it has wide, book-matched door frame veneers surrounding flush panels with cross-banded surrounds. The

Figure 20 Clothespress, Charleston, 1785–1790. Mahogany with white pine. H. 94", W. 51³/4", D. 24³/4". (Private collection; photo, Museum of Early Southern Decorative Arts.) The lower right brass has been digitally added to this image.

cross-banding of the drawers is especially wide, and the faces of the feet are both veneered and string-inlaid. All of these details are solid statements of Charleston's German school, as are the elliptical openings of the tympanum; however, the pediment scrolls exhibit much of the Massachusetts geometry of the secretary-press attributed to Jones (fig. 14), and the frieze

Figure 21 Detail of the pediment of the clothes-press illustrated in fig. 20.

is interrupted by two crossed strings that sprout husks at either side (fig. 21). This merging of stylistic influences is characteristic of transitional Charleston furniture made during the late 1780s or early 1790s.[26]

This stylistic transition was soon to be complete. By the 1790s, Charleston cabinetmakers were producing full-blown representations of furniture in the Salem manner. With the exception of scale and construction, they were virtually indistinguishable from Massachusetts work. For example, some of these pieces have no secondary wood other than white pine, which is found in Charleston furniture as early as the 1730s and, after the Revolution, was a major New England commodity in the southern coastal trade. Since white pine is much more easily worked than either yellow pine or cypress, it was preferred by joiners, carvers, and cabinetmakers in southern port cities, despite the cost of importing it. Cypress remained plentiful, but it was relegated to less labor-intensive positions and to architectural and maritime applications where resistance to damp rot was important. Despite the increasing use of white pine, the construction of Charleston furniture in the Massachusetts style is quite another matter. Old traditions persisted, exemplified by the full-bottom, three-quarter-depth dustboards and paneled upper and lower backs of the clothespress shown in figure 20; nevertheless, the facades of some Charleston pieces are so close to their northern counterparts that consideration has been given to the possibility that Salem cabinetmakers made large-scale furniture specifically for the South Carolina market. Although not true, if not for the strength of the cabinetmaking trade in Charleston, Salem cabinetmakers undoubtedly would have provided furniture to any specification. Just how a small New England port managed to make such an impression on the well-established regional styles of Charleston—and, for that matter, on other coastal southern cities as well, such as Norfolk and Wilmington, North Carolina—deserves examination.

After the Revolution, Salem was the first northern cabinetmaking center to engage in the venture cargo trade on a large scale. Her cabinetmakers became the earliest warehousemen and furniture shippers, buying finished goods from other shops specifically for export to an international market. A city of almost ten thousand by the mid-1790s, after the Revolution Salem launched into a frenzy of maritime mercantile activity that rivaled urban centers of much larger size. A European visitor noted in 1796 that the "uncommonly active and enterprising spirits" of the inhabitants of Salem was "the sole reason which can be ascribed for the great extent and rapid progress of its trade." Merchant shipping families who quickly developed international trade networks included the Bartons, Derbys, Wards, Crowninshields, Cushings, and Endicotts, all of whom amassed enormous fortunes by the beginning of the nineteenth century. Another interesting phenomenon in Salem was the substantial involvement of tradesmen in the export trade, a function typically associated with mercantile firms. In Salem, enterprising artisans not only actively participated in the venture trade in various goods but also engaged in co-ownership of vessels, with the intent of controlling sales of their products both in the coastal trade and abroad.[27]

Salem tradesmen involved in the venture trade included a significant number of cabinetmakers who, by the 1790s, had formed something approaching a cartel. Although the town had a sizable cabinetmaking trade before the Revolution, it was tiny compared to Charleston's. Between 1790 and 1800, twenty-eight cabinetmakers were working in Salem, and between 1800 and 1810, there were thirty-three. During the same decades Charleston cabinetmakers numbered sixty-four and 110, respectively. Charleston cabinetmakers, however, did not concern themselves with production for export, even though their northern counterparts seized upon this opportunity.

Over sixty cabinetmakers worked in Salem between 1790 and 1820, a substantial portion of whom engaged in the venture trade in one fashion or another. Prominent artisans, such as Elijah and Jacob Sanderson, William Appleton, and Nehemiah Adams, consistently produced furniture for export. The Sandersons maintained the largest cabinetmaking establishment in Salem, and as their voluminous records reveal, the brothers purchased prodigious quantities of cabinetware from other Salem artisans to augment their own consignments. By the late 1790s, the Sandersons co-owned several vessels with other cabinetmakers. Along with William Appleton, they owned the snow *Fanny*. Appleton and another prominent Salem cabinetmaker, Josiah Austin, owned the schooner *Olive Branch* in consort with the Sandersons. Nehemiah Adams joined the brothers in the co-ownership of the brig *Unicorn*. Such vessels joined the huge Salem mercantile fleet in exporting to the East and West Indies, to South and Central America, and to southern ports from Maryland to South Carolina. A study of over three hundred shipping manifests reveals repeated shipments of Salem furniture destined for Norfolk, Richmond, Edenton, New Bern, Wilmington, Georgetown, Charleston, Savannah, and New Orleans. The Sandersons even shipped furniture to Boston and Baltimore. The full extent of such shipments is unknown due to a great number of missing manifests, but the success of these ventures is evident in the remarkable quantity of Salem furniture with southern provenances that still survives in every southern coastal state.[28]

In Salem, a standard management for furniture ventures emerged by the late 1780s. Generally, ships leaving the port had cargoes consigned by a number of cabinetmakers, but in many instances one artisan or cabinetmaking firm shipped wares from other shops on commission, at the account and risk of the firm. Relatively little furniture appears to have been sent out of Salem to consignment merchants located in the various ports, and at least in the instance of Charleston, no merchants or cabinetmakers are known to have purchased shipments of Salem furniture for sale in their own establishments. Instead, the wares were typically sold at both public and private vendues, usually overseen either by the vessel's master or a supercargo. It was not unusual for a cabinetmaker to act as supercargo himself. Josiah Austin, for example, repeatedly served in that role, and even as shipmaster, in his ventures with the Sandersons and others.

One of the earliest furniture ventures of the federal period, but nevertheless typical of many that were to follow, sailed in the holds of the schooner *Ruth,* which left Salem in mid-December 1788 "bound to South Carolina and any of the other Southern States." Her cargo included "Sundry Cases and parcells of Household Furniture," supplemented by fourteen thousand bricks, window casings and sash, and ten casks of earthenware. At a manifest value of just under £522, the furniture comprised the most valuable portion of the cargo, which totaled £637.15.1. The cargo was shipped "one half on Account and Risk of . . . Josiah Austin and the other half on Account and Risk of . . . Elijah and Jacob Sanderson" and went "consigned to the said Elijah Sanderson for Sale and Returns." Elijah was aboard as supercargo to orchestrate the disposal of the venture goods and to purchase commodities for the return voyage.[29]

The timing of this venture was significant in relation to Charleston's financial health at that point. After a brief boom following the Revolution, in 1785 the city sank into an economic depression that was quickly fading by early 1789. When the *Ruth* dropped anchor in Charleston Harbor, the city's citizens were only just recovering from a grim purview of rice and indigo failures due to inclement growing seasons, new British restrictions on West Indian trade, and a general malaise in purchasing power. Indigo and rice exports had begun to rise to normal levels, and the cultivation of fine, long-staple, sea-island cotton, destined to be one of the state's most lucrative commodities, was well underway. Despite the depression, new boroughs were being added by developers and landowners during the 1780s: Cannonsborough, just north of Harleston Village on the Ashley side of the peninsula; Radcliffeborough, between the two rivers just north of the old city's northern line; and Mazyckborough and Wraggsborough on the Cooper side, north of Ansonborough. Fashionable, neoclassical dwellings were rising in each of these Charleston suburbs. The end of the 1780s marked the beginning of a renewed consumerism in the Low Country, which opened the door for the aggressive New England venturers who were to remain virtually unhindered until the Trade Embargo Act of 1807 and the end of the slave trade at the beginning of 1808.[30]

The invoice of furniture aboard the *Ruth* was quite specific, listing 177 pieces of case furniture, seating furniture, tables, and bedsteads. Included were four tall clocks with mahogany cases, twenty-six desks of mahogany, walnut, birch, maple, and cherry, and five desk-and-bookcases of mahogany and walnut. The desks ranged in value from £3.12 for plain maple examples to £12 for "Swelld mehogany" ones. Surprisingly, only four "bureaus" were listed, three of them "Swelld." The shipment also contained "Burch 3 1/2 ft tables," walnut and "mehogany 4ft tables," "side tables," breakfast tables, birch and mahogany card tables (both plain and swelled), a "stand table," and a "lightstand." Seating furniture consisted largely of inexpensive birch side chairs but also included three-dozen "common chairs" (ladderbacks), six "Black chairs" (probably Windsors or late iterations of "crook'd back" chairs), and two easy chairs valued at £4 each. The twelve mahogany bedsteads in the consignment varied in form and price from "4 oak plain bedsteads" worth a total of £3 to a "Mehogany Clawfoot Bedstead Compleat" valued at £7.10. The most expensive pieces in the cargo were three mahogany desk-and-bookcases, two of them described as "Swelld" and valued at £24 each. Elijah Sanderson was directed to dispose of these goods "to the best advantage you can for our interest & purpose" and, for the return, to purchase "Ceeder & Mahogany or other such goods as you may find best to answer this market."[31]

Sanderson carefully assembled all of the invoices of goods and services pertinent to the voyage. Eighteen days after departing from Salem, he paid John Ringal "some of Durty [thirty] Shilens Coinery in fool" for piloting the *Ruth* over the bar east of Charleston Harbor. During the same month he paid Thomas Bowen, publisher of the Charleston *Columbian Herald*, for "advertising Cabinet Furniture for Sale 3 times." Unfortunately, only three issues of that newspaper survive for 1789, none for the dates when Sanderson's advertisements ran. Sanderson established an account with the firm of N. & B. Perry & Co. for the purchase of ship's provender. Perry & Co. not only provided supplies but also warehouse space for the "Storage of Furniture from the 9th Jany," for which Sanderson paid £3 at the end of the month. On January 17, Sanderson listed "the Prise of the furnature Sold at Privat Sale," evidently one of several sales that either Sanderson or his Charleston agents held during that particular sojourn in the city. The items sold totaled only £29.5, but at the bottom of the sheet Sanderson noted an additional £178.5.11 for "furnature Soald at Oction bye Mr Dogit," indicating cabinetware sold at public vendue (probably by Henry Doggett, a Charleston vendue master).[32]

A third sale held on January 20, 1789, grossed £122.4. In this instance, the names of purchasers were listed, including members of the Simpson, Middleton, Smith, Ball, Dawson, Moncrieff, Martin, and Belcher families. The two most expensive items sold were desk-and-bookcases, which brought £12.15 each from Morton Brailsford and a "Mr Annister." These may have been the "2 Black Walnut Desks & Book Cases" listed at £30 in the ship's manifest, but other items fetched less than the Sandersons had valued them. Two walnut desks were on the manifest at £5.10 each, but together brought only £9.4 from the firm of Hume & Peacock, who presumably purchased them for resale. At the end of the day, Sanderson had grossed £329.14.11 from a furniture venture valued at £522, but evidently not all of the furniture, bricks, and window casings had been sold. Sanderson remained in Charleston until early March. On February 20, Roper's Wharf charged the

Ruth ten shillings ten and one-half pence for "3 days wharfage" and six shillings ten and one-half pence for drayage and loading "4700 feet mahogany." During the first week of March, Sanderson bought "3 Casks of Indico" from William Stephen, and another 113 pounds of indigo from the firm of Snowden, Lothrop & Forrest. Following the direction of his partners, he also purchased fifty-three cedar logs. As in Charleston, red cedar was favored in Salem for small drawer frames such as those in secretary interiors. Having wrung all the business possible from Charleston, the *Ruth* sailed on March 7, the day when Sanderson paid out 30 shillings for pilotage "over the Bar." There is no record of how much of his cargo remained unsold, but if furniture and other goods remained in the hold, the schooner no doubt put in at other southern ports on the return voyage to Salem in order to dispose of the balance.[33]

Such was the nature of the venture furniture trade early in the federal period. The furniture in the cargo of the *Ruth* probably consisted largely of pieces that either were still in the old-fashioned rococo style, such as the "Clawfoot Bedstead," or were transitional in nature, such as the "3 Swelld mehogany bureau[s]," all of which were still fashionable in the Massachusetts Bay region. A rococo mahogany desk dated 1789 and probably from Charlestown originally belonged to Samuel Gaillard, who engaged a Charleston cabinet shop to fit it with a restrained, classical bookcase. Other items in the Sanderson cargo, such as the breakfast tables and "Swelld Mahogany Card tables," could have been fully neoclassical in style, but the manifest and sale accounts do not verify that supposition. By 1789, however, Charlestonians were well acquainted with the new fashions, for they had been available in some of the city's cabinet shops for nearly two decades. It may be that the Sandersons and their colleagues learned a good deal about what sort of furniture was merchantable in the Low Country during this early venture. The Sandersons eventually owned four copies of Hepplewhite's *Guide*, although Salem neoclassical case furniture reveals no greater employment of Hepplewhite's designs than does work from Charleston shops of the same period. In any event, by the close of the 1780s, the Salem cabinet trade was on the brink of shifting fully to the production of wares in the new taste, which would have satisfied the most fashion-conscious of Charlestonians.[34]

By the end of the eighteenth century, Salem cabinetmakers were shipping astounding cargoes of furniture. The schooner *Two Brothers* out of Danvers sailed from Massachusetts in early January 1801, bound for Charleston with "Seventy nine cases Furniture" in her holds. Much larger ventures were not unusual. In 1809, the brig *Welcome Return* set sail for Brazil filled with furniture from the shops of the Sandersons, Appleton, Adams, Richard and Josiah Austin, Joshua Burbank, Francis Pulcifer, William Luther, and William Hook, the total value of cabinet goods aboard listed at $8,160.80. Elijah Sanderson drew up the invoice of the furniture and on the back of the document penned instructions to the shipmaster, Jeremiah Briggs:

> It often happens that furniture shipt by different people on board the same vessel is invoiced at different prices some higher and some lower of the same

kind and quality and sometimes there is a difference in the goodness of the work . . . therefore I wish you to sell mine by itself—not to mix it in a bargain with others . . . you will find that my furniture is marked with a brand ES on the back of each piece.

One carved card table of this period with the initials "E. S." painted in blue on the gate frame descended in a Wilmington, North Carolina, family. Cooperative ventures such as the 1809 voyage of the *Welcome Return*, though sailing with goods intended for a major market such as Rio de Janeiro, frequently called at intermediary ports at the discretion of the master or supercargo, including Wilmington and Charleston.[35]

Ingenious packing methods enabled Salem cabinetmakers to maximize their shipments. Within the "five Cases of Mehogany Furniture Shiped on Board the Schooner Greyhound . . . Bound to Georgetown South Carolina" in 1808 were:

three Small Righting Desk & Bookcases	[$]90.0
one Gentlemans Righting Desk with	17.0
one Ladies Work table in it	13.0
one pair Card tables Varnishd	36.0
	156.0

"Returns" were also important, for it was uneconomical for a vessel to cast anchor in her home port laden only with ballast. As we have seen, indigo and lumber were considered to be both profitable and useful commodities for purchase in the Low Country. In 1799, William Appleton and the Sanderson brothers paid Robert Cottle for "Truckage of 38 Casks Rice at Charleston at 9d per load." This purchase was not the only one that the cabinetmakers or their supercargo made after selling their furniture, for an additional charge for transporting 160 casks of rice from Charleston to Boston was appended to the bill. In 1817, Elijah Sanderson sent a venture of furniture to Charleston. As insurance against the possibility that the furniture could not be sold at invoice price, Sanderson instructed his consignee, Thomas Wheeler, to "leave it at Jos. Leland Commission Mercht. No. 87 East Bay . . . The returns to be made in Rice of the first quality." Trusting the sale of their furniture to commission merchants, however, seems to have been counter to the staunchly self-sufficient business methods of Salem cabinetmakers, regardless of the opportunity to have their goods constantly exposed to wealthy Charlestonians.[36]

Despite the considerable quantity of furniture shipped from Salem to Charleston, Salem cabinetmakers apparently had no business partners in South Carolina. The Massachusetts shops could have developed standing agreements with Charleston commission merchants but, instead, only occasionally used the services of such firms. The most likely Low Country agents for Salem furniture would have been Charleston cabinetmakers who, after the close of the eighteenth century, increasingly operated as warehousemen, often selling imported furniture cheaper than they could make it. A number of Charleston shops had close associations with the cabinet trade in both New York City and Philadelphia, and they sold prodigious quantities of furniture from those cities. This arrangement was particularly evident after about 1810 and during the boom years following the War of 1812, but the sale of furniture from the Massachusetts Bay region remained primarily a public sale business past 1820. Advertisements in Charleston newspapers typically gave notice of furniture to be sold right off the decks of merchant vessels, such as a cargo of "Mahogany Furniture" offered "on board the schooner Theoda" out of Salem in 1804, or the "5 Boxes CABINET FURNITURE, some very elegant," to be sold "on board the schooner Mehitabel, from Boston, lying at the Market Wharf" in January 1801. In contrast to Elijah Sanderson's two-month sojourn in Charleston in 1788, such brisk offerings appear to have best suited Massachusetts venturers bent upon a quick and profitable turnaround for furniture exports. After a week or so in Charleston, the Salem vessels sailed south to offer their remaining cargo in other ports.[37]

Even more surprising than the lack of trade ties between Charleston and Salem cabinetmakers is the scant documentation on masters or journeymen from Massachusetts cabinet shops emigrating to the South after the Revolution. During the colonial period, Boston cabinetmakers Charles Warham and Jonathan Badger plied their trade very successfully in Charleston. Such emigration was by no means typical later. With so much venture furniture leaving Salem for southern ports by the early 1790s, enterprising journeymen must have noted the potentially lucrative situations in the South, particularly in a large port such as Charleston; nevertheless, of the more than sixty cabinetmakers documented in Salem between 1790 and 1820, not a single individual is known to have emigrated to Charleston. The same is true of neighboring cabinetmaking centers in Massachusetts such as Dorchester, Lynn, and Beverly. Of over eighty individuals and partnerships engaged in the Boston cabinetmaking trade between 1780 and 1800, only one artisan appears to have moved to Charleston. In 1798, William Swaney was listed as a cabinetmaker on Newbury Street in a Boston city directory. He was in Charleston by 1803, and city directories list him on Magazine and Orange Streets, respectively, in 1806 and 1807. He died in Charleston in 1808.[38]

It is possible that other Massachusetts cabinetmakers moved to South Carolina and that their initial presence in Charleston was masked by their employment in one of the city's shops. A newly arrived workman seldom had the opportunity to announce himself as "late of" some fashionable cabinetmaking center unless he possessed the wherewithal to set up as a trade master on his own. In Charleston, apparently none did. The strong presence of Massachusetts Bay style in Charleston furniture made after 1790 suggests a more substantial influence than what is possible through tradesmen and their patrons ogling snappy venture furniture; however, the only documentation of the introduction of Salem style lies in specific design elements found on Charleston furniture.

Since no inclusive study of Massachusetts Bay furniture has been published, the extent of cross-pollination of regional styles between Boston and Salem is not perfectly understood. There are, nevertheless, salient features that furniture historians have long identified with Salem, largely due to the existence of signed and labeled pieces. The secretary-press attributed to William Jones (fig. 14) clearly relates to furniture signed by prominent artisans such as the Sandersons or William Appleton. Its pediment, which utilizes geometric formulas typical of Salem, compares very well with the head of a Salem secretary-and-bookcase with a Charleston history (fig. 26). Atypical of Salem production, however, are clothespresses, much less a press with a secretary drawer. Although made elsewhere, large clothespresses were commonly produced both in Charleston and in New York, and it has long been acknowledged that the finest American examples of the form usually are from those cities.

The intersecting string inlay on the friezes of the Salem secretaries shown in figures 26–29 is considered a hallmark of the Salem style. This frieze design was carried north to Portland and south through Virginia and the Carolinas. Curiously, it seems to skip past Boston and is foreign to New York, Philadelphia, and even Baltimore, where exuberantly inlaid friezes were common. Outside Massachusetts, Charleston furniture exhibits the most extensive use of this crossed stringing, which occurs in various combinations that often include horizontal husks separated by and even trailing inlaid pellets. The most common Charleston husk has broad curves at the sides and central points that are either flush with the flanking points or that hang only slightly below. The same is true of the shape of Salem husks, which are less likely to have the simple incising often found on Charleston examples. Even in Charleston, such incising occurs more often on table and sideboard leg inlays than in friezes, although there are exceptions. The usual formula for leg inlay in Boston and Salem—incorporating husks interspersed with long lenticular inlays and pellets—is less prominent on Charleston furniture, but it does occur, particularly on the legs of tables and sideboards.

The quarter-fans so prominently displayed on the drawers of the dressing chest attributed to Jones (figs. 11, 12) are occasionally found on Salem furniture, but they are more common on Boston, Portsmouth, New York, and Connecticut work. Figural inlays also are found on Salem furniture, but not with great frequency, just as they are relatively rare on furniture made in Rhode Island and further up Massachusetts's North Shore. They are far more common on Boston furniture owing to the presence of specialist inlay makers, although the size and strength of the inlay-making trade there remains to be researched. A good deal more is known about inlay makers in Baltimore; but the existing furniture from both Salem and Charleston uses sophisticated Massachusetts styles of figural inlay, particularly shells and, more rarely, federal eagles that appear to come from Boston. As noted earlier, white-background figural inlays, which appear frequently on Charleston furniture, do not have precise parallels in northern work. Other applied surface decoration such as the heavy drawer cross-banding typical of early Charleston neoclassical furniture is more common in Boston and Portsmouth than in Salem, but in New England it is considerably more restrained than in the bold South Carolina surrounds. Charleston cross-banding is more akin to British work of the 1770–1790 period.

Figure 22 Secretary-and-bookcase, Charleston, 1790–1800. Mahogany and mahogany veneer with red cedar and white pine. H. 104", W. 55⅜", D. 24⅜". (Private collection; photo, Museum of Early Southern Decorative Arts.)

Figure 23 Open view of the secretary-and-bookcase illustrated in fig. 22.

Salem cabinetmakers exported sideboards, pembroke tables, work tables, card tables, and side tables to Charleston. The double-tapered leg so characteristic of Salem and Boston table forms is absent in Charleston work. Low Country card tables, however, incorporate a variety of other Salem details, such as three-part skirt facades, with an inlaid tablet centering the frame, and the frequent use of lozenge-shaped inlay. As previously noted, all manner of chests of drawers were sent south from Massachusetts, includ-

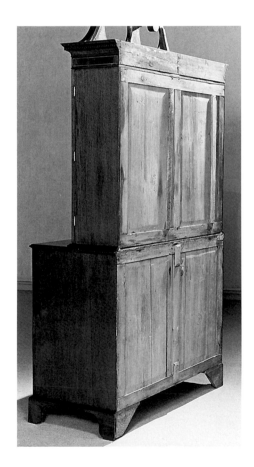

Figure 24 Detail of the pediment of the secretary-and-bookcase illustrated in fig. 22.

Figure 25 Rear view of the secretary-and-bookcase illustrated in fig. 22, showing the framed pediment and frieze and paneled upper and lower case backs.

ing, no doubt, the canted-corner examples that had been familiar in Charleston well before the Revolution. Desks, desk-and-bookcases, and, after 1790, secretary-and-bookcases were important venture items to Salem cabinetmakers. Although clothespresses were not sent south, relatively large case pieces such as gentlemen's secretaries were popular export items. Other Massachusetts furniture forms shipped to the Low Country but seldom adopted by Charleston cabinet shops were desks on tall, tapered legs with folding writing surfaces, including larger examples with bookcases and small pieces of the sort generally described as "ladies' writing desks." Tambour, which was particularly popular in Massachusetts by the beginning of the nineteenth century, was not especially favored by Charleston cabinetmakers, who may have been skeptical of the survival of a hide-glued assemblage of canvas and wood in a hot and damp climate.

The greatest stylistic impact from Massachusetts occurred during the 1790s. By the early 1800s, when Salem work began to be dominated by turned-leg case pieces and tables with carving by Samuel McIntire, Joseph True, and others, Charleston furniture increasingly focused upon New York details. In view of the continued importation of Massachusetts furniture well past 1800 and the presence of Charleston artisans, particularly carvers with the ability to duplicate evolving Salem and Boston tastes, the rapidly declining influence of Massachusetts styles between 1800 and 1810 seems surprising. By that time, however, New York was the rising star of the venture furniture business. This phenomenon was reinforced at the end of the eighteenth century by the arrival of cabinetmakers in Charleston who were more than willing to warehouse vast quantities of New York furniture and who quite naturally adopted New York details in their own products as well.

Seven case pieces attributed to the same anonymous shop illustrate some of the strongest expressions of the Massachusetts style to be found in Charleston neoclassical furniture. The group consists of a secretary-and-bookcase (figs. 22, 23), a desk-and-bookcase (fig. 31), two clothespresses (see fig. 30), and three chests of drawers (see fig. 33). Five of these pieces have

Figure 26 Secretary-and-bookcase, Salem, Massachusetts, 1790–1800. Mahogany and mahogany veneer with birch and white pine. H. 96³/₄", W. 43³/₄", D. 24¹/₄". (Private collection; photo, Gavin Ashworth.)

Figure 27   Detail of the pediment of the secretary-and-bookcase illustrated in fig. 26. (Photo, Gavin Ashworth.)

inlaid fluting either in the finial plinths or the cants of the feet (see fig. 33). Although the occurrence of this fluted inlay was apparently more common in Charleston than Massachusetts, a Salem chest of drawers (fig. 34) not only shares the same foot ornament but in many respects is almost identical to its Charleston counterpart. With the exception of the chest illustrated in figure 33, all of the pieces from this Charleston shop have dustboards and therefore follow the local norm rather than utilizing the simplified Massachusetts drawer support system, which consists of laths usually nailed to the case sides or, somewhat less commonly, glued and nailed into dadoes. Like many Low Country case pieces (see fig. 25), the Charleston chest has a paneled back. In Massachusetts work, this structural detail is usually confined to the top case of two-part pieces such as secretary-and-bookcases. The Salem example illustrated in figure 28 is exceptional in having a paneled lower case.

The stylistic tie between the Charleston secretary-and-bookcase illustrated in figure 22 and similar pieces made in Salem is remarkable. With the exception of the German-school, string-surrounded tympanum panels, the entire architectural composition of the pediment—including the sharp decreasing radius of the crown moldings where they meet the volutes, the circular cuts of the tympanum openings, the tall narrow plinth under the carved urn finial, and the crossed stringing of the frieze (fig. 24)—seem to have been lifted from the secretary-and-bookcase shown in figure 26. Clearly a Salem product, the latter example descended in the Dawson family of Charleston, bringing to mind the purchase by an unidentified member of that family of a "B[lac]k Walnut Bureau" at one of Jacob Sanderson's 1789 vendues. With a width of over fifty-five inches, the Charleston secretary-and-bookcase (fig. 22) is about ten inches wider than the Dawson example, approximately the width of two pigeonholes of the interior. Both pieces have similar feet, but the S-curve profiles of the Charleston ones are more akin to those on the clothespress illustrated in figure 20. Typical of both Charleston and Salem is the use of the single-string inlay to outline the feet and the tympanum (fig. 27). These details are shared by a secretary-and-bookcase labeled by Salem

Figure 28 Secretary-and-bookcase labeled by William Appleton, Salem, Massachusetts, 1795–1804 (based upon label address at Charter and Liberty Streets.) Mahogany and mahogany veneer with white pine. H. 97 1/2", W. 43 1/4", D. 24 3/8". (Courtesy, Winterthur Museum.)

cabinetmaker William Appleton (fl. ca. 1794–1822) (fig. 28). Were it not for the design of the prospect and shape of the pigeonhole valances, it would be tempting to attribute the Dawson secretary to Appleton's shop. The cabinetmaking community in Salem, however, was so tightly knit that separating the work of one cabinet shop from the next may be even more difficult than identifying furniture from different Charleston establishments. A secretary-and-bookcase labeled "MADE BY E. & J. Sanderson, CABINET AND CHAIR–MAKERS, In Federal Street, SALEM, MASSACHUSETTS" (fig. 29), has the same form of pediment as the Dawson and Appleton examples (figs. 26,

Figure 29 Secretary-and-bookcase labeled by Elijah and Jacob Sanderson, Salem, Massachusetts, 1790–1810. Mahogany and mahogany veneer with red cedar and white pine. H. 97⅝", W. 43⅜", D. 24¾". (Courtesy, Diplomatic Reception Rooms, U.S. Department of State.)

28), and the facing of its desk drawer is only slightly more elaborate than that on the Holmes secretary-and-bookcase (fig. 1). The Sanderson piece, however, has feet with spurred responds. Another Salem secretary-and-bookcase (in the Diplomatic Reception Rooms, U.S. Department of State) has feet like the Sanderson example, but its pigeonhole valances are identical to those on the Appleton secretary-and-bookcase and its carved and gilded eagle finial is similar to the one on the gentleman's secretary-and-bookcase shown in figure 36. Such finials were popular in Salem, but not in Charleston.[39]

The Dawson, Sanderson, and State Department secretaries (see figs. 26, 29) also have "pomegranate-style" rosettes. Those on the Sanderson and Dawson examples are virtually identical and are probably by the same carver (figs. 27, 29). The earliest occurrence of this type of rosette in Charleston graces the pediment of a German-school desk-and-bookcase of about 1785, the head of which is illustrated in figure 42 of *Charleston Furniture*. Similar rosettes occur on later Charleston pieces, including a library bookcase in the Governor's Mansion in Columbia, South Carolina.

Rosettes with shaded inlay, such as those on the secretary-and-bookcase shown in figure 22, are the most common type found on Charleston furniture, and they also occur on Salem work. Among the earliest examples from the Low Country are the rosettes on the clothespress illustrated in figures 4 and 5. Similar rosettes also occur on other pieces influenced by the German school, such as the secretary-press attributed to Jones (fig. 14) and the clothespress shown in figure 20. Most rosettes of this type have a small pellet of dark wood in the center, and each segment of the shaded fans terminates at the periphery with dark, convex or even elliptical inlays—probably ebony—that simulate shading. A more prominent version of this dark, convex "shading" occurs at the bottom of most of the fluted inlays used by this anonymous shop as well as by the shop that made the serpentine press (fig. 16). In this application, the dark shading simulates a stop-cut.[40]

The secretary-and-bookcase illustrated in figure 22 has doors with face veneers mitered at the corners in the usual Charleston manner. The doors of the Appleton secretary-and-bookcase are similarly finished, and, like the Charleston example, they have stringing outlining the stiles and rails (fig. 28). Although the doors of the Dawson secretary-and-bookcase have similar stringing, their frames are not veneered, and their corner joints (unmitered, unpinned, mortise-and-tenon joints) are visible (fig. 26). This structure was more common in Salem; however, veneering was usually a cost-driven option, and unveneered door frames also occur in Charleston furniture. The commodious writing compartment of the Charleston secretary-and-bookcase (fig. 23) follows the arrangement typical of post-Revolutionary pieces from the German school (fig. 15), but here the long drawers above the pigeonholes are placed at the top. The pigeonhole valances also are typical of that school, although the height of the pigeonholes is reduced. Even more closely allied with the earlier Charleston vernacular is the facade of the desk drawer, finished as a pair of sham drawers (fig. 22) in virtually the same proportional gradient as the Jones secretary-press (fig. 14).

Figure 30 Clothespress, Charleston, 1790–1800. Mahogany and mahogany veneer with yellow pine and white pine. H. 96", W. 50¼", D. 24¾". (Collection of the Museum of Early Southern Decorative Arts.) The inlaid rosettes and the finial are restorations.

Returning to the German-school format of wide edge-banding on the drawer faces is a clothespress (fig. 30) from the same shop as the Charleston secretary-and-bookcase (fig. 22). The press shares the Massachusetts architecture of the secretary, with the exception of the Gothic lancet arches with

Figure 31 Desk-and-bookcase, Charleston, 1790–1800. Mahogany and mahogany veneer with white pine. H. 98³/4" (including finial), W. 45", D. 25". The brasses are replaced. (Private collection; photo, Museum of Early Southern Decorative Arts.)

turned pendants that interrupt the cove molding (figs. 24, 30). Although traditionally considered a neoclassical detail on American furniture, an elaborate version of the same design occurs on the cornice of a "Gothick Bed" illustrated in the first edition of the *Director* (1754). Gothic cornices occur in most of the larger cabinetmaking centers of the eastern seaboard, including

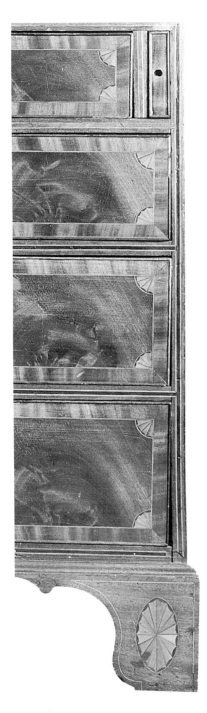

Salem. At least four Charleston shops used this form of cornice. One example occurs on the cornice of a secretary-press signed by Thomas Lee of Charleston, who, from 1804 to 1807, was in partnership with German cabinetmaker John Gros, a former apprentice of Jacob Sass.[41]

Neoclassical Charleston desk-and-bookcases are much rarer than secretary-and-bookcases. Except for merchants and cabinetmakers who were engaged in warehousing imported furniture, trade advertisements seldom mention desk-and-bookcases after the Revolution. As the example shown in figure 31 illustrates, however, some shops continued to produce them. Charleston cabinetmaker John Marshall charged a local attorney £18 for a "Mahoganey Desk & book case" in 1796, the same year Marshall took an immigrant German lad named Thomas Tennant as an apprentice. No document connects Marshall with the German-school cabinetmakers; however, despite its full-blown Salem-style pediment and frieze, the desk-and-bookcase shown in figure 31 quite clearly is the work of a German-school cabinetmaker, as is the secretary-and-bookcase from the same shop (fig. 22). On the surface, the secretary-and-bookcase reveals its "Charlestoness" principally in its massive, fifty-five-inch width. Although its secondary wood is entirely white pine (except for its solid, red cedar drawer cores), its full-bottom, three-quarter-depth dustboards, which match the construction of the desk-and-bookcase, have little to do with contemporary Massachusetts work.[42]

The wide edge-banding on the drawers of the desk-and-bookcase (fig. 31), here used with four-part, bookmatched veneers highlighted with quarter-fans, reveals the persisting aesthetic of a German-school shop. This style is

Figure 32   Detail of the lower case of the desk-and-bookcase illustrated in fig. 31.

Figure 33   Chest of drawers, Charleston, 1790–1800. Mahogany and mahogany veneer with red cedar, mahogany, and white pine. H. 37 1/4", W. 41 7/8", D. 22 1/2". (Courtesy, Yale University Art Gallery; gift of C. Stanford Bull.)

also evident in the paterae and stringing on the faces of the front feet, and especially in the heavy, contrasting triple-line inlay on the case stiles and rails (fig. 32). These particulars follow a tradition beginning in Charleston with the Edwards library bookcase and continuing past the Revolution with other German-school work, such as the clothespress illustrated in figure 16. Such details are as rare on Massachusetts Bay work as full dustboards, but they were standard drill in Charleston. Nail holes inside the door rails of this desk-and-bookcase indicate the early use of curtains or gathered fabric to conceal the bookcase interior. Considering the considerable expense of glazed doors with Chinese tracery, this practice seems an anomaly today, but, judging from the number of American pieces with similar evidence, such cloaking-off was common. The principal desire often was to parade an expensive facade, rather than exhibit the contents of a case piece.[43]

A canted-corner chest of drawers with a different foot pattern (fig. 33) is attributed to the same shop that produced the desk-and-bookcase (fig. 31). Like the labeled William Jones chest (fig. 8), it has equal-height drawers, which were relatively common in Charleston. Such drawers occur on British furniture, north German furniture in the British style, and American furniture from other regions. The Salem chest illustrated in figure 34 has equal-height drawers and fluted inlay in the foot cants. As on the Charleston chest (fig. 33), this cant inlay has dark, pointed ellipses at the bottom to simulate stop-cuts. The foot pattern of the Salem chest appears to match that of the Dawson and Appleton secretary-and-bookcases, but the string surround is not carried as far into the foot responds (figs. 26, 28).[44]

Figure 34 Chest of drawers, Salem, Massachusetts, 1790–1800. Mahogany and mahogany veneer with white pine. H. 36 7/16", W. 40 3/8", D. 22 3/8". (Private collection; photo, John Bivins.)

Another Salem-school, canted-corner chest (in the collection of the Society for the Preservation of New England Antiquities) has feet similar to the Charleston example, except that the inside profiles do not return as sharply at the bottom. This chest is documented to Langley Boardman, who left Salem about 1798, through an 1802 ledger entry made by John Rundlet of Portsmouth: "By Beaureau & handles [$] 28." Typical of neoclassical furniture from Portsmouth, but not from Salem, is Boardman's use of a full dustboard behind the center drawer rail—a structural feature employed earlier in Boston bombé furniture. Although strongly influenced by the Salem style, Portsmouth developed a distinctive regional cast of its own, both in style and construction.[45]

The marked similarity between the Charleston chest of drawers (fig. 33) and the Salem example (fig. 34) deserves further scrutiny. The Charleston chest has a more projecting serpentine front, which is a product of the standing patterns used to lay out the top, drawer fronts, and case rails. The top attachment is standard for most chests of drawers of the period; both pieces have laths blind-dovetailed to the top of the case sides at the front and rear, and the tops are held in place by screws inserted from underneath the laths. In addition to screws, the Charleston chest has three glue blocks positioned between the laths at each side to prevent the top drawer from tipping down when opened. The upper sides of the case and the underside of the top is extensively tooth-planed where these blocks are applied. Although tooth planes were used by most cabinetmakers for face-glued joints and for surfaces to be veneered, Charleston furniture exhibits a good deal more tooth-planing than normally expected. The Salem chest has no blocks between the top laths and therefore no tooth-planing on the top and sides.[46]

The bottoms of both chests are dovetailed to the sides of the cases, and full-width and full-depth blocks back up the base moldings. Both bottom drawers run on the case bottoms, and in both instances the chests have quarter-round, vertical foot blocks that abut the usual pair of horizontal blocks glued to the bed blocks as a bracing for the foot responds. The back feet of the Charleston chest have diagonal braces that are blind-dovetailed to the foot facings. This detail, which occurs sporadically in Charleston, is absent on the Salem chest. The Charleston chest also has heavier foot blocking than the Salem example and more extensive tooth-planing surrounding the blocks. The foot facings of the Charleston chest are three-quarters of an inch thick, whereas those of the Salem chest are little more than one-quarter-inch thick.

The drawer rails of the Charleston chest are made from two boards—a solid mahogany board with a serpentine face glued to a white pine board of the same thickness. The rails of the Salem chest are white pine veneered with mahogany. On both pieces, the drawer rails are half-dovetailed to the case sides, the joints covered in front with vertical facing strips glued to the edges of the case sides. Unlike other case pieces from the same shop, including a virtually identical chest with a history of descent in the Porcher family, the Charleston chest has no dustboards. The backings for its drawer rails are so deep they appear to be partial dustboards, and its drawer supports are set into dadoes and nailed in place. The drawer supports of the Salem chest are simply nailed to the sides of the case, which is typical of North Shore construction. There are, however, exceptions to this method; the Appleton secretary-and-bookcase (fig. 28) has drawer supports glued into half-dovetailed dadoes, and the supports of the aforementioned Langley Boardman chest are glued into plain dadoes.

From this point, construction of the Charleston and Salem chests diverges sharply (figs. 33, 34). The drawers of the Charleston chest are mahogany veneered on solid red cedar, the bottom and back of the drawers are white pine, and the sides of the drawers are red cedar, a more extensive use of the latter material than expected in New England. The drawer bottom is dadoed to the front and sides and nailed at the back in the usual fashion, and full-length glue blocks, cut through with a series of saw kerfs to aid expansion and contraction, are attached to the bevels next to the sides. The Salem chest has dado-fitted drawer bottoms, but without blocking at the sides, and its drawer fronts are veneered on four to five laminates of white pine, like those on the Boardman chest.

Despite the differences between these pieces, Charleston construction details can overlap with those found in Salem furniture. The drawer cores of the Salem secretary-and-bookcase illustrated in figure 26 are solid white pine, and the Appleton secretary-and-bookcase (fig. 28) has drawer blocking like the Charleston chest shown in figure 33. Similarly, the drawer fronts of the Porcher chest are composed of two or three laminates rather than being solid like most Charleston examples. The drawers of both the Salem and Boardman chests stop against vertical wooden strips glued to the back of the case. In usual Low Country fashion, the drawers of the Charleston chest are stopped by trapezoidal pieces of wood glued to the drawer rails. Since these stops engage the bottom inside face of the drawers, the drawer faces maintain a constant relationship to the front plane of the case, unaffected by expansion and contraction of the case sides. The Appleton secretary (fig. 28) also has stops glued to the rails.

The backs of both the Salem and Boardman chests are composed of horizontal boards nailed into rabbets in the case sides, whereas the back of the Charleston example, like other furniture from the same shop, is framed in two vertical panels (two rails and three stiles, assembled with unpinned mortise-and-tenon joints). The Charleston chest back is also screwed at the center into a top rabbet and to the case bottom and nailed into rabbets in the sides. Like the solid drawer cores on the Charleston chest, this panel construction is more indicative of Low Country work. The Appleton secretary-and-bookcase (fig. 28) is an exception in having a paneled lower case. Similarly, not every Charleston case piece has a paneled frame; the back boards of the Porcher chest and the example illustrated in figure 30 are composed of horizontally oriented boards that are nailed into rabbets.

Urban British pieces in the neoclassical style often have paneled backs, regardless of whether the back was applied to a chest of drawers or to a bookcase. The same is true of a great deal of Charleston furniture made between the 1770s and just past the end of the eighteenth century. Most American furniture tends to confine the use of paneling—which added to the cost of a piece—to the backs of bookcases or cupboards, where the back can be seen when the doors are either glazed or open. Paneled backs expand and contract with seasonal changes, whereas butted or even tongue-and-grooved or ship-lapped back boards can shrink, revealing a rather unworkmanlike gap. Single-piece case forms such as secretaries and chests of drawers did not readily reveal such sins.[47]

Other differences between the Charleston and Salem chests lie in the degree of finish, both inside and out (figs. 33, 34). The quality of the inlay of the Massachusetts example is somewhat better. The somewhat awkward incised husks on the cants of the Charleston chest differ from those on Massachusetts work; and the southern piece has a string-surrounded top, whereas the Salem chest has a plain top. The drawer dovetailing of the Salem piece is coarse compared to that of the Charleston chest, which has small pins typical of Low Country work. In addition, the unseen surfaces of the Salem chest, such as drawer bottoms, display the rough kerfs of a reciprocating saw, whereas all the inner surfaces of the Charleston piece are planed off. Very little Charleston furniture from any period exhibits saw kerfs. In short, the Charleston chest shows more care in finish and construction, which almost invariably is the case when Low Country furniture is compared with Massachusetts Bay work.[48]

Comparing the date of manufacture of the Charleston chest with its Salem counterpart is difficult (figs. 33, 34); however, the cut nails attaching the back of the Massachusetts chest probably indicate a later date for that piece. Like most of the surviving Charleston, canted-corner chests that retain their original brasses, this example has single-post ring pulls, one of the earliest forms of neoclassical brass (in use in Britain by the 1770s and common in America during the 1780s). The same type of hardware was used on the nearly matching Porcher chest of drawers mentioned earlier.

Over twenty Charleston shops utilized elements of the Massachusetts style to one degree or another. The "gentleman's secretary" illustrated in figure 35 is the only South Carolina example of this form known. Made like a small, three-bay library bookcase, this form seems to be particular to Salem, although Sheraton illustrated a fall-front version on plate 52 of *The Cabinet-Maker and Upholsterer's Drawing-Book* (1792). The Salem gentleman's secretary shown in figure 36 was owned by Joseph Manigault of Charleston, whose fine, three-story brick house on Meeting Street was designed by his brother Gabriel about 1803. Despite such eminent patronage for these expensive objects, Charleston cabinetmakers made little attempt to compete with Salem in their production. The Manigault gentleman's secretary exhibits much of the standard form for such pieces, with the exception of the arch at the bottom of the center bay, a space that more often than not is occupied by a drawer or cabinet. The Winterthur Museum, however, has a more elaborate example with a similar arch, and another labeled by Nehemiah Adams is entirely open below the secretary drawer. Another gentleman's secretary labeled by Edmund Johnson (also at Winterthur) is so

Figure 35 Gentleman's secretary, Charleston, 1790–1800. Mahogany and mahogany veneer with white pine. H. 115½", W. 76". (Private collection; photo, Museum of Early Southern Decorative Arts.) The door tracery is missing, and the two drawers below the desk drawer are replaced with a cabinet.

close to the Manigault example that it is tempting to make an attribution. As Charles Montgomery noted, however, although these pieces are "among the most important forms made by Salem and nearby cabinetmakers," they reveal "comparatively little variation in . . . over-all form." Most of these pieces have the parapeted cornice of the Manigault piece, a feature common in most American coastal cabinetmaking centers and certainly familiar in Charleston (see fig. 37).[49]

Both the Johnson and Manigault secretaries have thirteen-light Chinese tracery in each door, and the same originally was true of the Charleston-made example (fig. 35), which not only has lost its door tracery but also two drawers below the desk drawer (a space now occupied by a cabinet). The Charleston example has a history of descent from Judge Alfred Huger (son of John Huger, 1798–1853) of Charleston. Rather than a parapet, this secretary is finished with a scrolled pediment that incorporates a white-background floral patera in its finial plinth. Its pediment is related to the Charleston secretary-and-bookcase with elliptical door tracery illustrated in figures 34 and 43 in *Charleston Furniture*. The balance of the inlay is restrained, comprised of lunetted single stringing outlining the panels of the side bay doors, and the same stringing on the face of the desk drawer is augmented with a pair of Salem-like ovals of stringing. The desk drawer interior of the Charleston gentleman's secretary (fig. 35) has no prospect, but its pigeon-hole valances have the cyma shape favored by Charleston cabinetmakers of this period. Both the upper and lower backs of this gentleman's secretary are paneled, and unlike its Massachusetts prototypes, the bookcase has very little setback from the base.

The secretary-and-bookcase on legs illustrated in figure 37 is one of only five Charleston examples; however, the form was common in the Massachusetts Bay region. Also rare in Charleston is the tambour on this piece. The tambour on the Charleston example was destroyed, either by the elements or by ill use, but it has been reconstructed following the molded-element tambour of a very similar secretary from the same shop in the collection of the Charleston Museum. Other surviving work from this anonymous shop includes two scrolled-pediment secretary-and-bookcases. One of these has pomegranate-carved rosettes and incised husks aligned with each miter of the veneer covering the door rails and stiles, a German-school detail previously noted in the doors of the press shown in figure 16.[50]

The crossed diamond-shaped door tracery of the secretary-and-bookcase on legs (fig. 37) is a favored Salem pattern that occurs on two of the other three pieces from the same Charleston shop. Successful regional additions, however, are the inlaid spandrels at each corner of the doors. The sweeping curves of the cornice also follow Massachusetts style, as does the lavish use of satinwood veneer on the parapet, frieze, and interior drawer facings. The inlaid denticulation of this piece is repeated on the work of at least four Charleston shops and occurs both in Massachusetts work as well as in Britain. The writing surface pulls forward in the standard fashion for cylinder-fall and tambour secretaries, and it was originally fitted with a ratchetted reading rest that probably resembled the one on the Charleston Museum secretary-and-bookcase. The latter example is fitted with a prospect, the door of which is centered with a white-background paterae. The top and side edges of its lower case are faced with what appears to be West Indian rosewood in the same manner as the secretary shown in figure 37. The nicely drawn but simplified urns of the leg stiles, rendered in South American rosewood and maple with satinwood grounds, appear to be Charleston work. The unusual, face-applied cuffing at the feet are restorations.[51]

Similarly finished with an inlaid dentil course, but having far less delicacy in either proportions or detailing, is a secretary-and-bookcase signed and dated by the cabinetmaking firm of Philips and Welch (figs. 38–40). With the crossed triple string of its frieze repeated across its book-matched

Figure 36 Gentleman's secretary, Salem, Massachusetts, 1795–1805. Mahogany and mahogany veneer with white pine. H. 99⁵/₁₆", W. 67³/₁₆", D. 18³/₈". (Courtesy, Charleston Museum; photo, Gavin Ashworth.)

veneered drawer faces, the piece is a virtuoso display of the Salem idiom in Charleston. Not only the inlay design but also the architecture of the pediment continue the Massachusetts details that had begun to filter into the city over a decade earlier. The massive girth of the piece, however, speaks of the Teutonic penchant for square proportions and generously pragmatic storage space that Charlestonians appear to have been comfortable with. Naturally enough, that regional attitude extends to the construction of the piece, which has full dustboards, muntin-divided drawer bottoms, and a paneled lower case back. The original bookcase back almost certainly was treated in similar fashion, but it has been replaced. The piece was subjected to a number of traumatic indecencies in the 1940s, including the replacement of the pediment plinth tablet, bookcase doors, bed molding, and feet. There is no record of the original glazing plan. The sides of all the drawers

Figure 37   Secretary-and-bookcase on legs, Charleston, 1795–1800. Mahogany and mahogany veneer with white pine, tulip poplar, yellow pine, and red cedar. H. 92", W. 42", D. 24". (Courtesy, Sumpter Priddy, III, Inc.; photo, Katherine Wetzel.)

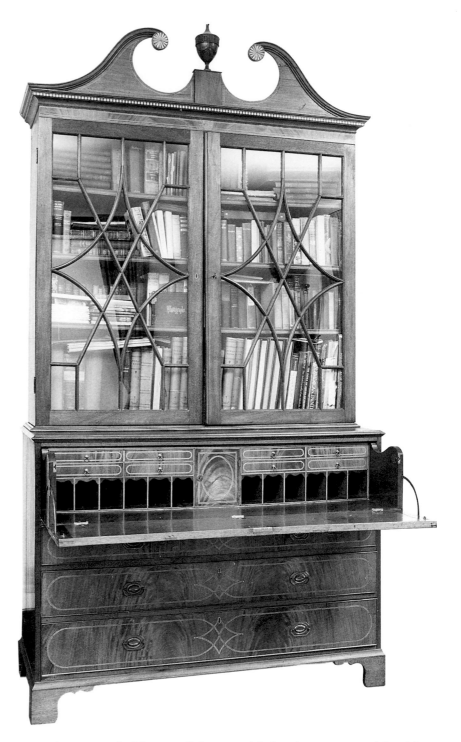

Figure 38 Secretary-and-bookcase signed by Philips & Welch, Charleston, 1800. Mahogany and mahogany veneer with mahogany, yellow pine, and white pine. H. 111$\frac{1}{2}$" (including finial), W. 58$\frac{1}{8}$", D. 24$\frac{1}{8}$". (Private collection; photo, Museum of Early Southern Decorative Arts.)

are mahogany, a lavish use of the material that is not unusual in either Charleston or New York, both of which boasted an enormous importation of the various mahoganies from Yucatan and the Caribbean islands.

The German-school proportions and retention of earlier British construction details on this piece are not surprising. John Michael Philips, who was the senior member of Philips and Welch, was born in 1773 and baptized the following year in St. John's Lutheran Church. Nothing is known of his apprenticeship. He was admitted to the German Friendly Society in 1796

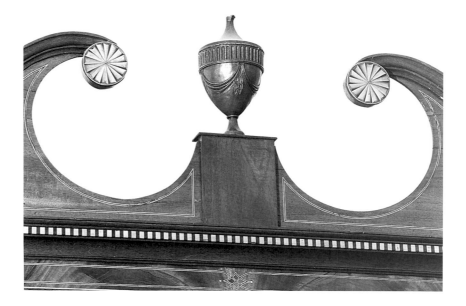

Figure 39   Detail of the pediment of the secretary-and-bookcase illustrated in fig. 38. The top of the finial is missing.

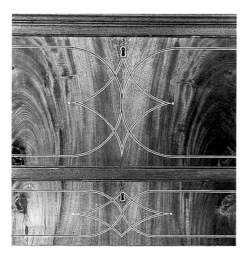

Figure 40   Detail of the lower case of the secretary-and-bookcase illustrated in fig. 38.

and placed what must have been his first advertisement in the spring of the same year, announcing that he carried on the cabinetmaking "Business in all its Branches" at his shop on Beaufain Street. Approximately three years later, his house and shop burned, reportedly due to a faulty cookstove. On the day following the report about the fire, however, Thomas Sigwald, another German cabinetmaker who boarded with Philips, published a notice that the fire must have occurred at the hands of "some evil-disposed persons, and not by accident, or carelessness."[52]

Following the 1799 fire, Philips formed a partnership with John Welch at the "uper End of King Street," as the June 18, 1800, signature on an interior drawer of the secretary reveals. Philips seems to have been plagued by the gods of fire, however, for his King Street establishment was consumed by flames in August 1800. A newspaper notice the following month indicated that the fire evidently brought an end to the short-lived Philips & Welch firm as well; accounts were to be rendered to "JOHN M. PHILIPS, who is fully authorized to settle" the business of the firm. Philips had already taken new quarters, advertising a scant week after the fire that he had "taken a small House, No, 131 King–street." Due to the "repeated losses" he had suffered from "having been burnt out last year, and now again by the late conflagration," he naturally solicited "the patronage and custom of the public and his friends." Philips was listed as a cabinetmaker in at least one city directory as late as 1813. Relatively little is known about John Welch. He is listed in city directories in 1803, when he was located at 80 Meeting Street, and in 1804, when he was listed as a principal of the firm of "J & G Welch" at 159 Meeting. George Welch, possibly the brother of John Welch, worked in the city from at least 1804 to as late as 1819. John Welch was last listed as a cabinetmaker and superintendent of the city burial ground in 1819.[53]

The secretary-and-bookcase illustrated in figure 38 does not signal the end of a stylistic era in Charleston, but it was made at a time when local cabinetmakers were taking more notice of other American styles. The Alston family galleried sideboard (in the Garvan Collection at Yale), for example, has a tripartite center drawer, arched central tambour cabinet, lozenge-shaped panels outlined with stringing, and reeded legs with carved capitals typical of both Salem and Boston. Its leg stiles, however, have long, elliptical veneers more typical of New York. After 1800, enormous quantities of New York furniture were sold by Charleston warehousemen. This practice was spurred not only by the more relaxed business attitudes displayed by New York cabinetmakers and shippers—in contrast to the virtually Puritan business ethics of Salem artisans—but also by the arrival in Charleston of cabinetmakers and other tradesmen well armed with New York business ties. One of these tradesmen was carver and gilder Richard Otis, who was in Charleston at least by 1816. A typical advertisement for his wareroom offered "An assortment of best N. York made FURNITURE, warranted to stand the climate, viz. Sideboards, Tea and Card Tables, Candle Stands, Bedsteads &c." Another announced the arrival of "10 dozen Cain and Rush bottom Chairs, with or without Settees to suit," along with "30 dozen Windsor Chairs," all in the "ship Corsair, from New-York." The seating furniture, which competed with the mass of Windsor and fancy chairs shipped to the Low Country from Philadelphia, filled a void in the marketplace since Charleston had virtually no specialist chairmakers.[54]

Although the evidence of converging and diverging stylistic traditions is clear in Charleston furniture from the last decades of the eighteenth century, interesting ironies and nagging mysteries remain. There is no question that the city's tightly knit, German cabinetmaking community was responsible for the earliest furniture in the neoclassical style. This, of course, is the height of irony since some of the most "British" aspects of Charleston neoclassical furniture were introduced by Germanic emigrés rather than by cabinetmakers from England, as was usually the case. To describe this furniture as purely British, however, would be a mistake, for Teutonic details of style and mass are equally discernable.

In contrast to the more stolid conservatism of upper New England, the cosmopolitan culture of the Low Country accepted new styles very quickly. Before the Revolution, a small group of Charleston shops was producing some of the earliest American furniture touched by what some unknown wag has called "the dead hand of Adam." German-school cabinetmakers were almost singlehandedly responsible for the emergence of neoclassicism in Charleston furniture, and they staunchly carried this banner to and past the end of the eighteenth century. That a large number of their apprentices, journeymen, and colleagues were of British extraction made no difference, for post-Revolutionary shopmasters like Sass, Gesken, Muckinfuss, and Gros were among the trendsetters in the cabinetmaking trade.[55]

The German influence on style leads to a second irony. Charleston cabinetmakers of the German school were the principal agents responsible for incorporating early neoclassical Massachusetts Bay forms and decoration into mainstream Charleston furniture fashions, but in a way never previously witnessed. Earlier trends can be charted more readily: British cabinetmakers came from London or some lesser urban center and brought styles familiar to them, designs eagerly sought after by fashion-conscious Charlestonians. The Germans then arrived, unwittingly bringing along the most recent utterings from St. Martin's Lane mixed in with a baroque, north German dialect. During the federal period, however, New England cabinetmakers came to Charleston solely for the purpose of selling furniture and filling their holds with profitable commodities for the return voyages. Although they did not remain, their style did. It was an extraordinary demonstration of the success of their exports, reflected a hundredfold in the Massachusetts Bay details strewn, first cautiously, then with abandon, across the face of Charleston furniture.

During the late eighteenth century, Salem cabinetmakers failed to develop commercial ties with their Charleston counterparts and the city's commission merchants. Although large quantities of Massachusetts furniture were shipped to Charleston, no Bay area artisans are known to have moved there. The considerable differences in patronage, culture, and climate between the the Low Country and New England may explain why Massachusetts cabinetmakers neglected to seek their fortunes in the moss-hung South.

Although the cabinetmaking trade in New England ports such as Salem was small in comparison to Charleston's, the cooperative nature of the venture cargo trade resulted in better profits for the cabinetmaking community as a whole. Trade masters like the Sandersons had a powerful motive for developing this enterprise: the opportunity to nudge out other cities by being the first to blanket the coastal community with attractive goods. Their plan was so successful that many shop masters became the owners of the vessels that carried their wares.

In Charleston, the senior members of the German school undoubtedly arrived with a common sense of community cohesiveness—the spirit that had created the *genossenschaften* of some German towns—but they established their cabinetmaking subculture in a city where satisfying a wealthy and materialistic local society was paramount. Even as the German community grew apace, and consequently had a very considerable effect on the city's furniture styles, no one in Charleston was bent upon efficient and highly productive manufacture for export. Instead, cabinetmakers had difficulty satisfying local demand. This concentration was intensified by the considerable technological changes of the neoclassical style—the problem of making complex forms that often required laminated coring, complex veneer applications, and intricate inlays, all of which required specialized labor. In some respects, the Germans arriving in South Carolina after the 1760s were the tradesmen most familiar with these techniques; however, the importation of specialized skills was not enough. As the historical events and administrative stumblings of the new republic unfolded during the first quarter of the nineteenth century, coastal southern cabinetmaking centers began to decline, particularly after the panic of 1819. With its heavy dependence on agricultural export, Charleston was devastated during that event, as were the tradesmen in the city. After 1820, however, the cabinetmaking trade in Salem grew faster than ever.

The "Salemizing" of Charleston furniture says a great deal about patronage and the cultivation of patronage. If a picture in a design book was worth a thousand words, then a three-dimensional object was worth ten thousand. An example of the importance of patronage is the much-quoted advertisement by Richard Magrath, a London immigrant who offered in 1771 "carved Chairs of the newest-fashion, splat Backs with hollow Seats and Commode Fronts, of the same pattern as those imported by *Peter Manigault, Esq.*" It would be interesting to know how similar Magrath's erstwhile samples were to the chairs that graced Manigault's apartments. In that particular instance, even the construction of the furniture may have been duplicated.[56]

The important point about Charleston furniture, however, is the degree to which artisans and their patrons were willing to accept outside influences. A whole succession of immigrant British cabinetmakers brought with them a long-standing tradition of conventional shop practices along with what they knew of current style. They may not have swayed Charlestonians toward crusts of applied carving and away from their prevailing sense of conservatism, regardless of the vast depth of Low Country wealth and its tight and direct links with London; but if the pediment of a Charleston double chest lacks a carved tympanum, it is by no means bereft of the focus upon structural dynamics so characteristic of urban British furniture. When the Germans came, facades became a bit more colorful, but usually not in an overly ostentatious manner. British construction aesthetic continued, for the Germans well understood such things themselves. When the Massachusetts style appeared in the late 1780s, no matter how fashionable it may have seemed or how quickly absorbed, it overlaid generations of long-established attitudes about workmanship. On closer examination, it often accompanied pre-existing elements of design and decoration rather than entirely ousting them. In doing so, the presence of the features exported from Massachusetts simply became another pretty powdering over a city style whose plate already was filled with a tasty ethnic pie, the recipe for which had been written thousands of miles to the northeast of Charleston.

ACKNOWLEDGMENTS For their assistance in varied but invaluable ways, I would like to thank Frank Horton, Brad Rauschenberg, Wendy Cooper, Mike Podminaniczky, Kemble Widmer, Dean Lahakainen, Alice Patrick, Thomas Savage, Robert Leath, David Beckford, Chris Loeblein, Harriet and Jim Pratt, Luke Beckerdite, Sumpter Priddy, and my favorite field researcher, my wife, Anne McPherson.

The material in this article is adapted from a manuscript under preparation by Bradford Rauschenberg and John Bivins for the forthcoming monograph *Charleston Furniture 1680–1820,* to be published by the Museum of Early Southern Decorative Arts and distributed by the University of North Carolina Press.

1. Walter B. Edgar, "South Carolina," unpublished manuscript, Institute of Southern Studies, University of South Carolina, 1996, pp. 61, 62, 83–85. This manuscript is scheduled for publication by the University of South Carolina Press. The biographical information on Charleston cabinetmakers presented in this article is derived from Bradford L. Rauschenberg, *Charleston Cabinetmakers, 1680–1820* (Chapel Hill: University of North Carolina Press for the Museum of Early Southern Decorative Arts [hereinafter cited as MESDA], forthcoming).

2. John Fyfe to Charles Desel, April 11, 1777, Charleston County Land Records, Miscellaneous (hereinafter cited as CCLRM), pt. 56, bk. P4, 1775–1777. Desel died in 1808 . His estate, worth nearly $15,000, included "A lot of Cabinet Maker's Tools [and] Benches" (Charleston County Inventories [hereinafter cited as CCI], vol. D, 1800–1810, pp. 450–51). On September 28, 1775, Henrich Christof "Kefkin," identified as a cabinetmaker of Osterholtz in Electoral Hanover, married Maria Margaretha Münch of Orangeburg County, South Carolina, in Charleston (St. John's Lutheran Church Records, 1755–1787, South Carolina Historical Society, Charleston). Desel & Gesken (spelled "Gaskin") are mentioned in 1784 in the Paul Cross Papers, 1768–1803, box 1, folder 8, 1783–1785, Manuscripts Department, South Carolina Library, Columbia. Jacob Sass emigrated from Hesse, Germany, to Charleston in 1773 at the age of twenty-three (N. Louise Bailey, ed., *Biographical Directory of the South Carolina House of Representatives,* vol. 4 [Columbia: University of South Carolina Press, 1984], p. 506). The cabinetmaking firm of Warner & Silberg is mentioned on October 25, 1788, in the South Carolina Court of Common Pleas, Judgement Rolls (hereinafter cited as SCCCPJR), box 135B, no. 25A, for a promissory note owed them since 1786. An announcement of the dissolution of their partnership appeared in the February 7, 1787, issue of the *Charleston Morning Post and Daily Advertiser.* Silberg died in December 1801, and his obituary described him as a native of Sweden (*South Carolina State Gazette and Timothy's Daily Advertiser,* January 5, 1802).

3. For more on the establishment of these townships, see Edgar, "South Carolina," pp. 92–111. Londonborough, whose populace was overwhelmingly German, was not founded until the 1760s. Information on the origin of the German settlers arriving during the 1760s is derived from MESDA research, which documents cabinetmakers from Hanover, Oldenburg, and Hesse-Cassel.

4. For Fisher, see *South Carolina Gazette,* May 16, 1771. For Thomas Hutchinson, see ibid., pp. 90, 97–98; Will of Thomas Hutchinson, July 16, 1782, Charleston County Wills (hereinafter cited as CCW), no. 2, 1783–1786, p. 318; and D. E. Huger Smith and Alexander S. Salley, Jr., *Register of St. Philip's Parish, Charles Town, 1754–1810* (1927; reprint ed., Columbia: University of South Carolina Press, 1971), p. 353. For Thomas Elfe, Sr., see *South Carolina Gazette and American General Gazette,* December 8, 1775. For Thomas Elfe, Jr., see CCW, no. 18, 1776–1784, p. 88; and *Gazette of the State of Georgia,* June 26, 1783. For Pearce, see Records of the Public Treasurers of South Carolina, 1725–1776, journal B, p. 352, nos. 79, 80; and Mabel L. Webber, comp., "The Thomas Elfe Account Book, 1768–1775," *South Carolina Historical and Genealogical Magazine* 38, no. 1 (January 1937): 39, 58, 61, 133. For Magrath, see *South Carolina Gazette,* August 8, 1771; and *Gazette of the State of South Carolina,* July 21, 1777. For Packrow, see *South Carolina and American General Gazette,* March 20, 1777; and *Gazette of the State of South Carolina,* August 7, 1778. For Townsend, see *South Carolina and American General Gazette,* June 3, 1771. For Axson, see *City Gazette of the Daily Advertiser,* May 28, 1788. For Finlayson, see Chancery Court Bill of Complaint, pt. 2, nos. 34–61, 1800 regarding a charge made by Finlayson against the estate of Andrew Hibben in 1784. For Gough, see deed from Gough to Eleanor Rust, March 16–17, 1777, CCLRM, pt. 3, bk. B5, 1776–1779, pp. 77–80. For Ralph, see *South Carolina and American General Gazette,* February 24, 1781. For Luyten, see *Charleston Morning Post and Daily Advertiser,* January 3, 1787. For Howe, see suit of William Donaldson vs. John Howe, March 29, 1779, SCCCPJR, box 105A, no. 104A. For Snead, see deed from Snead to Jacob Valk, September 16, 1779, CCLRM, pt. 66, bk. E5, 1781–1782, pp. 96–98. For Stewart, see appointment of Isabella Stewart as administrator of Stewart's estate, March 11, 1785, Charleston County Letters of Administration (hereinafter cited as CCLA), vol. OO, 1777–1785, p. 445. For Simmons, see mortgage of Simmons to John Croll, April 2, 1784, Charleston County Miscellaneous Records, 1784–1789, p. 69. For Philips, see letters of administration for the estate of Timothy Philips, July 16, 1784, CCLA, vol. K, 1778–1821, p. 92. For more on the aforementioned artisans, see their respective entries in E. Milby Burton, *Charleston Furniture, 1700–1825* (Charleston, S.C.: Charleston Museum, 1955), passim; and MESDA artisan files.

5. "Ralph and Dysell" were listed as plaintiffs in a Court of Common Pleas case against a British merchant (reported in the *South Carolina Weekly Gazette,* August 23, 1784). On March

31, 1784, Ann Cross paid "Desel & Gaskin" £10.17.6 for "Makeing a Mahogny Coffin full Trimd" for her husband (Paul Cross Papers, 1768–1803, box 1, folder 8, 1783–1785). In the April 22, 1789, *City Gazette of the Daily Advertiser,* merchant Thomas Corbett offered for sale "the lot and building, No. 44, in Church street . . . in the occupation of Messrs. Desel & Gasken, cabinetmakers." Desel was listed at both 44 Church Street and 15 Maiden Lane (probably his residence) in Milligan's city directory of 1790. By 1794, Desel had acquired cabinetmaker William Jones's shop and residence at 51 Broad Street (Jones, who died in 1792, was located at the corner of Broad and Tradd), where, according to city directories, he evidently remained until his death in 1807. In 1794, Gesken was listed by himself in Milligan's directory at 205 King Street. Inventory of Charles Desel, CCI, vol. D, 1800–1810, pp. 450–51.

6. Will of Benjamin Wheeler, April 30, 1784, CCW, no. 20, 1783–1786, p. 387. Warner & Silberg vs. James Brown, October 25, 1788, SCCCPJR, box 135B, no. 25A. *Charleston Morning Post and Daily Advertiser,* February 7, 1787. *City Gazette & Daily Advertiser,* October 1, 1793. *South Carolina Gazette and Timothy's Daily Advertiser,* January 5, 1802.

7. *South Carolina Gazette and General Advertiser,* December 18, 1783.

8. The Alston library bookcase is illustrated and discussed in Gerald W. R. Ward, *American Case Furniture in the Mabel Brady Garvan and Other Collections at Yale University* (New Haven, Conn.: Yale University Art Gallery, 1988), pp. 363–66, figs. 188, 188a. The Baltimore-like, scrolled pediment of the Alston library bookcase is a later addition, and evidence suggests that the piece originally had bracket feet below its base. These feet probably resembled those on the Edwards library bookcase. The secretary on legs is illustrated in Burton, *Charleston Furniture,* fig. 67, and William Voss Elder, III, and Jayne E. Stokes, *American Furniture 1680–1880* (Baltimore, Md.: Baltimore Museum of Art, 1987), p. 110.

9. Although the Alston and Holmes pieces are roughly contemporary with furniture associated with Jacob Sass (see fig. 16), a desk-and-bookcase signed by him and dated 1794 (at the Winterthur Museum) has different stylistic details. The differences between these pieces suggest that the Alston library bookcase and Holmes secretary are from another German-school shop of the early to mid-1780s, possibly one of the partnerships such as Desel & Gesken or Warner & Silberg.

10. The clothespress shown in figure 4 is illustrated in Burton, *Charleston Furniture,* figs. 15, 44. MESDA would like to locate this object so that it can be rephotographed for inclusion in the museum's forthcoming book on Charleston furniture.

11. A vast amount of furniture has been attributed to the shop of John and Thomas Seymour; however, other Boston cabinetmakers probably made a large percentage of the work assigned to their shop. John Seymour was in Portland, Maine, in 1785 and moved to Boston in 1794, where he was in partnership with his son, Thomas. An inlaid and mahogany-veneered coffer attributed to the Seymours has stringing in the center of its lid similar to that in the center of the friezes of the pieces illustrated in figures 4–6. The coffer is illustrated in Vernon C. Stoneman, *John and Thomas Seymour: Cabinetmakers in Boston 1794–1816* (Boston: Special Publications, 1959), p. 258, fig. 251. It is possible that this object was made in Charleston rather than in Boston.

12. The right foot of a "Commode Clothes Press" illustrated in plate 130 of the third edition of Thomas Chippendale's *The Gentleman and Cabinet-Maker's Director* (1762) follows this pattern. Presses made by Chippendale for Nostell Priory in 1771 and Harewood House in 1769–1770 have the identical foot (Christopher Gilbert, *The Life and Work of Thomas Chippendale,* 2 vols. [New York: Tabard Press, 1978], 2: 134, figs. 239, 241; 117, fig. 205; 60, fig. 94).

13. *South Carolina Gazette,* July 9, 1771.

14. Many of the German-school details, including profuse decoration with engraved ivory inlay, appear to center upon the duchy of Brunswick, which became a part of the Electorate of Hanover. See, for example, the ca. 1720 press-over-drawers, or *Aufsatz-Schrank,* from Braunschweig-Wolfenbüttel in Franz Swoboda, *Deutsche Möbel-Kunst Restauriert 1976–1980* (Mannheim: Städtischen Reiss–Museum Mannheim, 1981), pp. 10–11, fig. 3b. In the same style and collection is a desk-and-bookcase attributed to Brunswick. It has an English provenance and added English hairy-paw feet (Dr. Franz Swoboda, Director of Art and City Collections, Reiss-Museum, Mannheim, to the author, October 30, 1996). The desk-and-bookcase is illustrated in Heinrich Kreisel, *Die Kunst des deutschen Möbels: Spätbarock und Rokoko* (Munich: Verlag C. H. Beck, 1983), fig. 883.

15. For Muckinfuss, see *Charleston Courier,* August 5, 1808; and Muckinfuss's inventory, September 6, 1808, CCI, vol. D, 1800–1810, pp. 476–77. For Gros, see McIntosh and Gros vs. John Mushatt, June 10, 1815, SCCCPJR, 1815, no. 333A. For Sass, see *City Gazette and Commer-*

cial Daily Advertiser, July 3, 1815. For Philips, see ibid., August 11, 1800. For Sigwald, see letters of administration for the estate of Christian Sigwald, March 22, 1799, CCLA, vol. RR, 1797–1803, p. 147. For Rou, see John Christian Faber to George Daniel "Rowe," January 7, 1800, CCLRM, pt, 90, bk. A7, 1800, pp. 74–75. Demographics of the Charleston cabinetmaking community are derived from Rauschenberg, *Charleston Cabinetmakers, 1680–1820*.

16. *Charleston Morning Post and Daily Advertiser*, January 22, 1787. *City Gazette or the Daily Advertiser*, August 13, 1788. Ibid., May 19, 1789. Purchase of lot by Desel, CCLRM, pt. 80, bk. F6, 1791–1793, pp. 139–43. Mary Desel to Samuel Desel, February 5, 1810, CCLRM, pt. 100, bk. A8, 1809–1811, p. 170.

17. *City Gazette or the Daily Advertiser*, July 8, 1791. Ibid., November 9, 1790. *State Gazette of South-Carolina*, March 14 and April 8, 1791. Ibid., December 5, 1791. Jones became member 676 of the South Carolina Society on April 10, 1792 (J. H. Easterly, *Rules of the South Carolina Society, etc.*, 17th ed. [Charleston: South Carolina Society, 1937], p. 125). *State Gazette of South-Carolina*, November 10, 1792. Charleston County Letters Testamentary, 1792–1799, p. 33. Inventory of William Jones, February [16], 1793, CCI, vol. B, 1787–1793, p. 495.

18. Inventory of William Jones.

19. *Charleston Morning Post*, June 28, 1786. *South Carolina Gazette*, January 29, 1795. *Charleston Morning Post*, December 22, 1786. *South Carolina Gazette*, September 5, 1796. The advertisements are cited in Alfred Coxe Prime, comp., *The Arts & Crafts in Philadelphia Maryland and South Carolina, 1786–1800*, 2 vols. (Philadelphia, Pa.: Walpole Society, 1932), 2:64–65.

20. Brock Jobe, ed., *Portsmouth Furniture: Masterworks of the New Hampshire Seacoast* (Boston: Society for the Preservation of New England Antiquities, 1993), pp. 106–7. In comparing a ca. 1802 canted-corner chest of drawers by Langley Boardman (who trained in Salem, Massachusetts) with the Charleston example illustrated in figure 33 of this article, Jobe suggests that "closely related Charleston examples . . . may well be based on chests shipped by Boardman to that southern port" (entry by Brock Jobe in Alexandra W. Rollins, ed., *Treasures of State: Fine and Decorative Arts in the Diplomatic Reception Rooms of the U.S. Department of State* [New York: Harry Abrams, 1991], p. 179). Although structurally altered, a Boston-area chest with profusely carved cants and base in the Museum of Fine Arts, Boston, could date from the 1770s. The chest of drawers in *Charleston Furniture* has book-matched, veneered drawer faces with no inlay. The only stringing on the piece outlines the veneer on its canted corners. The top drawer frame is mahogany, whereas the other drawer frames are cypress; the drawer front cores are solid white pine. The drawers have no center muntins, and the bottoms are fitted to conventional dadoes at the fronts and sides. The writing slide in the top drawer is 1/2" thick and constructed with unmitred battens at each side. The case has full-bottom, three-quarter-depth, white pine dustboards. Evidently, the feet were replaced long ago. The facings are much thinner than expected for a Charleston piece of this type, and the foot cants show no evidence of veneering.

21. Charles Montgomery, *American Furniture: The Federal Period, 1788–1825* (New York: Viking Press, 1966), p. 185, fig. 142.

22. In Burton, *Charleston Furniture*, fig. 68, this exceptionally tall table is shown with a cabinet added at a slightly later date. A product of Charleston's German school, this table has carved brackets by the same artisan who executed all of the carving on both the pre-Revolutionary and neoclassical German-school furniture. This carver was probably Henry Hainsdorff, who in 1776 advertised that he had served as a journeyman for three years with London-trained carver John Lord (*South Carolina and American General Gazette*, October 2, 1776). Hainsdorff died in 1796 (Smith and Salley, *Register of St. Philip's Parish*, p. 355).

23. No research on the manufacture of white-background inlay in Britain is known (telephone conversation with Christopher Gilbert, Director Emeritus, Temple Newsam House, Leeds, September 1996). I would be grateful for any documented evidence of this work, since there is no documentation of post-Revolutionary inlay makers in Charleston. The "brittle-star-like" paterae on the front foot facings of the serpentine press occur on the frieze of a Norfolk corner cupboard in MESDA. These inlays may have been obtained from either Charleston or Britain, but whatever the source, they are rare in Norfolk.

24. The author thanks Thomas G. Sudbrink of the U.S. Department of State for his helpful examination of this object. Center-muntin drawer bottoms are comparatively rare on American furniture made outside Charleston. They occur occasionally in New York furniture made before and after the Revolution, and with some regularity in Norfolk, Virginia, during the late eighteenth and early nineteenth centuries. New York cabinetmakers frequently used half-bottom or paneled dustboards. Both dustboard systems are common in British furniture but com-

paratively rare in Charleston.

25. Thomas Sheraton, *The Cabinet-Maker and Upholsterer's Drawing-Book* (1793; reprint ed., New York: Dover Publications, 1972), p. 28 (original p. 10).

26. For the Strobel history, see MESDA research file S-8745.

27. The Duc de La Rochefoucault-Liancourt, as quoted in Margaret Burke Clunie, "Salem Federal Furniture" (master's thesis, University of Delaware, June 1976), p. 5. Clunie's thesis is the most detailed study of the post-Revolutionary cabinetmaking trade in Salem. It focuses on the trade structure of Salem rather than stylistic considerations.

28. Clunie, "Salem Federal Furniture," p. 14. Henry Wyckoff Belknap, "Furniture Exported by Cabinet Makers of Salem," *Essex Institute Historical Collections* 85 (October 1949): 336–37. Clunie, "Salem Federal Furniture," pp. 303, 45.

29. Mabel M. Swan, "Elijah and Jacob Sanderson, Early Salem Cabinetmakers," *Essex Institute Historical Collections* 70 (October 1934): 4–6.

30. Walter J. Fraser, Jr., *Charleston! Charleston!* (Columbia: University of South Carolina Press, 1989), pp. 173–75, 178, 192.

31. Swan, "Elijah and Jacob Sanderson," pp. 4–6.

32. Sanderson Papers, box 1, folder 3, J. D. Phillips Library, Peabody Essex Museum, Salem, Massachusetts.

33. Swan, "Elijah and Jacob Sanderson," pp. 6, 7. Sanderson Papers.

34. MESDA research file S-14,613. Entry by Brock Jobe in Rollins, ed., *Treasures of State*, p. 210.

35. This table is illustrated in John Bivins, *Wilmington Furniture 1720–1860* (Wilmington, N.C.: St. John's Museum of Art and the Historic Wilmington Foundation, 1989), p. 69. Several examples of Wilmington furniture in the Salem style are illustrated in this book. Records of the Collector of Customs for the Collection District of Salem & Beverly, Massachusetts, microfilm roll 28, National Archives, New England Region, Waltham, Massachusetts. Swan, "Elijah and Jacob Sanderson," pp. 8, 9. Belknap, "Furniture Exported by Cabinet Makers of Salem," p. 354. The card table signed by Elijah Sanderson is illustrated in Bivins, *Wilmington Furniture*, p. 69.

36. Invoice for furniture aboard the *Greyhound*, February 17, 1808, Sanderson Papers, box 2. Invoice by Robert Cottle to the Sandersons and Appleton, August 1799, Sanderson Papers, box 1. Invoice for furniture shipped to Charleston, December 5, 1817, Sanderson Papers, box 2.

37. *Charleston Courier*, September 4, 1804. *City Gazette and Daily Advertiser*, January 6, 1801.

38. For Warham, see *South Carolina Gazette*, November 9, 1734. For Badger, see Badger's purchase of a lot on Tradd St., CCLRM, pt. 22, bks. BB-DD, 1745–1748, pp. 77–85. Clunie, "Salem Federal Furniture," pp. 14, 87, 121. (Clunie notes that Dorchester Mills was particularly strong in the cabinet trade. Stephen Badlam, who executed commissions from Elias Haskett Derby, was there, along with William and Ebenezer Vose, Adam and Ebenezer Davenport, John and Benjamin Crehore, William Wadsworth, Lewis Leach, and Lewis Tucker.) Myrna Kaye, "Eighteenth-Century Boston Furniture Craftsmen," in *Boston Furniture of the Eighteenth Century*, edited by Walter Muir Whitehill, Brock Jobe, and Jonathan Fairbanks (Boston: Colonial Society of Massachusetts, 1974), pp. 267–302. Swaney was admitted to Masonic Lodge No. 14 on February 9, 1803, as recorded in *Historical Sketch of Orange Lodge, No. 14, A.F.M., Charleston, S.C.* (Charleston, S.C.: Lodge 14, 1911), p. 38. *Charleston Times,* February 18, 1808.

39. The Sanderson secretary and the unsigned example are illustrated in Rollins, ed., *Treasures of State*, p. 211, no. 121; p. 205, no. 116.

40. The rosettes on the pediment of the Appleton secretary have bicolor, fanlike inlays. Although atypical of Charleston, similar rosettes occur on Massachusetts-style furniture made in Wilmington, North Carolina, 160 miles north (John Bivins, *The Furniture of Coastal North Carolina, 1700–1820* [Chapel Hill: University of North Carolina Press for MESDA, 1988], p. 415, fig. 7.36c).

41. A Salem gentleman's secretary with this type of cornice is illustrated in fig. 67 of Richard H. Randall, Jr., *American Furniture in the Museum of Fine Arts, Boston* (Boston: Museum of Fine Arts, 1965). *Charleston Times*, May 24, 1804. Ibid., August 24, 1807. The secretary-press is recorded in MESDA research file S-14,656.

42. John Marshall vs. William Marshall, August 21, 1798, Charleston District Court of Common Pleas, Judgment Rolls, no. 657A. Charleston Orphan House, Indenture Book for Boys and Girls, p. 32, Charleston City Archives. Tennant continued in the trade until the 1830s. Inevitably, there are exceptions to almost every rule. In the Garvan Collection is a phenome-

nal double chest made by Stephen Badlam (1751–1815) of Dorchester Lower Mills and carved by John and Simeon Skillin of Boston in 1791 as a wedding present for Anstis Derby, the daughter of Elias and Elizabeth Derby. Both the upper and lower cases of this piece have full dustboards. See Ward, *American Case Furniture*, p. 172.

43. Pages 22 and 72 of *The New-York Revised Prices for Manufacturing Cabinet and Chair Work* (1818) indicate that the cost of the tracery for a pair of thirteen-light Chinese doors of this type was £1.10 compared to six shillings for flat panels. This publication supplanted the 1810 list of cabinetmakers' prices published by the city's "Society of Cabinet-Makers."

44. A clothespress and two other canted-corner chests of drawers are closely related to the chest (fig. 33) and have the same in-turned feet. The press is illustrated in *Antiques* 135, no. 5 (May 1989): 1133; one of the chest of drawers is illustrated in *Antiques* 91, no. 1 (January 1967): 19. This chest of drawers has wider cant faces than the one shown in figure 33 (which could indicate a different shop), fluted foot cants, and a top with edge-banding and a large central paterae of figured mahogany. A third chest of drawers (MESDA research file S-8740) virtually identical to the chest illustrated in figure 33 descended in the Porcher family of Ophir Plantation, St. John's Parish, Berkeley County, South Carolina. It has no inlay on its foot cants.

45. Jobe, ed., *Portsmouth Furniture*, pp. 106–7. Another canted-corner chest of drawers that can be attributed to Boardman was sold in New York in 1994 (Sotheby's, *Important Americana*, sale 6589, June 23–24, 1995, lot 520).

46. In colonial Charleston furniture, it is common to find tooth-planing inside drawer fronts and under table tops, even when no glue blocking is present. Cabinetmakers evidently preferred this tool (which has a nearly vertical iron and produces an essentially scraping cut) for cross-grain dressing of surfaces, particularly when hard, dense Santo Domingo mahogany was used.

47. The *New-York Revised Prices for Manufacturing Cabinet and Chair Work* lists an added cost of three shillings for "framing a back" of a bureau "with two panels extra from plain."

48. Exceptions can be found on finer Salem pieces, such as the Appleton secretary (fig. 28). Although its interior surfaces have prominent saw kerfs, the dovetailing of the drawers is very fine. Such variations suggest the need for caution in making blanket comparisons of structure and surface quality. Structural anomalies also occur in Charleston furniture, as exemplified by the absence of dustboards in the chest shown in figure 33 and the board backs (which were less expensive than paneled ones) of two other pieces from the same shop.

49. Montgomery, *American Furniture: The Federal Period*, p. 225, nos. 182; p. 224, no. 181; p. 222, no. 179.

50. This secretary, in the collection of the Historic Columbia Foundation, is located at the Robert Mills Historic House and Park. MESDA research file S-2422.

51 These inlays appear to be copies of Philadelphia work. A 1793–1797 card table by Adam Haines has leg stile inlay that is virtually identical. This table descended in the Maybank family of Charleston, and it has a label that reads: "ALL KINDS OF CABINET AND CHAIR-WORK DONE BY ADAM HAINES, NO. 135, NORTH THIRD-STREET, PHILADELPHIA." For the table, see MESDA research file S-23, 482.

52. St. John's Lutheran Church Records, 1755–1787, p. 42. Rules of the German Friendly Society, p. 122, no. 207. *City Gazette and Daily Advertiser*, May 23, 1796. Ibid., May 6 and 7, 1799.

53. *City Gazette and Daily Advertiser*, August 5, 1800. Ibid., September 5, 1800. Ibid., August 11, 1800. Burton, *Charleston Furniture*, p. 112, notes that Philips was listed as a cabinetmaker in city directories for 1809 and 1813 but does not specify what these publications were. Eleazer Elizer's Charleston directory for 1803. Negrin's *Social Magazine and Quarterly Intelligencer*, January 1804. Negrin's Charleston directory for 1806 and 1807. Schenck & Turner's Charleston directory for 1819.

54. *Charleston Courier*, October 20, 1818; Ibid., March 25, 1818.

55. Having long since lost a citation for this timeless description, the author would be most grateful if any reader could identify the source.

56. *South Carolina Gazette*, July 9, 1771.

J. Thomas Savage

The Holmes-Edwards Library Bookcase and the Origins of the German School in Pre-Revolutionary Charleston

▼ THE HOLMES-EDWARDS library bookcase in the collection of the Charleston Museum's Heyward-Washington House is arguably one of colonial America's greatest cabinetmaking masterpieces (fig. 1). It is also among the least understood. The library bookcase was made for Charleston merchant and South Carolina naval commissioner John Edwards (d. 1781), who emigrated from Bristol, England, about 1750 to engage in Charleston's burgeoning import and export trade. It is listed in his 1783 probate inventory as a "large Mahogany Book Case" valued at £100 South Carolina currency, and it stood originally in Edwards's handsome double house at 15 Meeting Street (fig. 2). The library bookcase descended through Edwards's daughter Elizabeth (ca. 1765–1836), who married attorney John Bee Holmes (1760–1827) on November 19, 1783. For generations in Charleston, it has been known as the "Holmes bookcase."[1]

Esther Singleton first published an illustration of the library bookcase in *The Furniture of Our Forefathers* (1901), where she described it as a pre-Revolutionary piece whose "drawers were used by the British officers for horse-troughs" (fig. 3). It appeared again in the January 1936 issue of *Antiques,* attributed to England and dated 1790. Subsequent publications perpetuated this date, although identification of the library bookcase's cypress secondary wood prompted scholars to reattribute it to Charleston. By January 1952, the piece had become an icon of Charleston cabinetmaking, appearing as the frontispiece in the thirtieth anniversary edition of *Antiques,* which featured "Furniture of the Old South, 1640–1820." More recently, systematic field research by the Museum of Early Southern Decorative Arts has placed the library bookcase at the inception of a cabinetmaking school representing several shops that flourished in Charleston between 1770 and 1795. Many of the details on this piece are repeated on late rococo and neoclassical furniture made just after the Revolution. Although the stylistic impact of the library bookcase has been acknowledged, its design origins and maker have remained elusive.[2]

The past difficulty with stylistic analysis and dating of the library bookcase is understandable, for it represents a synthesis of British and Continental structural and decorative features within the context of Charleston taste and patronage. Its secretary drawer, "Chinese" mullion design, and carved rosettes and basket ornament (fig. 4) are British details, whereas its complex, serpentine base, ogee head, contrasting panels of mahogany and burl veneers outlined with stringing, scrolled strapwork, elaborate floral marquetry, and extensive use of engraved ivory husks (figs. 5–8) are directly

Figure 1 Library bookcase attributed to Martin Pfeninger, Charleston, South Carolina, 1770–1775. Mahogany, mahogany and burl walnut veneer, and ivory and unidentified wood inlays with cypress. H. 128³/₄", W. 99", D. 20¹/₂". (Courtesy, Charleston Museum; photo, Gavin Ashworth.)

Figure 2 John Edwards House, 15 Meeting Street, Charleston, South Carolina, completed about 1770. (Photo, William Struhs.) This structure is the only surviving eighteenth-century Charleston frame house with a rusticated facade.

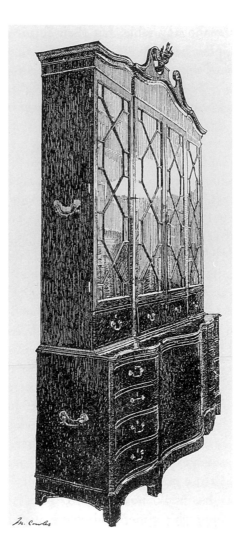

Figure 3 The Holmes-Edwards library bookcase as illustrated in Esther Singleton, *The Furniture of Our Forefathers* (New York: Doubleday, Page and Company, 1901), p. 150. This image indicates that the basket ornament was partially restored by the early twentieth century.

related to furniture produced in the German states of Brunswick and Hanover during the third quarter of the eighteenth century. Although the use of naturalistic floral marquetry in concert with scrollwork is found throughout Germany in both rococo furniture and the inlaid cabinet or *intarsia* rooms commissioned by German electors, dukes, margraves, and prince archbishops and was part of the standard repertoire of mid-eighteenth-century German woodworkers, its appearance on the library bookcase has no parallel in eighteenth-century American furniture.[3]

The construction of the Edwards piece also points to an artisan of Continental descent. The dustboards between the lower drawers are extremely thin, and their beveled edges engage grooves cut in the drawer rails and drawer supports, the latter of which are dadoed to the case sides (fig. 9). This type of "paneled" dustboard system, which also occurs on New York City furniture made between 1730 and 1780, may represent a northern European alternative to the full-bottom dustboards used in most of Charleston's pre-Revolutionary, British-tradition shops.

If a date of circa 1770 is accepted for its construction, several members of Charleston's pre-Revolutionary cabinetmaking community emerge as poten-

Figure 4 Detail of the pediment of the library bookcase illustrated in fig. 1. (Photo, Gavin Ashworth.) The five straight sprigs with leaves and flowers behind the rose of the basket-and-flower ornament are incorrect replacements.

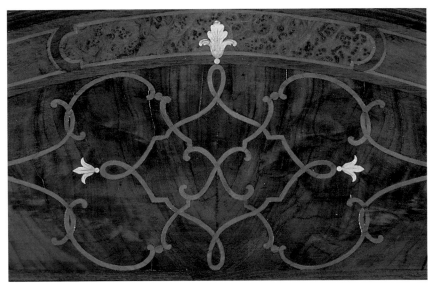

Figure 5 Detail of the scrollwork, mahogany and burl veneer panels, and engraved ivory husks on the frieze of the library bookcase illustrated in fig. 1. (Photo, Gavin Ashworth.)

Figure 6 Detail of the floral marquetry on the frieze and tympanum of the library bookcase illustrated in fig. 1. (Photo, Gavin Ashworth.) The color contrasts of the marquetry were originally stronger.

Figure 7 Detail of the floral marquetry on the tympanum plinth of the library bookcase illustrated in fig. 1. (Photo, Gavin Ashworth.)

Figure 8 Detail of an engraved ivory husk on a lower door of the library bookcase illustrated in fig. 1. (Photo, Gavin Ashworth.)

Figure 9 Detail of the dustboard construction on the library bookcase illustrated in fig. 1. (Photo, Gavin Ashworth.)

tial candidates for the maker of the library bookcase: Jacob Solvey, "a cabinetmaker" who married Barbara Schmidt in St. John's Lutheran Church on January 20, 1767; Martin Pfeninger, who first appears in the Thomas Elfe Day Book in May 1772; Jacob Sass, a native of Schenstad, Hesse, who emigrated to Charleston in 1773; Charles Lewis Desel, who married Elizabeth

Young in St. John's Church on March 20, 1774; and Henry C. Gesken, a cabinetmaker of "Osterholtz in Electoral Hanover, Prussia," who married Maria Margaretha Munch (Minnick) of Crims Creek, Orangeburg County, South Carolina, in St. John's Church on September 28, 1775.[4]

Two remarkably early references to inlaid work link Martin Pfeninger to the library bookcase. In the April 12, 1773, issue of the *South Carolina Gazette* and the April 13, 1773, issue of the *South Carolina Gazette and Country Journal*, he advertised "Cabinetmaking in all its branches, ALSO, INLAID-WORK in any TASTE, by MARTIN PFENINGER At his shop in New-Church-Street, adjoining the SCOTCH-MEETING and Parsonage-House, At the lowest Rates, and in the most expeditious Manner." The following November, he billed Charleston upholsterer Solomon Smith for "a fine Mahogany Bedstead with a Rich Cornice, Gothic Posts, Carved Swells & Caps, To Inlaid Pedestalls . . . £100." These documents reveal that Pfeninger was capable of producing highly finished and fashionable rococo forms embellished with a variety of inlaid decoration. His Germanic origins and stated ability to produce inlaid decoration "in any taste" make Pfeninger the leading candidate for the surface decoration, if not the construction, of the library bookcase.[5]

Although rarely produced in other colonial cities, library bookcases were popular in Charleston. The 1771 sale of Thomas Shirley's household furnishings included "A Mahogany Library case with eight Doors, four above and four below, is nine Feet two-Inches high, and seven Feet wide, has a scroll Pediment Head with dentiled Cornice and Frize; is in nine Pieces for the Convenience of moving, and fixed together with Screws." Thomas Elfe received £110 for a "Library Book Case" on February 12, 1772; £100 for a "Library Book Case wth Chineas doors & Draws under them" on November 14, 1772; and £110 for a "Library Book Case" on January 23, 1773. The latter example was for merchant Nicholas Langford who had imported "elegant mahogany . . . BOOK CASES, with glass doors and brass locks" from London five years earlier. An unusually large "Mahogany Library [bookcase], Glazed & Ceta 17 feet Long" valued at £100 was among the personal effects abandoned by South Carolina's last royal governor, Lord William Campbell, when he fled Charleston in 1775. Although the written record is rich in references to the form, only two Charleston library bookcases from the pre-Revolutionary period survive—the Edwards piece and an example based on a design that appeared in all three editions of Thomas Chippendale's *The Gentleman and Cabinet-Maker's Director*.[6]

The earliest reference to Martin Pfeninger is in the Day Book of Charleston cabinetmaker Thomas Elfe. On May 8, 1772, Elfe paid Pfeninger £40 "for work," a somewhat ambiguous entry since "work" could refer to either labor or a product such as inlay. Whether Pfeninger had just arrived in Charleston or was already established is unknown. Elfe's Day Book also illuminates the practice of commissioning piece work from specialized artisans such as carver William Crips, as well as from cabinetmakers with their own shops such as Abraham Pearce. Between 1768 and 1775, Pfeninger was one of thirty-eight tradesmen who either labored or provided piece work for

Elfe. These artisans included sixteen cabinetmakers, five carpenters, four carvers, three upholsterers, two blacksmiths, two turners, two painters, one joiner, one sawyer, one chairmaker, and one coachmaker.[7]

Pfeninger was almost immediately accepted by Charleston's Germanic community. On July 17, 1776, he was admitted to the German Friendly Society on the recommendation of tavern keeper Christian Sigwald. The following year, Pfeninger accepted a lot on King Street from Michael Kalteisen, the founder of the society, to settle a debt of £1000 South Carolina currency. Like many other Charleston artisans, Pfeninger suffered during the British blockade of Charleston during the Revolutionary War. In the October 28, 1777, issue of the *Gazette of the State of South Carolina*, he reported:

> MARTIN PFENINGER returns his sincere thanks to the Public in general, and to his Customers in particular, and is sorry the want of materials oblige him to leave off his business of Cabinet-making, &c. Such work as has been bespoke, and now in hand, will be finished as far as the materials he has will go. As soon as materials can be had, he will be obliged to the public and his customers for a continuance of their favours.

In 1781, Pfeninger's name was among the "List of persons desirous to shew every mark of allegiance to his Majesty." He died on September 20, 1782, and his will appointed his wife, Hannah, executrix and mentioned his son, Daniel Conrad (see appendix).[8]

Research in Germany and England has failed to identify either Pfeninger's birthplace or the town or city where he received his training. It is probable that he emigrated directly from Germany to Carolina where he joined Charleston's burgeoning Teutonic community. During the mid-eighteenth century, the Crown and colony recruited Protestants from the

Figure 10   *Dielenschrank*, Lubeck, Germany, 1760–1770. Woods not recorded. H. 95 5/8", W. 122 13/16", D. 32 1/4". (Illustrated in Wolfgang Schwarze, *Antike Deutsche Mobel: das Burgerliche und Rustikale Mobel in Deutschland von 1700–1840* [Wuppertal, Germany: by the author, 1977], p. 16, fig. 17.)

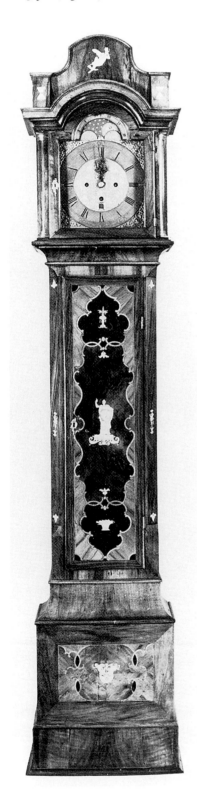

Figure 11 *Standuhr*, Brunswick, Germany, ca. 1770. Woods not recorded. H. 88¹/₂". (Illustrated in Wolfgang Schwarze, *Antike Deutsche Möbel: das Bürgerliche und Rustikale Möbel in Deutschland von 1700–1840* [Wuppertal, Germany: by the author, 1977], p. 70, fig. 177.)

German states, in part to create a buffer against Spanish encroachment and the Native American population on the frontier. On November 23, 1749, Governor James Glen reported: "Germany has been long the Seat of War, and has severely felt the calamities of it; and it may be presumed there are many of her People who wish for a place to rest in which they may enjoy the fruits of their own labour, as many of their countrymen do here." Assisted by promotional tracts depicting Carolina as a promised land for the poor Protestants of Europe, Charleston merchants rapidly developed a profitable business importing Germans. In 1751, the mercantile firm of Austin and Laurens advertised "about 200 German *Passengers* [including] . . . several handicraft Tradesmen and Husbandmen, and likely young Boys and Girls . . . to be indented for a term of Years, to any Person who will pay their Passages." Many of the early Germanic emigrés settled in towns such as Purrysburg and New Windsor on the Santee River, Orangeburg on the Edisto River, Amelia on the Santee River, and Saxe-Gotha on the Congaree River. By the late 1760s, however, some of these settlers had moved to Charleston, bolstering the city's Germanic population.⁹

St. John's Lutheran Church and the German Friendly Society served as the main support groups for German immigrants. The stated purpose of the society was to "relieve the distresses of our fellow creatures, and to promote their welfare . . . to support a falling brother—to save a sinking family from ruin—and father the helpless orphan." To become a member, one had to be at least twenty-one years old, have one parent of Germanic descent, and be able to "speak the German Language intelligibly." Like other ethnic societies in Charleston, the German Friendly Society advocated fellowship, secrecy, decorum, and a display of strict moral behavior in public. Although many of the early members had origins among the poor immigrant working class, the city's more successful and socially responsible German tradesmen and businessmen were attracted by the society's benevolence and philanthropy. Of all the Germanic cabinetmakers working in Charleston before the war, only Pfeninger and Jacob Sass (admitted July 9, 1777) were members.¹⁰

Although no documentary information regarding Pfeninger's early career is known, a study of mid-eighteenth-century Germanic cabinetmaking traditions offers clues to his place of origin and training. Given the northern Protestant origins of much of Charleston's Teutonic population, it is hardly surprising that the closest parallels with the Edwards library bookcase are found on furniture from the northern and northwestern German states. A three-part *dielenschrank* (fig. 10) from Lübeck is related in having a scrolled pediment and ogee-shaped cornice moldings on the side sections. Made of mahogany with carved and gilded capitals and foliate volutes, this cabinet has Palladian overtones like other German pieces influenced by English furniture styles. Following the accession of George I of Hanover to the British throne in 1714, there was a great deal of stylistic exchange between London and Hanover. Not only did some German cabinetmakers describe themselves as "English," the term was also applied to certain forms such as *Englische Stuhle*—a German interpretation of high-backed cane chairs popular in

Figure 12   Kommodenaufsatzschrank, Brunswick, Germany, 1750–1760. Woods and dimensions not recorded. (Illustrated in Wolfgang Schwarze, *Antike Deutsche Mobel: das Burgerliche und Rustikale Mobel in Deutschland von 1700–1840* [Wuppertal, Germany: by the author, 1977], p. 64, fig. 156.)

Holland and Britain from about 1680 to 1715. The British export trade in cabinetwares also facilitated the acceptance of English forms such as the bureau and bureau table into the German cabinetmaking tradition.[11]

The influence of German cabinetmakers on British furniture is the subject of Christopher Gilbert and Tessa Murdoch's *John Channon and Brass Inlaid Furniture, 1730–1760.* Their research has shown that Moravian artisans were instrumental in shuffling furniture styles between Germany and England during the eighteenth century. Both Abraham Roentgen (1711–1793), founder of the famous cabinetmaking business at Neuweid, and Johann Friedrich Hintz (d. 1772) were Moravians, and the production of British

Figure 13 *Kommodenaufsatzschrank*, Brunswick, Germany, ca. 1750. Woods not recorded. H. 100", W. 58¼", D. 29½". (Illustrated in Wolfgang Schwarze, *Antike Deutsche Mobel: das Burgerliche und Rustikale Mobel in Deutschland von 1700–1840* [Wuppertal, Germany: by the author, 1977], p. 70, fig. 176b.)

furniture with brass inlay and marquetry "mosaics" has been linked to their presence in London.[12]

Although there is no evidence that Pfeninger was a Moravian or that he spent time in England, there are similarities between the Edwards library bookcase and furniture associated with German cabinetmakers in London, particularly the engraved husks that appear in brass on British examples and in ivory on the Edwards piece. Roentgen specialized in the production of marquetry that combined exotic woods, brass, mother-of-pearl, and ivory. Ivory inlays were popular in Germany from the middle of the seventeenth century, and they remained fashionable in Brunswick and other northern states well into the third quarter of the eighteenth century. The retention of baroque architectural and ornamental details in parts of Germany has been

Figure 14 Chest of drawers with inlay attributed to Martin Pfeninger, Charleston, South Carolina, 1775–1782. Mahogany, mahogany veneer, ebonized beech and unidentified lightwood inlays with yellow pine and mahogany. H. 34", W. 41½", D. 24¼". (Courtesy, Colonial Williamsburg Foundation.)

Figure 15 Detail of a bracket foot on the chest of drawers illustrated in fig. 14.

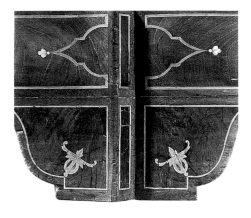

Figure 16 Detail of two bracket feet on the library bookcase illustrated in fig. 1, showing inlays and stringing. (Photo, Gavin Ashworth.)

attributed in part to the guild system, which required young tradesmen to produce presentation pieces built according to traditional specifications.[13]

An examination of case pieces made in Brunswick and Hanover during the third quarter of the eighteenth century provides convincing parallels to the Edwards library bookcase. A tall clock case or *standuhr* (fig. 11) made in Brunswick about 1770 is a standard British form adapted for German taste by the use of exotic veneers, scrolled strapwork, and floral and figural inlays. The inlaid ivory husks are very similar to those on the library bookcase, and the strapwork on both pieces, which features interlocking C and S scrolls connected by inlaid dots, appears to stem from the same shop tradition. Brunswick artisans typically used scrolled strapwork to frame panels of contrasting veneer, which were often made of exotic woods. A slightly earlier *kommodenaufsatzschrank* from Brunswick (fig. 12), for example, has scroll-outlined panels on the drawers, doors, canted corners, and tympanum, the latter of which are related to the strapwork and scroll-outlined mahogany and burl reserves on the library bookcase. Like many later pieces from

Figure 17 Detail of the base pendant on the chest of drawers illustrated in fig. 14.

Charleston's German school, the library bookcase has canted corners with string-inlaid panels of contrasting veneer. Although such corners are common on eighteenth-century British furniture, the use of cants for the display of elaborate marquetry and scroll- or strap-outlined panels of contrasting veneer is a hallmark of north German work. The canted corners of the library bookcase and related pieces from Charleston's German school are closer to the Brunswick prototypes (see figs. 11–13) than to most English examples. The Brunswick *kommodenaufsatzschrank* illustrated in figure 13 has cants with string-surrounded panels of contrasting veneer, scrollwork reserves on the frieze, and marquetry doors. Elaborate floral marquetry, like that on the frieze of the library bookcase, was extremely popular in the Brunswick region.[14]

The chest of drawers illustrated in figure 14 is closely related to the library bookcase and may be associated with Pfeninger's shop. Made about 1780, it falls within his Charleston period and exhibits several Germanic features imposed on an essentially British form. These features include the compartmentalization of the surface through the use of three-part string inlays on the edges of the top, sides, drawer fronts, and drawer rails. Also related to the Edwards piece is the use of single-line stringing to outline the veneer panels on the canted corners and bracket feet. Each of these surfaces is further embellished with inlaid rosettes, roundels, and husks, although the execution of these elements has little of the virtuosity displayed by the inlays on the library bookcase. The bracket feet of the two pieces (figs. 1, 15, 16) have

Figure 18   Schreibkommode, Brunswick, Germany, 1750–1760. Woods not recorded. H. 45¼", W. 43⁵/₁₆", D. 24¹³/₁₆". (Illustrated in Wolfgang Schwarze, *Antike Deutsche Mobel: das Burgerliche und Rustikale Mobel in Deutschland von 1700–1840* [Wuppertal, Germany: by the author, 1977], p. 64, fig. 154.)

a similar S-curve profile. This basic foot design, often with conforming string inlay, occurs on later examples from Charleston's German school as well as on coastal New England work. Similar feet occur on a secretary-and-bookcase made and labeled by Salem, Massachusetts, cabinetmaker William Appleton about 1795 (see John Bivins's article in this volume, p. 82, fig. 28) and on a chest made by Portsmouth, New Hampshire, cabinetmaker Langley Boardman (in the collection of the Society for the Preservation of New England Antiquities) about 1800. After the Revolution, New England styles had a powerful influence on Charleston furniture. The foot inlays on the Edwards library bookcase (fig. 16) also relate to the pendant inlay on the chest (fig. 17). Both designs may derive from *partie* and *contrapartie* marquetry, particularly those on the library bookcase that have fine shading cuts like metal engraving.[15]

The convex, canted corners on the front feet of the chest are another Germanic feature (fig. 15). Although baroque ball feet remained popular in the Brunswick-Hanover region through the third quarter of the eighteenth century (see figs. 12, 13), the *schreibkommode* and *kommodenschrank* illustrated in figures 18 and 19 indicate that bracket feet with convex cants were fashionable alternatives. The former piece also has a veneered base pendant and

Figure 20 Breakfast table with inlay attributed to Martin Pfeninger, Charleston, South Carolina, 1775–1782. Mahogany, mahogany veneer, and unidentified lightwood inlays with cypress and ash. H. 28⅞", W. 21½" (closed), D. 24¾". (Private collection; photo, Museum of Early Southern Decorative Arts.)

Figure 21 Detail of the leg and bracket inlay on the breakfast table illustrated in fig. 20.

panels of contrasting veneer with looped scrollwork like that on the frieze of the Edwards piece. The *kommodenschrank* is noteworthy in having a swelled molding above the doors—a common feature on north German case furniture and architecture—and in having floral marquetry on the tympanum, another feature associated with the library bookcase.

A serpentine breakfast table with floral inlays attributed to Pfeninger (fig. 20) is roughly contemporary with the chest of drawers, although its basic form relates to "Chinese" examples made during the mid to late 1760s. The dogwood-like blossoms on the upper leg stiles and brackets have fine shading cuts that resemble those on the foot inlays of the library bookcase and chest of drawers (figs. 15, 16, 21). Like the chest of drawers (fig. 14), the table also has double-ogee stringing with lightwood husk drops. The most elaborate neoclassical inlay in Charleston dates from the late 1770s and 1780s and includes both locally made products and the distinctive, white-background floral inlays traditionally considered a hallmark of Charleston work but probably imported from Britain.

Also illustrating the transition from late rococo to early neoclassical style is a group of sideboard tables, card tables, and breakfast tables, many of which have elaborate veneers, stringing, and carving. The card table illustrated in figure 22 is one of the earliest in the group. It is contemporary with the chest of drawers (fig. 14), and it has a "commode" front, pentagonal legs, string-outlined panels of contrasting mahogany veneer, an applied

Figure 22 Card table, Charleston, South Carolina, 1775–1785. Mahogany, mahogany veneer, and unidentified lightwood inlay with cypress and mahogany. H. 29⅜", W. 36", D. 17¹³⁄₁₆" (closed). (Courtesy, Charleston Museum; photo, Gavin Ashworth.)

Figure 23 Card table, Charleston, South Carolina, 1770–1785. H. 29⅜", W. 34½", D. 17½" (closed). (Collection of the Museum of Early Southern Decorative Arts.)

Figure 24 Detail of a carved bracket on the card table illustrated in fig. 23.

astragal molding on the lower edge of the rails, serpentine sides, and a conforming top with projecting rounded corners—details associated with pre-Revolutionary furniture from Charleston's German school and contemporary work from the Brunswick-Hanover region. The card table also has term feet like the breakfast table with inlay attributed to Pfeninger (fig. 20).

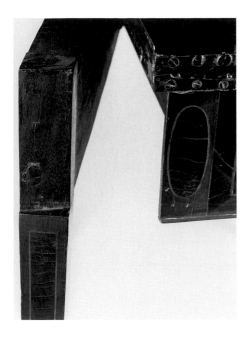

Figure 25 Detail of the swing-leg/rail joint of the card table illustrated in fig. 22. (Photo, Gavin Ashworth.)

Figure 26 Breakfast table, Charleston, South Carolina, 1775–1785. Mahogany, mahogany veneer, and unidentified lightwood stringing with cedrela, tulip poplar, and white pine. H. 28½", W. 36⅛" (open), D. 30". (Private collection; photo, Gavin Ashworth.)

Figure 27 Detail of a carved bracket on the breakfast table illustrated in fig. 26. (Photo, Gavin Ashworth.)

An early transitional card table (figs. 23, 24), with carved rococo brackets and cants similar to those of the chest of drawers and Edwards library bookcase, is related to the example shown in figure 22. It has similar serpentine side rails that are notched to house the swing leg rather than a swing leg notched to lap over the rail (fig. 25), but the tables are probably from different shops. This construction detail occurs on several Charleston card tables made during the 1770s and 1780s. On the table illustrated in figure 23, the rail veneers pass over the leg joints and those on the sides extend to the back edge of the frame. A Charleston breakfast table (fig. 26) combines elements of both card tables, including carved brackets (fig. 27), astragal rail moldings, and oval veneer panels.

A secretary-press (fig. 28) and a library bookcase (fig. 29) document the influence of Pfeninger's shop on post-Revolutionary furniture from Charleston's German school. The secretary-press is one of the earliest pieces of American neoclassical furniture and, viewed within the context of the Edwards piece, it represents a transition from the early phase of the German school, where Continental influences dominated, to the later phase, where coastal trade introduced late rococo and early neoclassical styles from the Massachusetts Bay region. The swelled head, inlaid cants with veneered panels and husks suspended from ogee-shaped stringing, and inlaid base pendant of the secretary-press have parallels on both the library bookcase and chest of drawers attributed to Pfeninger. Research by John Bivins sug-

Figure 28 Secretary-press, Charleston, South Carolina, 1780–1790. Mahogany, mahogany veneer, and unidentified lightwood inlays with white pine, cypress, and red cedar. H. 105 5/8", W. 56", D. 27 3/4". (Private collection; photo, Gavin Ashworth.) The pediment was altered during the late nineteenth or early twentieth century. Although portions of the swelled frieze are original, the tympanum, scroll moldings, and rosettes are modern restorations.

gests that the secretary-press may be associated with the shop of Jacob Sass, who was a contemporary of Pfeninger and who continued to work after the war. The case construction, foot and molding profiles, and "coopered," veneered doors are closely associated with those on a magnificent serpentine clothespress (see Bivins, p. 66, fig. 16.) The quarter-fans on the doors, urns (restored from evidence of the originals) on the bracket feet, and nine-husk drops suspended from inlaid rings on the cants of the lower case represent one of the earliest appearances of these motifs in Charleston, as well as document the assimilation of British neoclassical inlay styles that influenced other cabinetmaking centers including Norfolk, Virginia, and the Massachusetts Bay region.

Figure 29 Library bookcase, Charleston, South Carolina, 1790–1800. Mahogany, mahogany veneer, and unidentified lightwood inlays with red cedar, white pine, and cypress. H. 126 3/8", W. 117", D. 25". (Courtesy, Yale University Art Gallery, Mabel Brady Garvan Collection.) The broken-scroll pediment is a replacement.

The library bookcase (fig. 29) reportedly belonged to Colonel William Alston (1756–1839), a wealthy South Carolina planter whose primary country seat, Clifton, stood on the Waccamaw River near Georgetown. Following his marriage to Mary Brewton Motte in 1791, Alston purchased the Miles Brewton House (completed 1769) on King Street, arguably Charleston's most palatial, surviving pre-Revolutionary townhouse. He may have commissioned the library bookcase for his city residence shortly thereafter. Like the preceding secretary-press, the library bookcase probably represents the work of a journeyman associated with Pfeninger. The patterns used to lay out the lower case appear to be the same as those used for the Edwards piece. The ornament on the Alston example represents a significant departure from the baroque inlays and marquetry of Pfeninger. The cross-banding on the drawers and doors of the base, quarter-fan inlays, and neoclassical lightwood husks are Charleston interpretations of British neoclassical details. The only decorative similarity between the library bookcases is the husk placement and ogee termini of the stringing on their base plinths. During the twenty-year span between the production of the Edwards library bookcase and the Alston example, Continental influences waned as British and American neoclassical styles became more fashionable; yet, later reiterations of the late baroque details introduced by Pfeninger remained part of Charleston's unique neoclassical vocabulary.[16]

The written record of Martin Pfeninger's Charleston career documents his ability to produce inlay "in any taste," his pursuit of cabinetmaking "in all its branches," and his shop's completion of a sumptuous bedstead with carving, a rich cornice, Gothic clustered-column posts, and inlaid pedestals. After working for Thomas Elfe in 1772, he established a shop the following year on the corner of Tradd and Meeting (New Church) Streets, a highly visible location situated among the city's most impressive townhouses. Given this documentary evidence and his Germanic background, an attribution of the Edwards library bookcase, chest of drawers (fig. 14), and tables illustrated in figures 20–23 to Pfeninger's shop is reasonable and establishes his reputation as one of Charleston's most influential late colonial craftsmen.

ACKNOWLEDGMENTS   For assistance with this article the author thanks Luke Beckerdite, John Bivins, Johannes Emter Graf, the late Helena Hayward, Ronald Hurst, Robert Leath, Christopher Loeblein, Jonathan Poston, Jim and Harriet Pratt, Karen Rabe, Sigrid Sangl, and George Williams.

1. Charleston County, South Carolina, Inventories, A, 1783–1810, p. 142. For a genealogy of the Edwards family, see Mary Pringle Fenhagen, "John Edwards and Some of His Descendants," *South Carolina Historical Magazine* 55, no. 1 (January 1954): 15–27. For more on the John Edwards house, see John Bivins, Jr., "Charleston Rococo Interiors, 1765–1775: The 'Sommers' Carver," *Journal of Early Southern Decorative Arts* 12, no. 2 (November 1986): 84–90. The library bookcase was bequeathed to the Charleston Museum in 1947 by Mrs. George S. H. Holmes in "memory of George S. Holmes 1849–1922 and his ancestors of the Holmes and Edwards families bequeathed to his wife Nellie Hotchkiss Holmes and by her given in trust to the Charleston Museum."

2. Esther Singleton, *The Furniture of Our Forefathers: Part II* (New York: Doubleday, Page and Company, 1901), pp. 150–51. Homer Eaton Keyes, "The Present State of Early Furniture in Charleston, South Carolina," *Antiques* 29, no. 1 (January 1936): 19. E. Milby Burton, "The Furniture of Charleston," *Antiques* 61, no. 1 (January 1952): 38. John Bivins and Forsyth Alexander, *The Regional Arts of the Early South: A Sampling from the Collection of the Museum of Early Southern Decorative Arts* (Winston-Salem, N.C.: Museum of Early Southern Decorative Arts, 1991), p. 99.

3. Many of these details appear on furniture from Brunswick-Hanover by the 1720s.

4. St. John's Lutheran Church Records, 1755–1787, pp. 82, 88, 52. E. Milby Burton, *Charleston Furniture 1700–1825* (Charleston, S.C.: Charleston Museum, 1955), p. 118.

5. *South Carolina Gazette*, April 12, 1773; *South Carolina Gazette and Country Journal*, April 13, 1773. The bill is recorded in South Carolina Court of Common Pleas, Judgment Rolls, box 101A, no. 164A, November 17, 1774.

6. For the Shirley sale, see *South Carolina and American General Gazette*, June 10, 1771. Thomas Elfe Day Book 1768–1775, Charleston Library Society, account no. 63, February 12, 1772; account no. 131, November 14, 1772; and account no. 145, January 23, 1773. The Elfe Day Book is often erroneously described as an account book. For the Langford advertisement, see *South Carolina Gazette*, August 22, 1768. Inventory of the Goods and Chattels Left in the House of His Excellency The Right Honorable Lord William Campbell, Charlestown, South Carolina, T. 1/541, Public Record Office, London, transcribed as appendix 7 in Graham Hood, *The Governor's Palace in Williamsburg: A Cultural Study* (Williamsburg, Va.: Colonial Williamsburg Foundation, 1991), p. 308.

7. Elfe Day Book, account no. 63, May 8, 1772. The Elfe Day Book also records payment on a bond in the amount of £51 from "Martin Refinge" in October 1772. This was almost certainly

a reference to Pfeninger (account no. 140). For an excellent analysis of the Elfe Day Book, see John Christian Kolbe, "Thomas Elfe, Eighteenth Century Charleston Cabinetmaker" (master's thesis, University of South Carolina, Columbia, 1980).

8. German Friendly Society, Minutes, 1766–1787, South Caroliniana Library, Columbia, p. 244. Michael Kalteisen to Martin Pfeninger, Charleston County, South Carolina, Land Records, Misc., pt. 59, bk. W4, 1775–1778 (transcript), pp. 535–40. *Gazette of the State of South Carolina*, October 28, 1777, and *South Carolina and American General Gazette*, October 30, 1777. *Royal Gazette*, July 11, 1781. Rules of the German Friendly Society, p. 122, no. 87. Will of Martin Pfeninger, March 24, 1780, Charleston County, South Carolina, Wills, vol. 20, 1783–1786, p. 71.

9. According to Andrea Winter (author of *Meisterstuecke der Braunschweiger Tischlergilde* [1995]), there are lists of eighteenth-century Braunschweig masters but no list of apprentices. There is no one named Pfeninger on the list of masters. I am grateful to Dr. Winter for consulting her notes on this topic. An internet search of German telephone directories yielded 177 entries for the name "Pfenninger," but the addresses are representative of all areas of modern Germany. As quoted in Warren B. Smith, *White Servitude in Colonial South Carolina* (Columbia, S.C.: University of South Carolina Press, 1961), pp. 51–52. George C. Rogers, Jr., *Charleston in the Age of the Pinckneys* (Columbia, S.C.: University of South Carolina Press, 1980), pp. 6–7.

10. For a history of Charleston's German Friendly Society, see George J. Gongaware, *The History of The German Friendly Society of Charleston, South Carolina* (Richmond, Va.: Garrett & Massie, 1935). Michael Kalteisen, the founder of the German Friendly Society, was born in Machtolsheim in the Duchy of Wurtemburg in 1729. He arrived in South Carolina after 1743 and worked as an indentured servant for shoemaker John Clark of Ashley Ferry and for Dr. Frederick Holzendorff, surgeon at St. Philip's Hospital in Charleston (Helene M. Kastinger Riley, *Michael Kalteisen, Founder of the German Friendly Society* [Greenville, S.C.: by the author, 1995], pp. 1–3).

11. For a discussion of German influences on eighteenth-century British furniture, see Helena Hayward and Sarah Medlam, "The Continental Context: Germany," in *John Channon and Brass Inlaid Furniture, 1730–1760*, edited by Christopher Gilbert and Tessa Murdoch (New Haven, Conn. and London: Yale University Press, 1993), pp. 24–36. For British influence on German furniture, see Heinrich Kreisel and Georg Himmelheber, *Die Kunst des deutschen Mobels, Spatbarock und Rokoko* (Munchen, Germany: C. H. Beck, 1983).

12. Gilbert and Murdoch, eds., *John Channon*, pp. 21, 24–29. For more on the Moravian brotherhood and links between English and German craftsmen, see Lindsay Boynton, "The Moravian Brotherhood and the Migration of Furniture Makers in the Eighteenth Century," *Furniture History* 29 (1993): 45–58.

13. Engraved and inlaid brass husks on British furniture are illustrated in Gilbert and Murdoch, eds., *John Channon*, pp. 80, 81, 111.

14. For illustrations of eighteenth-century case pieces from the Brunswick-Hanover region of Germany, see Wolfgang Schwarze, *Antike Deutsche Mobel; Das Burgerliche und Rustikale Mobel in Deutschland von 1700–1840* (Wuppertal, Germany: by the author, 1977), pp. 62–71; and Kreisel and Himmelheber, *Die Kunst des deutschen Mobels,* figs. 882–86.

15. The Appleton secretary-and-bookcase is illustrated in Charles F. Montgomery, *American Furniture: The Federal Period* (New York: Viking Press, 1966), p. 222. The Langley Boardman chest is illustrated in Brock Jobe, ed., *Portsmouth Furniture: Masterworks from the New Hampshire Seacoast* (Hanover, N.H.: University Press of New England, 1993), p. 65. Although Jobe suggests that the canted corner foot with inlaid stringing was probably introduced into Charleston by Portsmouth imports, the fully developed form was utilized in Charleston by the early 1770s.

16. The Alston library bookcase is illustrated and discussed in Gerald W. R. Ward, *American Case Furniture in the Mabel Brady Garvan and Other Collections at Yale University* (New Haven, Conn.: Yale University Art Gallery, 1988), pp. 363–366.

Appendix

Will of Martin Pfeninger

In the Name of God Amen. I Martin Pfeninger of the Town of Charles town Cabinet Maker, being in perfect Health of Body and of sound Mind and Memory, Thanks be unto God for the same; but calling to Mind the Uncertainty of this transitory Life, and knowing that it is appointed for all Men once to die, do make and ordain this my last Will and Testament, that is to say principally and first of all, I give and recommend my Soul into the Hands of Almighty God that gave it, and my Body I recommend to the Earth to be buried in a decent Christian Burial at the Discretion of my Executor, and as these troublesome Times will admit. Nothing doubting but at the general Resurrection I shall receive the same again by the mighty Power of God. And as touching such worldly Estate wherewith it has pleased God to bless me in this Life, I give demise and dispose of the same in the following Manner and Form. Imprimis. I give and bequeath to Hannah my dear beloved Wife one Negro Fellow named London, and a Negro Woman named Chloe to her own proper Use and Behoof for ever, the rest of my Property what remains, after my Son's Share which I hereafter bequeath to him excepted, shall remain in the said Hannah's Hands paying out of the same all my just and lawful Debts, not to be done by public Vendue, but only sell so much as is sufficient to pay said Debts, and do with the rest according as she may please. Secondly I give and bequeath unto my Son Daniel Conrad, a Negro Wench named Byna, and a Negro Girl named Hannah, also the House and Lott adjoining to Mrs. Burn's near the Draw-gate in Charlestown, containing 150 feet in Depth, and 53 feet in front, also my Gildt Watch, my Riding Horse Hunter and black Colt, likewise my new Rifle and Shot Gun him and his lawful Heirs for ever. But in Case the said Daniel Conrad should happen to die before his Mother, then it is my Will and Desire that the aforesaid Hannah his Mother shall inherit what is bequeathed to him, and in the like Case if the Mother Hannah should happen to die before him, the said Daniel Conrad, then this is my Desire that he shall inherit all what the said Hannah his Mother is possess'd of at the Time of her Decease. But should it happen that they both of them die in a single State of Life, in that Case it is my Desire that my Estate shall be divided in three Parts or Shares VIZ. Sarah Fowler one Share, Sophia West one Share and Martin West one Share, with this Provise that he retains the Name of Martin, otherwise that Share to be divided between Elizabeth west and the said Martin or her Brother. And I do hereby constitute make and ordain the aforesaid Hannah my Wife the sole Executrix of this my last Will and Testament. And I do hereby utterly Disallow, revoke and disannul all and every other former Testaments, Wills, Legacies Bequests and Executers, by me in any wise before named, willed and bequeathed, ratifying and confirming this, and no other, to be my last Will and Testament, IN WITNESS whereof I have hereunto set my Hand and Seal, this twenty fourth day of March in the Year of our Lord one thousand seven hundred and eighty,

Martin Pfeninger (LS)

Signed Sealed Published pronounced and Declared by the said Martin Pfeninger as his last Will and testament, in the Presence of us, who in the Presence of each other, have hereunto subscribed our Names, VIZt.

John Christian Smith   George F. Dener   James Carmichael

Proved before Charles Lining Esq r O.C.T.D. April 2d 1783.
At same Time qualified Hannah Pfeninger Exix.

Examined   )
)
8 Co. Sh.   ) C.L.

Source: Charleston Will Book A, 1783–86, p. 64.

Sumpter Priddy III and Joan K. Quinn

Crossroads of Culture: Eighteenth-Century Furniture from Western Maryland

The mechanics are numerous, in proportion to the aggregate; and the Spirit of Industry seems to pervade the place.

George Washington, August 7, 1785

▼ THE BOUNDARIES OF western Maryland have never been clearly defined. To many, this geographic designation suggests the lands beyond the Blue Ridge Mountains, but historically "western Maryland" encompassed the entire territory beyond the "fall line"—where ships could continue no further upriver, where rolling hills and gentle mountains emerged from the landscape, and where people, goods, and ideas moved over land (fig. 1). Like other inland regions where geography inhibited access, this area of Maryland was referred to in eighteenth-century parlance as the "backcountry," "backlands," and "backwoods."[1]

Maryland's backcountry was sparsely populated during the early eighteenth century. As early as 1732, Governor Charles Calvert attempted to attract colonists to the region by offering land on favorable terms. Like other colonial officials, he hoped that these settlers would secure raw materials for British manufacturers, constitute a new market for British goods, and provide a buffer against French forces on the western frontier. After a 1748 Act of Assembly established the boundaries of Frederick County (which encompassed Frederick, Washington, Allegheny, Garrett, Montgomery, and portions of Carroll and Howard Counties today) and made Frederick Town the county seat (fig. 2), the region's population grew dramatically as large numbers of settlers arrived from eastern Maryland, southern Pennsylvania, Virginia, and Europe.[2]

Because of its growing population, Frederick County was partitioned in 1776, with the formation of Washington and Montgomery Counties, and in 1787, with the formation of Allegheny County. In 1790, Frederick County had 30,971 inhabitants, Washington County had 15,822, Montgomery County had 18,003, and Allegheny County had 4,809. In 1791, Frederick County had four hundred stills, eighty grist mills, two glass houses, two iron furnaces, two forges, and two paper mills. Agriculture was the foundation of the region's economy, and Frederick County led the state in grain production. In 1813, William Harris Crawford (1772–1834) observed that "the crops of wheat and other grains from Monocacy river to Frederick Town to Woodville . . . [were] superior to any thing I had ever seen." These agricultural and manufacturing industries created a strong economic base

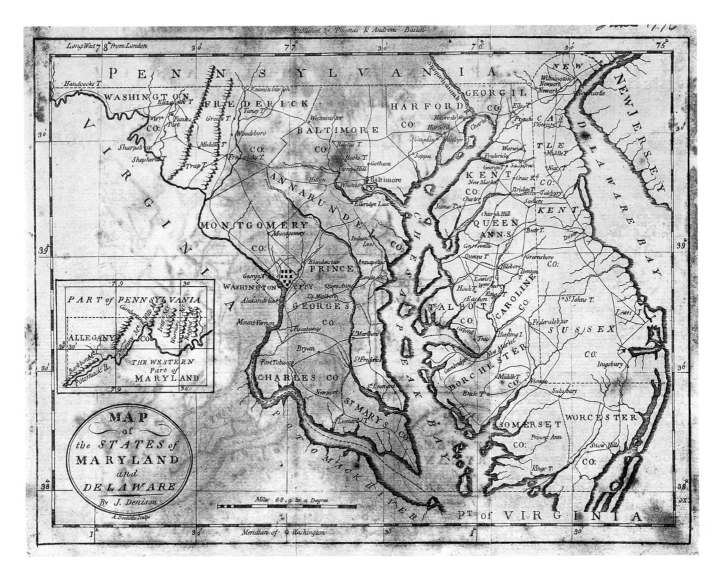

Figure 1 J. Denison, MAP of the STATES of MARY-
LAND and DELAWARE, published in Jedidiah
Morse's *American Geography,* 3d ed., 1796. (Cour-
tesy, Maryland Hall of Records.)

in western Maryland. With prosperity came a demand for furnishings that
surpassed those produced in most rural communities.[3]

During the eighteenth century, western Maryland had two principal trading centers—Frederick Town and Hagerstown. Frederick Town was founded
by Irish immigrant Daniel Dulany (1685–1753) in 1745. Although Dulany
lived and practiced law in Annapolis, he acquired a vast tract of land in "the
backwoods" as a speculative investment. He described this region as a
"delightful Country . . . that Equals . . . any in America . . . well furnished
with timber of all sorts, abounding with . . . stone fit for building . . . and
to Crown all, very healthy." After dividing Frederick Town into 351 lots,
Dulany sold most of the property to freeholders of Germanic and British
descent. Many of the town's earliest residents were tradesmen, including
seven cabinetmakers and two joiners. In 1771, Annapolis customs inspector
William Eddis wrote, "from an humble beginning, has Frederick Town
arisen to its present flourishing state. . . . Provisions are cheap, plentiful, and
excellent. . . . [H]ere are to be found all conveniences, and many
superfluities."[4]

Hagerstown was founded by Jonathan Hager, a German immigrant who arrived in Philadelphia in 1736. He purchased two hundred acres of land from Daniel Dulany in 1739 and, after acquiring additional tracts, founded Elizabeth Town (named after Hager's wife) in 1762. Elizabeth Town was renamed "Hagerstown" and made the seat of Washington County at the beginning of the Revolution. Because of its location and date of settlement, Hagerstown grew more slowly than Frederick Town. In 1771, William Eddis noted that Hagerstown had "more than a hundred comfortable edifices" and that it was "making quick advances to perfection." He also believed that Hager's "encouragement to traders" was critical to the town's success.[5]

Although Frederick Town and Hagerstown were in the heart of Maryland's backcountry, they were not isolated. Western Maryland was crisscrossed by old roads built on ancient Indian trails and new roads chartered by the colony and state. The "Old Indian Trail," or Monocacy Road, led from Frederick Town into south central Pennsylvania, and the "Great Wagon Road" ran from Pennsylvania through Hagerstown, Martinsburg and Winchester, Virginia, and down the Shenandoah Valley four hundred miles into Tennessee. Travelers from eastern Maryland came by two separate routes—one from Baltimore and one from Annapolis—that converged in Frederick Town then continued over the mountains to Hagerstown, Pittsburgh, and the Ohio territory. From eastern Virginia, settlers followed the trails that led from Fredericksburg to the headwaters of the Rappahannock, then across the piedmont to Winchester. Others came by the "River Road" that ran near the Potomac from Alexandria and Georgetown. Frederick Town and Hagerstown were often a final destination for many of the artisans who traveled these roads, but others stayed only a brief time. The furniture produced in both towns reflects this constant influx of new tradesmen and patrons.[6]

The culture and economy of western Maryland were linked to Pennsylvania, eastern Maryland, and northern Virginia. Chambersburg, Carlisle, and Gettysburg, Pennsylvania, were important commercial centers within fifty miles of Frederick Town. Although slightly more distant, York and Lancaster were points of departure for many of the Germanic settlers who moved from Pennsylvania to western Maryland. Along the Potomac River in (West) Virginia were Harper's Ferry and Shepherdstown, and slightly further inland were Charlestown and Martinsburg. Nestled in the rolling hills of Virginia's northern piedmont were Winchester, Berryville, Middleburg, and Leesburg. In western Maryland, Sharpsburg, Margaretsville (Boonsboro), Cumberland, Emmitsburg, Liberty Town, Taney Town, and New Market emerged as small but important economic centers. Artisans moved freely within this larger region, living at one time in Maryland, at another in Virginia, at another in Pennsylvania. Over 150 cabinetmakers and joiners worked in western Maryland before 1820.[7]

Most of the Germanic settlers in western Maryland were from Protestant families who came to the colonies to escape religious persecution in the Palatinate during the seventeenth and eighteenth centuries. The earliest emigrés arrived in Philadelphia. Although some remained in the city, most traveled westward, settling in the countryside or in one of the inland towns like Lancaster or York. From the outset, the colony's Germanic community was culturally diverse. In addition to refugees from the German states, a large number of Mennonites from the valley of the upper Rhine and Switzerland emigrated to Pennsylvania.[8]

As the population of southeastern and western Pennsylvania grew and land became more expensive, many of these Germanic people moved south, settling in western Maryland, the Shenandoah Valley of Virginia, the Carolina backcountry, and Tennessee. To encourage settlement in western Maryland, Lord Baltimore offered colonists two-hundred-acre tracts of inexpensive land "in fee simple." Although most of the Germanic settlers in Maryland came from Pennsylvania, evidence suggests that over a thousand Teutonic immigrants arrived in Annapolis during the first half of the 1750s and countless others followed. Later in the century, Baltimore became an important port of entry for European immigrants. John Frederick Amelung, who established the New Bremen "Glassmanufactory" in Frederick County, arrived in Baltimore on August 31, 1784. Fifteen of his workers arrived there later in that year. The influx of Germanic artisans continued through the end of the eighteenth century. On October 6, 1792, the ship *Waaksaamheyd* arrived with "German redemptioners," including glassmakers, potters, stonecutters, whitesmiths, carpenters, cabinetmakers, and "a single Man of approved Abilities in making of Varnishes, Gilding, Carving, ornamental stone cutting and coach painting." William Eddis attributed the "advancement of settlements" in western Maryland to "the arrival of many emigrants from the palatinate, and other Germanic States [who] . . . had been disciplined in the habits of industry, sobriety, frugality, and patience" and who were responsible for creating "the first improvements."[9]

The fact that Teutonic immigrants arrived in many American ports complicates the study of Germanic furniture in America. Cultural expressions are rarely respectful of political boundaries, and many objects traditionally

Figure 3 Chest, Lancaster, Pennsylvania, 1776. White pine and white oak with yellow pine and walnut. H. 23½", W. 44⅞", D. 22¾". (Courtesy, Yale University Art Gallery, Mabel Brady Garvan Collection.)

attributed to Germanic artisans in Pennsylvania were actually produced in other colonies. To further illustrate the point, some artisans who lived in Pennsylvania came to western Maryland for training. On December 29, 1761, Mathias Baker, Sr., of York County, Pennsylvania, bound his son Mathias to Godfrey Brown of Frederick County, Maryland, "to learn the trade of a Joyner." A group of Germanic chests from Pennsylvania and Maryland share a common cultural background. The chest illustrated in figure 3 has elaborately decorated panels, the center of which is initialed "•C•B••H•B•," and an interior inscription identifying its original owner, Casper Hildebrand of Lancaster. Like other chests produced by immigrant Palatinate artisans, it has details that resemble those on Continental German examples made from the late seventeenth through the late eighteenth centuries. Dozens of closely related chests, constructed of painted softwoods or of walnut, were made in Pennsylvania—particularly around Lancaster County.[10]

A similar chest associated with "White Oak Forest Farm," near Hagerstown, represents either Pennsylvania or Maryland production (fig. 4). This piece may have descended in the Beachtel family, who purchased the property in 1738, or in the family of Joseph Loose, who was born in Pennsylvania in 1810 and married Henrietta Beachtel in 1844. The iron handles on the ends of the case, the profiles of the lid and base moldings, and the design of the facade vary little from the Pennsylvania example shown in figure 3. Subtle differences can be found in the dentil course added to the base molding,

Figure 4 Chest, probably Frederick County, Maryland, 1770–1780. Walnut with tulip poplar. H. 23¼", W. 51¼", D. 23". (Private collection; photo, Gavin Ashworth.)

in the slightly smaller feet, and in the pilaster flutes, which abut the capitals rather than terminate below them.[11]

A slightly later chest that descended in the Beachtel family (fig. 5) was undoubtedly made in the Hagerstown area; however, it clearly emanates from the same cultural tradition, if not shop tradition, as the preceding example (fig. 4). The joiner substituted five ogee feet for the turned feet on the earlier example and added two lipped drawers. The medial and base moldings on the later chest are interrupted at their junctures with the drawer divider, feet, and plinths of the outer pilasters. One of the most intriguing design elements on this chest is the scalloped appliqué above the drawer divider, which presages the carved ornament on a later western Maryland chest (fig. 7). The joiner's use of ribbon-figured walnut is also associated with furniture made in the vicinity of Hagerstown and Frederick Town. The fluted pilasters on the facade are a more generic detail. Chests from Pennsylvania, western Maryland, and the Valley of Virginia occasionally have this feature.

Chests or *kistch* were the most common storage forms in Germanic households. Young women of Germanic descent typically received chests as gifts for dower goods before their marriage. This tradition was such an integral part of German culture that even female servants often received chests when their indentures expired. On February 25, 1805, Tille Dorff was bound to John Martin of Frederick County. In exchange for performing "all kinds of House and out of Door work," she was to receive a "Common Chest

Figure 5 Chest, Frederick County, Maryland, 1770–1780. Walnut with yellow pine. H. 29³/₈", W. 56", D. 28¹/₂". (Private collection; photo, Museum of Early Southern Decorative Arts.) The lower portions of the feet are restored.

Figure 6 Schrank, Frederick County, Maryland, 1775–1785. Walnut with tulip poplar. Dimensions not recorded. (Courtesy, Maryland Historical Society.) The turned feet are restored.

without Drawers," a bedstead, two "common Stools," a blanket, a bed quilt, a new spinning wheel, and "a new suit of cloaths, such [as] is common for farmers."[12]

Schranken were also traditional storage forms, and like chests, they had important cultural connotations as symbols of cleanliness, prosperity, continuity, and order. A schrank found in Libertytown (fig. 6) is roughly con-

Figure 7 Chest, Hagerstown, Maryland, 1785. Walnut. H. 24½", W. 31", D. 22½". (Courtesy, Sotheby's.)

temporary with the Beachtel family chests. All three pieces have fluted pilasters and moldings that are secured with large, diamond-shaped pins. Intentionally exposed structural details, such as these pins and the dovetails on the frieze of the schrank, are typical of Germanic work. Like the schrank, many corner cupboards from western Maryland have pilasters flanking the doors.[13]

A chest and desk with their production dates and owners' initials inlaid in white putty (probably white lead, calcium carbonate, or sulfur) show how Frederick County furniture styles evolved during the 1780s. The chest is initialed "HS" and dated "·17·85" (fig. 7). Like the chests that descended in the Hildebrand and Beachtel families (figs. 3, 4, 5), this example has a dovetailed case underlying an architectural facade. Its straight bracket feet are made from the same piece of wood as the ovolo-and-ogee base molding. These molding/foot components are mitered at the corners, pinned to the bottom board of the case (without overlapping the front or sides), and reinforced at each corner with large, wrought-nailed blocks that extend diagonally toward the center of the chest. Like the ogee-foot chest from the Beachtel family (fig. 5), the "HS" example has an astragal molding that separates the drawers from the chest section and forms capitals for the fluted plinths below. The carved fans above the plinths are one of the most distinctive features of this chest. Although fan ornaments are relatively common in neoclassic architecture, they are seldom encountered on furniture. In western Maryland, however, they occasionally occur on joiners' work, particularly on the doors of neoclassical corner cupboards.[14]

The drawers of the "HS" chest (fig. 7) have several features found on other pieces from the region. The drawer fronts have ovolo lip moldings that overlap the case on all four sides like those on the ogee-foot chest from the Beachtel family (fig. 5). Also typical of Frederick County work, the drawer frames of the "HS" chest have three large dovetails at each corner. The dovetails at the front are conventional, but the ones at the back are reverse-pinned—a relatively common Germanic detail shared by another chest from the same shop. The drawers of the "HS" chest run on their bot-

Figure 8 Desk, Hagerstown, Maryland, 1796. Cherry with yellow pine and cherry. H. 37⅝", W. 44½", D. 20¾". (Courtesy, Washington County Historical Society, Hagerstown; photo, Gavin Ashworth.) The desk originally had bracket feet.

Figure 9 Detail of the prospect door of the desk illustrated in fig. 8. (Photo, Gavin Ashworth.)

toms, which are nailed into an open rabbet in the front and directly to the bottom of the sides and the back.[15]

A desk made in the same shop has an elaborately shaped prospect door dated "1796" and initialed "M•R•" for Martin Rohrer of Hagerstown (figs. 8, 9). Rohrer's father, Jacob, purchased Jonathan Hager's stone house in 1745 and subsequently raised his family there. Although the desk has lost its original feet, the inlaid numerals and drawer construction of the desk are virtually identical to those on the "HS" chest (fig. 7). The curvilinear design of the inlay on the prospect door resembles the applied panels on the plinths of several Frederick County tall case clocks.[16]

Western Maryland artisans used both putty compounds and contrasting woods for inlay. The chest illustrated in figure 10 has elaborate script initials inlaid in maple or another light-colored hardwood. The letters "DS" refer to the original owner, Daniel Sayler (1775–1850) of Beaver Creek in Frederick County (figs. 11, 12). The inlay maker used gouges and a V-shaped parting tool to define and shade the letters, then he filled the cuts with a putty similar to that used on the preceding chest and desk (figs. 7, 8). Not only do the carving techniques resemble those used by regional gunmakers, but the practice of inletting colored fillers has antecedents in European arms and armor. Although elaborate script letters occasionally appear on Pennsylvania furniture, they do not usually exhibit this degree of detail.[17]

The painted decoration on the chest illustrated in figure 13 is also unusual from a technical standpoint. As its inscription suggests, it was made in 1791 for Adam Neff of Frederick County. Colorful and expressive, this simple

Figure 10 Chest, Frederick County, Maryland, 1780–1790. Walnut; maple and putty inlay. H. 29¼", W. 51", D. 24¾". (Private collection; photo, Gavin Ashworth.)

Figure 11 Detail of the inlay on the chest illustrated in fig. 10. (Photo, Gavin Ashworth.)

Figure 12 Detail of the inlay on the chest illustrated in fig. 10. (Photo, Gavin Ashworth.)

Figure 13 Chest, Frederick County, Maryland, 1791. Tulip poplar. H. 25¾", W. 49", D. 22⅞". (Collection of the Museum of Early Southern Decorative Arts.) The feet and base molding are restored.

dovetailed case has sgraffito decoration: the design was incised through a coat of damp green paint to reveal the brilliant orange color beneath. Although sgraffito-decorated earthenware was prized by the Palatinate Germans and was relatively common in Europe and Pennsylvania, only a few pieces of furniture have figural decoration in this technique alone. Variations of this vase-and-flower design appear on other furniture from western Maryland.[18]

Further insight into the work of Germanic artisans in western Maryland is provided by the ledger of Frederick Town joiner Joseph Doll (1747–1819). His parents, Johannes and Catharina (Hartmann), emigrated to Pennsylvania in 1741 from Bretten, in the Palatinate. By 1747, they had settled in Lancaster, Pennsylvania. Their son Joseph was baptized in the First Reformed Church in Lancaster in May of that year. Johannes Doll's trade is

not specified in any record, but circumstantial evidence suggests that he may have been a joiner. His oldest son, Johannes (b. 1736), was schoolmaster at Lancaster's First Reformed Church, but his next two sons worked in the woodworking trades. Conrad (b. 1739) was a cabinetmaker, and Joseph was a house joiner who occasionally made furniture. The younger Johannes's son Conrad (1772–1819) was also a joiner and cabinetmaker, and he is the only member of the family for whom documented work is known. A highly carved organ case that the younger Conrad designed and constructed for Peace Church in Hampden Township, Cumberland County, Pennsylvania, still survives in its original location (fig. 14). Its paneled pilasters, carved rococo C scrolls, and pitch pediment have much in common with early cabinetmaking in western Maryland.[19]

Figure 14　Conrad Doll, organ case for Peace Church, Hampden Township, Cumberland County, Pennsylvania, 1807. Painted softwoods. Dimensions not recorded. (Courtesy, Friends of Peace Church and the Pennsylvania Historical and Museum Commission; photo, Gavin Ashworth.)

Figure 15 Tall clock with a thirty-hour movement by John Fessler, Sr., Frederick Town, Maryland, ca. 1785. Painted softwoods. H. 84$^{1/2}$", W. 20$^{3/4}$", D. 10$^{7/8}$". (Private collection; photo, Museum of Early Southern Decorative Arts.)

Like many Germanic families that settled in Pennsylvania during the eighteenth century, the second generation of the Doll family headed west and then south. Johannes's sons Joseph and Conrad both moved to Maryland in the 1760s. Conrad arrived by 1761, when he married Anna Maria Schisler in the Evangelical and Reformed Church in Frederick Town. Joseph joined his brother later in the decade, probably after the death of their father on February 3, 1765. He married Charlotte Storm in Frederick Town and helped raise a family of fourteen children.[20]

Joseph Doll's ledger (written in phonetic English) indicates that he provided a wide range of products and services for his Germanic and British neighbors between 1761 and 1789. The largest portion of his business involved the production of an astonishing variety of building materials, including sills, joists, flooring, studs, lath, rafters, and shingles. Except for an occasional door or window sash, Joseph Doll was not involved with finish carpentry or interior woodwork. Similarly, furniture making was only a small part of his business. His ledger indicates that he constructed less than twenty pieces between 1773 and 1777 and a few scattered examples in the following years.[21]

Doll produced more bedsteads than any other form: Six had low posts, one had high posts, and two were cradles. The low-post bedsteads ranged in price from eleven shillings to twelve shillings eight pence. Four were made in pairs, one of which was "Painted Green." The "bedStid with high Posts painted blue with four Scroos" was the only example assembled with bed bolts. Made in 1787, it cost £2.7.6—over twice as much as any bedstead from the prior decade. The second most expensive bedstead was purchased by Christian Weaver. In 1774, he paid £1 for a "Greadle to Rog his Chylde." The other cradle, made the following year, cost John Brunner 18 shillings.[22]

Doll's ledger also records the production of seven tables that ranged in price from £1 to £1.8. Although two of the tables were not described, two were "walnut," one had "2 Drawers and brass hands," one was referred to as a "Kitchin Table," and one was described as a "Larch Pobler Table for a workebench with Two Trawers in it with divicions." John Hoober, a glass engraver at Amelung's New Bremen Glassmanufactory, paid Doll £1.7 for the latter in 1775. [23]

Doll produced only four case pieces, but they were the most expensive furniture forms recorded in his ledger. John Brunner paid £3.15 for a "Kitchin Cobert" in 1775; Casper Mantz paid £3.5 for a "Chest with drawers" for his "Daughter Caety" in 1775; Peeter Brunner paid £7 for a "Kitchen

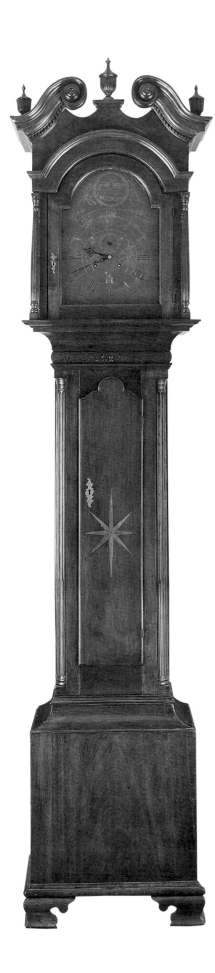

Figure 16 Tall clock with an eight-day movement by George Schnertzel, Frederick Town, Maryland, ca. 1780. Walnut with yellow pine. H. 104", W. 19½", D. 11½". (Private collection; photo, Gavin Ashworth.) The base is restored.

Figure 17 Detail of the frieze of the tall clock illustrated in fig. 16. (Photo, Gavin Ashworth.)

Dresser with glas and furniture" in 1776; and John Kyle paid £4.10 for a "Corner Cobbert" in 1789. The dresser Doll made for his neighbor Brunner was twice as expensive as any piece he had made prior to that time, and over two and a half pounds more than any recorded later in his career.[24]

Like many other woodworkers, Doll made coffins. Between 1775 and 1789 he made seven at prices ranging from five shillings to £1.15. He also repaired furniture and made a variety of kitchen goods, including a door for a fireplace, a cutting box, and a bread tray with a lead liner. His ledger indicates that he mended several chairs and made Henry Cronier "a Sidepeese to his bedStid paint blue." Regrettably, none of the surviving household furnishings from western Maryland can be associated with Doll's ledger entries.[25]

Although the products of most of the Germanic artisans who moved from Pennsylvania to western Maryland remain anonymous, a large group of tall case clocks made by Germanic clockmakers and cabinetmakers in Frederick County survives. These cases range from simple, flat-top examples to carved ones with elaborate scrolled pediments. The simpler end of the spectrum is represented by a case with a thirty-hour, brass dial movement by John Fessler, Sr. (1760–1820), one of the most productive clockmakers in Frederick Town (fig. 15). His parents were Swiss immigrants who arrived in Pennsylvania in 1760 and subsequently settled in Lancaster. Fessler served in the Continental Army from 1777 to 1782, and, like many of his contemporaries from Europe, he moved to western Maryland after the Revolution.[26]

The case for Fessler's clock has a flat hood with a broad cove cornice, a plain frieze, a square door conforming to the brass dial, a rectangular waist door with Germanic "rat-tail" hinges, and a paneled plinth with an ogee base molding. The front of the case that surrounds the waist door consists of a mortise-and-tenon frame that is pinned to the case sides. Like the simplest chests from the region, such cases are derived almost verbatim from their European counterparts. Numerous flat-top cases with thirty-hour, or "long-day," movements were made in western Maryland, but most have imported British hinges, thinner stock, and other concessions to Anglo-American style.

One of the most expensive Germanic cases from western Maryland (fig. 16) has an eight-day movement by George Schnertzel of Frederick Town (fl. 1772–1810). This clock case is the only example from the region with a leaf-carved, pulvinated frieze (fig. 17)—a feature that appears on a few Philadelphia clock cases made during the 1760s and 1770s. The pediment scrolls on the Schnertzel clock are unusually low, as are those on several similar cases with movements by Eli Bentley of Taney Town, Maryland, and Arthur Johnson and George Woltz of Hagerstown.[27]

The tall case clock illustrated in figure 18 has a thirty-hour movement signed "George Woltz Hagers Town" and dated "1789." Woltz's parents were Swiss immigrants who settled in York, Pennsylvania, by 1731. Woltz (1744–1812) purchased a lot in Hagerstown in 1774 and served as a major in the Maryland Militia in Annapolis in 1776. After the Revolution, he returned to Hagerstown, where he worked until his death in 1813. The earliest documented clock by Woltz descended in his family.[28]

Although local tradition maintains that Woltz made clock cases and other household furniture, there is no documentary evidence that he was a cabinetmaker. The cherry and walnut furniture listed in his probate inventory and cited by one scholar as evidence of his woodworking skills was nothing more than the personal possessions of a prosperous artisan. He did not own any chisels, molding planes, or other specialized tools necessary for the production of case furniture. His inventory listed only clockmaking tools and an "unfinished" movement.[29]

Movements by Woltz and his competitors are often housed in cases from the same cabinet shops. The clock case illustrated in figures 19 and 20 has a thirty-hour movement by Jacob Young, who worked in Hagerstown from the late 1770s until his death in 1792; however, the case is clearly by the same hand that made the one for the signed Woltz movement (fig. 18). A less expensive but related case has a thirty-hour movement by Hagerstown clockmaker John Itnyer (d. 1786).[30]

Most of the early Hagerstown cases with movements by Woltz and his competitors have bold ogee feet, a scalloped panel applied on the plinth, fluted quarter-columns, a waist door with an arched head with ogee-shaped shoulders, an astragal molding below the frieze, and broad cove moldings above. The principal differences between the cases for the Woltz and Young clocks occur on their hoods. The hood on the Woltz clock has simple baluster colonettes and a flat top, whereas the one on the Young example has

Figure 19 Tall clock with a thirty-hour movement by Jacob Young, Hagerstown, Maryland, ca. 1785. Walnut. Secondary woods and dimensions not recorded. The feet and rosettes are restored. (Private collection; photo, Gavin Ashworth.)

Figure 20 Detail of the hood of the tall clock illustrated in fig. 19. (Photo, Gavin Ashworth.)

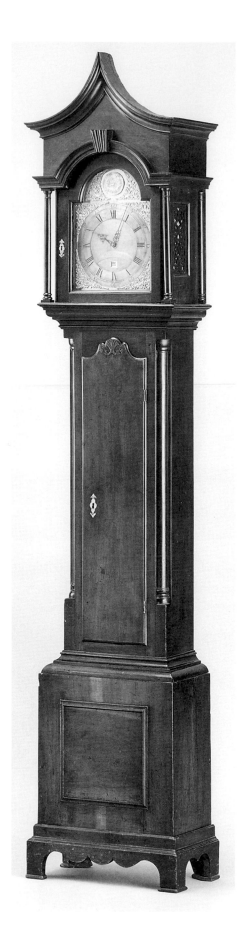

Figure 21 Tall clock with a thirty-hour movement signed "John Myer, Frederick Town," Maryland, 1770–1790. Cherry with tulip poplar. H. 97⅝", W. 20⅛", D. 10⅝". (Courtesy, Colonial Williamsburg Foundation.)

Figure 22 Detail of the waist door of the tall clock illustrated in fig. 21.

fluted colonettes and a broken-scroll pediment. The scrolled pediment has an unusually deep tympanum and a decidedly vertical thrust—features that occur on closely related cases with movements by several other Hagerstown clockmakers. On the Young case, the shell-shaped keystone and molded, tulip-shaped plinth for the central finial signify the work of an accomplished joiner. Several clock cases and related desk-and-bookcases with similar pediments were made in Lancaster, Pennsylvania, during the last three decades of the eighteenth century. The Woltz and Young cases may represent the work of a joiner who trained or worked as a journeyman there.[31]

Although none of these cases are signed, several Hagerstown cabinetmakers were capable of producing them. William Conrad, who was described as a "joiner," purchased a town lot in 1775. His 1790 inventory lists one of the most complete sets of molding planes recorded in the region and "2 Books called Swans Architecture" valued at £6.5. More importantly, the cabinetwork in his shop included "2 falling unfinished Tables" and "1 Cherry Clock Case" that, together with "a piece of iron," were valued at £9.4.6. The wide variety of clock cases and movements made in the Hagerstown area suggests that a high degree of craft specialization existed there by the end of the Revolutionary era.[32]

Throughout western Maryland, joiners who had trained in vernacular traditions worked in close proximity to cabinetmakers, chairmakers, and other tradesmen with urban backgrounds. In contrast to the Germanic work discussed at the beginning of this article, other Frederick County furniture reflects the influence of British design and construction techniques. Much of this furniture, however, may have been produced by tradesmen working outside the English mainstream, including artisans of Scottish and Irish descent and Germanic tradesmen working in a British style.

Although a large number of artisans from different cultures worked in western Maryland, much of their work can be separated into individual shop groups. Structural and stylistic details shared by these groups also indicate that a distinctive regional taste emerged during the last quarter of the eighteenth century. Many of the surviving pieces have strong family provenances or other histories that place them within the boundaries of old Frederick County. These objects provide a solid foundation for understanding how the convergence of artisans and cultures influenced furniture styles and trade practices within the region.

Two tall clock cases—one with a thirty-hour movement by John Myer (figs. 21, 22) and the other with an eight-day movement by Elijah Evans (fig. 24)—introduce this diverse group of early Frederick County furniture. Despite the outward differences of their pediments and bracket feet, these cases evidently represent the work of a single artisan or shop. Both cases have unfluted quarter-columns, and their moldings, keystones, Doric colonettes, and waist doors are virtually identical. All of these details were clearly inspired by British tall clocks of the 1760–1790 period.

The pagoda-shaped pediment of the Myer clock (fig. 21) suggests that the case maker had access to British design books or, at the very least, that he had an acute awareness of rococo furniture and architectural styles. Similar pediments appear on a clock case with a movement by Robert Grieff of Beath, Scotland; a clock case illustrated on plate 163 in the third edition of Thomas Chippendale's *The Gentleman and Cabinet-Maker's Director* (1762) (fig. 23); a "china case" shown on plate 49 in the Society of Upholsterers's *Houshold Furniture in Genteel Taste* (1760); and a variety of buildings and interior details illustrated in English architectural design books, such as Sir William Chambers's *Designs of Chinese Buildings, Furniture, Dresses, Machines, and Utensils* (1757) and William Paine's *Builder's Companion and Workman's General Assistant* (1758).[33]

The waist door of the Myer case is capped with a small carved shell and flanking acanthus leaves (fig. 22). The cabinetmaker used a gouge to hollow out the lobes of the leaves rather than flute and shade them in a conventional manner. His techniques produced a stylized design that contrasts with the naturalistic carving from most urban centers and larger towns on the periphery of western Maryland, such as York, Lancaster, and Reading. Several other pieces of Frederick County furniture have carving that is conceived and executed in a similar manner, possibly owing to the lack of professional carvers there.[34]

Although British influences are apparent in the design of the Myer and Evans cases, the small carved tulip below the center finial on the Evans clock (fig. 24) and the wedged dovetails and thick stock of both pieces are Ger-

Figure 23 Design for a tall clock illustrated on pl. 163 in the third edition of Thomas Chippendale's *Gentleman and Cabinet-Maker's Director* (1762). (Collection of the Museum of Early Southern Decorative Arts.)

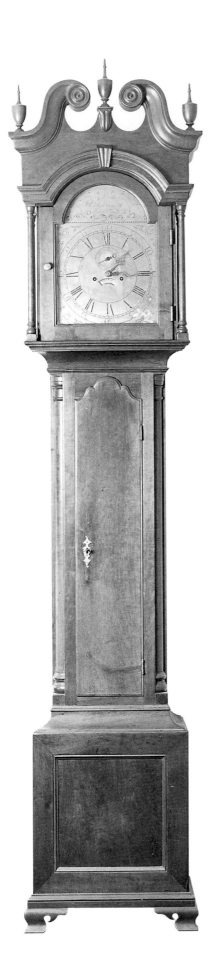

Figure 24 Tall clock with an eight-day movement signed "Elijah Evans Frederick Town," Maryland, 1780–1789. Cherry with tulip poplar. H. 98¼", W. 21½", D. 11½". (Private collection; photo, Museum of Early Southern Decorative Arts.)

manic stylistic and structural conventions. History suggests that understanding these overlays of culture is more complex than identifying the origins of individual details. North German styles were introduced into England with the crowning of George I and the subsequent influx of Hanoverians into Britain. Conversely, Germanic artisans returning home carried British details with them.

A clock case with a movement inscribed "Thos. Liddell Frederik Town 1760" is from a different cabinet shop (fig. 25), but it shares several important features with the Evans and Myer examples. It has a waist door with a small shell like the Myer clock (fig. 21) and ogee feet with spurlike cusps, a high arched pediment, and a tympanum similar to those on the Evans example (fig. 24). On the Liddell case, however, the side moldings of the cornice return partially around the front and function as imposts for the scroll moldings above. Below each cornice return is a fluted block intended to represent a pilaster. Similar blocks appear on the pediments of other case pieces from the region as well as on numerous Pennsylvania examples. High arched pediments and tympana with tight, semicircular cutouts like those on the Liddell and Evans clocks are common on other furniture from the Frederick Town area. These profiles also have numerous parallels in case furniture from Pennsylvania; however, it is unclear whether the designs came from England, the Continent, or the Middle Atlantic region.

The Liddell case has several other details that appear repeatedly on furniture from western Maryland. The overlapping-diamond fretwork on the frieze (fig. 26) is repeated in various forms on at least a half-dozen case pieces made in the vicinity of Frederick Town during the last quarter of the eighteenth century. The incurved ogee feet on the Liddell clock, which are the earliest and most pronounced of their form, are probably based on British prototypes. Incurved ogee feet occur on furniture from southeastern Pennsylvania, the Tidewater region of Virginia, northeastern North Carolina, New York, and Connecticut. They are, however, unusual in Frederick County, where straight bracket feet or conventional ogee feet were the norm.

As the preceding clock cases suggest, the convergence of tradesmen and patrons from different cultures resulted in the production of distinctive and surprisingly creative furniture forms in western Maryland. This diversity is further illustrated by a group of desk-and-bookcases, clock cases, and corner cupboards made in or near Frederick Town during the last quarter of the eighteenth century. Collectively, these objects reveal a great deal about the cabinetmaking trade in the town and the evolution of furniture styles within the region.

Figure 25 Tall clock with an eight-day move-
ment signed and dated "Thos. Liddell Frederik
Town 1760," Maryland. Walnut with tulip poplar
and yellow pine. H. 102³/8", W. 20¹/4", D. 10¹/2".
(Courtesy, Historical Society of Frederick County,
Maryland; photo, Gavin Ashworth.)

Figure 26 Detail of the waist door of the tall
clock illustrated in fig. 25. (Photo, Gavin Ashworth.)

Frederick Town cabinetmakers made desk-and-bookcases with complex
interiors prior to the Revolutionary War. In 1770, Henry Wilson sold his
neighbor John Fillson "one Black Walnut Desk carved work in the Inside
with a prospect door." The desk-and-bookcase illustrated in figure 27 has a
history of ownership by Barbara Fritchie, a nineteenth-century resident of
Frederick Town. It has a writing compartment with concave-blocked
drawer fronts, elaborately shaped pigeonhole dividers, and a prospect door
flanked by pilasters and surmounted by a dentiled architrave (figs. 27, 28).
Both the pilasters and architrave pull out to reveal document drawers, and
the entire prospect section conceals ten secret drawers. The spandrels, keystone, moldings, and facade of the prospect door are carved from the solid.
The shells and leaves resemble those on the doors of the Myer and the Liddell clocks (figs. 22, 26), and the fluted pilasters and dentils of the architrave
have parallels in early dower chests and clock cases from the region (see figs.
4–7, 25). The cases are constructed using full-depth dustboards that are thinner than the drawer rails. Like the "HS" chest (fig. 7) and the Rohrer desk
(fig. 8), the bottoms of the large drawers of the desk-and-bookcase are
nailed from beneath to the lower edges of the drawer sides, but here, small
strips are attached to the bottoms to serve as runners.[35]

The desk-and-bookcase illustrated in figure 29 has doors with highly
figured walnut panels and circular carved fans. No other furniture from
western Maryland or the Middle Atlantic region has fans that are comparable in size or placement. Small carved fans were popular furniture ornaments in both regions, but they were usually limited to the valances of
pigeonholes, small interior or exterior drawers, and prospect doors. Quarter-fans and half-fans were the most common varieties, but examples carved
in the round were occasionally employed.

Figure 27 Desk-and-bookcase, Frederick Town, Maryland, 1780–1800. Walnut with tulip poplar. H. 96½", W. 45", D. 21⅞". (Collection of the Museum of Early Southern Decorative Arts.) The bookcase section has been shortened.

Figure 28 Detail of the prospect of the desk-and-bookcase illustrated in fig. 27.

Figure 29 Desk-and-bookcase, Frederick Town, Maryland, 1780–1800. Walnut with tulip poplar. H. 94", W. 42¹/₂", D. 23¹/₂". (Courtesy, Carlyle House Historic Park, owned by the Northern Virginia Regional Park Authority; photo, Gavin Ashworth.)

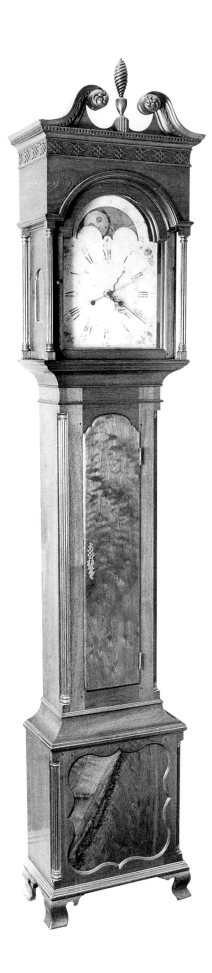

Figure 30 Tall clock, Frederick Town, Maryland, 1780–1800. Walnut with yellow pine. H. 104¼", W. 21¼", D. 11¼". (Private collection; photo, Museum of Early Southern Decorative Arts.)

Figure 31 Detail of the hood of the tall clock illustrated in fig. 30.

Figure 32   Tall clock with an eight-day movement signed "John Fessler," Frederick Town,
Maryland, 1780-1810. Cherry with tulip poplar.
Dimensions not recorded. (Private collection;
photo, Baltimore Museum of Art.)

Figure 33   Detail of the hood of the tall clock
illustrated in fig. 32.

Although different in form, the pediments of these desk-and-bookcases
are related in having both a frieze and cornice below their scroll pediments.
The pediment of the fan-carved example is similar in shape to those on a
number of Frederick Town case pieces derived from German prototypes, as
exemplified by the Schnertzel clock case (fig. 16). The pediment on the
Fritchie desk-and-bookcase (fig. 27) has higher scrolls, a tympanum with
broad, elliptical openings, and a fluted, half-round plinth for the central
finial. Variations of these last details also occur on an unsigned tall clock that
descended in the Schley family of Frederick County (figs. 30, 31) and on a
later example with a movement by John Fessler, Sr. (figs. 32, 33). These historical associations are extremely important because the Schley and Fessler
families were associated. In 1811, John Fessler, Jr., set up his clockmaking
business in the house of George Schley, whose brother John Jacob (1751–
1829) was a "Joynter."[36]

Figure 34 Corner cupboard, Frederick County, Maryland, 1780–1800. Walnut with tulip poplar. H. 91". (Courtesy, Historical Society of Frederick County, Maryland; photo, Gavin Ashworth.) The feet are old replacements.

The Schleys' parents, John Thomas (1712–1789) and Marta Margareta (Wintz von Wintz) (1712–1790), emigrated from Weurtzheim, Germany, and settled in Frederick Town in 1745. The records of the German Reformed Church refer to the father as a "schoolmaster," but in the first list of lot holders he is also described as an "innholder." John Thomas reportedly built the first house in Frederick Town in 1746.[37]

Figure 35 Detail of the carving on the corner cupboard illustrated in fig. 34. (Photo, Gavin Ashworth.)

John Jacob presumably served a seven-year apprenticeship beginning at the age of fourteen and probably began working independently about 1772. In that year, he received 250 board feet of walnut from Joseph Doll. In 1778, Schley married Anna Maria Shellman (1754–1843). Her father, John Mattheus (1724–1795), was a Rhenish joiner who arrived in Frederick Town by 1751. It is possible that Schley trained with Shellman since apprentices often married into the families of their masters.[38]

A tall clock with a movement by John Fessler, Sr., and a history of descent in the Shellman family (figs. 32, 33) provides an additional link between the desk-and-bookcases (figs. 27, 29) and the Schley family clock case (figs. 30, 31). All of these pieces have similarly shaped tympana, and the clock cases have rosettes with spiraling leafage, fretwork friezes, and cornice moldings with small ogee elements, broad flat dentils, and deep coves. Although it is impossible to attribute this furniture to a particular artisan, the physical evidence and histories associated with these objects point to a member (or members) of the Schley or Shellman families.[39]

Closely related to the preceding group are two corner cupboards (figs. 34–36), one of which was found near Myersville in Frederick County (fig. 34). Both cupboards have finials similar to the one on the Fritchie desk-and-bookcase (fig. 27), and one has a boldly carved fan in the arch of its upper door (figs. 36, 37). In form, the cupboards are virtually identical. Both have a pitched pediment with a Corinthian entablature, an arched, glazed door flanked by fluted pilasters, and a single drawer and paneled door below. The cupboard illustrated in figure 34 has replaced feet, but the original ones undoubtedly resembled those on the other example.[40]

The pediments and doors of these cupboards have a variety of classically inspired architectural details that set them apart from other western Maryland furniture: inlaid dentils and carved borders, finials, modillion blocks, rosettes, and Corinthian capitals. The only other Corinthian capitals in the

Figure 36 Corner cupboard, Frederick County, Maryland, 1780–1800. Walnut with tulip poplar. H. 89½". (Private collection; photo, Museum of Early Southern Decorative Arts.) The flame sections of the finials are missing.

region are on the entrance to Thomas Maynard's stone house built near New Market, Maryland, in 1809. His house has an eight-panel front door flanked by fluted Corinthian pilasters and capped by a six-light transom with a dentiled hood. Designs for architectural "frontispieces" may have provided the inspiration for these cupboards. Their overt architectural char-

Figure 37 Detail of the carved fan and mullions on the door of the corner cupboard illustrated in fig. 36.

Figure 38 Corner cupboard, Frederick County, Maryland, 1780–1800. Woods and dimensions not recorded. (Illustrated in Wallace Nutting, *Furniture Treasury* [New York: MacMillian Co., 1928], fig. 534.)

acter, relationship to the entrance of the Maynard house, and relatively coarse construction suggest that they were made by house joiners rather than cabinetmakers.[41]

Because the backboards extend only as high as the upper edge of the canted corners, the pediment head of each cupboard has a central ridge that slopes downward and flattens as it approaches the back corner. To provide an additional nailing surface and to reinforce the joint along the upper back edge, the joiner attached beaded battens at the juncture of the backboards and top. He also fitted each cupboard with serpentine shelves (with serpentine spoon slots), aligning them with the muntins of the doors.

With their complex ogee feet and superimposed pilasters, the corner cupboards illustrated in figures 38 and 39 are stylistically related to the preceding examples (figs. 34, 36). Both have molded keystones and double rows of offset dentils—details that occur with some frequency on other pieces from Frederick County. R. T. Haines Halsey probably purchased the cupboard illustrated in figure 38 in Maryland during the 1920s for collector Francis P. Garvan. The other example (fig. 39) descended in the Mahoney family of Frederick County. Several related cupboards have appeared in the marketplace over the last several years, including one inscribed "Frederick, Maryland."[42]

A tall chest inscribed "Francis Keyes" (figs. 40, 41) has several details that tie it to the Garvan and Mahoney cupboards. Keyes was an attorney who lived in Loudon County, Virginia, directly across the Potomac River from Frederick County. His chest has a broad, coved cornice, offset dentils, an applied shell with convex lobes on the top center drawer, and stop-fluted quarter-columns. The latter detail is common on furniture from northern

Figure 39 Corner cupboard, Frederick or Washington County, Maryland, 1790–1810. Tulip poplar. H. 100", W. 48½". (Private collection; photo, Museum of Early Southern Decorative Arts.)

Figure 40 Chest of drawers, Frederick County, Maryland, or Washington County, Virginia, 1780–1800. Walnut with yellow pine. H. 77⅞", W. 39¼", D. 23¼". (Private collection; photo, Greg Vaughan.) The feet and base molding are replaced.

Figure 41 Detail of the shell appliqué and cornice molding on the chest illustrated in fig. 40.

Figure 42 Tall clock, Frederick Town, Maryland, 1785–1800. Walnut with tulip poplar. H. 106", W. 23", D. 11⅛". (Private collection; photo, Gavin Ashworth.)

Figure 43 Detail of the hood of the tall clock illustrated in fig. 42. (Photo, Gavin Ashworth.)

Virginia, particularly the Winchester area, and it may have been introduced to western Maryland by tradesmen migrating up the Shenandoah Valley (figs. 16, 47). The chest also has a drawer support system commonly found on furniture from the Valley of Virginia, southeastern Pennsylvania, and Tennessee. The supports are dadoed and nailed to the sides of the case and tenoned into rails at the front and rear. This framework helps stabilize the case and provides a nailing surface for the vertical backboards.[43]

A related group of furniture made in Washington County, Virginia, in the southeastern corner of the state, has offset dentils, stop-fluted quarter-columns, and construction details similar to the Keyes chest and the corner cupboards illustrated in figures 38 and 39. These relationships may be more than circumstantial. Francis Keyes owned land in Washington County, Virginia, and married there in 1801. His wife, Polly, was the daughter of Joseph Meek of Hagerstown. Members of the Meek family and certain relatives in the Grubbe family were cabinetmakers who moved from Maryland to Washington County, then to Missouri during the late eighteenth and early nineteenth centuries.[44]

Like styles and construction techniques, furniture also moved from region to region. An exceptional tall case clock with unusual appliqués on

Figure 45 Tall clock with an eight-day movement signed "Valentine Steckell," Frederick Town, Maryland, 1790–1810. Walnut with tulip poplar. Dimensions not recorded. The feet and base molding are restored. (Courtesy, Historical Society of Frederick County, Maryland; photo, Gavin Ashworth.)

Figure 44 Tall clock with an eight-day movement signed "John Fessler," Frederick Town, Maryland, 1785–1800. Walnut with tulip poplar and white pine. H. 103¹/₂", W. 23", D. 11¹/₈". (Private collection; photo, Museum of Early Southern Decorative Arts.)

its tympanum (figs. 42, 43) is one of two related examples found in Shepherdstown, (West) Virginia. Although several scholars have attributed the clocks to Shepherdstown, evidence suggests that they were influenced by styles from western Maryland if not actually made there. The profile of the pediment, fluted appliqués on the edges of the tympanum, urn finials with broad, undercut rims, and superimposed quarter-columns (fluted above plain) are details associated with early Frederick Town production. The clock also has several highly individualistic features, including the stylized, chip-carved volutes at the scroll junctures, the magnolia pods (or stylized pine cones) capping the finials, the fluted, cylindrical pediment scrolls, and the stylized baroque keystone squeezed between the open rounds of the pediment.

A Frederick Town origin for the preceding clock (fig. 42) is strongly suggested by a related case with a movement by John Fessler, Sr. (fig. 44), and another, derivative of the previous two, with a movement by Valentine Steckell of Frederick Town (figs. 45, 46). Many artisans and their appren-

Figure 47 Corner cupboard, Frederick County, Maryland, 1780–1800. Walnut with yellow pine. H. 89¹/₂", W. 50¹/₂", D. 32¹/₄". (Courtesy, Sumpter Priddy III, Inc.) The upper case has been shortened.

Figure 48 Detail of one of the tympanum appliqués of the corner cupboard illustrated in fig. 47.

tices moved freely throughout the southern backcountry. Hagerstown clockmaker George Woltz owned several pieces of property in Shepherdstown, and other Maryland artisans are known to have spent time along the southern banks of the Potomac.[45]

An elaborate architectural corner cupboard (figs. 47, 48) provides additional evidence for attributing the clock case shown in figure 42 to western Maryland. Although the spandrel appliqués on the cupboard are considerably more sophisticated than the tympanum carving on the clock (figs. 43, 48), both designs feature C scrolls connected by chip-carved volutes. Another cupboard with related tympanum carving, stop-fluted pilasters, and gadrooned moldings has a history of descent in the Brindle family of

Figure 49 Corner cupboard, Frederick County, Maryland, 1780–1800. Yellow pine; polychrome paint. H. 96", W. 56½". (Private collection; photo, Gavin Ashworth.)

Figure 50 Detail of the entablature and cornice of the corner cupboard illustrated in fig. 49. (Photo, Gavin Ashworth.)

Hagerstown. Like other cupboards from the region, the example shown in figure 47 has plinth feet, an interior pilaster at the apex of the back, and stop-fluted pilasters. Similar details also occur on corner cupboards from northern Virginia.

The painted corner cupboard shown in figures 49 and 50 illustrates the difficulty of separating furniture made in western Maryland from contemporary northern Virginia work. The cupboard shares a number of stylistic features with Frederick County examples, including an elaborate, stepped cornice with an applied fret and Greek key molding, a large molded keystone surmounted by a truss with guttae blocks and a fluted plinth, stop-

Figure 51 Windsor chair, Frederick County, Maryland, ca. 1810. Maple and tulip poplar; painted. H. 33½", W. 21¼", D. 16". (Private collection; photo, Gavin Ashworth.)

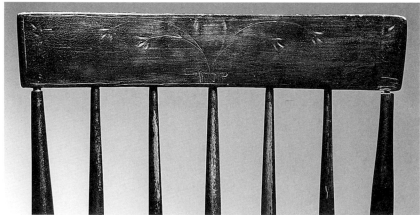

Figure 52 Detail of the carving on the crest rail of the Windsor chair illustrated in fig. 51. (Photo, Gavin Ashworth.) The chip carving on the crest rail has flowers that turn outward like the relief carving on a group of Frederick County cupboards.

fluted pilasters and cants, and a crossetted architrave. The floral carving is related in design to that of two corner cupboards (figs. 34–37) and a Windsor chair with a Frederick Town history (figs. 51, 52). No other Frederick County cupboard has complex mullions like this example; however, a desk-

Figure 53   Armchair, Frederick County, Maryland, 1770–1790. Walnut with yellow pine. H. 39⅛", W. 22⅜" (seat). (Private collection; photo, Museum of Early Southern Decorative Arts.) This chair descended in the Tyler family of "The Shelter," in Prince William County, Virginia.

Figure 54   Side chair, probably Hagerstown, Maryland, 1770–1790. Walnut. Secondary woods and dimensions not recorded. (Illustrated in Pauline Pinkney, "George Woltz, Maryland Cabinetmaker," *Antiques* 35, no. 3 [March 1939]: 124–27.)

and-bookcase by Martinsburg, (West) Virginia, cabinetmaker John Shearer has doors that are similar. He made furniture for several Frederick Town residents and is believed to have moved there during the early nineteenth century. Although many furniture historians have described Shearer's work as "bizarre" and "eccentric," furniture historian Philip Zea has shown that his furniture has Scottish antecedents. The Scots-Irish were clearly a powerful cultural force in the southern backcountry, but their specific contributions to regional British material culture remain poorly understood.[46]

In addition to case furniture, cabinetmakers in western Maryland constructed a large number of chairs. The most common chair design in the region has a straight crest rail and a solid vase splat with a half-round bead on the shoulders (fig. 53). Although the basic design of the back appears to be derived from British or Chesapeake Bay region chairs, the shape of the arms and arm supports and the wedged, through-tenon construction (the seat rails pierce the back stiles) probably reflect Pennsylvania influences. Several variations of this chair design exist. An example that belonged to George Woltz has pointed "beads" on the shoulders of the splat (fig. 54), and a related set with pierced splats and serpentine crests has a Frederick Town history (fig. 55).

Figure 55   Side chair, Frederick Town, Maryland, 1770–1790. Walnut. H. 40½", W. 22¼", D. 19". (Courtesy, Colonial Williamsburg Foundation.)

Another group of straight-leg chairs differs only slightly from the standard Frederick County model (fig. 56). These chairs have a saddle-shaped crest rail with flared ears and a simple flared splat with three vertical piercings, each interrupted with a rounded ball or arch. Simple box stretchers and more complex "H" stretchers both appear on chairs in this group. When arms are added, they roll gently outward and have simple, rounded supports. Like the previous group, these chairs also have through-tenons at the juncture of the seat rails and rear stiles.

Figure 56 Armchair, Frederick Town, Maryland, 1770–1790. Walnut with white pine. H. 37¼", W. 21⅞" (seat). (Private collection; photo, Museum of Early Southern Decorative Arts.)

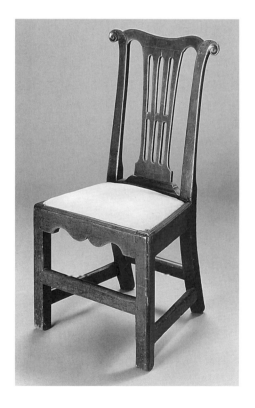

Figure 57 Side chair, Frederick County, Maryland, 1770–1800. Walnut. H. 37½", W. 18⅝", D. 14⅝". (Private collection; photo, Sumpter Priddy, Inc.)

Figure 58 Side chair, Frederick Town, Maryland, 1780–1800. Walnut with yellow pine. H. 39½", W. 17¼" (seat). (Courtesy, All Saints Parish; photo, Gavin Ashworth.)

The chair illustrated in figure 57 is clearly related to the previous examples in the shape of the splat, in the configuration of the legs and stretchers, and in the through-tenons of the seat frame. It differs from them, however, in

Figure 59   Corner cupboard, Frederick County, Maryland, 1780–1800. Cherry with tulip poplar and yellow pine. H. 107", W. 47½". (Courtesy, Henry Ford Museum and Greenfield Village.)

having parallel stiles, heavier stock, scrolled ears, and ogee shaping on the seat rail. The latter detail brings to mind the ogee shaping between the feet of the Myer clock (fig. 21).[47]

The finest Frederick County chairs, and those most clearly based upon Pennsylvania examples, consist of a set of six carved examples with pierced splats, shell-carved crests and knees, and claw-and-ball feet (fig. 58). They were apparently presented to All Saints Parish in Frederick Town by vestryman George Murdock (1768–1804). That these chairs were actually constructed for the church is strongly suggested by the symbolic dogwood blossom carved in the front rail. Dogwood blossoms are well documented on furniture made specifically for an ecclesiastical context. A chancel chair ordered by the vestry of Saint Michael's Church in Charleston, South Carolina, from the Philadelphia firm of Beal and Jameison in 1816 has dogwood blossoms carved on the crest and arm terminals.[48]

A remarkable corner cupboard (figs. 59, 60) with a variety of details garnered from different sources shows how the distinct character of western

Figure 60   Detail of the pediment of the corner cupboard illustrated in fig. 59.

Maryland furniture reflects the complex overlay of cultures within the region. Although its form and specific details suggest the work of a creative, and perhaps eccentric, artisan, the cupboard is, nevertheless, a composite of regional influences. The claw-and-ball feet, cabriole legs, and shell-carved knees, which resemble those on the chairs from All Saints Parish, are clearly based on Pennsylvania prototypes. Other details, however, are borrowed from the larger vocabulary of ornament popular in western Maryland and northern Virginia during the late eighteenth century. The three floral finials on the corner cupboard are related in concept to the frieze appliqués on the cupboard shown in figures 49 and 50, to the carved crest rail of the Windsor chair illustrated in figures 51 and 52, and to the carved mullions on the doors of the cupboards shown in figures 34–37. Like the corner cupboard with the C-scroll appliqués (figs. 47, 48), this example has a gadrooned ovolo capping the cornice (figs. 59, 60). It also has intaglio carving on the tympanum, which reflects the strong regional taste for naturalistic ornament on friezes and pediments. Other western Maryland details on the corner cupboard include the layered rosettes, shaped dentils, and crossetted architrave for the arched door. Similarly, the arched panels of the lower doors echo the Gothic interiors of fall-front desks made by John Shearer of Martinsburg, (West) Virginia. Other features of the cupboard appear to be unique in this region's furniture: the carved bead-and-reel molding on the cornice, the drill-work ornament on the outer finial plinths, and the unconventional mullion design.

Like the corner cupboard, many of the pieces discussed in this study represent the work of regional artisans who were challenged by the influx of people from Pennsylvania, eastern Maryland, and northern Virginia, who constantly weighed the new ideas they introduced, and who blended Germanic and British cultural traditions with their own personal experiences. Collectively, these influences compelled these artisans to produce objects that were distinctively their own yet reflected the tastes of the larger region in which they lived. This formula, repeated time and again at the crossroads of western Maryland, produced one of the most distinctive schools of furniture in eighteenth-century America.

ACKNOWLEDGMENTS   For assistance with this article the authors thank Joseph Adkins, John Bast, James Beachley, Luke Beckerdite, Collin Clavenger, Mary Ruth Coleman, Janet Davis, Julie Dennis, Gail Denny, William Voss Elder, III, Rebecca Fitzgerald, J. Michael Flanigan, Elizabeth Graff, Lisa Grygiel, Sean Guy, Wesley Harding, Ronald Hurst, Carrol H. Hendrickson, Jr., Sally and Roddy Moore, Jonathan Prown, Jackie Rogers, Susan Shames, N. Kenzie Smith and Sons, Bruce Shuettinger, John J. Snyder, Jr., Christine Steltzer, Marie Washburn, Gregory Weidman, James Whisker, Jean Woods, and Mr. and Mrs. William Yinger. We are especially grateful to the staff at the Museum of Early Southern Decorative Arts—Jennifer Bean, Frank Horton, Brad Rauschenberg, Martha Rowe, and Wesley Stewart—and to Edward and Helen Flanagan.

1. Donald Jackson and Dorothy Twohig, eds., *The Diaries of George Washington*, 6 vols. (Charlottesville: University Press of Virginia, 1978), 4:176. In Maryland, the towns below the fall line included Port Deposit on the Susquehanna and Georgetown on the Potomac. In Vir-

ginia, they included Fredericksburg on the Rappahannock, Richmond on the James, and Petersburg on the Appamattox. For examples of these period references to western Maryland, see *Archives of Maryland, Proceedings of the Council of Maryland*, 72 vols. (Baltimore: Maryland Historical Society, 1908), 28:25–26; and Daniel Dulany to Lord Baltimore, November 24, 1744, as quoted in Aubrey C. Land, *The Dulanys of Maryland* (Baltimore: Maryland Historical Society, 1955), p. 172.

2. *Archives of Maryland, Proceedings of the Council of Maryland*, 28:25–26. Lord Baltimore described this area as "the back lands on the Northern and Western boundaries of our said province not already taken up between the Rivers Potomack and Susqauehana." *Archives of Maryland, Proceedings of the Council of Maryland*, 46:142–44.

3. *Heads of Families at the First Census of the United States taken in the Year 1790, Maryland* (Baltimore, Md.: Southern Book Company, 1952), p. 9. J. Thomas Scharf, *History of Western Maryland*, 2 vols. (1882; reprint ed., Baltimore, Md.: Regional Publishing Company, 1968), 1:36, 396. William Harris Crawford Journals, June 4, 1813, Crawford Papers, Library of Congress, Washington, D.C.

4. Land, *Dulanys of Maryland*, p. 172. Between 1748 and 1764, the lot holders in Frederick Town included cabinetmakers, joiners, chairmakers, carpenters, gunmakers, blacksmiths, glassmakers, glasscutters, and other tradesmen (Amy Lee Huffman Reed and Marie LaForge Burns, *In and Out of Frederick Town, Colonial Occupations* [Frederick: by the authors, 1985], pp. 34–43). William Eddis, *Letters from America, Historical and Descriptive: Comprising Occurrences to 1777, Inclusive* (London: by the author, 1777), pp. 101–2.

5. Daniel Wunderlich Nead, *The Pennsylvania-German in the Settlement of Maryland* (1914; reprint ed., Baltimore, Md.: Genealogical Publishing Co., 1975), pp. 54–55. The name "Elizabeth Town" fell from favor during the 1780s, appears only sporadically during the 1790s, and all but disappears by 1800. Eddis, *Letters from America*, pp. 133–34.

6. Route 11 follows the path of the "Great Wagon Road" from Carlisle, Pennsylvania, into eastern Tennessee.

7. Artisan database, Museum of Early Southern Decorative Arts (hereinafter cited as MESDA), Winston-Salem, North Carolina.

8. For more on Germanic immigrants in Maryland, see Dieter Cunz, *The Maryland German, A History* (Princeton, N.J.: Princeton University Press, 1948).

9. *Archives of Maryland, Proceedings of the Council of Maryland*, 28:25–26. Thomas C. Williams and Folger McKinsey, *History of Frederick County, Maryland*, 2 vols. (1910; reprint ed., Baltimore, Md.: Regional Publishing Company, 1967), 1:7. Dwight P. Lanmon, Arlene Palmer Schwind, Ivor Hoel Hume, Robert H. Brill, and Victor F. Hanson, *John Frederick Amelung, Early American Glassmaker* (Corning, N.Y.: Corning Museum of Glass Press, 1990), p. 22. *Baltimore Daily Repository*, October 6, 1792, as quoted in H. E. Comstock, *Pottery of the Shenandoah Valley Region* (Chapel Hill: University of North Carolina Press for MESDA, 1994), p. 11. Eddis, *Letters from America*, p. 99.

10. Frederick County Court (Land Records) Book G, 1761–1762, p. 351 [MSA C485]. The document was signed in German script. For other related chests, see Monroe Fabian, *The Pennsylvania German Painted Chest* (New York: Main Street Press, 1978).

11 For information on the Loose and Beachtel families and "White Oak Forest Farm," see David and Susan Miller, Loose Family Genealogy, unpublished, undated manuscript on file at the Washington County Historical Society, Hagerstown, Maryland.

12. Indenture of Tille Dorff, February 25, 1805, Frederick County Register of Wills (indentures), GMC 1801–1808, p. 466 (MSA C799-1).

13. Easton, Maryland, collector Benjamin Palmer purchased this *schrank* during the 1960s from dealer Stoll Kemp of New Market in Frederick County. A western Maryland corner cupboard with three fluted pilasters was sold at Sotheby's, *Fine Americana*, New York, June 23 and 24, 1994, lot 466.

14. Inlaid diamonds were commonly used between numbers and letters on Pennsylvania German pieces. See, for example, a tall case clock with a movement by Benjamin Morris of New Britain, Bucks County, Pennsylvania, in Israel Sack, Inc., *American Antiques From the Israel Sack Collection* (Alexandria, Va.: Highland House, 1979), vol. 10, p. 1502, no. P4581.

15. A much simpler chest by the same maker is in a private collection. It is inlaid with the initials "SB" and dated "17•81." It has the same base molding and foot blocking as the chest shown in fig. 7, and very similar feet. The authors thank Edward and Helen Flanagan for this information.

16. For the history of the desk, see MESDA research file S-9745.

17. The authors thank Edward and Helen Flanagan for bringing this chest to their attention. Seventeenth-century arms makers occasionally used colored mastic fillers. The authors thank Wallace Gusler for this comparative information.

18. One or two other chests by this decorator are known; one is in a private collection, and the other is pictured in Gregor Norman-Wilcox, "American Furniture, Noteworthy and Unrecorded," *Antiques* 36, no. 5 (December 1939): 283, fig. 3.

19. Charles Edward Doll III, 300 Years of the Doll Family, unpublished manuscript, Mount Clemens, Michigan, p. 4. John J. Snyder, Jr., "Carved Chippendale Case Furniture from Lancaster, Pennsylvania," *Antiques* 107, no. 5 (May 1975): 975.

20. Doll, 300 Years of the Doll Family, pp.5–7.

21. Joseph Doll Ledger, 1772–1805, Historical Society of Frederick County, Inc., Frederick, Maryland.

22. Joseph Doll's ledger contains the following entries for bedsteads: Henry Shover, October 1773, "one pair of bedSteds Painted Green... £1.5"; Francis Mantz, January 10, 1775, "one bedstid . . . 12s"; John Brunner, Jr., July 8, 1775, "one pair of bedStids at 3 dollars . . . £1.2"; John Hummel, March 29, 1777, "one Little bedStid . . . 12s"; Michael Christ, February 1787, "one bedStid with high Posts painted blue with four Scroos . . . £2.7.6. "Doll's ledger contains the following entries for cradles: Christian Weaver, November 26, 1774, "one Greadle to Rog his Chylde . . . £1"; John Brunner, Jr., July 8, 1775, "a Creadle . . . 18s."

23. Joseph Doll's ledger contains the following entries for tables: Francis Mantz, September 1773, "one Walnut Table with Two Drawers . . . £1.5"; John Brunner, Jr., July 8, 1775, "making a Table at 20 . . . £1"; Caspar Mantz, September 26, 1775, "one Table for his Daughter Caety . . . £1.2.6"; Jacob Stealey, October 11, 1775, "one Table with 2 Drawers and brass hands . . . £1.7.6"; Peeter Brunner, March 18, 1777, "one Walnut Table at Three dollars . . . £1.2.6"; Mathias Zimmer, February 10, 1786, "one Kitchin Table . . . £1.5.0"; John Hoober, February 2, 1775, "one Larch Pobler Table for a workebench with Two Trawers in it with divicions . . . £1.7."

24. Joseph Doll's ledger contains the following entries for case furniture: John Brunner, Jr., February 6, 1775, "one Kitchin Cobert . . . 3.15"; Caspar Mantz, September 26, 1775, "one Chest with drawers for ditto [daughter Caety] . . . £3.5"; Peeter Brunner, February 16, 1776, "one Kitchen Dresser with glas and furniture . . . £ 7"; John Kyle, March 7, 1789, "one Corner Cobbert . . . £4.10."

25. Joseph Doll's ledger contains the following entries for coffins: John Breidenbach, May 15, 1775, "To one Coffin . . . 10s"; Peeter Brunner, December 8, 1775, "To one Coffin . . . 10s"; Peeter Brunner, February 16, 1776, "To one Coffin for his Son John at 25/ . . . £1.5"; Christian Weaver, November 26, 1776, "One Smol Coffin for his Childe . . . 5s"; Peeter Brunner, March 18, 1777, "To one Coffin for his Father . . . 1.15"; John Brunner, Jr., undated, "one Coffin for his Father . . . £1.10"; Phillip Friegi, January 14, 1788, "One Coffin for M [illegible] Wittman . . . £1.5." In 1774, Doll charged Thomas Preise 1s 6d for "mending Two Chairs." On June 16, 1790, Doll charged Henry Cronier 2s 9d for "Making a Sidepeese to his bedStid paint blue."

26. James Biser Whisker, Daniel David Hartzler, and Steven P. Petrucelli, *Maryland Clockmakers* (Cranberry, N.J.: Adams Brown, Co., 1996), pp. 30–31. Fessler served his apprenticeship in Lancaster.

27. Ibid., pp. 113, 227, 335, and figs. 15, 16, 245, 246, 226–69.

28. Deed from Jonathan Hager to George Woltz, Frederick County Land Records, bk. 5, 1773–1774, p. 205 The tall clock illustrated in fig. 18 is illustrated and discussed in Pauline Pinkney, "George Woltz, Maryland Cabinetmaker," *Antiques* 35, no. 3 (March 1939): 124–25. See also James W. Gibbs, *Dixie Clockmakers* (Gretna, La.: Pelican Publishing Co., 1979), p. 83.

29. Gibbs, *Dixie Clockmakers,* p. 83. Pinkney attributes a small but fine group of local furniture to Woltz and notes that "he advertised in contemporary papers that he made chairs and spinning wheels." None of the advertisements abstracted from local newspapers by MESDA refer to the manufacture of chairs or spinning wheels, thus it is likely that Pinkney was mistaken. Furniture historian Gregory R. Weidman also suggested that Woltz may have been a cabinetmaker in *Maryland Furniture, 1740–1790: The Collection of the Maryland Historical Society* (Baltimore, Md.: Maryland Historical Society, 1984), pp. 130–31.

30. For more on Itnyer, see Whisker, Hartzler, and Petrucelli, *Maryland Clockmakers*, pp. 46, 170, figs. 124–25.

31. For information on related cases from the Lancaster area, see John J. Snyder, "The Bachman Attributions: A Reconsideration," *Antiques* 105, no. 5 (May 1974): 1056–66.

32. Inventory of William Conrad, July 1, 1780, Washington County, Maryland, Inventories No. B, 1785–1803, pp. 99–101. We do not believe that Woltz made the cases for his movements. These cases, which date between 1780 and 1810, were made by a group of artisans working in the Hagerstown area. For examples, see William Voss Elder III, *Maryland Queen Anne and Chippendale Furniture* (Baltimore, Md.: Baltimore Museum of Art, 1968), p. 100, fig. 69; MESDA research files S-9702 and S-9764 (by the same case maker as the example illustrated in figs. 19–20 of this article); Israel Sack, Inc., *American Antiques From the Israel Sack Collection*, vol. 5, p. 1169, no. P4030; Maryland Historical Society, acc. 63.19.1; Colonial Williamsburg Foundation, acc. 1980-200. The aforementioned examples are in approximate chronological order.

33. The Grieff clock was owned by antique dealer Andrew Golding of Charleston, South Carolina, in the summer of 1996.

34. Pennsylvania tall clocks often have carved shells on the waist door. Occasionally they have shells used as keystones over the hood door. A Pennsylvania clock case with a shell-carved door descended in the Dorsey family of Frederick County. It is virtually identical to examples with movements signed by Isaac Thomas, a clockmaker and case maker who worked in Willistown in Chester County, Pennsylvania (MESDA research file S-9546). For more on Thomas, see Arthur E. James, *Chester County Clocks and Their Makers* (1946; reprint ed., Exton, Pa.: Schiffer Publishing Co., 1976), pp. 188–89.

35. The purchaser of Wilson's desk was probably John Fillson (b. 1747) of East Fallowfield, Pennsylvania. Fillson spent much of his early life on his father's lands on the Brandywine, but he attended Reverend Samuel Finley's school in Nottingham, Maryland (Willard Rouse Jillson, *Filson's Kentucky* [Louisville, Ky.: John P. Morton and Co., 1929], pp. 139–49). Fillson lived in Frederick County, Maryland, in 1770 (Frederick County Land Records, March 6, 1770, bk. N, 1770–1772, p. 38), then moved back to Pennsylvania and on to Kentucky. A Henry Wilson owned fifty acres in two tracts of land called "Stoney Point" and "Labyrinth" (Donna Valley Russell, "Frederick County Debt Book, 1756–1757," *Western Maryland Genealogy* 8, no. 3 [July 1992]: 131). A Henry Wilson also appears in Frederick County in the 1776 census of Maryland (Bettie Stirling Carothers, comp., *The 1776 Census of Maryland* [Westminster, Md.: Family Line Publications, 1992], p. 72), but no one by that name is listed in the *Heads of Families at the First Census of the United States taken in the Year 1790*. MESDA acc. file 3985. Barbara Fritchie, a local Civil War heroine and Yankee sympathizer, was the subject of John Greenleaf Whittier's 1863 poem "Barbara Fritchie." She and her husband, John, lived in a small brick cottage at 154 West Patrick Street in Frederick.

36. For the history of the Schley family clock, see MESDA research file S-9693. For an illustration, see Whisker, Hartzler and Petrucelli, *Maryland Clockmakers,* p. 214, figs. 219–20. *Frederick Herald*, November 2, 1816. Although the *Herald* reported that Fessler had set up shop "in the house of Mr. John Schley," family genealogy indicates that "John" Schley was the nickname of George Thomas Schley. John Thomas Schley is commonly referred to in documents as "Thomas" and John Jacob Schley as "Jacob." Tyre Lee Jennings III, The Schley Family, unpublished manuscript, Houston, Texas, 1990. Joseph Doll Ledger, p. 27.

37. Scharf, *History of Western Maryland*, 1:485. John Jacob Schley moved to Georgia in the winter of 1793 (Jennings, Schley Family, p. 101). Reed and Burns, *In and Out of Frederick Town,* pp. 34–36, 40.

38. Joseph Doll Ledger, p. 27. Jennings, Schley Family, p. 101. Reed and Burns, *In and Out of Frederick Town*, p. 51. Williams and McKinsey, *History of Frederick County*, 2:1314.

39. An early twentieth-century document indicates that the Fessler clock was purchased at the estate sale of John Jacob Shellman by his daughter, Mrs. George Harris, and that it remained in the care of her daughter until the 1880s. It was then purchased by Dr. Daniel J. Hanes. It subsequently descended to his daughter, Miss Maria W. Hanes.

40. For the history of the cupboard illustrated in fig. 34, see MESDA research file S-9263.

41. For more on the Maynard's house, see Historic Sites Survey, New Market Region, August 1994, Frederick County Department of Planning and Zoning. A small group of freestanding cupboards and a built-in cupboard from Frederick County, Virginia, are the only other pedimented examples with peaked roofs known to us. Although relatively little work has been done to trace the movement of artisans between the upper Valley of Virginia and western Maryland, several artisans are known to have worked in both areas, including members of the Krebs family, who were both gunmakers and cabinetmakers during the late eighteenth century.

42. Garvan loaned the cupboard to the Hammond-Harwood House in Annapolis during the 1930s and 1940s. A founder of the Metropolitan Museum's American Wing, Halsey was a professor at St. John's College in Annapolis. The records related to his collecting are preserved in the Archives of American Art, Washington, D.C. For more on Halsey as a collector, see Elizabeth Stillinger, *The Antiquers* (New York: Alfred Knopf, 1980). The cupboard inscribed "Frederick, Maryland," was owned by San Francisco antiques dealer Thomas Livingston in 1995.

43. Loudoun County Court Order Book G, 1776–1783, p. 75.

44. For information on the Meeks and Grubbe families, see Danny Morris Fluhart, *The Meek Family of Washington County, Virginia* (Waldorf, Md.: by the author, n.d.), n.p. The authors thank Roddy Moore for information on the Keyes, Meeks, and Grubble families and the group of furniture from Southwest, Virginia.

45. Whisker, Hartzler, and Petrucelli, *Maryland Clockmakers*, pp. 102–3.

46. For more on Frederick County Windsor chairs, see Nancy Goyne Evans, *American Windsor Chairs* (New York: Hudson Hills Press for the Winterthur Museum, 1996), pp. 117–23. John J. Snyder, Jr., "John Shearer, Joiner of Martinsburg," *Journal of Early Southern Decorative Arts* 5, no. 1 (May 1979): 1–25. Philip Zea and Donald Dunlap, *The Dunlap Cabinetmakers: A Tradition in Craftsmanship* (Mechanicsburg, Pa.: Stackpole Books, 1994), pp. 40–41.

47. A set of Philadelphia area chairs with cabriole legs and trifid feet, originally owned by Benjamin Franklin, have a virtually identical splat, ears, crest, and front rail. These chairs, however, are considerably lighter in construction and have typical Philadelphia blocking inside their seat frames. It is likely that both groups have a common British prototype.

48. George W. Williams, *St. Michael's Charleston, 1751–1951* (Columbia: University of South Carolina Press, 1951), p. 175.

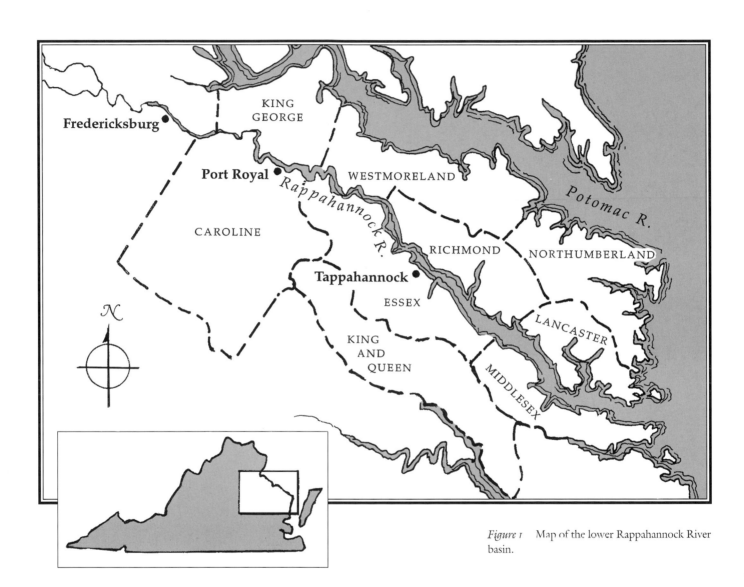

Figure 1 Map of the lower Rappahannock River basin.

Ronald L. Hurst

Irish Influences on Cabinetmaking in Virginia's Rappahannock River Basin

▼ DURING THE LAST twenty-five years, research has dramatically increased our understanding of the furniture trade in eighteenth-century Tidewater Virginia. In the course of this work, scholars have rightly looked to contemporary England as the main source of stylistic and structural detailing in Tidewater furniture, a pattern that mirrors the Anglocentric focus of many southern historians. Because England was the dominant economic and cultural force in the eastern part of the colony, the elite routinely ordered cabinetwares from London, Liverpool, and other English ports until the outbreak of the Revolution. An even greater impact on eastern Virginia's furniture industry came from the significant numbers of English joiners and cabinetmakers who emigrated to the towns and rural districts of the coastal plain during the second and third quarters of the century. These transplanted artisans continued to make vast quantities of furniture in the English taste, and they trained hundreds of Virginia-born apprentices to carry on the same traditions.[1]

Perhaps because of England's preeminent role in the development of the Virginia furniture industry, little attention has been given to the role played by immigrant cabinetmakers from other parts of the British Isles. The dearth of published information about the furniture of Ireland, Scotland, and Wales has certainly hindered such research. However, as furniture historians on both sides of the Atlantic have begun to identify specific Irish, Scottish, and Welsh cabinetmaking traditions, it has become apparent that artisans from those places did shape some localized cabinetmaking practices in Virginia and the other southern colonies. One of the clearest examples of this phenomenon is found in the lower Rappahannock River basin, where a remarkable body of cabinetwares made in several shops from the 1750s to the 1770s exhibits strong evidence of Irish design influence.[2]

Almost entirely rural in the eighteenth century, the narrow peninsulas on both sides of the Rappahannock River supported a mix of small and middling farms and sizable plantations (fig. 1). The landowners grew tobacco and, later, grain for export to Europe and the West Indies. Ships from British ports commonly sailed directly to local river landings where they off-loaded imported manufactured goods and took on cash crops in return. Considerable commercial activity also occurred in Fredericksburg at the falls of the Rappahannock. The area's largest market center, it had a population of about fifteen hundred by 1775. Much smaller but still important to local commerce were the villages of Port Royal in Caroline County and Tappahannock in Essex County, each with an estimated population of a few hundred.[3]

Structural and stylistic analysis indicates that Irish-influenced furniture from the Rappahannock basin was made in three or more shops. The exact locations of these businesses are unknown, but Tappahannock is the best candidate since much of the furniture in question was originally owned within the adjacent counties of Essex and Richmond. Despite its small size, Tappahannock was an official port of entry where as many as a half-dozen ships were commonly anchored. The town had a Masonic Lodge, an impressive brick courthouse, a room for public balls or "assemblies," and a number of gentry residences. Cabinetmaker John Nesmith is known to have worked in Tappahannock from 1778 to 1789, and there were almost certainly others. On the other hand, some of the furniture in this study may have been made in nearby rural shops. Between 1730 and 1790, the counties of Essex and Richmond alone were home to at least ten artisans who called themselves cabinetmakers. Some of these tradesmen probably made furniture during the winter months but farmed during the spring, summer, and fall.[4]

Figure 2 Card table, Ireland, ca. 1760. Mahogany with deal. H. 29", W. 33", D. 17½". (Courtesy, Malahide Castle, Ron and Doreen McDonnell Collection; photo, Gavin Ashworth.)

Figure 3 Detail of a foot on the card table illustrated in fig. 2. (Photo, Gavin Ashworth.)

The most obvious evidence of Irish influences on Rappahannock cabinetwares is found in the local popularity of several standard Irish foot forms, including one that Irish furniture historians term the trifid foot. Not to be confused with the American interpretation of that word, the Irish trifid features a large, rounded central lobe flanked by a pair of small, tightly scrolled volutes. Only occasionally encountered in England, the trifid was one of the two or three most widely used foot forms in Ireland from the 1720s to the

Figure 4 Side chair, lower Rappahannock River basin, Virginia, 1760–1775. Cherry. H. 37³/₈", W. 21¹/₂", D. 17³/₄". (Private collection; photo, Hans Lorenz.)

Figure 5 Detail of a foot on the side chair illustrated in fig. 4.

1780s. Trifid feet could be plain or exuberantly carved, depending on the overall ornamentation of the object, but the voluted form remained relatively constant. A representative example of the Irish trifid foot appears on the card table illustrated in figures 2 and 3. This foot is remarkably similar to those on a set of side chairs made in the lower Rappahannock basin during the 1760s or 1770s (figs. 4, 5). Originally upholstered over-the-rail, the chairs descended in the Beverley family of Blandfield plantation in Essex County. Outside the Rappahannock basin, the scrolled trifid foot is unknown in Virginia, and it is rare in other American centers except for Philadelphia, where the form was employed thirty to forty years earlier.[5]

The same Rappahannock shop that made the trifid-foot chairs also made furniture with paneled feet, to use the current Irish term. Examples include a second set of side chairs with a history in the Beverley family (figs. 6, 7) and a corner chair originally owned by the Garnett family at Peach Grove

Figure 6   Side chair, lower Rappahannock River basin, Virginia, 1760–1775. Cherry. H. 37½", W. 21½", D. 18". (Private collection; photo, Hans Lorenz.)

Figure 7   Detail of a foot on the side chair illustrated in fig. 6.

plantation in King and Queen County about fifteen miles from Tappahannock (fig. 8). All of these chairs have splats cut from the same template, and all were made of cherry, one of the area's most popular primary woods. The paneled feet on the Beverley and Garnett chairs nearly match those on a circa 1750 game table at Glin Castle in County Limerick (figs. 9, 10). Found on hundreds of other surviving Irish tables and chairs, the paneled format was easily the most common Irish foot form of the day. Again rare in English furniture, its scattered appearance in American cabinet centers such as Philadelphia is usually associated with the presence of immigrant Irish artisans.[6]

The dressing or writing table shown in figure 11 also appears to be from a contemporary Rappahannock shop. The paneled feet, while not identical, are quite similar to those on the Beverley and Garnett chairs. Although the early history of the table is unknown, it features important structural characteristics associated with eastern Virginia furniture. In particular, the thin

Figure 8 Corner chair, lower Rappahannock River basin, Virginia, 1760–1775. Cherry with yellow pine. H. 35⅝". (Private collection; photo, Hans Lorenz.)

Figure 9 Game table, Ireland, ca. 1750. Mahogany with deal and oak. H. 27", W. 31", D. 21⅜". (Courtesy, Glin Castle Collection; photo, Gavin Ashworth.) The table is shown without its reversable top.

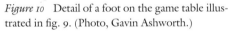

Figure 10   Detail of a foot on the game table illustrated in fig. 9. (Photo, Gavin Ashworth.)

Figure 11   Writing or dressing table, lower Rap-
pahannock River basin, Virginia, 1760–1775.
Cherry with yellow pine. H. 28³/₈", W. 35¹/₄",
D. 19¹/₂". (Courtesy, Colonial Williamsburg
Foundation; photo, Hans Lorenz.)

Figure 12   Detail of a knee block from the table
illustrated in fig. 11.

Figure 13 Tea table with drawer, Ireland, 1750–1765. Mahogany with deal and oak. H. 28⅝", W. 32", D. 20⅜". (Courtesy, Colonial Williamsburg Foundation; photo, Hans Lorenz.)

Figure 14 Detail of a carved knee from the table illustrated in fig. 13.

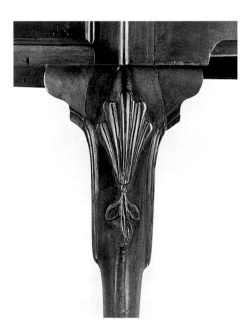

Figure 15 Detail of a carved knee from the table illustrated in fig. 11.

knee blocks are glued directly to the front of the rails, an English technique transplanted to parts of the coastal South (fig. 12). The knee blocks on tables and chairs from other American cabinet centers, including those in the Delaware Valley, generally are much heavier and are glued and nailed to the underside of the rails. Contemporary, single-drawer Irish tables akin to the Rappahannock example survive in large numbers (fig. 13). Their cabriole legs frequently have elongated, carved scallop shells and pendant leaves flanked by pairs of partial knee scrolls, a particularly popular combination in Ireland (figs. 14, 15). Similar ornament appears on the tables illustrated in figures 2, 22, and 24. The pairing of a straight front apron with slightly shaped side aprons also parallels Irish precedent. Although many of these individual details can be found on English furniture, their combined use here argues for an Irish design source.

Representing the work of a different Rappahannock shop, but similarly Irish influenced, are the remains of a high chest of drawers that descended in the Finch family of King George County, across the river from northern Essex (fig. 16). The chest has lost its upper case and its lower drawers. The drawer supports were incorrectly replaced during the 1950s when the knee blocks and the center section of the front rail were conjecturally restored. Despite its poor condition, the object still speaks to its cultural origins. In particular, its heavily articulated paneled feet and the pronounced, deeply molded partial knee scrolls that end abruptly above the ankle suggest strong ties to Irish furnituremaking traditions. In addition to these ornamental details, the mere presence of a high chest of drawers in colonial eastern Virginia points toward an Irish connection. Only two Tidewater high chests

Figure 16 Base of a high chest of drawers, Rappahannock River basin, Virginia, 1745–1760. Black walnut with yellow pine. H. 31", W. 41½", D. 23". (Courtesy, Colonial Williamsburg Foundation; photo, Hans Lorenz.)

survive—both in fragmentary condition. The form was considered old-fashioned in English urban centers by the 1720s or 1730s and was succeeded by case forms such as the clothespress. Most middling and gentry householders in coastal Virginia willingly followed the English lead, as demonstrated by the large number of Virginia clothespresses that survive. The high chest, however, remained in production in Irish cities as late as the 1780s, which probably accounts for its late appearance in the Rappahannock basin.[7]

The dressing table illustrated in figure 17 is from the same shop that produced the Finch high chest. Although it stands on simply turned pad feet and lacks the diminutive, carved scallop shell on the knee, the cabriole legs exhibit deeply molded partial knee scrolls identical to those on the high chest. Other parallels are found in the similarly shaped side and front rails and the construction of the side and back panels, the latter identical down to the placement of the triple joint pins. Fragments of the original drawer supports in the high chest suggest that they matched those in the dressing table. The table has long been attributed to Williamsburg because of its discovery in the Wornom family of nearby York County in the 1930s, but a recent survey of early Virginia tax, census, and court records reveals that all identifiable members of the Wornom family lived in Northumberland County during the eighteenth century. Situated at the tip of Virginia's Northern Neck, Northumberland shares its southwestern border with Richmond County, where a number of the objects in this study were first owned.[8]

A tea table recorded in the J. K. Beard photographic collection at Colonial Williamsburg may well be from the shop that produced the Finch and Wornom pieces (fig. 18). Until his death in 1940, Beard was Virginia's most active and noted dealer in southern furniture. With a base of operations in

Figure 17 Dressing table, Rappahannock River basin, Virginia, 1745–1760. Black walnut with yellow pine. H. 28½", W. 29⅞", D. 20⅞". (Collection of the Museum of Early Southern Decorative Arts, gift of Mr. and Mrs. Thomas S. Douglas, III.)

Figure 18 Tea table, Rappahannock River basin, Virginia, 1745–1760. Woods and dimensions not recorded. (Courtesy, Colonial Williamsburg Foundation; photo, J. K. Beard collection, ca. 1935.)

the city of Richmond, forty miles southeast of Tappahannock, Beard's early photographs confirm that he handled many of the most important pieces of southern furniture now in the region's public and private collections. The boldly formed rectangular tea table illustrated in figure 18 was among the objects Beard owned in the 1920s or 1930s. Its cabriole legs and heavily molded partial knee scrolls are remarkably similar to those on the high chest and the dressing table, and its deep, shapely aprons are reminiscent of those on both pieces. The tea table features the so-called slipper foot, another typically Irish form. Widely popular in the lower Rappahannock basin, the slipper foot, again, is unknown in the rest of Virginia and rare elsewhere in America except for early eighteenth-century Philadelphia and New York and midcentury Newport, Rhode Island.[9]

Irish slipper-foot tables often have sparely ornamented but well-shaped cabriole legs like those on a table found in Dublin early in this century (fig. 19). Similarly conceived legs and feet appear on a group of Rappahannock tables from the third quarter of the eighteenth century, among them a tea table with a history in the Beverley family at Blandfield (fig. 20). An identical table by the same artisan was acquired by Colonial Williamsburg in 1928 from Bessie Brockwell, a Petersburg dealer in Virginia antiquities (fig. 21). Both tables exhibit simplified versions of the busily shaped aprons seen on many Irish tea tables (figs. 22–24), as well as the indented corners common to both Irish and English forms (figs. 25, 26). The artisan responsible for the two Rappahannock tea tables used the same foot and leg designs on a dining table with deep, well-shaped end rails (figs. 27, 28). Brockwell sold the latter table to the Colonial Williamsburg Foundation in 1932.[10]

Figure 19 Tea table, Ireland, 1740–1770. Mahogany with deal. Dimensions not recorded. (Private collection; courtesy, Glin Castle Irish Furniture Archive.)

Yet another Irish-influenced Rappahannock shop was responsible for a much larger dining table that descended in the Bates family of Essex County (fig. 29). Like the previous example, this piece has deep rails with shaped cut-outs at each end, and it stands on slipper feet. The frame and gate construction of the two dining tables is different, however, as are the details of their legs and feet. The cabriole legs on the Bates table are much straighter and stiffer than those on the tables shown in figures 20, 21, and 27, and the rear face of the slipper foot does not curve as sharply forward. A compara-

Figure 20 Tea table, Rappahannock River basin, 1755–1770. Black walnut. H. 28¹/₂", W. 38¹/₄", D. 22³/₄". (Private collection; photo, Hans Lorenz.)

Figure 21 Tea table, Rappahannock River basin, 1755–1770. Black walnut. H. 29", W. 38³/₄", D. 23⁵/₈". (Courtesy, Colonial Williamsburg Foundation.)

Figure 22 Tea table, Ireland, 1735–1750. European walnut with deal and other woods. Dimensions not recorded. (Private collection; courtesy, Glin Castle Irish Furniture Archive.) This table was found at Newbridge, County Dublin.

Figure 23 Detail of an end rail from the tea table illustrated in fig. 20.

tively plain, mahogany tea table with a history at Sabine Hall plantation, the Richmond County estate of the Landon Carter family, may well be associated with the Bates piece (fig. 30). Below the abruptly shaped knees, the legs are almost perfectly straight, and there is only a trace of the forward curve behind the slipper foot. The porringer top on the table is a modern, and probably inaccurate, replacement.[11]

Only one set of Virginia-made slipper-foot chairs is known, but their execution in black walnut and their history in the prominent Chinn family of Tappahannock argue for production in the Rappahannock basin (fig. 31). Although the chairs were not available for examination and have not been publicly seen since the 1952 exhibition, "Southern Furniture," at the Virginia Museum of Art, the minimally curved rear face of their feet points to a connection with the Bates and Carter family tables. The central drop on the front rail of the Chinn chairs is reminiscent of those on other Rappahannock furniture, including the Wornom dressing table, the Beard tea table, and the Beverley tea table (figs. 17, 18, 20).[12]

Figure 24 Tea table, Ireland, 1750–1760.
Mahogany. H. 30", W. 30", D. 21". (Courtesy,
Malahide Castle, Ron and Doreen McDonnell
Collection; photo, Gavin Ashworth.)

Figure 25 Detail of a corner on the top of the tea table illustrated in fig. 24. (Photo, Gavin Ashworth.)

Figure 26 Detail of a corner on the top of the tea table illustrated in fig. 20.

Figure 27 Dining table, Rappahannock River basin, 1755–1770. Black walnut with yellow pine. H. 29¹/₄", W. 44³/₄", D. (closed) 17", D. 46¹/₈" (open). (Courtesy, Colonial Williamsburg Foundation; photo, Hans Lorenz.)

Figure 28 Detail of an end rail from the dining table illustrated in fig. 27.

Figure 29 Dining table, Rappahannock River basin, 1755–1770. Black walnut with yellow pine. H. 28¹/₂". (Private collection; photo, Gavin Ashworth.) The top is replaced.

Figure 30 Tea table, Rappahannock River basin, 1750–1760. Mahogany. H. 26½", W. 24", D. 16½" (all dimensions are from the frame). (Private collection; photo, Museum of Early Southern Decorative Arts.) The top is replaced.

Figure 31 Side chair, Rappahannock River basin, 1745–1760. Black walnut. H. 39". (Private collection; photo, *Antiques* 61, no. 1 [January 1952]: 66, fig. 48.)

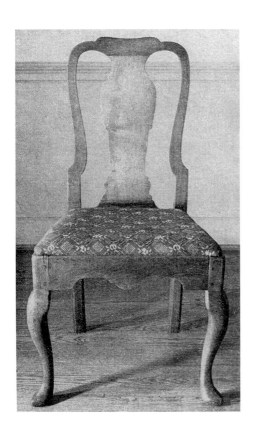

Evidence of Irish influence in the Rappahannock basin is not confined to individual details but also is seen in the presence of at least one typically Irish furniture form, the chest with drawers on cabriole stand. The example illustrated in figure 32, which descended in the Jeffreys family of Richmond County, stands on short cabriole legs with slipper feet similar to those on the Beverley tea table group. The chest on cabriole stand, only occasionally encountered in England and rare in America except in areas of Irish settlement, was one of the most frequently encountered case furniture forms in eighteenth-century Ireland. Irish examples more often have one tier of drawers instead of two, but variations in the stands are seemingly endless (fig. 33). Many feature carved and shaped skirts, which may be the inspiration for the extensively shaped front apron on the Jeffreys chest (figs. 32, 34). Two other southern chests feature double tiers of drawers, shaped aprons, cabriole legs, and slipper feet. Produced in a different shop, they are more coarsely constructed and probably later than the Jeffreys piece. Even so, they exhibit similar exposed dovetails and may well be from the Rappahannock basin.[13]

Most of the Irish-influenced furniture illustrated thus far fits into the east-

Figure 32 Chest on stand, Rappahannock River
basin, 1750–1765. Black walnut with yellow pine,
tulip poplar, and oak. H. 46¹/₂", W. 50⁵/₈",
D. 20¹/₈". (Private collection; photo, Gavin
Ashworth.)

Figure 33 Chest on stand, Ireland, 1740–1760. Mahogany. H. 41", W. 47", D. 25". (Private collection; courtesy, Sotheby's.)

Figure 34 Chest on stand, Ireland, 1740–1760. Mahogany. H. 39", W. 51", D. 35". (Private collection; courtesy, Sotheby's.)

ern Virginia preference for cabinetwares in the neat and plain style. One of the hallmarks, however, of eighteenth-century Irish furniture is the abundance of shallow but florid carving that decorates the often deep aprons of tea, card, and sideboard tables, chest on stands, and some other kinds of case furniture (fig. 35). These heavily ornamented goods were primarily made for

Figure 35 Writing table and bookcase, Ireland, 1740–1760. Mahogany with oak. H. 83¹/₄", W. 34³/₄", D. 30". (Courtesy, Colonial Williamsburg Foundation, gift of Hiram J. Halle; photo, Hans Lorenz.)

the Irish gentry and nobility and were quite costly. Though there is little evidence of such work in the Irish-influenced furniture of the Rappahannock basin, one exception survives in the form of an extraordinary armchair that descended in the Carter family at Sabine Hall in Richmond County (fig. 36).

The basic shape of the Carter chair reflects a standard and widely employed British design. Similar tapered legs with block feet appear in the third edition of Thomas Chippendale's *Gentleman and Cabinet-Maker's Director* (1762). The deep front and side aprons are also typical of close stool chairs, like this one, and were intended to conceal the tall, cylindrical chamber pot housed within. In an eastern Virginia context, however, the carving that is lavishly distributed over the aprons is without parallel. It lacks the background punchwork and/or diapering often seen on the fully carved

Figure 36 Armchair, Rappahannock River basin, ca. 1765. Mahogany with white pine (by microanalysis). Dimensions not recorded. The splat is an old replacement. (Private collection; photo, Gavin Ashworth.)

aprons of Irish pieces, but the overall design of the carved ornament is quite close to that on a number of Irish tables. In particular, the symmetrical acanthus sprays with voluted terminals on the Carter chair are remarkably similar to those on the front apron of a midcentury Irish card table (figs. 37–39). The enormous wealth of the Carter family likely accounts for this uncharacteristically profuse display of carved ornament.[14]

As noted, many of the details observed on the furniture in this study also appear on contemporary English pieces; however, the elements in question—trifid, paneled, and slipper feet, pronounced knee scrolls, and the like—are seen only sporadically in England, where dozens of other ornamental options were far more popular. On the other hand, these designs, particularly the foot forms, were enormously popular in Ireland. That all of them appear together in the small geographic confines of the Rappahannock basin, but are found nowhere else in the Chesapeake, argues convincingly for the presence of an Irish connection.

Figure 37 Card table, Ireland, 1750–1765. Mahogany. Dimensions not recorded. (Private collection; courtesy, Glin Castle Irish Furniture Archive.)

Figure 38 Detail of the front rail carving on the card table illustrated in fig. 37.

Figure 39 Detail of the front apron carving on the armchair illustrated in fig. 36.

The stylistic parallels between furniture attributed to the Rappahannock River basin and to Philadelphia also raise a question as to whether any of the pieces attributed to Virginia could have been made in Pennsylvania. Furniture was occasionally shipped to Virginia from Philadelphia, but for a variety of reasons the objects illustrated here do not fit that pattern. Although the trifid and paneled feet on the cherry chairs made for the Beverley and Garnett families (figs. 6, 8) are analogous to those from Philadelphia and other Delaware Valley centers, the scale of the Virginia chairs is smaller and more delicate than that of eastern Pennsylvania seating furniture. The through-tenons, nailed-on knee blocks, and vertical, quarter-round glue blocks common to Delaware Valley chairs do not appear on the Rappahannock examples. Moreover, the splat pattern on the Virginia pieces clearly places their date of production in the third quarter of the eighteenth century, well after the foot forms in question had largely disappeared from Philadelphia furniture. The same is true of the slipper-foot tea and dining tables. Use of the slipper foot was never widespread in the Delaware Valley, and it went out of fashion there before the Virginia tables were made. Although cherry was a popular primary wood in both eastern Pennsylvania and the Rappahannock River basin for much of the eighteenth century, the pithy, relatively poor-quality cherry that grew in the sandy soils along the Rappahannock is usually easy to distinguish from the hard, clear cherry grown in Pennsylvania's loamy, rocky soils and cooler climate.

How, then, do we account for the presence of several Irish-influenced cabinet shops in the rural Rappahannock basin? The answer lies in the regular but little recognized trade relationships that existed between Ireland and the Chesapeake colonies for much of the eighteenth century, particularly between the 1720s and the 1770s. Irish linen, highly salable because of its consistent quality and competitive pricing, was the principal manufactured commodity in this trade. In fact, the Chesapeake was one of Ireland's largest regional American markets for linen, a necessary commodity widely used in the fabrication of bedding and all grades of clothing. Most Irish cloth came to the Chesapeake on Irish ships and was sold directly to consumers along the Rappahannock and other rivers. Norfolk, Virginia's largest port, also did a brisk trade in Irish linen, averaging nearly 157,000 yards per year between 1769 and 1772.[15]

Chesapeake exports to Ireland included tobacco, which was a staple in that trade for much of the eighteenth century, but as Maryland and Virginia planters began shifting to grain production in the 1750s, shipments of wheat also took on a central role. In 1768, more than 11,000 bushels of wheat were shipped to Irish ports from the upper district of the James River alone. Two years later, Virginia planters sent three times that amount to merchants in Ireland. Baltimore, an increasingly significant market center for Chesapeake planters as far south as the Rappahannock, played an even larger part in the Irish wheat and flour trade. In 1770, 102,000 bushels of wheat, or about 40 percent of Baltimore's tonnage, was shipped directly to Ireland. Much of that grain came from Virginia farms and plantations.[16]

The healthy economic exchange between Ireland and the Chesapeake certainly fostered contacts that might have led to the immigration of Irish artisans, including cabinetmakers; however, an even more important factor in the arrival of Irish craftsmen was the staggeringly high trade in indentured servants, which continued unabated until the end of the eighteenth century. It is estimated that fifty thousand Irish immigrants came to America during the particularly intensive years between 1760 and 1775, and most arrived as indentured servants. By this time, indentured service no longer carried the stigma it once had but was instead seen as a practical means of securing passage to Britain's American colonies. Because servants were in demand, the terms of indenture were often favorable for the "adventurer." Except for convicts, service rarely exceeded four years, and contracts were no longer sold at auction on American docks; many Irish servants renegotiated their own contracts upon arrival in the colonies.[17]

During the last decades of the colonial period, America's servant trade with Ireland was dominated by three immigrant Irish merchant communities: one in New York, another in Philadelphia, and the third in the thriving Chesapeake port of Baltimore. The volume in Baltimore was significant. In 1774, an Irish merchant living in the Maryland port wrote to an associate in Drogheda: "We are sure that within these two Years there has been 6000 servants sold in this Town from England and Ireland." Although many indentured servants worked off their time in agricultural pursuits, during the 1760s a Philadelphia merchant wrote to a colleague in Ireland that "Tradesmen of all Sorts sells very high." Records confirm that incoming Irish and other servants seldom stayed in the ports where they first landed. Their time, instead, was often purchased by individuals from other areas, who periodically went to cities like Baltimore in search of laborers.[18]

The nationality of immigrant cabinetmakers in the Chesapeake is often difficult to determine, even under the best of circumstances. With Irish artisans, this determination is complicated by the fact that Ireland was heavily colonized by the English in the seventeenth century so that, by the mid-eighteenth century, many native Irishmen bore English and other British surnames. It is known, however, that some Irish artisans who disembarked at Baltimore eventually moved south in search of opportunities. An example is cabinetmaker James McCormick, who arrived in Baltimore in 1785 or 1786 and advertised that he had "for some Years past worked in the first Shops in Dublin." Within a few months, McCormick moved his business south to Alexandria, Virginia, on the Potomac River, and in time he relocated to Norfolk before finally settling in Petersburg.[19] Other Irish artisans clearly followed similar paths.

Traditional historians usually rely on surviving written documents to prove the theories advanced in their research, a luxury frequently unavailable to students of material culture. Even so, a close examination of three-dimensional objects and the context of their use and ownership can often provide the evidence needed to substantiate a theory or explain a seemingly abberant pattern. Such is the case with the cherry and walnut furniture made in the lower Rappahannock basin and the Irish cabinetmaking practices that shaped it.

ACKNOWLEDGEMENTS For their generous assistance, I wish to thank Luke Beckerdite at the Chipstone Foundation; Carey Howlett, Jonathan Prown, and Susan Shames at Colonial Williamsburg; Sally Gant and Martha Rowe at the Museum of Early Southern Decorative Arts; Paul Doyle and Mairead Dunlevy at the National Museum of Ireland; John Bivins; Anne Rogers Haley; and Sumpter Priddy. I am particularly grateful to Desmond Fitz-Gerald, Knight of Glin, who not only shared his own extensive knowledge of Irish furniture but opened the photographic archives at Glin Castle and arranged access to several important public and private collections of Irish furniture.

1. In 1764 George Washington ordered "Two Elbow — & Ten common sitting Chairs for an Entertaining Room" from a factor in Liverpool. The same year, London upholsterer Edward Polhill supplied Washington with "12 Chairs covered with Leather and brass nail'd, 2 Elbows to ditto, 6 Windsor Chairs painted Green." Helen Maggs Fede, *Washington Furniture at Mount Vernon* (Mount Vernon, Va.: Mount Vernon Ladies' Association of the Union, 1966), p. 22.

2. Clear evidence of Irish furniture design also has been observed in the piedmont region of North Carolina. See Michael H. Lewis, "American Vernacular Furniture and the North Carolina Backcountry," *Journal of Early Southern Decorative Arts* 20, no. 2 (November 1994): 1–38.

3. William H. Seiner, "Economic Development in Revolutionary Virginia: Fredericksburg, 1750–1810" (Ph.d. diss., College of William and Mary, 1982), p. 20.

4. James B. Slaughter, *Settlers, Southerners, Americans: The History of Essex County, Virginia, 1608–1984* (Tappahannock, Va.: Essex County Board of Supervisors, 1985), pp. 36–40. Hunter Dickinson Farish, ed., *Journal & Letters of Philip Vickers Fithian, 1773–1774* (Williamsburg, Va.: Colonial Williamsburg, 1957), p. 154. Information about Nesmith was extracted from the Museum of Early Southern Decorative Arts's (hereinafter cited as MESDA) computerized *Index of Early Southern Artists and Artisans*. The practice of farming during the growing season and following another trade during cold weather was widespread in eighteenth- and nineteenth-century America. A southern example of this pattern was cabinetmaker and carpenter Joseph Freeman (1772–1842) of Gates County, North Carolina. (John Bivins, Jr., *The Furniture of Coastal North Carolina, 1700–1820* [Chapel Hill, N.C.: University of North Carolina Press for MESDA, 1988], pp. 374–76, 468–69).

5. American furniture historians use the term trifid to describe feet like those on the high chest base shown in figure 16. For the purposes of this essay, I will use trifid in the Irish sense. For an example of a Philadelphia foot of this form, see Joseph Downs, *American Furniture, Queen Anne and Chippendale Periods* (New York, N.Y.: MacMillan Co., 1952), no. 73.

6. The corner chair is recorded in MESDA research file S-5643, where conflicting notes indicate that the chair was owned in Fredericksburg or King and Queen County. However, the present owner, a descendent of the original owner, confirms that the chair came from Peach Grove near the town of Owenton in King and Queen County.

7. The Finch high chest of drawers is tentatively attributed to Williamsburg, Virginia, in Wallace Gusler, *Furniture of Williamsburg and Eastern Virginia, 1710–1790* (Richmond: Virginia Museum, 1979), pp. 21–23. The attribution was based on the reported York County, Virginia, history of a dressing table from the same shop, but new research suggests that the table was originally owned in the Rappahannock basin vicinity. See figure 17 and note 8 of the present essay. In addition to the Finch chest, a second, unrelated example is recorded in MESDA research file S-2169. Made of black walnut and yellow pine, the second chest is missing its upper case, lower case top board, lower case drawers and drawer supports, and one of its front legs. For examples of Irish high chests of drawers, see John T. Kirk, *American Furniture and the British Tradition to 1830* (New York, N.Y.: Alfred A. Knopf, 1982), p. 195, figs. 560–61.

8. For sample references to the Wornom family in Northumberland County, see T. L. C. Genealogy, *Virginia in 1740: A Reconstructed Census* (Miami Beach, Fl.: T. L. C. Genealogy; 1992), p. 305; Netti Schreiner-Yantis and Florene Speakman Love, comps., *The 1787 Census of Virginia*, 3 vols. (Springfield, Va.: Genealogical Books in Print, n.d.), 2:1270, 1998; and Government Printing Office, *Heads of Families at the First Census of the United States taken in the Year 1790, Virginia* (Washington, D.C., 1908), pp. 38, 75, 188. Despite the survival of York County records as far back as the 1630s, the earliest reference to the Wornom family in that jurisdiction is a marriage record in 1825. W. B. Crindlin, "York County Marriages," *Virginia Magazine of History and Biography* 25 (December 1917): 420.

9. The city of Richmond, located in central Virginia on the James River, should not be confused with Richmond County on the Rappahannock River. The slipper foot also appears in the piedmont region of North Carolina, where other Irish-influenced furniture designs have been recorded. See Lewis, "American Furniture and the North Carolina Backcountry," pp. 29–33. For an example of a Philadelphia slipper foot, see Downs, *American Furniture*, no. 112. For a Newport slipper-foot high chest of drawers dated 1748, see Brock Jobe and Myrna Kaye, *New England Furniture: The Colonial Era* (Boston: Houghton Mifflin Co., 1984), p. 34, fig. I–38.

10. The thin pads beneath the feet on the Beverley table are twentieth-century additions.

11. For the histories of the Bates and Sabine Hall tables, see MESDA research files S-3894 and S-4045. The rear face of each foot on the Sabine Hall table exhibits a short, vertical flute executed with a gouge. Pairs of wider but equally short flutes appear on the backs of the paneled feet on the Finch family high chest. The objects do not appear to be otherwise connected, but the fluting may represent a local practice employed in several shops. A now-lost eastern Virginia dressing table made of black walnut and yellow pine had turned pad feet with single, broad flutes on the back. MESDA research file S-5300.

12. The Chinn chair was illustrated in Helen Comstock, "Furniture of Virginia, North Carolina, Georgia, and Kentucky," *Antiques* 61, no. 1 (January 1952): 66, fig. 48. The inverted baluster-form splat, rare in Virginia, is similar to those on a set of black walnut chairs originally owned by the Tayloe family at Mount Airy plantation, directly across the river from Tappahannock. MESDA research files S-5422, 6057, and 7080. Initial testing suggested that one of the Tayloe chairs was made of European walnut, but it is now believed that all of these chairs are of American black walnut.

13. For the history of the Jeffreys chest with drawers on cabriole stand, see MESDA research file S-4567. The two other chests are from a second unidentified shop. One is made of yellow pine, and the other of black walnut. See Comstock, "Furniture of Virginia, North Carolina, Georgia, and Kentucky," p. 70, fig. 68; and Paul H. Burroughs, *Southern Antiques* (New York, N.Y.: Garrett & Massie, Inc., 1931), p. 151, pl. 4.

14. Thomas Chippendale, *The Gentleman and Cabinet-Maker's Director*, 3d. ed. (London, 1762), pls. 9, 19, 25.

15. Thomas M. Truxes, *Irish-American Trade, 1660–1783* (Cambridge, Eng.: Cambridge University Press, 1988), pp. 20, 34–35, 39, 66, 69, 79–80, 171, 181–83.

16. Truxes, *Irish-American Trade,* pp. 122–24, 187.

17. Truxes, *Irish-American Trade,* pp. 128–39.

18. Truxes, *Irish-American Trade,* pp. 123, 141.

19. McCormick's career is summarized in Ronald L. Hurst, "Cabinetmakers and Related Tradesmen in Norfolk, Virginia: 1770–1820" (master's thesis, College of William and Mary, 1989), pp. 123–25.

Figure 1   Detail of Edward Crisp, *A Compleat Description of the Province of* CAROLINA *in 3 Parts. 1st The Improved part from the Survey's of Maurice Mathews & Mr. John Love. 2ly. the West part by Capt. Thos. Narin. 3ly A Chart of the Coast from Virginia to Cape Florieda.* Colored engraving. 32³/₄" × 40". (Courtesy, South Caroliniana Library; photo, Museum of Early Southern Decorative Arts.) This map was engraved by John Harris in London and published by Crisp about 1711.

Luke Beckerdite

Religion, Artisanry, and Cultural Identity: The Huguenot Experience in South Carolina, 1680–1725

The place called Charles Town . . . [is] very commodiously scituated from many other Navigable Rivers that lie near it on which the Planters are seated; by the Advantage of Creeks, which have a Communication from one great River to another . . . the Planters may bring their Commodities to the Town . . . for Trade and Shipping. . . . At our being there was judged in the Country a 1000 or 1200 Souls; but the great Numbers of Families from England, Ireland, Berbadoes, Jamacia, and the Caribes, which daily Transport themselves thither, have more than doubled that number.

Carolina
Thomas Ashe, 1682

▼ IN DECEMBER 1679, Thomas Ashe and forty-five French Protestant refugees sailed for Carolina aboard the royal frigate *Richmond*. They landed the following April, shortly before the seat of government moved to the "Poynt of Land" dividing the Ashley and Cooper Rivers (fig. 1). Instructed "to enquire into the State of the Country, by his Majesties Special Command," Ashe meticulously catalogued commodities suitable for export and speculated about products that could be manufactured in Carolina, particularly naval stores, wine, olive oil, and silk.[1]

The Low Country's semitropical climate and diverse natural resources were foreign to most European emigrés, but no more so than the human landscape. By the time Ashe published *Carolina*, the region was inhabited by settlers from the British West Indies, England, Ireland, France, and Switzerland; by American Indians; and by African slaves. Soon to follow were immigrants from Scotland, the Netherlands, Portugal, and Germany; colonists from other areas of North America; and vast numbers of slaves whose ethnic backgrounds were as diverse as the white population. The patterns of interaction and cultural exchange that emerged among these diverse people during the first sixty years of settlement were remarkably fluid. Each group maintained a degree of ethnic and cultural identity; yet, at the same time, the challenges of early colonial life bound them together.[2]

This article explores the social and cultural context of Low Country decorative arts from 1680 to 1735. Only a handful of objects from this period are known, but they document the presence of diverse European craft traditions and the adaptation of those traditions to the environment and the demands of a pluralistic society. More importantly, they illuminate the dynamic process of cultural transfer, confrontation, and accommodation that began with the first organized efforts to colonize the region.

Settlement

In 1663, Charles II rewarded eight political allies with a vast proprietary grant that included South Carolina. After two failed attempts to colonize Carolina from Barbados, Lord Ashley persuaded his fellow proprietors to contribute £500 each to purchase passage, equipment, and provisions for two hundred colonists. The first settlers landed about sixty miles northeast of Port Royal in March 1670, but soon moved to a neck of land on the west bank of the Ashley River. By 1672, they had laid out town lots and built a palisade fort and approximately thirty houses. For the following eight years, this village served as the capital and as a commercial center for the farms and plantations along the Ashley and Cooper Rivers.[3]

By colonizing Carolina, the proprietors hoped to profit from the development of large personal estates, from the collection of quit-rents from each landowner, and from the production of commodities not yet raised or manufactured in Britain. To encourage settlement by "men of estate," they awarded sizable grants to individuals or partners who transported large numbers of indentured servants. Seth Sothell, for example, received twelve thousand acres in 1675 for agreeing to build thirty houses and "seat" 120 colonists. Although several members of the "lesser" gentry came to Carolina, most of the early immigrants were yeomen, tradesmen, and indentured servants—all attracted by the availability of inexpensive land and the commercial opportunities that Carolina offered.[4]

A large percentage of the colonists who arrived during the first decade of settlement were Barbadians. Unlike their English counterparts, many of the Barbadians were from prominent planter families. The introduction of sugar cultivation had caused land prices on the island to rise geometrically between 1640 and 1670. As smaller tracts became consolidated into large estates, displaced Barbadian planters, smaller landowners, and freemen looked to Carolina for new economic opportunities. The wealthiest individuals arrived with slaves and servants, acquired vast tracts of land, and formed a powerful political faction during the first forty years of settlement.[5]

Dutch, Swiss, and French colonists also settled in the Low Country during the late seventeenth century. *A Compleat Description of the Province of* CAROLINA, published by Edward Crisp about 1711, shows two Dutch residences near Charleston on the Ashley River (fig. 2). The Dutch represented only a small fraction of the population and were primarily merchant-traders and yeomen. Only a few tradesmen, such as joiner John Vanderhorst (d. 1715), are identified in seventeenth-century records. He arrived with a small group of Dutch immigrants in 1694.[6]

The Huguenots who emigrated to South Carolina during the 1680s and 1690s were far more numerous and diverse. Approximately 56 percent were from western coastal provinces of France, 31 percent were from inland provinces or from southeastern France, and 13 percent were born outside France. Most of the Huguenots from the western provinces sought refuge initially in England or the Netherlands. Merchant Isaac Mazicq fled from Isle de Ré to Amsterdam with £1500 sterling. From there he traveled to London, where he purchased interest in a cargo and passage on a ship

Figure 2   A Plan of the TOWN & HARBOUR of CHARLES=TOWN, shown on the map illustrated in fig. 1. The Dutch residences are designated "Vnderwood" and "Vandross." Joiner Pierre Le Chevalier's house in Charleston is 4, and the Huguenot church is R. By 1704, there were two churches—French and English—and three meeting houses—Presbyterian, AnaBaptist, Quaker—in the Charleston vicinity.

bound for Charleston. In 1685, he wrote, "God gave me the blessing of . . . escaping the cruel persecution . . . and . . . I promise . . . to observe the anniversary . . . with a fast." Protestants from the southeastern provinces typically fled to Switzerland or Germany. Silversmith Solomon L'Egaré was away at college when he received word that his parents had escaped from their home at Lyons in Champagne and that he was to disguise himself as a peasant and flee to Geneva. Solomon subsequently joined his family in Bristol, England, where they resided for several years before emigrating to America. His father, François, and two of his brothers went to Massachusetts in 1691, and Solomon went to Charleston.[7]

Huguenots such as Mazicq and L'Egaré probably had knowledge of Carolina before the diaspora. French perceptions of the New World were shaped by late sixteenth-century publications such as Jacques Le Moyne de Morgue's illustrated account of the French expedition to Florida and South Carolina (fig. 3), by promotional tracts such as Ashe's *Carolina* and Charles de Rochefort's *Histoire naturelle et morale des Iles Antilles* (1652), and by the personal experiences of "old" diaspora Huguenots, conveyed through friends and family members living in sympathetic Protestant countries. In 1685, Judith Giton wrote:

> For eight months we had suffered from the. . . . soldiers. . . . We therefore resolved on quitting France at night . . . and abandoning the house with its

Figure 3 Jacques Le Moyne de Morgue, *Réné de Laudonniére and the Indian Chief Athore Visit Ribaut's Column,* probably Paris or London, 1565–1586. 4" × 10". Watercolor on vellum. (Courtesy, New York Public Library.) Le Moyne was a member of the French expedition that settled at Fort Caroline on the St. John's River in 1564. Although the colony failed in less than a year, Le Moyne survived and returned to Paris. In 1572, he escaped the Massacre of St. Bartholomew's Day and fled to London. Encouraged by Sir Walter Raleigh, Le Moyne began drawing and painting plants, insects, and scenes of Indian life remembered from his voyage. His watercolor of commander Réné de Laudonniére and Chief Athore visiting the column erected by the first French expedition is an idyllic depiction of Europeans and Native Americans sharing the riches of the New World. This imagery must have held special meaning for Le Moyne and other Huguenots, who undoubtedly saw America as a place of opportunity and sanctuary (Jessie Poesch, *The Arts of the Old South: Paintings, Sculpture, Architecture & the Products of Craftsmen, 1560–1860* [New York: Harrison House, 1983], pp. 3–7).

furniture. We went to Romans . . . and there contrived to hide ourselves for ten days, whilst a search was made . . . we passed on to . . . Cologne, where we left the Rhine and took Wagons to Wesel. . . . [A] host who spoke a little French . . . told us that we were only thirty leagues from Lunenburg. We knew that you [her brother] were there. Our deceased mother and I entreated my eldest brother to . . . go that way; or else . . . to go himself to see you. . . . But he would not hear of it, having nothing on his mind but 'Carolina'. . . . After this, we passed into Holland, in order to go to England. We were detained in London for three months, waiting for a vessel to set sail for Carolina.

Although Giton's sojurn in London was brief, nearly half of the Huguenots who emigrated to South Carolina had lived in England more than five years. The growing population of Protestant refugees and the attendant decline in jobs undoubtedly influenced their migration to the colonies. Unlike Quakers, Presbyterians, AnaBaptists, and other "dissenters," the Crown placed few religious or civil restrictions on the Huguenots. This tolerance suggests that economic opportunity was the primary motive for emigration.[8]

The first contingent of Huguenots arrived in 1680 on the *Richmond*. Organized by René Petit and Jacob Guérard, this group included a high percentage of families and tradesmen "skilled in ye manufacture of silkes, oyles, and wines." To minimize conflicts with their English-speaking neighbors, most of the Huguenots settled north of Charleston on a tributary of the Cooper River, later known as French Quarter Creek. Immigration increased following Louis XIV's revocation of the Edict of Nantes in 1685, and by 1700 over 325 refugees had arrived in Charleston. During the seventeenth and early eighteenth centuries, the principal Huguenot-settled areas were along the south bank of the Santee River, on Goose Creek, on the eastern and western branches of the Cooper River, and in Charleston (see French names and "French Settlement" designated in fig. 1). This pattern probably resulted from the availability of land, since the Huguenots never attempted to isolate themselves from the British population.[9]

Huguenot Artisans and Artisanry

Of the twenty-one joiners and carpenters known to have worked in the Charleston area before 1700, ten were British, nine were Huguenots, and two were of undetermined descent. In many respects, the diaspora of the Huguenot joiners is representative of the Carolina refugees as a whole (fig. 4). Jacques Varine, Pierre Le Chevalier, Jacques Lardan, and Abraham Lesueur were from Normandy. Varine (fl. 1680–1688/89) and his family were among the French Protestants who arrived on the *Richmond* in 1680. Born in Rouen, he resided in London for at least six years before emigrating to South Carolina. Pierre Le Chevalier (fl. 1692–1712) came from Saint Lo, about 150 miles west of Rouen. Although his arrival date is not known, he purchased a lot in Charleston on October 19, 1692, and his residence is shown on Edward Crisp's map (see fig. 2). Jacques Lardan was born in the port of Dieppe, a major point of departure during the Huguenot diaspora. He acquired a lot in Charleston in 1694, applied for naturalization in 1696/97, and died the following year. Abraham Lesueur (fl. 1696–1740) came from Harfleur, near the mouth of the Seine. He also appears on the 1696/97 list of French and Swiss refugees in Carolina, and he had an unusually long career in Charleston.[10]

Pierre (1664–1729) and Gabriel (ca. 1666–ca. 1702) Manigault were born in La Rochelle, the great Protestant fortress on the coast of Aunis. They probably arrived in Charleston about 1695. In June of that year Gabriel received a warrant for one hundred acres for the arrival of himself and a "negro" named Sambo. Pierre married Judith Giton in 1699, and he fathered two children—Gabriel (1704–1781) and Judith. Pierre Galliard (fl. 1693/94–1710) was from the village Cherveaux, about fifty miles northeast of La Rochelle in Poitou. He and his wife, Magdelane, came to South Carolina in 1693/94 and subsequently purchased land in Jamestown, a French and Swiss settlement on the south bank of the Santee River. Étienne Tauvron was born on Isle de Ré, off the coast of La Rochelle, and arrived in Charleston by 1696/97. He helped inventory the estate of Jacques Lardan in 1698, and he witnessed the will of Pierre Le Chevalier in 1702.[11]

Jean Guibal (1696–1703) and Moise Carion were from the southeastern province, Languedoc. Guibal was born in Saint André de Valborgne. He received a warrant for land in Carolina in January 1695/96 and was one of five individuals commissioned to sell lots in Jamestown. Carion (fl. 1696–1697) was born in Faguère, about forty miles from Saint André de

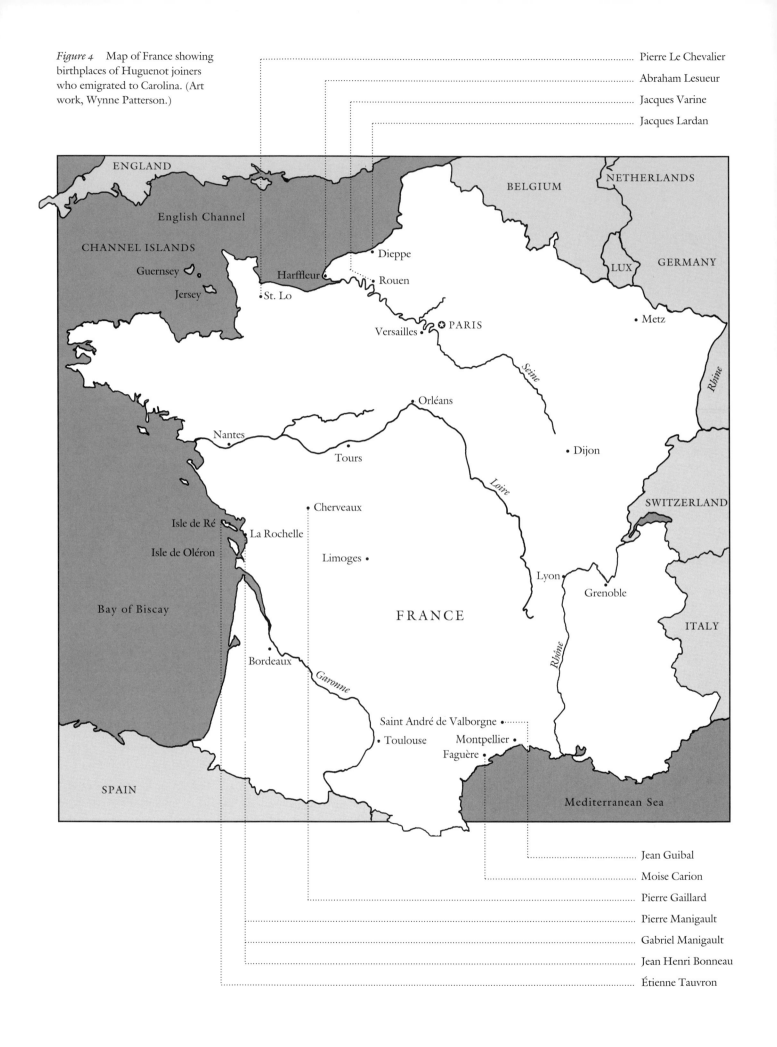

Figure 4 Map of France showing birthplaces of Huguenot joiners who emigrated to Carolina. (Art work, Wynne Patterson.)

Figure 5 Armchair, coastal South Carolina, 1680–1700. Cherry with ash. H. 41¼", W. 23", D. 16¼". (Private collection; courtesy, Museum of Early Southern Decorative Arts.)

Valborgne. He, his wife, Ann (Riboteau), and son, Moise, were among several Santee-area Huguenots who petitioned for naturalization in 1696/97. Carion purchased three adjoining lots in Jamestown in 1705/6, but the town failed owing to frequent flooding of the Santee.[12]

A massive great chair with a South Carolina recovery history probably represents the work of a first-generation Huguenot joiner (fig. 5). The spindle-and-rail construction of the back is repeated on vernacular French chairs depicted in mid-seventeenth-century paintings by the Le Nain brothers and on French-style chairs (fig. 6) illustrated in Søren Terkelsen's *Dend hydrinade Astrea* (1645). The latter also have small spindles pinned to their upper rails like those of the great chair. Unlike turned armchairs from the northern and middle colonies, which typically have arms tenoned into the front posts, the great chair has large turned arms that extend beyond the front posts. Chairs with overpassing arms from Normandy and Brittany are illustrated in early volumes of *Vie à La Campagne*, but similar examples were probably made throughout the provinces as well as in other areas of north-

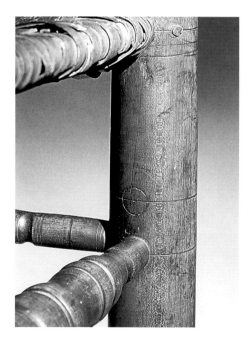

ern Europe. Related arms also occur on chairs from southeastern Virginia and eastern North Carolina, the earliest of which have spindle-and-rail backs, turned feet, or other details associated with Continental furniture-making traditions.[13]

With the exception of the long back spindles and upper stretchers, every joint on the great chair is pinned (figs. 7, 8). The pins securing these joints are set at acute angles, and their use may stem from the earlier practice of pinning rectangular and round through-tenons. The holes for the tenons were drilled with a center bit (fig. 8) rather than a pod auger, or spoon bit, which was used by most chairmakers during the late seventeenth century. The presence of this tool and the fact that the chair was turned on a great wheel lathe suggest that it is an urban product, despite its nonarchitectural turnings. The seat is lower than normal and may have been fitted with a thick cushion.[14]

In early South Carolina inventories, turned chairs are generally described by their paint color or by their seat material, whereas joined chairs are more often identified by their wood. In 1692, merchant William Dunston owned ten "palmato chaires" valued at £1.6.15. Three years later, Joseph Penderves's inventory listed "2 permeto chaires" valued at 2s 6d, "1 Great Sedar Elbo Chaire" valued at 5s, "1 Small Sedar Ditto" valued at 1s 6d, "1 Chaire Cushion" valued at 1s, and two hammocks valued at £1. "Palmetto chairs" and hammocks are among the most common seating and sleeping forms listed in seventeenth-century South Carolina inventories. Both were relatively inexpensive and well suited to the Low Country's sultry climate.[15]

No early Carolina bedsteads survive, but seventeenth- and early eighteenth-century forms included "Cott Bead[s]," "Cabin bead[s]," and "Standing Bed Stids." Most bedsteads, however, were simply described as "new" or "old," with appraisals ranging from a few shillings to around £3. Almost invariably, the bed furniture was more expensive than the frame. In 1686, merchant Paul Grimball submitted an account of losses sustained when a Spanish raiding party from St. Augustine ransacked his house on

Figure 9   Couch, coastal South Carolina, 1700–1725. Walnut. H. 38⅞", W. 27¼" (seat), L. 80¾". The upper portion of the crest rail is missing. (Collection of the Museum of Early Southern Decorative Arts.)

Edisto Island. His inventory included "1 hammock 1.0.0 . . . 5 beedsteads broke & spoyld 0.15.0 . . . 7 beeds bolsters & pillows 30.0.0 . . . 2 large wosted Ruggs & Cadoes 3.0.0 . . . 14 blankets for beeds 12.0.0 . . . 4 cors Ruges 3.0.0 . . . 30 pr. sheets 30.0.0 . . . 20 pillobears 5.0.0 . . . 1 sheet of Reed serge curtains & valians last & fringed wth silk 10.0.0 . . . [and] 3 sheets of Bed curtains more 12.0.0." The curtains appear to have been for his personal bedstead, whereas the remaining items were stock.[16]

Couches, or "day-beds," were used in place of bedsteads and hammocks in some households. John Boyden's inventory listed one "couch bedstead . . . £2.10" in 1726, and William Ramsey's listed "3 old beds, couch beds, pillows & bolsters . . . £35" in 1733. The couch illustrated in figure 9 is the only

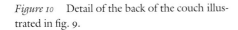

Figure 10   Detail of the back of the couch illustrated in fig. 9.

Figure 11 Gateleg table, probably New York City, 1700–1725. Mahogany with maple and tulip poplar. H. 30⅛"; top: 58" × 72¼" (open). (Courtesy, Historic Hudson Valley, Tarrytown, New York; photo, Gavin Ashworth.) The original owners may have been Philip Van Cortlandt (1683–1748) and his wife, Catherine De Peyster (1688–ca. 1766), who were married in 1710.

surviving example from the Low Country. It is considerably larger than most colonial couches, and it has a fixed back rather than an adjustable one. The spindles flanking the splat (fig. 10) resemble the legs on a gateleg table that descended in the Van Cortlandt family of New York (fig. 11). Both sets of turnings have superimposed balusters with distinctive cup-shaped elements. Similar turnings also occur on a contemporary New York draw bar table that almost certainly represents the work of a northern European immigrant. A French or Germanic origin for the maker of the couch is suggested by its serpentine stiles—intended to represent twisted columns—and fleur-de-lis carving (figs. 10, 12). Although few Germanic people emigrated to the Low Country before 1730, Teutonic styles may have arrived earlier with Huguenots who had sojourned in one of the Protestant states or in countries influenced by them. Regional settlement patterns and material culture both suggest that the Huguenots introduced a variety of north European details, not all of which were purely French.[17]

Figure 12 Conjectural drawing of the back of the couch illustrated in fig. 9, showing how the missing carved components on the crest rail probably appeared. (Drawing by Luke Beckerdite, artwork by Wynne Patterson.)

Figure 13 Detail of the nailing evidence for a sacking bottom on the rails of the couch illustrated in fig. 9. The holes adjacent to the beaded edges are from a later cane bottom.

Figure 14 Conjectural drawing of a pavilion based on diagrams in Peter Thornton, *Seventeenth-Century Interior Decoration in England, France and Holland* (New Haven, Conn.: Yale University Press, 1978), p. 158. (Artwork by Wynne Patterson.)

The caned seat on the couch replaces its original "sacking," which was tacked into the rabbets on the inner edges of the rails (fig. 13). Sacking typically consisted of a canvas edge with sewn grommets and rope lacing; however, some systems had a central canvas panel suspended by the roping. Ornate couches like this example frequently had a costly suite of cushions, often including a squab, bolster, and pillows. Some may have been fitted with "pavilions," or canopies, like the one that accompanied Daniel Gale's hammock in 1725. Low Country inventories and correspondence indicate that most pavilions were simple, utilitarian devices made of netting or other thin, inexpensive fabrics (fig. 14) rather than the costly textiles used on their court counterparts. In 1725, Margaret Kennet wrote, "we have . . . a very troublesome . . . Insect which are called the muschatoe . . . so that all the Hott months we are forced to use pavilions made of Catgut Gause. Twenty yds. maks a Pavilion." During the seventeenth century, "pavilion" was the French term for a cone- or dome-shaped fixture suspended from the ceiling by a cord, "with a valence . . . and with two or three large curtains that . . . had to drag on the ground . . . to be long enough to . . . encompass the foot end." Textile historian Audrey Michie has suggested that Huguenots may have introduced the term "pavilion" in the Carolinas.[18]

Figure 15 Armchair, possibly coastal South Carolina, 1690–1720. Walnut. H. 45¹/₂" (feet restored), W. 22", D. 16³/₄". This chair originally had a plank seat. During the nineteenth or early twentieth century, the seat boards were removed and the upper edges of the beaded seat rails were rounded to accommodate a woven seat. (Courtesy, Colonial Williamsburg Foundation.)

Figure 16 Detail of the back of the armchair illustrated in fig. 15.

Although no netting was listed among Paul Grimball's losses, his stock included a variety of textiles, materials, and tools for the production of upholstered furniture: "12 1/2 hids of english tand sole leather . . . 12 Rich new backes & seats of Turky work: for chear . . . 3: doz of reed lether backes & seates for cheares . . . Tooles for Carpendors Joyners Turnors . . . [and] a parsell new bras nailes 2 sorts for cheares." As these references suggest, seventeenth-century patrons often purchased upholstery materials before commissioning the seating frames. Rather than altering the textile, most chairmakers made their frames fit the upholstery. This practice was particularly common for turkeywork, which was woven into panels and had a selvage suitable for nailing. The "backs & seats" in Grimball's inventory were probably for low-backed stools—commonly referred to as "farthingale" or "Cromwellian" chairs—or for their more fashionable high-backed counterparts, occasionally referred to in English inventories as "French chairs." Parisian upholsterers began making *gands fauteuils*, or "grand chairs," with high, raked backs during the early 1670s, and variations of the form remained popular on the Continent and in Britain through the seventeenth century.[19]

Figure 17 Armchair, probably New York City, 1685–1700. Maple stained red. H. 44", W. 22½", D. 17¼". (Private collection; photo Christopher Zaleski.)

Figure 18 *Escabeau*, Charleston, South Carolina, 1695–1725. Cypress. H. 24¾", W. 15¼", D. 11¾". (Collection of the Museum of Early Southern Decorative Arts.)

The turned and joined armchair illustrated in figure 15 may be a rural South Carolina interpretation of the grand chair. It first surfaced in the "Questions and Answers" section of *Antiques* in August 1926. Judging from the editor's response, the owner asked if the chair could be "associated with the early coming of Huguenot settlers to the South." Five years later, furniture historian Paul Burroughs attributed the chair to South Carolina in *Southern Antiques*. Most of his attributions were based on family or recovery histories.[20]

The maker of the Carolina chair angled the arm, seat rail, and stretcher joints to create a backward list rather than by sawing the rear posts out of wide boards or by using double-axis turning. The stretchers join the posts at the same level on all four sides, and the seat rails have half-inch-wide beads and rabbeted edges that originally supported a plank seat. The open back frame provides little support for the sitter (fig. 16), which suggests that the chair had a tied-on squab, or *carreau*, and a matching one for the plank seat. Furniture historian Peter Thornton has noted that French upholsterers "fitted both seat and back with squabs, which were tied on with ribbons . . . [but] there appears to be no English parallel for this French practice before the . . . early nineteenth century." A similar complement of cushions evidently accompanied a contemporary New York armchair (fig. 17). Next to South Carolina, New York had the largest Huguenot population in colonial America.[21]

Low Country appraisers typically used prevailing English terms for furniture. French forms, such as *gands fauteuils, coffres, armoires*, and *escabeaux*, were probably referred to as elbow chairs or great chairs, chests, presses or cupboards, and stools. *Escabeaux* were simple stools used in houses and in churches where they may have functioned as coffin, or "bier," stands. The cypress example illustrated in figure 18 has a history of use in the Miles Brewton house in Charleston (completed 1769), but its original context was much earlier. Although it is thought to have come from an earlier dwelling in the Brewton family, it may have descended in the Manigault family who occupied the house from the late nineteenth century until the present. Like many French *escabeaux*, it has splayed legs and a top with a shaped cut-out (fig. 19). Its elongated baluster turnings suggest a date of 1700–1720, making it roughly contemporary with the French-Canadian example illustrated in figure 20.[22]

Figure 19 Detail of the top of the *escabeau* illustrated in fig. 18.

Figure 20 *Escabeau*, Quebec, 1690–1700. Birch, maple, and pine. H. 22⅝". (Courtesy, Historic Deerfield.)

The only cultural designation for furniture in early Carolina inventories is "Dutch"—a term that had both specific and generic meanings depending on its usage. "Dutch chairs" and "Dutch tables," for example, probably referred to objects perceived as having Continental details rather than being literally Dutch in origin or form. The "old Round Dutch flap table" listed in the 1726/27 inventory of Alice Hogg's estate may have resembled a late seventeenth- or early eighteenth-century falling-leaf (or gateleg) table that descended in the Manigault family (fig. 21). Attached to the end rail is a nineteenth-century plaque engraved "Gabriel Manigault/1739." This inscription and the Manigault family genealogy suggest that the table belonged to the immigrant Gabriel or that it descended from his brother Pierre to his nephew Gabriel. Both Pierre and his brother were joiners, and either could have constructed this table if they had learned turning or if they purchased the turned components from a specialist. Alternatively, they could have purchased the table from a local turner or joiner.[23]

Figure 21 Gateleg table, Charleston, South Carolina, 1690–1710. H. 29½"; top: 52¼" × 67⅛" (open). Cypress and red cedar. (Courtesy, Charleston Museum; photo, Gavin Ashworth.)

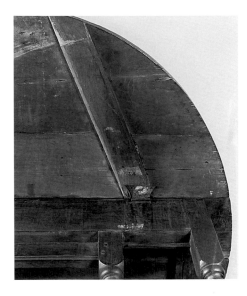

Figure 22 Detail of a batten on the gateleg table illustrated in fig. 21. (Photo, Gavin Ashworth.)

Figure 23 Detail of the end of a batten on the gateleg table illustrated in fig. 21. (Photo, Gavin Ashworth.)

Figure 24 Gateleg table, northern Europe, 1680–1720. Red pine. H. 28½"; top: 38" × 67¼" (open). (Courtesy, Charleston Museum; photo, Gavin Ashworth.) Damage to the rail below the replaced drawer suggests that the original was missing for some time; however, the current cypress drawer appears to be an early eighteenth-century Carolina replacement. The battens under the leaves are chamfered and dovetailed in the same manner as those illustrated in figs. 22 and 23. The turnings of this table are very similar to those on late seventeenth-century chairs from southwestern France.

The Manigault table has an oval top with butt-joints between the leaves and center section, random-width boards, long tongue-and-groove joints, and wide dovetailed battens that prevent the top from warping (figs. 22, 23). This distinctive batten system also occurs on a northern European gateleg table with an early eighteenth-century cypress drawer (fig. 24). The remaining structural and stylistic details on the Manigault table are somewhat more generic. The top and drawer runners are attached with nails rather than pins, and wear marks on the legs indicate that the missing drawer had a front that extended below the drawer bottom. The lower edge of the drawer may have been shaped, and it almost certainly had an ogee molding like the end rail.[24]

The primary woods of the Manigault table—red cedar and cypress—are the most common ones specified in early inventories. Ashe wrote that Carolina was "cloathed with odoriferous and fragrant . . . Cedar and Cyprus Trees, of . . . which are composed goodly Boxes, Chests, Tables, Scrittores, and Cabinets. . . . Carolina [cedar] is esteemed equal . . . for Grain, Smell and Colour . . . [to] Bermudian Cedar, which of all the West Indian is . . . the most excellent." During the seventeenth and early eighteenth centuries,

Figure 25 Table, Charleston or Berkeley County, South Carolina, 1695–1715. Walnut. H. 29³/₄", W. 51" (frame), D. 41¹/₂" (frame). (Private collection; photo, Gavin Ashworth.) The legs of this table were turned from 3 1/2" stock.

Figure 26 Henrietta Johnston, *Thomas Broughton*, Charleston, South Carolina, 1710–1711. Crayon on paper. 10⁵/₈" × 7³/₄". (Private collection; photo, Museum of Early Southern Decorative Arts.)

regional merchants and tradesmen maintained large stocks of these and other woods. In 1694, merchant John Vansusteren's inventory listed "900 foot of Ceader bords . . . [and] 80 foot of Ceader Plank," and joiner James Beamer's listed two hundred feet of cedar boards and a large "parcel of Cedar." Twelve years later, joiner Jean du Brevill sold two thousand feet of cypress boards to merchant Francis LeBrasseur.[25]

Contemporary promotional tracts and surviving furniture also document the presence of trees not commonly associated with the Low Country. *A Brief Description of the Province of Carolina* (1666) stated that "*Walnut-trees* of great growth" and cherry thrived in "the barren sandy ground." Although the preceding armchairs and a small group of tables support that claim, the easternmost supplies of black walnut and cherry may have been exhausted by the middle of the eighteenth century.[26]

The walnut stretcher table illustrated in figure 25 reportedly belonged to Colonel Thomas Broughton (fig. 26) of Mulberry Plantation (see "Mulbery" on the Cooper River at the top of fig. 1). Its ogee rail moldings, baroque, baluster-shaped turnings, and compressed, ball-shaped feet resemble those of the Manigault table, though the Broughton example may be at least a decade later. The top of Broughton's table also has an ogee molding identical to those on the rails and stretchers below, and it has one-inch-thick, dovetailed cleats that were originally secured to the frame with three pegs each (fig. 27). Tables with dovetailed cleats were produced throughout northern Europe from the Renaissance to the nineteenth century.[27]

Broughton (d. 1737) emigrated from the Leeward Islands before January 20, 1696. He held several ranks in the South Carolina militia, served intermittently as an assemblyman for Berkeley and Craven Counties, and amassed a sizable fortune in the Indian trade. In 1706, he purchased land on the northwestern branch of the Cooper River in Berkeley County and became a planter. Five years later, Anglican minister Francis LeJau wrote, "I now have no leading man or men of authority in my Parish, Col. Broughton had left us 3 months ago to go and live upon his fine seat fourteen miles off."[28]

Figure 27 Detail of a leg, ogee-molded top, and a dovetailed cleat on the table illustrated in fig. 25.

Figure 28 Thomas Coram, *Mulberry Plantation*, painted in Charleston or Berkeley County, South Carolina, 1778–1780. Oil on paper. 4^{1}/₁₆" × 6^{11}/₁₆". (Courtesy, Carolina Art Association/Gibbs Museum of Art; photo, Museum of Early Southern Decorative Arts.)

Broughton's "fine seat" is depicted in a late eighteenth-century watercolor by Charleston artist Thomas Coram (fl. 1769–1780) (fig. 28). In the foreground are rows of slave houses with high, steep roofs, small windows, and arched doors. These dwellings appear to be somewhat later than Broughton's house, Mulberry, which probably dates to 1711–1714. Partially shown in the background, Mulberry is a one-and-a-half-story, English bond, brick building with a jerkin-head gambrel roof and four adjoining, single-story pavilions. The house originally had a gable roof, but it was altered to the present form before Coram's painting (fig. 29). Architectural historian Thomas Waterman argued that Mulberry's design derived from

Figure 29 Mulberry, Berkeley County, South Carolina, ca. 1714. (Photo, Gavin Ashworth.)

Figure 30 Detail of a second-floor room in Mulberry. (Photo, Gavin Ashworth.)

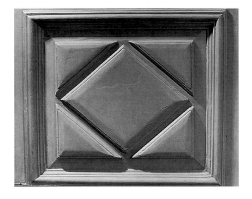

Figure 31 Detail of the central panel of the door illustrated in fig. 30. (Photo, Gavin Ashworth.)

Figure 32 *Buffet bas*, Quebec, ca. 1700. Red pine painted red. H. 39³/₄", W. 41⁵/₈", D. 19". (Courtesy, Historic Deerfield.)

sixteenth-century French chateaux and pointed out similarities between Mulberry and vernacular houses in French-settled areas of Virginia and the West Indies. Other scholars have suggested that late seventeenth-century Netherlandish and French tower houses may have provided the inspiration for Mulberry's distinctive pavilions.[29]

The interior was extensively remodeled during the nineteenth century, but remnants of original woodwork on the second floor document the involvement of European-trained joiners (fig. 30). The doors have central panels with molded, lozenge-shaped designs, or *pointes des diamant*, and complex applied moldings around the panel fields (fig. 31)—details that occur frequently on late seventeenth- and eighteenth-century French furniture (fig. 32) and architectural woodwork. The presence of such details should come as no surprise given Berkeley County's large Huguenot population and Broughton's ties to that community. He was, for example, acquainted with refugee artisans, including joiner Pierre Le Chevalier, and Broughton's son, Nathaniel, married Henriette Charlotte de Chastaigner (fig. 33), whose father, Alexander, was from Rochelais nobility.[30]

Contemporary Huguenot houses provide an interesting contrast with Mulberry. Daniel Huger's (1688–1754) house, "Limrick" (fig. 34), was built between the Cooper and Wando Rivers about fifteen miles southeast of Mulberry. His parents, Daniel (1651–1711) and Margaret (Perdriau), were born at Loudun in Poitou. Like many Huguenots from that province, they subsequently moved to La Rochelle, where their daughter Marguerite was born. In 1682 they boarded a ship at Isle de Ré and escaped to England, where they resided for approximately twelve years. The Hugers' early flight may have enabled them to preserve some of the wealth that Daniel, Sr., had accumulated in his mercantile business. He purchased three lots in Charleston in 1694 and several hundred acres of land in Craven County between 1696 and 1709. Daniel, Jr., inherited a portion of this land in 1711 and subsequently acquired additional acreage in Craven County and Berkeley County.[31]

Figure 33 Henrietta Johnston, *Henriette Charlotte de Chastaigner*, Charleston, 1711. Crayon on paper. 11⁵/₈" × 8⁷/₈". (Courtesy, Carolina Art Association/Gibbs Museum of Art; photo, Museum of Early Southern Decorative Arts.)

Figure 34 Limrick, Berkeley County, South Carolina, ca. 1711. (Courtesy, Library of Congress.)

Figure 35 Detail of the stair in Limrick. (Courtesy, Library of Congress.)

Figure 36 Table, probably Berkeley County, South Carolina, ca. 1711. Cypress with traces of original red paint. H. 27⁷⁄₈", W. 36³⁄₁₆", D. 23¹⁄₄". (Courtesy, Charleston Museum; photo, Gavin Ashworth.

Figure 37 Table, coastal South Carolina, 1780–1820. Cypress painted blue. H. 28¹⁄₄", W. 37¹⁄₂", D. 22¹⁄₂". (Courtesy, Charleston Museum; photo, Gavin Ashworth.)

Limrick was built on Daniel's Berkeley County plantation about 1713. The house burned in 1945, but photographs reveal that it was a two-story, frame structure with a tall gable roof, enclosed chimneys, and a central hall (fig. 35). The principal rooms of the first floor had fireplace walls with raised paneling and bolection-molded surrounds that resemble the earliest ones in Mulberry. The stair balusters in the hall were probably turned by the same artisan that made a tea table reportedly from Limrick (fig. 36). Both sets of

Figure 38 Dressing table, probably Charleston, South Carolina, 1700–1720. Mahogany with red bay. H. 28", W. 32³⁄₄", D. 18¹⁄₂". (Courtesy, Colonial Williamsburg Foundation.)

turnings feature an elongated ogee baluster over a compressed smaller one. In the colonies, superimposed balusters occur primarily on furniture from New York and South Carolina (see figs. 10, 11). As the table illustrated in figure 37 demonstrates, this pattern remained fashionable in rural areas of the Low Country well into the nineteenth century.³²

The most prevalent turning on early Carolina tables is a long slender baluster with a thin collarino just below the capital. A dressing table and two small side tables illustrate three different interpretations of this regional pattern (figs. 38–40). The dressing table is made of mahogany and red bay, a local hardwood that naturalist Mark Catesby described as "fine gran'd, and of excellent use for cabinets, &c." (fig. 38). Although mahogany first appears in Charleston records in 1730, it was probably being imported by the beginning of the eighteenth century. The feet of the dressing table resemble those of the *escabeau* (fig. 18), but they have a distinct cavetto below the torus rather than a simple fillet. Torus-and-cavetto moldings also function as capitals for the balusters of the table. The side tables (figs. 39, 40) have compressed, ball-shaped feet that are more closely allied to those of the

Figure 39 Table, probably Charleston, South Carolina, 1700–1720. Cypress painted black. H. 27⁵⁄₈", W. 26", D. 21". (Collection of the Museum of Early Southern Decorative Arts.)

Figure 40 Table, coastal South Carolina, 1700–1720. Walnut and tulip poplar with yellow pine. H. 29¹⁄₂", W. 27¹⁄₂", D. 21¹⁄₄". (Courtesy, George Washington Birthplace National Monument; photo, Museum of Early Southern Decorative Arts.)

Manigault, Broughton, and Limrick tables (figs. 21, 25, 36), and their delicate leg turnings, crisp, ogee-molded rails and stretchers, and finely cut dovetails mark them as urban products. Tables similar to these were undoubtedly made by artisans of both British and Continental descent.³³

Although northern European and English styles were dominant in the Low Country, a Charleston gateleg table with an oral tradition of ownership by Henry Laurens (1724–1792) probably represents the work of a joiner trained in the Massachusetts Bay region (fig. 41). With its bilaterally symmetrical baluster turnings, separate feet tenoned into the stretcher block under the pivot legs, channel-molded end rails, and a central drawer support dovetailed to the front rail and nailed up to the back rail, it is virtually indistinguishable from gateleg tables made in Boston during the first quarter of the eighteenth century. Judging from the table's date of manufacture, it probably descended from Laurens's father, John, or his grandfather, André (Laurent). André was born in Saint Sauveur, a small Aunisian village

Figure 41 Gateleg table, Charleston, South Carolina, 1700–1725. Walnut with yellow pine and cypress. H. 29½"; top: 47¾" × 57½". (Collection of the Museum of Early Southern Decorative Arts.)

near La Rochelle. He escaped to England in 1682, married Marie Lucas in London in 1688, and emigrated to New York City shortly thereafter. By 1696, they had settled in South Carolina where John was born. John reportedly converted to Anglicanism during his youth and later served as church-warden for St. Philip's Parish.[34]

Patronage, Culture, and Community
As the preceding objects reveal, stylistic influences from Europe, Britain, and the northern colonies converged in the Low Country during the late seventeenth and early eighteenth centuries. Much of this diversity can be attributed to Huguenot tradesmen, who historian Neil Kamil asserts were part of a "dispersed . . . culture of almost pure contingency, of infinite adaptation to the niches made available by their craft." Other decorative arts from the Low Country show how artisanry and patronage enabled the Huguenots to maintain their cultural identity while interacting with surrounding cultures.

Huguenots account for a disproportionately large percentage of the sitters in surviving pastel portraits by Henrietta de Beaulieu Johnston. Henrietta was probably born near Saint Quentin in Picardy about 1674. In 1708, she, her second husband, the Rev. Gideon Johnston, and their four

Figure 43 Henrietta Johnston, *Susanne Le Noble*, Charleston, South Carolina, 1710. Crayon on paper. 10⁷/₈" × 6³/₄". (Private collection; photo, Museum of Early Southern Decorative Arts.)

Figure 42 Henrietta Johnston, *Samuel Prioleau*, Charleston, South Carolina, 1715. Crayon on paper. 12" × 9". (Collection of the Museum of Early Southern Decorative Arts.)

children emigrated from Ireland to Charleston, where Gideon was to serve as the Bishop's Commissary. From the outset, the Johnstons had financial problems, exacerbated by church politics and Gideon's frequently poor health. In 1709, he wrote, "were it not for the Assistance my wife gives me by drawing . . . Pictures . . . I shou'd not have been able to live."[35]

Most of Johnston's sitters were government officials, clerics, merchants, planters, prominent tradesmen, and their wives and children. Samuel Prioleau, for example, was a South Carolina–born silversmith, jeweler, and planter (fig. 42). His parents were refugees from Saintonge, and his father, Elias, was the first minister of the Huguenot Church in Charleston. Susanne Le Noble (fig. 43) was also from a prominent Huguenot family. Gideon Johnston noted that her father, Henry, was one of several French gentlemen "that have distinguished themselves in my favour." Gideon's highest praise, however, was for Huguenot physician John Thomas: "he has been extremely kind and generous to me; . . . he has constantly attended us on all occasions. . . . When I call'd for a Bill . . . he told me he wou'd take not one single farthing."[36]

The Johnston's experiences suggest that the Huguenots in Charleston had a strong sense of community and ethnic identity. Cultural bonds may have been even stronger among those who settled outside the city. In *A New Voyage to Carolina* (1702), John Lawson described the French settlers on the Santee as "one Tribe or kindred, every one making it his Business to be assistant to the Wants of his Country-Man, preserving his Estate and Reputation with the same Exactness and Concern as he does his own; all seeming to share in the Misfortunes, and rejoyce at the Advance, and Rise, of their Brethren."[37]

Apprenticeships were another means by which the Huguenots interacted with each other and with the English-speaking community. During the late seventeenth century, three of the four silversmiths documented in Charleston were French— Pierre Jacob Guerard, Solomon L'Egaré, and Nicholas

(a)

(b)

(c)

Figure 44 Sacramental plate for Biggin Church, St. John's Parish, South Carolina, including: (*a*) Standing cup by Miles Brewton, Charleston, South Carolina, ca. 1711. Silver. H. 7⅝". (*b*) Paten by Miles Brewton, ca. 1711. Silver. H. 2¹⁵/₁₆", Diam. 5¾". (*c*) Cup, Paris, seventeenth century. Silver gilt. Dimensions unrecorded. (Courtesy, Museum of Early Southern Decorative Arts.)

de Longemare. The fourth was Miles Brewton, who arrived in Charleston with his parents in 1684 and evidently trained with one of the aforementioned men, beginning about 1686. The earliest silver surviving from the Low Country is attributed to Brewton, whose mark—MB within a shield—appears on a standing cup and paten made for Biggin Church in St. John's Parish about 1710 (fig. 44*a, b*). Both of these forms are similar to standing cups and patens made by Huguenot silversmiths for French churches in England as well as to corresponding forms made and used by Anglicans.[38]

Brewton's silver was subsequently moved to Strawberry Chapel, which was built about 1725 to accommodate parishioners who were unable to travel to Biggin Church. During the Civil War, the silver was hidden in a nearby rice mill, where it remained until 1946. The standing cup and paten were discovered with several other pieces of sacramental plate, including two alms basins, a London flagon dated 1724/25, and a late seventeenth-century Parisian cup (fig. 44*c*). Church tradition maintains that the French cup was brought to Carolina by a Huguenot minister and subsequently presented to St. John's Parish, where it served as the first communion cup.[39]

Like Brewton's sacramental plate, the presence of French silver in an Anglican church suggests that a process of Anglo-French "creolization" was occurring in the religious and material life of the Low Country. Gideon Johnston, for example, was shocked that the Anglican congregations in South Carolina elected their ministers as did the Protestants. Similarly, some Huguenots attended Anglican services and even joined Anglican congregations; however, their actions did not necessarily mean that they abandoned French Protestantism. When Pierre Manigault died in 1729, he bequeathed £10 to the poor of St. Philip's Church and £10 to the poor of the Huguenot Church.[40]

Figure 45   Dressing table, Charleston, South Carolina, 1725–1735. Walnut. H. 31⅝", W. 31¾", D. 21". (Collection of the Museum of Early Southern Decorative Arts.) The dressing table has an illegible inscription written in French.

Centuries of persecution had taught the Huguenots how to accommodate other cultures while maintaining their own identity through language, religion, marriage, and material life. Expressions of cultural identity could be as subtle as the carved fleur-de-lis and French-style intaglio shell on the Charleston dressing table illustrated in figure 45 or as obvious as the Huguenot organizations and institutions that have survived from the seventeenth century to the present. Although historians have argued that the Huguenots in Carolina were rapidly assimilated by the English-speaking population, evidence suggests that they were active participants in the development of a multicultural, regional identity.

ACKNOWLEDGMENTS   For assistance with this article, the author thanks Gavin Ashworth, John Bivins, Mr. and Mrs. Parker Gilbert, Ralph Harvard, Frank Horton, Neil Kamil, Peter Kenny, Robert Leath, Jonathan Poston, Mr. and Mrs. McColl Pringle, Bradford Rauschenberg, Martha Rowe, J. Thomas Savage, Wes Stewart, and Robert Trent.

1. Unless otherwise noted, the primary sources cited in this article are transcribed on index cards in the artisan files and personnel files in the Museum of Early Southern Decorative Arts (hereinafter cited MESDA), Winston-Salem, N.C. Several of the inventory references to furniture forms cited here were transcribed by Director of Research Bradford Rauschenberg and are in folders adjacent to the South Carolina furniture files. Thomas Ashe, *Carolina, Or a Description of the Present State of that Country* (London, 1682) in *Narratives of Early Carolina, 1650–1708,* edited by Alexander S. Salley, Jr. (New York: Charles Scribner's Sons, 1911), pp. 138–159.

2. For emigration to Carolina, see Richard Waterhouse, "South Carolina's Colonial Elite: A Study in the Social Structure and Political Culture of a Southern Colony, 1670–1770" (Ph.D. dissertation, Johns Hopkins University, 1973); Richard S. Dunn, *Sugar and Slaves: The Rise of the Planter Class in the English West Indies, 1624–1713* (Chapel Hill: University of North Carolina Press, 1973); Charles E. Baird, *History of the Huguenot Emigration to America*, 2 vols. (1885; reprint ed., Baltimore, Md.: Genealogical Publishing Co., 1991); Arthur Henry Hirsch, *The Huguenots of Colonial South Carolina* (1928; reprint ed., Baltimore, Md.: Genealogical Publishing Co., 1991); Amy Ellen Friedlander, "Carolina Huguenots; A Study in Cultural Pluralism in the Low Country, 1679–1768" (Ph.D. dissertation, Emory University, 1979). The ethnic background of the African population in South Carolina is discussed in Daniel C. Littlefield, *Rice and Slaves: Ethnicity and the Slave Trade in Colonial South Carolina* (Urbana: University of Illinois Press, 1991).

3. Waterhouse, "South Carolina's Colonial Elite," pp. 8–12. A smaller number of settlers came from Jamaica, Bermuda, Montserat, Antigua, Nevis, and New Providence. Mills Lane, *Architecture of the Old South: South Carolina* (New York: Abbeyville Press, 1989), p. 10.

4. Curtis P. Nettles, *The Roots of American Civilization: A History of American Colonial Life* (New York: Appleton-Century-Crofts, Inc., 1947), pp. 126, 139. Waterhouse, "South Carolina's Colonial Elite," pp. 12–17: "The [Proprietors'] instructions to Governor Sayle in 1669 directed that grants of 150 acres be made to each free person, the same for each male servant, 100 acres for each woman servant, 100 acres for each male servant under sixteen and 100 acres to servants when their time expired. Those arriving in subsequent years were to receive smaller grants."

5. Waterhouse, "South Carolina's Colonial Elite," pp. 30–32. Of the twenty governors that served between 1664 and 1730, six were Barbadians (Dunn, *Sugar and Slaves*, p, 114; William Young Prior, Grahame Thomas Smallwood, Jr., John Frederick Dorman, and Timothy Field Beard, comps., *The List of the Colonial Governors and Chief Executives of America Prior to 4 July 1776* [Lancaster, Va.: Hereditary Order of Descendants of Colonial Governors, 1989], n.p.).

6. MESDA artisan files. Dara L. D. Powell, *The Flagg Family: An Artistic Legacy and the Provenance of a Collection* (Pound Ridge, N.Y.: Countess Anthony Szápáry, 1986), p. 69.

7. Friedlander, "Carolina Huguenots," pp. 86–89. Mazicq may have been one of the founders of the Huguenot Church in Charleston. In his will, he left the church £100 and specified that the interest be used for the support of a Protestant minister (Baird, *Huguenot Immigration to America*, 1:310–11). For the emigration of the L'Egaré family, see ibid., 2:111. In his will, François left Solomon twenty shillings "to cutt him off . . . for . . . deserting my Service . . . before he was of age, and marrying utterly against my will and consent" (MESDA artisan files). In early South Carolina records, Solomon's last name is often spelled "Legare."

8. For Le Moyne, see Jessie Poesch, *The Arts of the Old South: Paintings, Sculpture, Architecture & the Products of Craftsmen, 1560–1860* (New York: Harrison House, 1983), pp. 3–7. Charles de Rochefort was a Huguenot minister living in Holland. His *Histoire naturelle* was published at Rotterdam in French in 1658 and in Dutch in 1662; at London in English in 1666; at Lyons in French in 1667; and at Rotterdam in French in 1681 (St. Julien Ravenel Childs, "French Origins in Carolina," *Transactions of the Huguenot Society of South Carolina* 50 [1945]: 30). Judith Giton's letter is translated in Baird, *Huguenot Emigration to America*, 2:114–15, 396–97. Friedlander, "Carolina Huguenots," pp. 88–90.

9. Friedlander, "Carolina Huguenots," pp. 2–4, 67–70, 106–8.

10. MESDA artisan files. Joiners Richard Batin (fl. 1672–1681) and Francis Gracia (fl. 1681–1703) may have been French, but conclusive evidence is lacking. Richard Batin, his wife, Rebecca, and a servant named George Prideaux arrived in the colony by May 1672 (Agnes Leland Baldwin, *First Settlers of South Carolina, 1670–1680* [Easley, S.C.: Southern Historical Press, Inc., 1985], p. 16; Hirsch, *Huguenots of Colonial South Carolina*, pp. 8, 11; MESDA artisan files). Francis Gracia (fl. 1681–1703) was a resident of South Carolina by June 1681, and his wife, Elizabeth, immigrated three years later (Baldwin, *First Settlers of South Carolina*, p. 105; MESDA artisan files). Although Gracia's origin is not known, his name could be a corruption of François Grascherie. Members of the Grascherie family of La Rochelle were naturalized in England in 1687 (Baird, *Huguenot Emigration to America*, 1:293). For Varine, see St. Julien Ravenel Childs, "The Petit–Guérard Colony," *South Carolina Historical and Genealogical Magazine* (hereinafter cited SCHGM) 43, no. 1 (January 1942): 1, 2, 16, 17; Alexander S. Salley, Jr., ed., *Warrants for Land in South Carolina* (Columbia: University of South Carolina Press,) pp. 335–36, 467; Deed from Theophilus Paty to James Varien, October 20, 1685, "Abstracts from the Records of the Court of Ordinary of the Province of South Carolina, 1692–1700,"

SCHGM 9, no. 1 (January 1908): 119–20; Deed from "Susan Varine . . . Executrix of the last will . . . of James Varine" to unidentified grantee, March 1688/89 in Records of the Secretary of the Province and the Register of the Province of South Carolina, 1696–1703 (hereinafter cited as *RSPRPSC*), pt. 3, p. 376. For Le Chevalier, see Baird, *Huguenot Emigration to America*, 2:80; Land Warrant to "Peter le Chevalier," October 19, 1692, Charleston County, South Carolina Wills (hereinafter cited CCSCW), 1687–1710, vol. 53, p. 542; Town lots 162, 163, and 168–170 granted to Le Chevalier between October 19, 1692, and November 16, 1693, *RSPRPSC*, *1714–1719*, pt. 4, pp. 31–32; Will of "Peter Le Chevalier," April 30, 1712, Charleston County, South Carolina Miscellaneous Records (hereinafter cited CCSCMR), 1711–1718, p. 33. At least two other joiners named Le Chevalier worked in the colonies (Neil D. Kamil, "Hidden in Plain Sight: Disappearance and Material Life in Colonial New York," in *American Furniture*, edited by Luke Beckerdite and William N. Hosley [Hanover, N.H.: University Press of New England for the Chipstone Foundation, 1995], pp. 212–14, 217–19, 231, 237, 245 n. 32). For Lardan, see Baird, *Huguenot Emigration to America*, 2:79; Hirsch, *Huguenots of Colonial South Carolina*, pp. 118–19 n. 58; Land Warrant to "James Larden," March 31, 1694, *RSPRPSC, 1714–1719*, p. 41; *"Liste des François et Suisses" From an Old Manuscript List of French and Swiss Protestants Settled in Charleston, on the Santee and the Orange Quarter in Carolina who Desired Naturalization (1696/97)* (1868; reprint ed., Baltimore, Md.: Genealogical Publishing Company, 1968), p. 41; and E. Milby Burton, *Charleston Furniture, 1700–1825* (Charleston, S.C.: Charleston Museum, 1955), p. 100. For Lesueur, see Baird, *Huguenot Emigration to America*, 2:82; Hirsch, *Huguenots of Colonial South Carolina*, pp. 57–58, n. 32; *Liste des François et Suisses*, p. 50; "Abstracts from the Records of the Court of Ordinary of the Province of South Carolina, 1692–1700," *SCHGM*, 10, no. 1 (January 1909): 137 (Governor Blake directs "Abraham Leswear" to appraise the estate of Jacques Lardan, along with joiners Pierre Le Chevalier and Steven [Étienne] Tauvron); Will of Jacques de Bordeaux, December 20, 1699, CCSCW, 1692–1693, vol. 53, p. 481; Bradford L. Rauschenberg, "Coffin Making and Undertaking in Charleston and its Environs, 1705–1820," *Journal of Early Southern Decorative Arts* 16, no. 1 (May 1990): 19–20; Alexander S. Salley, Jr., ed., *Register of St. Philip's Parish, Charles Town, S.C., 1720–1758* (Columbia: University of South Carolina Press, 1971), p. 264.

11. For Pierre Manigault, see Baird, *Huguenot Emigration to America*, 1:279, 326; Beatrice St. Julien Ravenel, *Architects of Charleston* (1945; reprint ed., Columbia: University of South Carolina Press, 1992), p. 55; and MESDA artisan files. For Gabriel Manigault, see Baird, *Huguenot Emigration to America*, 1:279, 326; Ravenel, *Architects of Charleston*, p. 55; and MESDA artisan files. For Galliard, see Baird, *Huguenot Emigration to America*, 2:32, 59; Warrant granted to Isaac Cailleboeuf of Sainte Soline in Poitou for bringing six persons including Galliard to Carolina (Salley, ed., *Warrants*, p. 446); Deed involving town lot owned by "Peter Girard and Peter Galliard," December 1696, RSPRPSC, Miscellaneous Records, 1682–1690, pt. 4, p. 22; *Liste des François et Suisses*, pp. 52–53; Deeds from Paul Bruneau and John Gaillard to "Peter Gaillard," RSPRPSC, 1707–1711, pt. 1, pp. 155–56; Warrants for land in Craven County received by Galliard between November 24, 1707, and April 14, 1709, ibid., pp. 45, 155–56, 259; and Hirsch, *Huguenots of Colonial South Carolina*, pp. 16–17. For Tauvron, see "Abstracts from the Records of the Court of Ordinary of the Province of South Carolina, 1692–1700," *SCHGM*, 10, no. 1 (January 1909): 137; Will of Pierre Le Chevalier, September 1, 1702, CCSCW, 1671–1731, vol. 1, p. 48; Baird, *Huguenot Migration to America*, 1:311; Will of Stephen (Étienne) Tauvron, July 19, 1729, CCSCW, vol. 63, p. 148; and Salley, ed., *Register of St. Philip's Parish*, p. 234.

12. For Guibal, see Baird, *Huguenot Migration to America*, 2:106, 134; Warrants to "John Guppell" for land on the east side of the western branch of the Cooper River, January 9, 1695/96, and February 24, 1696/97 (Salley, ed., *Warrants,* pp. 528, 570); Hirsch, *Huguenots of South Carolina*, pp. 16–17. For Carion, see *Liste des François et Suisses*, p. 62; Hirsch, *Huguenots of South Carolina*, pp. 16–17.

13. For a later child's slat-back armchair with turned arms that pass over the front posts, see *Vie à La Campagne*, December 1920 (reprinted 1982), p. 42. A seventeenth-century French armchair with a rail-and-spindle back and turned arms that pass over the front posts is illustrated in *Vie à La Campagne*, December 1922 (reprinted 1976), p. 30. The French counterparts of British "Cromwellian" chairs typically have turned or rasp-shaped arms that pass over the front supports (see Monica Burckhardt, *Moblier Louis XIII Louis XIV* [Paris: Charles Massin, undated]: pp. 10, 31). For more on French-influenced seating from southeast Virginia and eastern North Carolina, see John Bivins, Jr., *The Furniture of Coastal North Carolina, 1700–1820* (Chapel Hill: University of North Carolina Press for MESDA, 1988), pp. 115–17; John Bivins,

Jr., "The French Connection," *The Luminary* 8, no. 2 (Summer 1987), pp. 1–3; John Bivins, Jr., and Forsyth Alexander, *The Regional Arts of the Early South* (Chapel Hill: University of North Carolina Press for MESDA, 1991), p. 21; and Ronald L. Hurst and Jonathan Prown, *Southern Furniture, 1680–1830: The Colonial Williamsburg Collection* (New York: Harry Abrams, 1997). See, for example, the armchair and side chair in Philippe de Champaigne's *Ex-Voto* (1662), illustrated in Alain Mérot, *French Painting in the Seventeenth Century*, translated by Caroline Beamish (New Haven, Conn.: Yale University Press, 1995), p. 187.

14. For more on the use of the center bit in the seventeenth century, see Benno M. Forman, *American Seating Furniture, 1630–1730* (New York: W. W. Norton, 1988), pp. 254–55. The author thanks John Alexander for his thoughts on the use of this tool.

15. Inventory of Wilson Dunston, April 27, 1692, CCSCW, 1687–1710, vols. 52–53, pp. 117–32; Inventory of Joseph Penderves, July 13, 1695, CCSCW, 1687–1710, vols. 52–53, pp. 301–4. In 1725, Richard Woodward's estate included "12 Black Permatto Bottom chares" (CCSCMR, 1726–1729, pp. 122–26); and in 1733, John Gardner's estate included "2 Elbow and 27 plain Parmatoce Botsd. Chairs" (CCSCW, 1732–1737, vols. 65–66, pp. 139–40), and John Lewis's estate included "12 black chairs Carolina Make . . . £6"(CCSCW, 1732–1737, vols. 65–66, pp. 112–15). Hammocks occur sporadically in seventeenth-century European inventories. A "cotton hamocke" was at Knole in 1645, and Prince Maurice of Nassau presented a hammock to the King of France (Peter Thornton, *Seventeenth-Century Interior Decoration in England, France and Holland* [New Haven, Conn.: Yale University Press, 1978], pp. 169, 172).

16. For different forms of bedsteads, see Inventory of Nicholas Mardin, March 3, 1696/97, CCSCW, 1687–1710, vols. 53–53, pp. 418–20; and Inventory of Richard Phillyps, February 20, 1694/95, CCSCW, 1687–1710, vols. 52–53, pp. 287–90. "Paul Grimball's Losses by the Spanish Invasion in 1686," *SCHGM* 29, no. 1 (January 1928): 233–36.

17. One of the earliest references to a couch in South Carolina is the "cain" one owned by William Rhett in 1719 (Thayer Hall Indenture to Col. William Rhett, January 8, 1718/19, Register of the Province of South Carolina, 1714–1719, (hereinafter cited RPSC) pp. 353–55. Cane couches probably appeared about the same time as cane chairs. Francis Turgis's inventory of March 19, 1696/97, listed a dozen cane chairs (CCSCW, 1687–1710, vols. 52–53, pp. 429–31). Inventory of John Boyden, September 5, 1726, CCSCMR, 1726–1727, pp. 130–35. Inventory of William Ramsey, July 4, 1733, CCSCW, 1732–1737, vols. 65–66, pp. 46–49. The gateleg table illustrated in fig. 11 is discussed in Peter M. Kenny, "Flat Gates, Draw Bars, Twists, and Urns: New York's Distinctive, Early Baroque Oval Tables with Falling Leaves," in *American Furniture,* edited by Luke Beckerdite (Hanover, N.H.: University Press of New England for the Chipstone Foundation, 1994), pp. 109, fig. 2; 116. A New York draw-bar table by the same turner is in a private collection. For an excellent discussion of the Carolina couch, see Bivins and Alexander, *The Regional Arts of the Early South,* p. 72. Most of the colony's Germanic immigrants settled in Purrysbury, New Windsor, and rural communities along the Savannah River.

18. Andrew Allen's October 18, 1735, inventory listed a couch and squab valued at £10 (CCSCW, 1732–1737, vols. 65–66, pp. 331–34). Charleston upholsterer Robert Hunt advertised "couches, matrasses, [and] squabs" in the August 10, 1734, issue of the *Charleston Gazette.* Inventory of Daniel Gale, January 26, 1725, CCSCMR, 1726–1727, pp. 24–26. As quoted in Audrey Michie, "Charleston Upholstery in All Its Branches, 1725–1820," *Journal of Early Southern Decorative Arts* 11, no. 2 (November 1985): 57. Pavilions are discussed in detail in Thornton, *Seventeenth-Century Interior Decoration,* pp. 159–60. Michie, "Charleston Upholstery," p. 60.

19. "Grimball's Losses," pp. 233–36. For more on turkeywork chairs, see Margaret Swain, "The Turkey-work Chairs of Holeyrood House," in *Upholstery in America & Europe from the Seventeenth Century to World War I,* edited by Edward S. Cooke, Jr., (New York: W. W. Norton & Co., 1987), pp. 51–63. The influence of French seating on chairmaking in Holland and England is discussed in Thornton, *Seventeenth-Century Interior Decoration,* pp. 192–203; Peter Thornton, "Upholstered Seat Furniture in Europe, 17th and 18th Centuries," in Cooke, ed., *Upholstery in America & Europe,* pp. 29–34; and Robert F. Trent, "17th-Century Upholstery in Massachusetts," in ibid., p. 40.

20. *Antiques* 10, no. 2 (August 1926): 141. Paul H. Burroughs, *Southern Antiques* (Richmond, Va.: Garrett & Massie, Inc., 1931), pp. 161, 166. For more on the southern chair, see Hurst and Prown, *Southern Furniture, 1680–1830* pp. 52–54.

21. Thornton, "Upholstered Seat Furniture," p. 33; and Thornton, *Seventeenth-Century Interior Decoration,* pp. 180, 181, 202, 207. The New York chair is illustrated and discussed in

Kamil, "Hidden in Plain Sight," pp. 201–7. The bulbous finials, compressed baluster turnings, and flat scrolled arms on the Carolina chair are reminiscent of those on an eighteenth-century, Danish slat-back chair illustrated in Forman, *American Seating*, p. 172, fig. 87. French styles had a tremendous influence on Scandinavian furniture.

22. French and French-Canadian *escabeaux* are illustrated in Jacqueline Boccador, *Le Moblier Français Du Moyen Age à la Renaissance* (Saint Just en Chaussée, Fr.: Monelle Hayot, 1988), p. 306, fig. 259; and Jean Palardy, *The Early Furniture of French Canada* (1963; reprint ed., New York: St. Martin's Press, 1965), pp. 205–6.

23. For references to "Dutch" chairs and tables, see especially Thayer Hall Indenture to Colonel William Rhett, January 8, 1718, RPSC, 1714–1719, pp. 353–55; and Inventory of Alice Hogg, March 10, 1726/27, photocopy on file at MESDA. During the seventeenth and early eighteenth centuries, gateleg tables were generally identified by their woods or the shape or action of their tops (Kenny, "Flat Gates, Draw Bars, Twists, and Urns," pp. 107–8). The Manigault example would probably have been referred to as a "cedar," "oval" (or possibly round), "flap," or "falling leaf" table. The 1692 inventory of Wilson Dunston listed a "ceadar ovell table" valued at £1.10 (see note 15 above).

24. A French-Canadian gateleg table similar to the European example (fig. 24) is illustrated in Palardy, *The Early Furniture of French Canada*, fig. 382. The turnings on the European table are very similar to those on many late seventeenth-century "Ile D'Oléron" chairs (MESDA research file S-9119; conversation with Robert F. Trent).

25. Ashe, *Carolina,* in Salley, ed., *Narratives of Early Carolina,* p. 142. Bradford L. Rauschenberg, "Timber Available in Charleston," *Journal of Early Southern Decorative Arts* 20, no. 2 (November 1994): 53, 61.

26. *A Brief Description of the Province of Carolina* (London: Robert Horne, 1666), in *Historical Collections of South Carolina: Embracing Many Rare & Valuable Pamphlets and Other Documents Relating to the History of that State From its First Discovery to its Independence in the Year 1776*, 2 vols. (New York: Harper & Brothers, 1836), p. 12. The latest pieces of Charleston furniture with walnut primary are a desk signed by cabinetmaker William Carwitham (fl. 1730–1770) (MESDA collection) and the dressing table illustrated in fig. 45. Both date to about 1740–1745.

27. Similar details also occur on contemporary tables from French- and Dutch-settled areas of New York (Kenny, "Flat Gates, Draw Bars, Twists, and Urns," pp. 110, fig. 4; 112, fig. 10; 130). For French and French colonial tables with dovetailed cleats, see Boccador, *Le Moblier Français Du Moyen Age à la Renaissance*, p. 22; and Palardy, *Furniture of French Canada*, figs. 376, 379, 398, 410.

28. For Broughton, see Dunn, *Sugar and Slaves,* p. 112, n. 41; Baldwin, *First Settlers of South Carolina,* p. 36; MESDA, *Henrietta Johnston* (Winston-Salem, N.C.: by the museum, 1991), pp. 51–52; and Waterhouse, "South Carolina's Colonial Elite," pp. 69–70. Broughton dealt in furs and Indian slaves who were sent to the West Indies. As quoted in Lane, *Architecture of the Old South: South Carolina,* p. 22.

29. Thomas Tileston Waterman, *The Dwellings of Colonial America* (Chapel Hill: University of North Carolina Press, 1950), pp. 32–37. Conversations with J. Thomas Savage and Jonathan Poston of the Historic Charleston Foundation and architectural historian Ralph Harvard. For a structural analysis of Mulberry, see George T. Fore and Associates, Report on Mulberry Plantation, Goose Creek, South Carolina, Raleigh, N.C., 1989.

30. On September 17, 1703, Broughton and Le Chevalier executed a bond to Governor Nathaniel Johnson, Broughton's father-in-law, for Peter Jacob Gurrard's proper administration of the estate of his father, Jacob, of Berkeley County ("Abstracts from the Records of the Court of Ordinary of the Province of South Carolina, 1700–1712," *SCHGM* 12, no. 1 [January 1911]: 208). *Henrietta Johnston*, pp. 39, 51, 53. Baird, *Huguenot Emigration to America*, 1:284, 297.

31. Baird, *Huguenot Emigration to America*, 1:310, 2:50–51. Daniel, Sr., and his wife were naturalized in England on March 8, 1682. Daniel, Jr., and his sister, Madeleine, were born in South Carolina.

32. Lane, *Architecture of the Old South: South Carolina,* pp. 22, 27–29. Burton, *Charleston Furniture*, fig. 76; MESDA research file, S-8157. New York tables with stacked balusters are illustrated in Kenny, "Flat Gates, Draw Bars, Twists, and Urns," pp. 109, fig. 2; 110, fig. 3; 112, fig. 9; 119, fig. 23; 121, figs. 26–27; 124–25; and Dean F. Failey, *Long Island Is My Nation: The Decorative Arts & Craftsmen, 1640–1830* (Setauket, N.Y.: Society for the Preservation of Long Island Antiquities, 1976), p. 28, fig. 27.

33. The author thanks Ronald L. Hurst for the information on the dressing table. Rauschenberg, "Timber Available in Charleston," pp. 70–71. Mahogany appears in Boston fur-

niture during the late seventeenth century and in New York furniture by the first decade of the eighteenth century. Given the Low Country's familial and trade connections with the West Indies, it is likely that mahogany came into use in Charleston at about the same time. Although the drawer has been altered, the red bay components appear to be original. They support a Charleston attribution, since this wood seldom appears on furniture made elsewhere. Naturalist Mark Catesby wrote: "in Carolina [red bay is] everywhere seen. . . . [T]he wood is fine grain'd, and of excellent use for cabinets, &c." (Rauschenberg, "Timber Available in Charleston," pp. 46–47). On January 23, 1733/34, joiner Thomas Blythe mortgaged property including "36 mahogany boards and red bay boards" (ibid).

34. The earliest joiner known to have moved from New England to Charleston is Charles Warham (1701–1779). Born in London, Warham worked in Boston for at least a decade prior to his arrival in Charleston about 1733 (MESDA artisan files; Myrna Kaye, "Eighteenth-century Boston Furniture Craftsmen," in *Boston Furniture of the Eighteenth Century*, edited by Walter Muir Whitehill, Brock Jobe, and Jonathan Fairbanks [Boston: Colonial Society of Massachusetts, 1972], p. 300). In the November 2, 1734, issue of the *South Carolina Gazette*, he advertised, "Charles Earham, Joiner, late from Boston, N. England, maketh all sorts of Tables, Chests, Chest of Drawers, Desks, Book-cases . . . [and] Coffins of the newest fashion, never as yet made in Charlestown." Baird, *Huguenot Emigration to America*, 1:282, 2:315, 333. Joyce D. Goodfriend, *Before the Melting Pot: Society and Culture in Colonial New York City, 1664–1730* (Princeton, N.J.: Princeton University Press, 1992), p. 49.

35. Twenty-two of Johnston's sitters were of British descent, seventeen were of French descent, and three are unidentified (*Henrietta Johnston*, pp. 42–72). For Johnston's origins, see Martha R. Severens, "Who was Henrietta Johnston?" *Antiques* 148, no. 5 (November 1995): 704–9. As quoted in Whaley Batson, "Henrietta Johnston (c. 1674–1729)," in *Henrietta Johnston*, p. 10. For more on Johnston and her patrons, see ibid.; Forsyth Alexander, "Henrietta's Charles Town: Charleston in the First Quarter of the Eighteenth Century"; and "The Crayon Drawings of Henrietta Johnston and Related Works, " in *Henrietta Johnston*.

36. *Henrietta Johnston*, p. 50.

37. John Lawson, *A New Voyage to Carolina*, edited by Hugh Talmedge Lefler (Chapel Hill: University of North Carolina Press, 1967).

38. For more on Guerard, de Longemare, and L'Egaré, see Baird, *History of the Huguenot Migration*, 2:52, 77, 80, 111–12; Samuel Gaillard Stoney, "Nicholas de Longuemare," *Transactions of the Huguenot Society of South Carolina* 55 (1950): 38–69; and MESDA artisan files. Frank Horton, "Miles Brewton, Goldsmith," *Journal of Early Southern Decorative Arts* 7, no. 2 (November 1981): 1–13. Museum of London, *The Quiet Conquest: The Huguenots, 1685–1985* (London: by the museum, 1985), pp. 72–76. The aforementioned silversmiths are often referred to as "Peter Jacob Girrard," "Solomon Legare," and "Nicholas de Longuemare" in South Carolina records.

39. Horton, "Miles Brewton, Goldsmith," pp. 9–12. For the history of the French cup, see Frederich Dalcho, *An Historical Account of the Protestant Episcopal Church in South Carolina* (1820; reprint ed., New York: Arno Press, 1970), p. 273; and MESDA research file S-10933.

40. Batson, "Henrietta Johnston (c. 1674–1729)," p. 10. "Will of Peter Manigault," *Transactions of the Huguenot Society of South Carolina* 30 (1925): 40. The Manigault family's connection to the French church persisted throughout the eighteenth century. On March 2, 1774, the *Georgia Gazette* reported, "the body of the Honourable Peter Manigault, Esq. who lately died in London arrived [in Charleston] . . . and the same evening was deposited in the family vault in the cemetery belonging to the French Church."

Appendix

Huguenot Joiners in the Low Country, 1670–1730

Name	Alternative Spelling	Birthplace	Working dates
Jacques Varine	James Varien	Rouen, Normandy	1680–1689
Pierre Le Chevalier	Peter Le Chevallier	St. Lo, Normandy	1692–1712
Pierre Gaillard	Peter Gaillard	Cherveaux, Poitou	1694–1710
Jacques Lardan	James Lardant	Dieppe, Normandy	1694–1698
Pierre Manigault	Peter Manigault	La Rochelle, Aunis	1695–1718
Gabriel Manigault		La Rochelle, Aunis	1695–1709
Moise Carion	Moses Carion	Faguère, Languedoc	1696–1697
Abraham Lesueur	Abraham Lesware	Harfleur, Normandy	1696–1740
Étienne Tauvron	Steven Tauvron	Isle de Ré	1696–1729
Jean Guibal	John Guppell	Saint André de Valborgne, Languedoc	1698–1703
Anthoine de Bordeaux	Anthony De Bordeaux	South Carolina	1709–1725
Jean du Brevill	Jean du Breuill	Unknown	1713–14
Isaac Chovin	Isaac Shauvin	Unknown	1714
Jean Henri Bonneau	John Henry Bonneau	La Rochelle, Aunis	1717–1753

Sources: Artisan files, Museum of Early Southern Decorative Arts, Winston-Salem, North Carolina; Charles W. Baird, *History of the Huguenot Emigration to America*, 2 vols. (1885; reprint ed., Baltimore, Md.: Genealogical Publishing Co., 1991); Arthur Henry Hirsch, *The Huguenots of Colonial South Carolina* (1928; reprint ed., Baltimore, Md.: Genealogical Publishing Co., 1991); *Transactions of the Huguenot Society of South Carolina.*

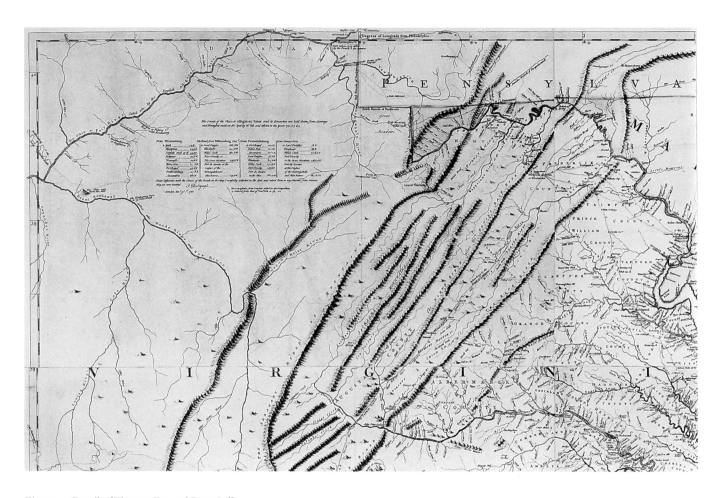

Figure 1 Detail of Thomas Fry and Peter Jefferson's *A MAP of the most INHABITED part of VIRGINIA containing the whole PROVINCE of MARYLAND with part of PENSYLVANIA, NEW JERSEY and NORTH CAROLINA*, London, 1768. (Courtesy, Colonial Williamsburg Foundation.)

Wallace Gusler

The Furniture of
Winchester, Virginia

▼ THE MODERN REALTOR'S axiom "location, location, location" certainly applied to the thriving, eighteenth-century town of Winchester, Virginia. Strategically situated on the "Great Wagon Road"—the longest and most traveled highway in colonial America—Winchester was a major center of frontier development (fig. 1). The town was also a crossroads, connected to eastern Virginia by Ashby's Gap and to the western frontier by the Potomac River Valley and several gaps in the Allegheny Mountains. This location facilitated trade and attracted settlers from the Delaware River Valley, the piedmont and Chesapeake Bay regions of Virginia and Maryland, and other areas of the southern backcountry. By 1776, Winchester was one of the largest backcountry towns in the colonies.

The earliest European exploration of the Shenandoah Valley occurred during the late seventeenth century, when the area had few permanent inhabitants and was principally a hunting ground for Native Americans. Winchester was apparently established at the site of Shawnee Springs, an Indian village located near the warriors' path. This path, which traversed the length of the valley and connected the "Northern" and "Southern" Indians, eventually became the "Great Wagon Road."[1]

Popular literature credits Virginia Lieutenant Governor Alexander Spotswood's 1716 expedition by the "Knights of the Golden Horseshoe" with the official discovery of the Shenandoah Valley, but Indian traders and explorers had penetrated the area much earlier. The northern end of the valley was mapped by Louis Michell in 1707. Spotswood was, however, instrumental in changing the land granting policies of the General Assembly to encourage settlement in western Virginia. Whereas the old "head right" system allotted fifty acres for every settler, the new system allotted fifty acres and gave individuals the option to purchase an unlimited number of fifty-acre tracts for five shillings each.[2]

During the late 1720s, settlers began to move into the northern Shenandoah Valley. Wealthy eastern Virginians also capitalized on the more liberal land granting policies by surveying and buying extensive tracts as speculative investments. In 1728, Tidewater planters Robert Carter and Mann Page purchased 50,000 acres in the Shenandoah Valley. During the following decade, Jacob Stover, Joist Hite, Robert McKay, and John and Isaac Van Meter acquired large tracts to settle German, Swiss, and Scots-Irish families.[3]

As settlement increased, the Virginia legislature made provisions for the establishment of new counties. Frederick County was established in the northern valley in 1738, and Augusta County was established in the central and southwestern valley in 1745. Orange County, Virginia, surveyor James Wood laid out the first town in the Shenandoah Valley in 1744. Originally named Frederick Town, it became the seat of Frederick County and was subsequently incorporated as Winchester.[4]

Among the earliest settlers in the valley were Germanic and Scots-Irish immigrants, most of whom were second-generation Pennsylvanians. They accounted for about two-thirds of the population prior to the Revolution. British colonists from eastern Virginia made up the remainder, along with a few settlers from other areas such as New York and Maryland. By the third quarter of the eighteenth century, the Shenandoah Valley's population was a mosaic of diverse peoples and religions—Presbyterians, Lutherans, Anglicans, Quakers, Dunkards, and Mennonites. This diversity brought together numerous cultural lifestyles and trade traditions. Eventually these cross-currents of style and function merged British and Germanic traditions.[5]

Many objects produced in the region show the duality of these influences. Germanic craftsmen contributed strongly to the establishment of trades in Winchester and the Shenandoah Valley. Their conservative lifestyle and strong work ethic was often in sharp contrast to that of the Scots-Irish, as pointed out by an early nineteenth-century observer:

> you can always tell when you get among the Dutch and the Quakers, for there you perceive that something has been done for posterity. Their houses are of stone, and built for duration, not for show. If a German builds a house, its walls are twice as thick as others—if he puts down a gate-post, it is sure to be nearly as thick as it is long. Every thing about him, animate and inanimate, partakes in this character of solidity. His wife is even a jolly, portly dame—his children chubby rogues, with legs shaped like little old-fashioned mahogany bannisters—his barns as big as fortresses—his horses like mammoths . . . his cattle enormous—It matters not to him, whether the form of sideboards or bureaus changes, or whether other people wear tight breeches or Cossac pantaloons in the shape of meal-bags. Let fashion change as it may, his low, round crowned, broad brimmed hat keeps its ground—his galligskins support the same liberal dimensions, and his old oaken chest and clothespress of curled maple, with the Anno Domini of their construction upon them, together with the dresser, glistening with pewter plates, still stand their ground, while the baseless fabrics of fashion fade away. . . . Ceaseless and unwearied industry is his delight, and enterprise and speculation his abhorrence. Riches do not corrupt, nor poverty depress him; for his mind is a sort of Pacific ocean . . . unmoved by tempests, and only intolerable from its dead and tedious calms. . . . [W]hen he dies, his son moves on in the same pace, till generations have passed away, without one of the name becoming distinguished by his exploits or his crimes.

Although this amusing characterization is obviously prejudiced, a tendency toward excessive technology and stylistic conservatism is manifest in Germanic architecture and decorative arts from the Shenandoah Valley as well as from other areas of America and Europe.[6]

The "ceaseless and unwearied industry" of the region's Teutonic settlers undoubtedly contributed to the region's economy, which was largely based on the cultivation and export of grain, hemp, and livestock. Wheat, corn, and cattle were marketed in Philadelphia and eastern Virginia, and hemp was exported for the manufacture of rope. The Indian trade in furs and deerskins was also important in the development of the region. The earliest white settler at Winchester was probably an Indian trader. One of the most typical patterns of settlement in the backcountry began with the establishment of an Indian trader at a critical geographic location. Eventually his trading post became a store, and a settlement or town developed around it. As the town grew, merchants and tradesmen supplied and produced goods for the frontier trade. The rapid growth of settlement in the Shenandoah Valley and western territories also provided an expanding market for the vast array of imported items required by hunters, farmers, and tradesmen.[7]

During the French and Indian War (1754–1763), Winchester was the headquarters for General Edward Braddock's campaign against Fort Duquesne. The building of Braddock's Road, which cut through the mountains to the west, was important to settlement after the war. The town also profited from the construction of Washington's headquarters, Fort Loudon, just north of Winchester in 1756 and the subsequent quartering and provisioning of troops and refugees. In 1760, Andrew Burnaby noted that Winchester had about two hundred houses and was "the place of general rendezvous of the Virginia troops, which is the reason of its late rapid increase and present flourishing condition."[8]

Later in the century, the production of cast-iron stoves, firebacks, utensils, and pig and bar stock became integral components of the regional economy. In 1767, Isaac Zane of Philadelphia purchased a "Mansion House," a "Furnace Called Marlboro," and several hundred acres of land about twelve miles from Winchester. Because the ore near the furnace produced pig and bar iron that was brittle and unsuitable for "American Consumption," Zane built a new furnace near beds of more malleable ore in 1772. The following year, Zane's common-law wife, Sally, reported that they could "not keep any Great Stock of Iron on Hand there being so many Customers ready for it almost as fast as it is made." In 1781, Thomas Jefferson estimated that Marlboro Furnace was producing 600 tons of pig iron and 150 tons of bar iron annually.[9]

Descriptions of Winchester changed markedly during the third quarter of the eighteenth century. In 1755, English visitor Lord Adam Gordon remarked that the town was built of limestone and "inhabited by a spurious race of mortals known by the appellation of Scotch-Irish." Twenty years later, Philip Vickers Fithian referred to it as "a smart village nearly half a mile in length, and several streets broad and pretty full. . . . The land is good, the country pleasant, the houses in general large." Fithian also wrote that "we see many everyday, traveling out and in, to and from Carolina, some on foot with packs, and some in large covered wagons. The road here is much frequented, and for 150 miles farther [south] . . . thickly inhabited."[10]

The pace of settlement expanded dramatically after the Revolution. As the mercantile importance of Winchester grew, the town's society became increasingly cosmopolitan and complex. Mrs. Susanna Knox described the elegant lifestyle and cultural diversity of the town at the turn of the century.

> I have already experienced more true politeness, hospitality and attention in the short time I have been here than I ever did . . . in Fredericksburg where

I was bred. I went first to Dr. Mackeye, he has a handsome house elegantly furnished. I think his drawing room is one of the genteelest I ever saw. . . . Yesterday we drank tea with a Mrs. Tidbald, another most delightful woman. She was bred in Philadelphia. Her husband is a merchant of prominence, and she made the greatest display of plate at her tea table that ever I saw—a large silver tea urn, coffee pot, tea pot, cream pot, sugar cup, slop bowl, and a large silver goblet on the side table all beautifully ornamented. They live in a large stone house. I was only in the drawing room—that was a very handsome one elegantly furnished with mahogany—a settee covered with copper plate calico, red and white, the window curtains the same, with white muslin falls drawn up in festoons, with large tassels as big as my two fists. . . . Mr. Peacock has just made a purchase of a beautiful lot with a very pretty house, a number of fine fruit trees, a good garden and a well on it—and gives only 200 for it and that to be paid off in so easy a manner that it will be no more than paying rent. . . . It provokes me to think how much dearer the lots are in Falmouth, and this town is larger than Fredericksburg and it put together. I was at the Dutch church last Sunday, a very handsome stone building. . . . It has a fine steeple [and] . . . is nicely finished off within. . . . There is one of the finest organs in it I ever heard, so you may perceive that I am quite in my element. Fine society, charming music, excellent living, and no trouble about it. I wish to God all my family . . . were well settled up here. . . . I would be bound never to want to cross the Ridge again.

Although one may doubt that Winchester was as perfect as Mrs. Knox depicted it, the account of her visit is revealing. Her references to inhabitants from Baltimore and Philadelphia alluded to the cosmopolitan composition of Winchester's "higher class." She also acknowledged that the inhabitants were extremely hospitable and that "many of [the] . . . lower order who are entirely strangers . . . seem anxious for the welfare of my children." Her references to the different social classes and her description of the Dutch church and the minister's sermon "preached in English that day" are evidence of the social and cultural diversity that made Winchester a thriving town.[11]

By the end of the colonial period, Winchester was the largest town west of the Blue Ridge Mountains. The same social, cultural, and economic forces that propelled its development are embodied in the material culture of the region—particularly in the furniture made in and around Winchester during the late eighteenth and early nineteenth centuries. The cabinetmaking trade profited from the patronage of a strong middle and upper class, and a great variety of sophisticated furniture survives. The town's diverse cultural traditions and mercantile and family connections with Philadelphia and Baltimore are reflected in both the style and construction of this material. A strong Delaware Valley influence is evident in the earliest furniture, whereas Baltimore styles influenced the inlay and veneering practices of many later neoclassical pieces.

The key to identifying early Winchester-school furniture is a desk (figs. 2–4) inscribed "Christopher Frye Cabinet Maker Fauquire August 25 1797—James Lee Martin His Shop." The earliest reference to James Lee Martin in Fauquier County, Virginia, is the tax list for 1794. Although generally referred to as "James L. Martin," the 1798 records list him as "James Lee Martin" and note that "Christopher Frye" was a tithable member of his household. Frye is not listed in Martin's tax entry for the following year, but

Figure 2 Desk signed by Christopher Frye and James Lee Martin, Fauquier County, Virginia, 1797. Walnut with yellow pine and tulip poplar. H. 41³/₄", W. 43³/₄", D. 21¹/₂". (Private collection; photo, Craig McDougal.) The desk originally had a bookcase, and its feet are replaced.

Figure 3 Detail of the interior of the desk illustrated in fig. 2.

Figure 4 Detail of the inscription on the secret drawer of the desk illustrated in fig. 2.

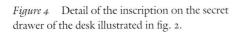

Martin did have a tithable household member named "Presley Foley." Like Frye, Foley was probably an apprentice or journeyman in Martin's shop.[12]

Frye was the son of Christopher Frye, Sr., of Winchester and appears as a tithable individual on his father's tax records in 1794. The following year, the younger Frye began working in Martin's Fauquier County shop. Christopher Frye, Sr., was probably a cabinetmaker. In his 1801 will, he directed Christopher Frye, Jr., "to look after [his] . . . business." Christopher Frye, Sr., was listed as a farmer from Holland when he served in the

Figure 5 Desk-and-bookcase attributed to the Frye-Martin shops, Winchester area, Virginia, 1791–1794. Cherry with yellow pine. H. 103³/₄", W. 42¹/₄", D. 24¹/₂". (Courtesy, Colonial Williamsburg Foundation.) This example and the high chests illustrated in figs. 9 and 14 have their original finials and most of their original brasses.

Figure 6 View of the desk-and-bookcase illustrated in fig. 5 with door and fallboard open.

Figure 7 Detail of the interior of the desk-and-bookcase illustrated in fig. 5, showing a fluted document drawer and the prospect compartment open. The mitered molding above the door is the face of a secret drawer. A card table that descended in the Lupton family (CWF 1987-725) has a top with a molded edge of the same configuration as the molding around the prospect door.

Figure 8 Detail of the pediment of the desk-and-bookcase illustrated in fig. 5.

Seventh Company of the Virginia Regiment in 1756; however, the fact that he had a "business" and lived in Winchester at the time of his death indicates that he was not principally a farmer in his later life. He may have learned his trade after serving in the military, or he could have been listed as a farmer because of a dual occupation. A casual approach to trade designations was common in eighteenth-century recordkeeping.[13]

The elder Frye left land to his son, Christopher, his daughter, Polly, and his son-in-law, James Lee Martin. Apprentices and journeymen frequently married into their master's family. Perhaps this practice applies here, since Martin married Mary (Polly) Frye in Frederick County, Virginia, on May 21, 1793, the year before he moved to the shop in Fauquier County. He was probably one of the James Martins who worked in the cabinetmaking and chairmaking trades in Baltimore during the 1780s and 1790s.[14]

A desk-and-bookcase made for Frederick County farmer and entrepreneur David Lupton (figs. 5–8) shares several features with the Frye-Martin desk (fig. 2). Lupton family tradition maintains that the desk-and-bookcase and two related cabriole-leg high chests (figs. 9, 14) were made by an itinerant cabinetmaker from Baltimore. The "itinerant" aspect of the history is

Figure 9　High chest with cabriole legs attributed to the Frye-Martin shops, Winchester area, Virginia, 1791–1794. Cherry with yellow pine. H. 97", W. 44", D. 24¼". (Courtesy, Colonial Williamsburg Foundation.)

misunderstood, since Martin worked in the area for over twenty years; how-ever, the physical and documentary evidence associated with these pieces suggests that this tradition is essentially correct. Lupton was also acquainted with the Frye family. In 1790, Christopher Frye, Sr., and his wife, Mary, sold Lupton a half-acre lot in Winchester.[15]

The Lupton desk-and-bookcase and the Frye-Martin desk have prospect doors with nearly identical molded surrounds and wide fluted document drawers without bases or capitals. On both desks, the molding above the prospect door is the front of a shallow drawer, and inside the prospect com-partment, a small panel beneath the drawer pulls out to access a small, "secret" well. The construction of the Lupton and Frye-Martin pieces is vir-tually identical. The only significant difference is in the base and capital moldings of the quarter-columns. Those of the signed example are larger and less academic than the turnings on the Lupton group. The base and cap-ital moldings on the Frye-Martin desk appear to be scaled for a full column rather than for a quarter-column, whereas those on the Lupton pieces are remarkably similar to imported brass bases and capitals commonly found on urban British and American case pieces. These differences could signify the work of two different turners in or contracted by the Frye-Martin shop; they could represent different options available to patrons; or they could reflect different approaches to the application of architectural details, one type by Frye and the other by Martin.

James Lee Martin died in 1815 at Berryville, Virginia, a few miles north-east of Winchester. His extensive inventory indicates that he was working as a cabinetmaker until his death. His wife, Mary, bought most of the household furniture, and their son Wilford purchased the majority of the woodworking tools and workbenches, presumably to carry on the cabinet-making business. Christopher Frye, Jr., resided in Winchester at least until 1815 when he sold land.[16]

The furniture attributed to the Frye-Martin shops is part of a large school of cabinetmaking that flourished in the northern Shenandoah Valley during the late eighteenth and early nineteenth centuries. At least forty-five related pieces survive, and approximately two-thirds of these examples were found in or have histories associated with Winchester and/or Frederick County. Included in this group are high chests with cabriole legs, high chests of drawers (three drawers over two drawers over four long drawers), conven-tional four-drawer chests, desks, desk-and-bookcases, tall clock cases, card tables, clothespresses, and corner cupboards.[17]

Although several cabinet firms were operating in the Winchester area, the products of the Frye-Martin shops have several consistent structural and stylistic features:

1. Desk-and-bookcases, cabriole-leg high chests, and corner cupboards have upper sections that are taller in proportion to the lower sections than on most American examples (see figs. 5, 9, 14). This trait appears to have originated in the Winchester school and is found on furniture made as far south as Rockingham and Augusta Counties in the Shenandoah Valley.

2. Scroll pediments have over-arcing ends with rosettes centered lower

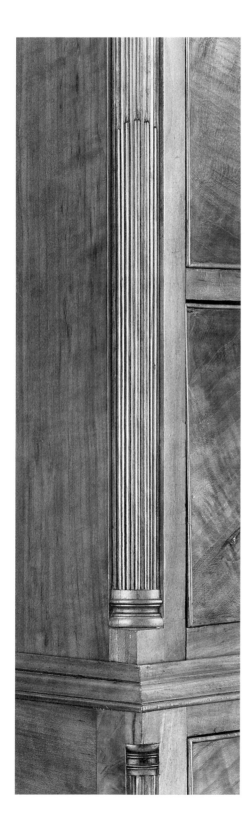

than on comparable Philadelphia examples. The Winchester pediments are also more open because the tympanum intersects the scroll moldings at a point lower than on examples from other areas (see figs. 8, 10, 15).

3. Scroll pediments usually have an astragal molding a few inches below the crown and scroll moldings. This astragal is single- or double-swagged beneath the center scroll section (see figs. 8, 10, 15, 33). Straight astragal moldings also occur below the hoods of tall clock cases (see fig. 22) and below the cornice moldings of high chests (fig. 39).

4. The central plinths of scroll and pitch pediments often have applied carving designed in two layers—a convex shell overlapping a flaring stylized foliage (figs. 8, 10, 15, 25). On Tennessee furniture in the Winchester style, these elements are reversed (see fig. 53).

5. Neoclassic, urn-style finials are usually atop fluted plinths positioned on the corners of the crown molding, not lined up with the corners of the main case below as in more academic examples.

6. Paneled doors usually have two panels, a tall vertical rectangle and a smaller square or horizontal rectangle. This combination probably resulted from the attenuated design of the upper cases (see figs. 5, 33).

7. Quarter-columns and pilasters often have arched stop-fluting (see figs. 11, 12, 34).

8. Claw-and-ball feet have talons ending short of the bottom of the balls (see figs. 13, 16). The rear talon is shorter than the front and side talons, almost doubling the distance from the end of its talon to the floor level.

9. Desk interiors frequently have prospect doors flanked by document drawers that are unusually wide (see figs. 3, 6, 7). The faces of the document drawers are often fluted, but they do not have base and capital moldings. This stylized representation of a pilaster also has parallels in the fluting of door rails (fig. 33).

10. The full-depth dustboards are thinner than the drawer rails but do not have kickers. This dustboard design is typical of Philadelphia and probably

Figure 11 Detail of an arched, stop-fluted quarter-column on the upper section of the high chest with cabriole legs illustrated in fig. 9.

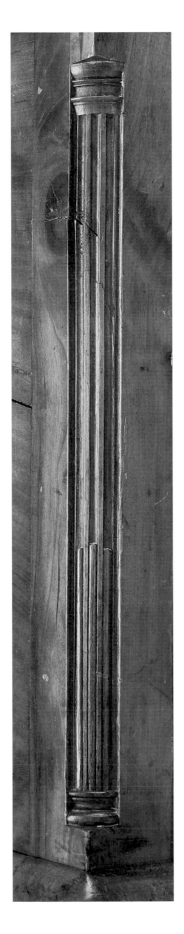

Figure 12 Detail of an arched, stop-fluted quarter-column on the lower section of the high chest with cabriole legs illustrated in fig. 9. This quarter-column is carved from the stile rather than being turned and fluted on a lathe like the columns on the upper section.

Figure 13 Detail of a claw-and-ball foot of the high chest with cabriole legs illustrated in fig. 9.

represents an influence from that city. Backboards are nailed into rabbets in the case sides and top and to the bottom of the case.

11. Feet are usually set on flat boards that are mitered at the front corners and have the base molding cut on their projecting edge. These boards are glued and nailed to the bottom of the case. Both ogee and straight bracket feet are backed by a single, weight-bearing vertical block, and two horizontal flanker blocks support the brackets.

12. Cornices are usually nailed and glued.

13. On drawers with cockbeading, the bottoms often have two cross-grain, planed furrows cut to clear the drawer stops that are nailed and glued to the top of the drawer blades. This feature was necessary because the drawer bottom was too thick and/or not set high enough to clear the stops.[18]

14. Tall clock cases have several horizontal backboards rather than the usual single vertical board. This feature appears almost exclusively in the Frye-Martin group.

15. Clock hood doors frequently have a name written with quill and ink across the top inside of the arch. These names were written in the cabinet shop and appear to be those of the customer.

16. Yellow pine is the dominant secondary wood; occasionally poplar is used throughout, and sometimes it is combined with black walnut and yellow pine.

Figure 14 High chest with cabriole legs attributed to the Frye-Martin shops, Winchester area, Virginia, 1791–1794. Cherry with yellow pine. H. 97¹/₂", W. 44", D. 24". (Courtesy, Colonial Williamsburg Foundation.)

Because some of these features are found on furniture from other areas, they must be considered collectively or corroborated by histories or other evidence before making an attribution to a specific place, school, or shop. The furniture made for David Lupton provides an excellent case in point and serves as a springboard for examining other shop traditions that relate to and diverge from the Frye-Martin group.[19]

The desk-and-bookcase and high chests shown in figures 5, 9, and 14 were

Figure 15 Detail of the pediment of the high chest with cabriole legs illustrated in fig. 14.

made for Lupton's house, Cherry Row (figs. 17, 18), which is situated on Apple Pie Ridge about a mile west of Winchester. Although the high chests are very similar, they have slightly different drawer graduations, different brasses, and different finials (figs. 9, 14). Their upper cases contain four long drawers rather than three as in contemporary Philadelphia examples. The extra drawer probably accounts for the more attenuated proportions of the Winchester chests. Apparently, the design was achieved by using a standard high chest format for the upper sections. High chests made in the back-country usually have four large drawers surmounted by two small ones.

The forward facing rear feet on these chests could reflect the maker's lack of familiarity with Philadelphia examples, or they may have been specified by the patron. A related high chest base with correctly positioned rear feet supports the latter hypothesis (fig. 19). It has a history of descent in the Bailey, Parkins, and Solenberger families who lived south of Winchester in Shenandoah County. The feet have well defined knuckles and are among the finest produced in the Winchester area (fig. 20). The retracted talons relate to those on the Lupton chests (figs. 13, 16), but the feet of the base are

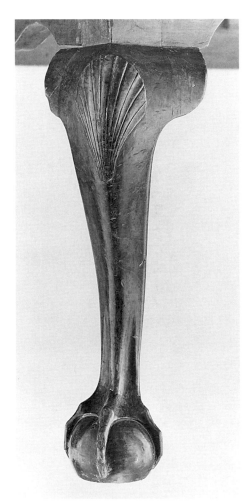

Figure 16 Detail of a front leg of the high chest with cabriole legs illustrated in fig. 14.

Figure 17 Cherry Row, Frederick County, Virginia, completed 1794. (Photo, Gavin Ashworth.)

Figure 18 Detail of the carved date board on the exterior of Cherry Row. (Photo, Gavin Ashworth.)

Figure 19 Base of a high chest with cabriole legs, Winchester area, Virginia, 1791–1794. Walnut with tulip poplar. Dimensions not recorded. (Private collection; photo, Wallace Gusler.) This base may have supported a separate case of drawers, or it may be the lower part of a single-piece form.

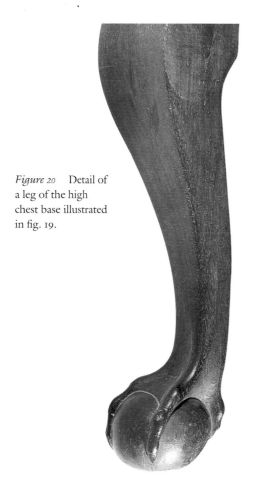

Figure 20 Detail of a leg of the high chest base illustrated in fig. 19.

Figure 21 Detail of the right side of the high chest base illustrated in fig. 19.

Figure 22 Tall clock case attributed to the Frye-Martin shops, Winchester area, Virginia, ca. 1795. Walnut with yellow pine. H. 99½". (Private collection; photo, Craig McDougal.) The movement is not signed. The tips of the ogee feet are missing. The door has scars from modern, surface-mounted false hinges, but the original hinges are intact.

Figure 23 Detail of the hood of the tall clock case illustrated in fig. 22.

clearly by a different hand. They probably represent the work of a carver rather than a cabinetmaker who occasionally did carving. The design and construction of the base is also less sophisticated than that of the Lupton chests. The maker failed to take advantage of the height of the front skirt and used linear scalloping rather than a more centralized and more conventional arched design. In addition, he cut the side scalloping above the level of the outer drawer supports and installed an inset panel to correct his mistake (fig. 21). Despite these differences, the tradesmen responsible for the base were clearly influenced by the work of the Frye-Martin shops.

The tall clock case illustrated in figure 22 has all of the structural details associated with the Frye-Martin shops. Its finials and rosettes match those

Figure 24   Corner cupboard attributed to the Frye-Martin shops, Winchester area, Virginia, ca. 1790. Cherry and mahogany (capitals) with yellow pine. H. 125", W. 61", D. 24". (Courtesy, Colonial Williamsburg Foundation.) The shelves are faced with applied strips with scalloped lower edges.

Figure 25 Detail of the pediment of the corner cupboard illustrated in fig. 24.

on the Lupton suite (figs. 8, 10, 15, 23), and it has arched, stop-fluted quarter-columns on the waist and fluted quarter-columns on the plinth below. This quarter-column arrangement, which is relatively common in Winchester-school work, may relate to the superimposition of orders in classical architecture. The name "Anderson," written in quill script across the inside arch of the hood door, probably refers to the original owner.

The corner cupboard illustrated in figures 24 and 25 has pilasters with arched stop-fluting, finials like those on the clock case and high chests shown in figures 8, 10, 15, and 23, and a tympanum appliqué by the same hand that carved the appliqués and rosettes on the clock case and all of the pieces in the Lupton suite. Antique dealer Joe Kindig, Jr., purchased this cupboard and the overmantle shown in figure 26 out of the James Hamilton House in Kernstown, about a mile south of Winchester. The overmantel is one of the most elaborate examples of carving from the Winchester area. The leaves and flowers rising from the basket on the overmantel are considerably more naturalistic and more skillfully rendered than the primitive foliage on furniture in the Frye-Martin group.[20]

Another corner cupboard (fig. 27) is attributed to the Frye-Martin group based on its relationship to the Hamilton example and to a built-in cupboard with a pitch pediment (fig. 28) in David Lupton's house. Like the Hamilton cupboard (figs. 24, 25), these examples have Ionic capitals with flat arched scrolls and shallow, relatively naive egg-and-dart moldings (figs.

Figure 26 Overmantle from the James Hamilton House, Kernstown, Virginia, ca. 1800. Painted yellow pine. (Courtesy, Winterthur Museum.) The eagle has been removed from its original position shown here and reinstalled in another location in the Winterthur Museum.

29, 30). On the cupboards illustrated in figures 27 and 28, the applied molding that runs over the door and joins the top molding of the capitals (figs. 27, 28) is a variation of the astragal molding found on the pediments of several other pieces in the Frye-Martin group. These cupboards are the only examples from the Winchester school with a barrel back terminated in a large, carved shell in the top (fig. 31).

Although the cupboards shown in figures 27 and 28 are principally made of yellow pine, the capitals of the former example are walnut and those of the latter are maple (figs. 29, 30). Walnut and maple take carving much better than yellow pine, which is heavily layered with hard (summer growth) and soft (spring growth) rings. On both cupboards, the contrasting woods would have been covered by their original blue paint. This wood usage is consistent with that of the Hamilton cupboard, which has cherry primary wood and mahogany capitals. Mahogany is an excellent wood for carving, but cherry tends to be brittle and splits easily. Because the colors of mahogany and cherry are compatible, they could pass for the same wood.

Another parallel to this practice is found in Belle Grove Plantation, a massive, Georgian-style stone house built by Major Isaac Hite to the south of Winchester during the 1790s. Its neoclassical woodwork is largely constructed of yellow pine, but at least one carved capital (others not examined)

Figure 27 Corner cupboard, Winchester area, Virginia, ca. 1790. Yellow pine, walnut (capitals), and maple (shell) with yellow pine; linen lining; traces of original blue paint inside and out. Dimensions not recorded. (Courtesy, Piaget, St. Louis.)

is either walnut or mahogany (fig. 32). Although the use of cabinet woods for carved capitals and other architectural details occurs in other areas, the corner cupboards illustrated in figures 24, 27, and 28 and Belle Grove present a strongly defined pattern. When compared with other areas of Virginia, the use of cabinetmaking woods for carved as opposed to structural components is unusual. In this instance it suggests that a cabinetmaker

Figure 28 Corner cupboard in Cherry Row, Frederick County, Virginia, completed ca. 1794. Yellow pine and maple (capitals) with yellow pine; linen lining; traces of original blue paint inside and out. Dimensions not recorded. (Private collection; photo, Gavin Ashworth.)

either from or familiar with the practices of the Frye-Martin shops was involved in the construction of Belle Grove. The parallels between the movable cupboards and the architectural example in Cherry Row (figs. 24, 27, 28) also suggest that tradesmen from the Frye-Martin shops were responsible for many of the architectural details in Lupton's house.

The Frye-Martin shops had a tremendous influence on furniture made in

Figure 29 Detail of a capital on the corner cupboard illustrated in fig. 28. (Photo, Gavin Ashworth.)

Figure 30 Detail of a capital on the corner cupboard illustrated in fig. 27.

Figure 31 Detail of the carved shell in the interior of the corner cupboard illustrated in fig. 27.

Figure 32 Detail of a carved capital in Belle Grove, Frederick County, Virginia, ca. 1795. (Courtesy, Belle Grove Plantation; photo, Wallace Gusler.)

the Shenandoah Valley and as far west as Nashville, Tennessee. In some instances it is difficult to separate the products of the principal shops from those operated by journeymen and apprentices. A desk-and-bookcase with a Greene County, Virginia, history (fig. 33) is closely related to the Lupton example (fig. 5). It has arched, stop-fluted quarter-columns on both sections of the case (fig. 34) and a double-swagged, astragal molding (fig. 35) similar to the one on the tympanum of the Lupton desk-and-bookcase (fig. 8). The interior is plain but distinguished in having fine cockbeads on the partitions around the drawers and pigeonhole valances made from a single piece of wood that crosses all of the apertures on each side (fig. 36). The interior drawers have nailed frames rather than dovetailed ones like desks documented and attributed to the Frye-Martin shops. Other structural variations suggest that this desk-and-bookcase represents the work of a journeyman associated with the Frye-Martin shops. Rather than having conventional dustboards like the signed Frye-Martin desk and Lupton pieces, the desk-and-bookcase has dustboards that are set in grooves in the drawer rails and drawer supports.

As the preceding desk-and-bookcase suggests, the Frye-Martin shops appear to have been the genesis for many of the stylistic and structural details associated with the Winchester school. A clothespress with a history of ownership at Belle Grove shows how certain mainstream details, such as

Figure 33 Desk-and-bookcase, Winchester area, Virginia, ca. 1800. Walnut with yellow pine. H. 93", W. 41¼", D. 23". (Private collection; photo, Craig McDougal.) The feet, finial, and rosettes are restorations based on the Lupton desk-and-bookcase (fig. 5) and the tall clock case shown in fig. 22.

Figure 34 Detail of an arched, stop-fluted, quarter-column on the desk-and-bookcase illustrated in fig. 33. (Photo, Museum of Early Southern Decorative Arts.)

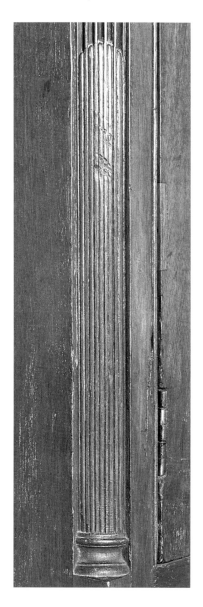

arched, stop-fluted quarter-columns, were reinterpreted by the tradesmen in the Frye-Martin shops and by other artisans in the Winchester school (fig. 37). The quarter-columns below the waist molding are carved with stops, and those above are carved with flutes (fig. 38). The waist molding serves as the termination of the stops when the corners are viewed as a single column; however, the capital of the stopped section and the base of the fluted section partially contradict this perception.

High chests were among the most common forms produced by cabinet-makers in the Winchester school. Most of these chests have ogee feet and conventional drawer arrangements—three small drawers over two small drawers over four large drawers—and some examples are virtually indistinguishable from high chests made in Pennsylvania, western Maryland, and other regions of the southern backcountry. The high chest illustrated in figure 39, however, has several distinctive features. The patron probably specified the six upper drawers and cornice drawer (the front of the cornice is the front of the drawer). Late seventeenth- and early eighteenth-century high chests occasionally have cornice drawers. By contrast, the arched stop-fluting and astragal molding under the cornice are typical Winchester-school details.

Figure 37 Clothespress, Winchester area, Virginia, ca. 1815. Mahogany and mahogany veneer with yellow pine. Dimensions not recorded. (Courtesy, Belle Grove Plantation.)

Figure 38 Detail of the capitals on the upper and lower sections of the clothespress illustrated in fig. 37.

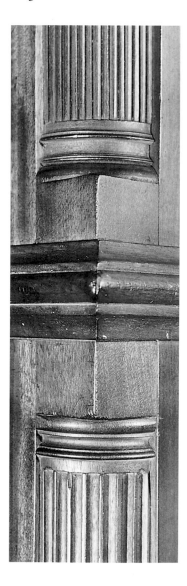

Figure 39 High chest, Winchester area, Virginia, ca. 1795. Walnut with yellow pine. H. 84", W. 48", D. 23". (Private collection; photo, Wallace Gusler.) The feet are replacements.

Figure 40 Chest of drawers, Winchester area, Virginia, ca. 1790. Mahogany, mahogany veneer, and apple with yellow pine. H. 36 1/8", W. 39", D. 20 3/4". (Private collection; photo, Craig McDougal.)

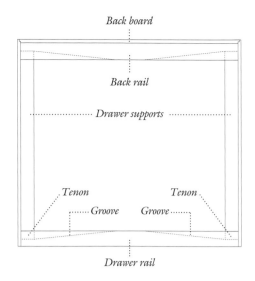

Figure 41   Plan of the drawer support system of the chest of drawers illustrated in fig. 40. (Drawing, Wallace Gusler; artwork, Wynne Patterson.)

Figure 42   Chest of drawers, Winchester area, Virginia, ca. 1810. Walnut with yellow pine. H. 37⅝", W. 38", D. 21⅞". (Courtesy, Colonial Williamsburg Foundation.)

Figure 43   Detail of the foot of the chest of drawers illustrated in fig. 42.

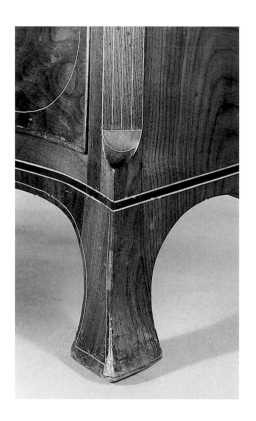

A serpentine chest that reportedly came from "Rockville," the Hite family home in Frederick County (destroyed during the twentieth century), has several construction details commonly found on case pieces from the northern Shenandoah Valley (fig. 40). Instead of having dustboards, the chest has a framed drawer support system: The drawer supports are dadoed to the case sides and tenoned to the drawer dividers and to horizontal back rails (fig. 41). Most Winchester-school tradesmen used a groove plane to cut the mortises for the tenons of the drawer supports. Rather than run the groove the full length of the drawer dividers, these artisans typically left a blank or very shallow section in the middle and cut the groove full-depth at the ends alone.

The basic design of this chest is derived from rococo examples, which have the sides and middle of the serpentine on the same frontal plane. On most neoclassical chests, however, the center of the serpentine curve projects well beyond the sides (see fig. 42). The drawer construction of the Hite chest also has earlier precedents. The fronts are composed of horizontally grained, vertically laminated, yellow pine planks. After gluing up the fronts, the cabinetmaker sawed them into serpentine shapes, just as he would have for a solid drawer front. By contrast, the serpentine drawer front of the neoclassical period is typically composed of many strips of wood that were sawn to a serpentine shape before being stacked and glued together. The frontal serpentine plane and drawer construction of the Hite chest suggest that it dates from the late 1780s or early 1790s and that its maker trained or worked earlier in the century.

Figure 45   Detail of the hood of the tall clock case illustrated in fig. 44.

Figure 44   Tall clock case, Winchester area, Virginia, ca. 1790. Curly maple with yellow pine and walnut. H. 87³/₄", W. 22¹/₄", D. 12¹/₄". (Courtesy, Colonial Williamsburg Foundation.)

With their straight outer edge and sharp curve at the bottom, the feet of the Hite chest are similar to those on furniture from the Shenandoah Valley and Tennessee. The early features of the Hite chest and related pieces from Frederick County suggest that this foot pattern originated in the Winchester vicinity. The use of unconventional hardwoods for contrasting veneers is also characteristic of the Winchester school. The Hite chest has apple wood cross-banding, but other pieces with ash and buckeye are known. On the most expensive examples, these local woods are often used in conjunction with imported mahogany veneer.

The chest illustrated in figure 42 is a more typical neoclassical example from the Winchester school. Its drawer fronts are veneered with curly walnut, and all of its secondary wood is yellow pine. The chest has drawer bottoms that are planed to clear the drawer stops, like those on case pieces in the Frye-Martin group, and flared, hoof-like feet similar to those on other chests from the Winchester area (fig. 43).

The stylistic influences that affected the Winchester school came from both outside and within the region. Occasionally the influence of local gunmakers is evident in Winchester furniture. The curly maple tall clock case illustrated in figures 44 and 45 has a basket ornament with spiraled, four-petal flowers that are remarkably similar to those on the capitals of the Lupton cupboard (fig. 29) and on the floral finial of the brass patchbox (also engraved near the door hinge) of a rifle signed by John Haymaker (d. 1804) of Winchester (fig. 46). Haymaker also carved the same flower on the forestock; however, the carving is extremely worn. Dozens of Shenandoah Valley riflemakers used this finial and carved detail, indicating that the motif was popular throughout the region. The rifle stock, clock ornament, and capitals are also related in being made of curly maple, the standard wood

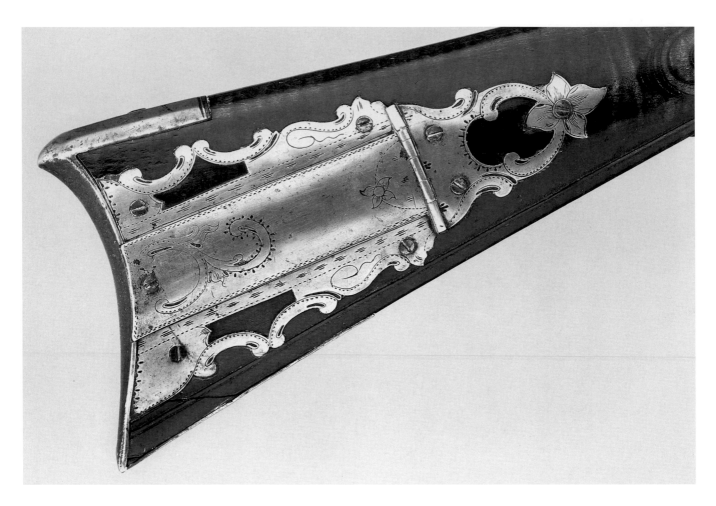

Figure 46 Detail of the brass patchbox on a rifle signed "J. Haymaker," Winchester, Virginia, ca. 1790. Curly maple, iron, steel, brass, and silver. L. 60". (Private collection; photo, Craig McDougal.) Haymaker's work reflects an acute understanding of the rococo style and its application to woodcarving, brass work, and engraving. From the standpoint of design and workmanship, the products of the city's riflemaking school are far more sophisticated than those of the furniture-making school.

used by Shenandoah Valley riflemakers. Associated style and technology linked the riflemaking, cabinetmaking, and house joinery trades. Artisans in backcountry towns, particularly those of Germanic descent, often maintained close ties. John Haymaker, for example, witnessed Christopher Frye, Sr.'s, will.[21]

A different association between the gunmaking and cabinetmaking trades is evident in the career of riflemaker George Krepps (fl. ca. 1790–1820). He began his career in or near Winchester, moved to Hagerstown, Maryland, during the 1790s, and returned to Winchester by 1820, when he advertised as a cabinetmaker. Although none of his furniture has been identified, several finely carved and engraved rifles survive from his Maryland period.[22]

Like the preceding tall clock case, the desk illustrated in figure 47 has details borrowed from long rifle design. It is related to the Frye-Martin group, and its history in Upperville in Fauquier County supports that association. The stars on the fallboard (fig. 48) are elongated and have distended points like the stars on long rifles (fig. 49). Stars of this basic form originated in German rifle decoration of the seventeenth and eighteenth centuries. They are usually inlaid on the cheek rest and made of variegated horn, with each point composed of half-white and half-black segments. Although not a part of the Winchester school, a remarkable tall clock case from Pulaski County in southwestern Virginia has a star similar to the ones

Figure 47 Desk, Winchester area, Virginia, ca. 1800. Walnut and maple inlay with yellow pine and tulip poplar. H. 44³/₈", W. 40³/₄", D. 21³/₄". (Private collection; photo, Craig McDougal.) The desk has arched, stop-fluted quarter-columns and other features associated with the Frye-Martin shops. The interior has a central prospect door flanked by four equal-sized drawers (two over two). Above the drawers are three pigeonholes with arched valances. The prospect door of the interior has the initials "I·F" inlaid in maple.

Figure 48 Detail of the star inlay on the fallboard of the desk illustrated in fig. 47.

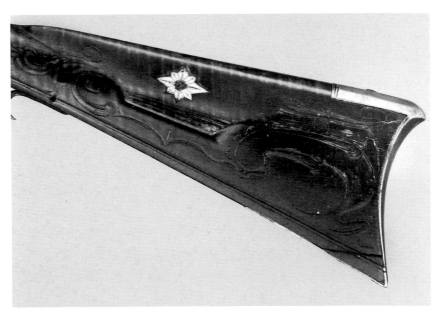

Figure 49 Detail of the cheek rest of the rifle illustrated in fig. 46, showing the silver "hunter's star" inlay.

on the desk (figs. 50, 51). This clock shows the influence of rifle, powder horn, and musical instrument making in its design and materials. The maker of its brass movement, Peter Whipple, was probably a member of the John Whipple family of Winchester. John was working in the shop of Winchester clockmaker Goldsmith Chandlee in 1787.[23]

Figure 50 Tall clock case attributed to Peter Raff with movement attributed to Peter Whipple, Pulaski County, Virginia, ca. 1815. H. 108¹/₂", W. 24", D. 15". (Courtesy, Colonial Williamsburg Foundation.)

Figure 51 Detail of the hood of the tall clock case illustrated in figure 50.

Winchester influences clearly extended far beyond the town. Furniture with Winchester structural and stylistic details was produced in western Maryland, Shenandoah and Washington Counies, Virginia, Monroe County, West Virginia, and Middle and East Tennessee. The distribution of this furniture shows the same basic patterns documented for the movement of Winchester riflemakers. Jacob Gabott apprenticed to Christopher Heskill in Winchester in 1758. At the beginning of the Revolution, he was part owner of a gun factory at Staunton in Augusta County, Virginia. During the 1790s, apprentices and journeymen from Simon Lauck's shop in Winchester set up shops in other areas: John Sheets moved to Staunton, Jacob Funk and Henry Harding moved to Strasburg in Shenandoah County, and Nicholas Chisler moved to Morgantown, (West) Virginia. Winchester riflemakers and cabinetmakers moved down the Great Wagon Road to markets in the southwest or up the Potomac River Valley along the old Braddock Road and west into the Ohio Valley, following the general migration routes for the settlement of the frontier. In 1809, John Eastely (b. 1786) of Tennessee wrote Newmarket, Virginia, riflemaker Henry Spitzer:

> Sir I am still calculating to come and work with you During the next winter Season . . . if you employ me and will give me any Kind of a living chance which I do not in the least doubt that you will I do not calculate on gain my principle motive in comming will be to reside where information of every Kind necessary can be had.

Figure 52   Desk-and-bookcase, Knoxville, Tennessee, ca. 1810. Cherry with yellow pine and tulip poplar. H. 96" (minus feet), W. 42", D. 20". (Courtesy, Lawson-McGhee Library; photo, Museum of Early Southern Decorative Arts.)

Figure 53 Detail of the pediment of the desk-and-bookcase illustrated in fig. 52.

Apparently Eastely had worked for Spitzer before; however, his desire "to reside where information of every Kind necessary can be had" suggests that the inhabitants of the frontier considered Shenandoah Valley towns such as New Market and Winchester to be cultural, stylistic, and technological centers.[24]

Winchester influences are apparent in a large group of furniture made in the Nashville and Knoxville areas of Tennessee. A high chest of drawers and two desk-and-bookcases (see figs. 52, 53) from the Knoxville area appear to be the work of a cabinetmaker trained in the vicinity of Winchester. Furniture historians Derita Coleman Williams and Nathan Harsh have attributed all of these examples to Thomas Hope, largely on the basis of family traditions. Hope was principally a house joiner. He was working in Knox County by 1797 and is thought to be the Thomas Hope listed in the Charleston, South Carolina, directory of 1790. If these objects are from Hope's shop, he must have employed a journeyman from Frederick or Shenandoah County, Virginia. The construction and carving of these examples are clearly related to furniture from the Frye-Martin shop tradition. William Wright, who is documented in the Knoxville area in 1798, is a possible candidate for this Tennessee work. A cabinetmaker by the same name worked in Shenandoah County, Virginia, from 1790 to 1825. The Knoxville cabinetmaker may have been a member of the same family. The other Knoxville desk-and-bookcase (not illustrated) has a vertically fluted finial that is identical to many Shenandoah County examples.[25]

Similarly, Samuel Williams may have introduced Winchester styles to the Nashville area. An individual by that name appears in the 1815 settlement of James Lee Martin's estate: "to Samuel Williams Journeyman's acct . . . $133.00." On June 10, 1817, a Samuel Williams in Nashville advertised that he had "lately arrived from the eastern States and is in possession of the newest fashions." Although Williams sold his Nashville shop in 1818, he probably continued working as a journeyman there just as he had in Virginia. If these references are to the same Samuel Williams, the Nashville pieces related to the Frye-Martin group may represent his work or influence.[26]

Figure 54 Desk, Virginia or Tennessee, 1808. Walnut and maple inlay with tulip poplar. H. 47¼", W. 42", D. 20". (Courtesy, Winterthur Museum.)

Figure 55 Detail of the writing compartment of the desk illustrated in fig. 54. The mitered molding above the door is the face of a secret drawer.

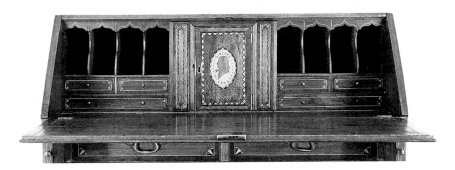

The desk shown in figure 54 illustrates the difficulty of identifying the precise origins for some objects related to the Winchester school but made in areas far removed from the town. Like many desks associated with the Frye-Martin group, it has wide document drawers, a prospect door with a molded surround concealing a "secret" drawer (figs. 55, 56), and a hidden well beneath the drawer inside the prospect. Its pigeonhole valances are constructed in single units that cross all four openings on each side, like those on the Winchester desk-and-bookcase illustrated in figures 33 and 36. The extensive inlay on this desk represents a departure from Winchester work, with the exception of the stars on the fallboard. The placement of the stars is remarkably similar to that of the Winchester desk shown in figure 47. The distance between the stars on the Winchester example is more

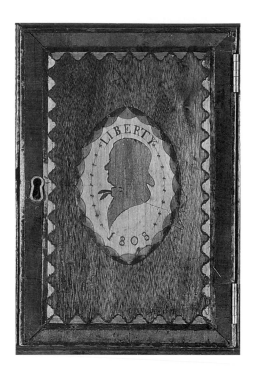

Figure 56 Detail of the prospect door of the desk illustrated in fig. 54.

understandable when compared with the fallboard inlay on the other desk, which centers around an eagle (fig. 54).

The case construction of the preceding desk is more primitive than that usually found in Winchester work. The drawer rails and supports, for example, are lapped onto the drawer rails and nailed to the sides of the case. The fan inlays on the drawer fronts and scalloping on the edges of the prospect door are associated with East Tennessee work. Inlaid profiles also occur on an East Tennessee chest (not illustrated) with feet that are virtually identical to those on the Hite example (fig. 40). Although these decorative features are relatively common in East Tennessee furniture, similar details are found on pieces from the lower Shenandoah Valley, particularly from the area between Augusta and Washington County bordering on Tennessee. The desk was purchased in Wythe County, Virginia, but it does not have a family history to help substantiate its origin.[27]

The 1808 date and nationalistic references on the desk refer to the year when James Madison of Virginia defeated Charles Cotesworth Pinckney of South Carolina in the presidential election, thus continuing the "Virginia Dynasty." Although the features of the profile are not distinctive enough to identify the subject with any degree of certainty, it probably represents James Madison (fig. 56). The seventeen stars on the fallboard over the eagle and those on the prospect door represent the seventeen states of the Union in 1808. Regardless of whether the desk originated in southwestern Virginia or in East Tennessee, it remains important as an election year icon and as an example of the dissemination of Winchester style.[28]

The furniture and tradesmen of Winchester had a wide sphere of influence during the late eighteenth and early nineteenth centuries. Winchester was an important backcountry commercial and style center. The town's cabinetmakers produced furniture for local demand and trained apprentices and journeymen who carried Winchester style and technology to new markets in the Shenandoah Valley and western frontier. The influence of these transplanted artisans was far more profound than the written record suggests. Like their contemporaries in Winchester, they rarely mentioned their training and tended to advertise that they employed workmen from Philadelphia, Baltimore, Norfolk, and New York. These cities were considered the leading style centers during the early federal period, as was London during the colonial period. Although Philadelphia and Baltimore influences were important in the development of the Winchester school, new styles were invariably adapted and reinterpreted to suit local cabinetmaking traditions and tastes. Whether made in the northern Shenandoah Valley, southwest Virginia, or East Tennessee, Winchester-school furniture bears the clear imprint of that city's diverse culture and cabinetmaking traditions.[29]

ACKNOWLEDGMENTS   For assistance with this article, the author thanks Bill and Hazel Adams, Richard Adams, Georgia Allen, Mark Anderson, Luke Beckerdite, Stewart Bell, John Bivins, Laurie Bonbright, Mrs. Allen Bond, Margaret Gill, Liza Gusler, Mack Headley, Tim Hodges, Diane Hudgins, Charles Hummel, Ronald Hurst, Roger and Mary Lou Koontz, Craig McDougal, Jim and Marilyn Melchor, Roderick Moore, Fred Painter, Jonathan Prown, and Byron Smith. I am especially grateful to Betty Stvan for her assistance with numerous details pertaining to this article and to the Reverend William Hill Brown, III, for making his desk available for this study.

1. Richard L. Morton, *Colonial Virginia* (Chapel Hill: University of North Carolina Press for the Virginia Historical Society, 1960), pp. 40–41. Frederick Morton, *The Story of Winchester in Virginia* (Strasburg, Va.: Shenandoah Publishing House, 1925), p. 37.

2. Morton, *Story of Winchester*, pp. 40–41. John W. Wayland, *A History of Shenandoah County, Virginia* (Strasburg, Va.: Shenandoah Publishing House, 1927), p. 47. Morton, *Colonial Virginia*, p. 539.

3. F. B. Kegley, *Kegley's Virginia Frontier* (Roanoke: Southwest Virginia Historical Society, 1938), p. 33. Morton, *Story of Winchester*, p. 544.

4. Morton, *Colonial Virginia*, pp. 546–47. Disputes over the boundaries of these counties and the overlaid Lord Fairfax Grant (1685) continued from the 1720s to 1754, with some settlers purchasing land from Fairfax and others from the government of Virginia. The new name may have been derived from Wood's birthplace, Winchester, England. For more on the development of towns in the Virginia backcountry, see Christopher Edwin Hendricks, "Town Development in the Colonial Backcountry—Virginia and North Carolina" (Ph.d. diss., College of William and Mary, 1991), see esp. pp. 64–78.

5. Morton, *Colonial Virginia*, p. 551.

6. John Kirke Paulding, *Letters from the South Written During An Excursion In the Summer of 1816*, 2 vols. (New York: James Eastburn & Co., 1817), 1:142–43.

7. The British government placed a bounty on the production of hemp, and certificates were issued and recorded in the county courts. The court order books of Frederick County and Augusta County contain annual entries recording the number of pounds produced by individuals. In 1770, Botetourt County was established from the lower part of Augusta. In that year, the new county produced 170,000 pounds of hemp. See Robert Douthat Stoner, *The Seed Bed of the Republic, Early Botetourt* (Kingsport, Tenn.: Kingsport Press, Inc., 1962), p. 47. Although records of the Indian trade in the Shenandoah Valley are scarce, some revealing examples survive. John Frazier set up a trading post at Franklin (Venango County, Pennsylvania) about 1740 but moved to Winchester after losing his establishment at the beginning of the French and Indian War. He married and ran a shop in Winchester during the late 1750s. He also guided and repaired arms for Washington and was involved in the disastrous defeat of Braddock's forces. Frazier's schedule of losses lists a set of armorers' tools, dozens of knives, tomahawks, trade silver, saddles, gunlocks, a belt of wampum, rifles, smooth-bore guns, and gunpowder (see *Man at Arms* 16, no. 5 [September/October 1994]). The records of the Greenbrier store in present-day Greenbriar County, West Virginia (Virginia State Library [hereinafter cited as VSL], Richmond), show how imported goods were traded for deer skins during the 1770s. The Greenbrier store was a branch of Sampson and Matthew's store in Staunton, Virginia. Goods were shipped by pack horse from Staunton to Greenbriar. The records of the Pitzer store in Covington, Virginia (private collection), document similar trading patterns during the 1790s. Deerskins, furs, guns, gunpowder, and flints were important trade goods in the backcountry throughout the eighteenth century.

8. Hendricks, "Town Development in the Colonial Backcountry," p. 75.

9. *The Virginia Magazine* 77 (1969): 291–306. John Bivins, Jr., "Isaac Zane and the Products of Marlboro Furnace," *Journal of Early Southern Decorative Arts* 11, no. 1 (May 1985): 20–23.

10. Morton, *Colonial Virginia*, pp. 84–86.

11. Fitz Knox, comp., *Genealogy of the Fitzhugh, Knox, Gordon, Selden, Horner, Brown, Baylor, (King) Carter, Edmonds, Digges, Page, Tayloe, and Allied Families* (Atlanta, Ga., 1932), pp. 19–20. The author thanks Wendy Cooper and Liza Gusler for this reference.

12. Fauquier County Personal Property Tax Records, 1799, VSL. The case of this desk is constructed with hidden dovetails at the top and bottom. These were originally covered at the top by a bookcase (small nail holes from the waist molding are visible.) At the bottom, the hidden dovetail is covered by the base frame. The base frame is approximately 3$\frac{1}{2}$" wide and 1" thick.

It is mitered at the front corners and continues to the back on the sides. Along the back, two frame elements butt to the sides and do not extend across the back, being only long enough to support the rear foot brackets. These frame elements are made of walnut and have the base molding cut on their outer edges. The case has walnut drawer rails that are notched at the corners to receive the quarter-columns (the columns cover the rail joints) and full- to ³/₄-depth dustboards that are dadoed to the sides and tongue and grooved into the rails. The dustboards are flush with the drawer rails on the top and slightly thinner at the bottom. The dadoes for the dustboards are approximately ¹/₄" narrower than the rails. Drawer guides are glued on top of the dustboards at each side behind the quarter-columns. The vertical back boards are nailed into rabbets at the top and sides and face nailed to the bottom of the case. The fall board support partitions are blind-mortised into the bottom of the writing surface, and are though-tenoned into the drawer rail. The walnut supports for the fall board are faced with vertically grained walnut and edged with applied cock beading. The large case drawers also have walnut fronts and applied cock beading. The drawer sides have wide dovetails and pins. The top three drawers have three tails in front and two in back, whereas the bottom drawer has four front tails and three back tails. The drawer sides and front are grooved to receive the chamfered edges of the bottoms. The bottom boards run parallel to the sides of the drawer and extend past the drawer backs. The center section of the extended bottom is cut away to the edge of the drawer back leaving the sides extended to stop against the back boards. The bottoms are nailed along the back edges. The fallboard has battens that are mitered at the top on both sides. The interior drawer bottoms are set into rabbets in the front and sides, overlap the back, and are nailed with small wrought sprigs. The bottoms are flush with the back and have small blocks glued to them to serve as drawer stops.

The desk has had at least one campaign of restoration in which most of the original nails were lost and some repairs were made. Several pieces of wood in the dustboards and drawer bottoms have nail holes that are not related to the construction of the desk. Several of these appear to be in elements of the first construction and must represent the use of salvaged wood by Frye and Martin. The only conjectural restoration is the feet.

13. Winchester Personal Property Tax Records, 1794, VSL. Will of Christopher Frye, Sr., February 13, 1801, Frederick County, Virginia, Will Book 6 (1795–1802), pp. 642–44. *Virginia Magazine of History*, vol. 1, p. 389. For Frye's military service and the reference to his being a farmer, see *Virginia Magazine of History*, vol. 1, p. 389, as cited in Mary Goodwin, Research Report Prepared for John Graham, Colonial Williamsburg Foundation, February 14, 1969. In 1780, Christopher Frye of Winchester proved his service in Colonel William Byrd's Seventh Company of the Virginia Regiment (*Shenandoah Valley Pioneers and their Descendants—A History of Frederick County* [Berryville, Va., 1963], p. 90, as cited in Goodwin, Research Report).

14. Frederick County Marriage Bonds, 1771–1825, VSL, as cited in Margaret Gill, Research Report Prepared for Wallace Gulser, Colonial Williamsburg Foundation, May 18, 1973. John Hill, "The Furniture Craftsman in Baltimore, 1783–1823" (master's thesis, University of Delaware, 1967). Hill's thesis includes references to the following James Martins: James Martin, cabinetmaker, Frederick, Maryland, n.d., p. 440; James Martin, Sr., cabinetmaker, Lovely Lane between Calvert and South Streets, Baltimore, 1796, p. 440; James Martin, cabinetmaker, Dugans Wharf, Baltimore, 1799, p. 441. The following individuals served apprenticeships with one of the Baltimore James Martins: Daniel H. Bateman, 1802, p. 366; John Henry Lancaster, 1802, p. 365; George Kennedy, 1794, p. 358; John Stricher, 1799, p. 360. The author thanks Philip Zimmerman for information from this thesis. Coffins provided by James Lee Martin of Winchester were generally more expensive than those furnished by his contemporaries, which suggests that he was at the pinnacle of his trade. The author thanks Dr. H. E. Comstock for this information.

15. Wallace Gusler interview with Mrs. Allen Bond (1973), the last member of the Lupton family to own the high chest illustrated in figure 14. Christopher and Mary Frye to David Lupton, January 16, 1790, Winchester City Deed Book 1, p. 8.

16. Inventory of James Lee Martin, June 6, 1815, Frederick County, Virginia, Will Book 9 (1810–1816), pp. 421–25, VSL. Winchester City Deed Book 3, March 14, 1815, p. 177, Winchester Corporation Records, Judicial Center, Winchester, Virginia.

17. Since 1973, the author has examined over forty-five pieces in this group. Only a small number are illustrated in this article.

18. This approach to cutting clearance channels across the bottom relates to similar cuts made in floorboards to level them on the joists, a practice common in house joinery. Several variations of this problem with proper installation of drawer stops have been encountered. In one

instance, the stops were put on the bottom of the drawer blades, making it necessary to cut shallow notches in the top of the back of the drawer in order to clear the stops when installing the drawer. Sometimes support blocks were glued in the corner between the drawer front and the bottom of the bottom. This support block was then carved away to adjust the drawer fit.

19. In this article, I use "Frye-Martin shops" and "Frye-Martin group" to designate the products of the multigenerational shop tradition that included the Fryes, Martin, and their journeymen.

20. Wallace Gusler interview with Joe Kindig, Jr., 1970; Accession files, Winterthur Museum, Winterthur, Delaware.

21. John Haymaker was identified as a gunsmith when he sold his share of town lot 202 to his father, Adam (John Haymaker to Adam Haymaker, October 22, 1799, Winchester City Records, Deed Book 1, p. 165). This lot was the same one that Lord Fairfax granted to Adam Haymaker in 1753. Adam was a gunsmith who worked from the 1750s to his death in 1808. For references to Adam Haymaker's work and apprentices, see Harold B. Gill, Jr., *The Gunsmiths of Colonial Williamsburg* (Charlottesville: University of Virginia Press for the Colonial Williamsburg Foundation, 1974). Goodwin, Research Report.

22. In the April 1, 1820, issue of the *Winchester Gazette*, George Krepps gave his location as opposite the courthouse and listed cabinetwork. For more on Krepps's change of trades, see Daniel D. Hartzler, *Arms Makers of Maryland* (Mechanicsburg, Pa.: George Schumway, 1977), pp. 204–7.

23. John Whipple is listed as a tithable individual in Chandlee's tax entry. Winchester City Personal Property Tax Records, March 25, 1787, Library of Virginia, Richmond.

24. For the Jacob Gabott apprenticeship, see Gill, *Gunsmiths of Colonial Virginia*, pp. 82, 90. All of Lauck's apprentices disappear from the records by 1796 (Simon Lauck Personal Property Taxes, Frederick County Tax Records, 1794–1796, VSL). John Sheets is listed in the Augusta County tax records after 1796 and is cited as residing in Staunton in the governor's papers, VSL. Jacob Funk and Henry Harding are listed together in the Shenandoah County Personal Property Tax Rolls of 1797–1800, VSL. A signed rifle by Funk is also dated 1796 and signed "Strasburg Va. State." Nicholas Chisler is mentioned in correspondence during the War of 1812. He made rifles in Morgantown for the state of Virginia. Executive Papers, VSL. The Spitzer letter is in a private collection. The author thanks Dr. H. E. Comstock for this reference.

25. Derita Coleman Williams and Nathan Harsh, *The Art and Mystery of Tennessee Furniture and Its Makers Through 1850* (Nashville, Tenn.: Tennessee Historical Society, Tennessee State Museum Foundation, 1988), pp. 65, 87, 99; see p. 65 for the desk-and-bookcase with the fluted finial. The authors did not associate these pieces and the Winchester school. The histories of the desk-and-bookcase and high chest are intriguing since the arched, stop-fluted quarter-columns of both pieces and the pediment rosettes, applied carving, and interior of the desk-and-bookcase are clearly associated with Winchester work. For the William Wright from Knoxville, Tennessee, see ibid., p. 323. For the William Wright from Shenandoah County, see artisan files, Museum of Early Southern Decorative Arts, Winston-Salem, North Carolina.

26. For the Nashville, Tennessee, Samuel Williams, see Williams and Harsh, *The Art and Mystery of Tennessee Furniture*, pp. 322. For the Frederick County Samuel Williams, see Inventory of James Lee Martin.

27. The desk-and-bookcase shown in figures 33–36 has interior drawers with nailed frames, indicating that a wide range of work existed in the Winchester area and that attributions based on such variations can be tenuous. For the Tennessee chest, see Williams and Harsh, *The Art and Mystery of Tennessee Furniture*, p. 88, pl. 24. Wallace Gusler interview with Joe Kindig, Jr., 1970. Mr. Kindig stated that he purchased the desk illustrated in figure 54 from Wytheville, Virginia, antique dealer Garland Stevens.

28. Joseph Nathan Kane, *Facts about the Presidents,* 5th ed. (New York: H. W. Wilson Co., 1989), p. 29. Winterthur student Johana Ruth Harris was unable to identify positively the subject of the silhouette (Johana Ruth Harris, Research Paper, Winterthur Museum, 1995).

29. In the January 30, 1790, issue of the *Virginia Gazette and the Winchester Advertiser,* cabinetmaker William King advertised that he made Windsor chairs, common chairs, spinning wheels, and cabinet work and employed "well experienced hands from the city of Philadelphia." Nashville, Tennessee, cabinetmaker Samuel Williams, who was probably a journeyman from James Lee Martin's shop, advertised that he had "several of the best workmen from the shops in New York and Philadelphia" (Williams and Harsh, *The Art and Mystery of Tennessee Furniture*, p. 322).

Figure 1 Easy chair, England or eastern Virginia, ca. 1745. Walnut with beech; original upholstery with later additions. H. 45³/₄", W. 30¹/₄", D. 30¹/₂". (Courtesy, Colonial Williamsburg Foundation; photo, Hans Lorenz.)

*Leroy Graves and
F. Carey Howlett*

Leather Bottoms, Satin Haircloth, and Spanish Beard: Conserving Virginia Upholstered Seating Furniture

Figure 2 Matthew Pratt, *Mary Jemima Balfour,* Hampton, Virginia, 1773. Oil on canvas. 49" × 39¹⁄₂". (Courtesy, Virginia Historical Society.)

▼ BY THE MID-1760S, Richmond County, Virginia, planter John Tayloe II (1721–1779) had completed his elegant Georgian house, Mt. Airy. His furnishings included pier tables designed by architect William Buckland, whose shop produced much of the interior woodwork in Mt. Airy, and other furniture that he and his wife, Rebecca, had purchased or inherited. The easy chair illustrated in figure 1 may have been purchased by Tayloe during the late 1740s or early 1750s, or it may have been a bequest or gift from his father, John Tayloe I (1687–1747), whose 1747 estate inventory listed "a doz Dammask Bottom'd Chairs & two Easy ditto." It descended in the Tayloe family for several generations and oral tradition maintains that it came from Mt. Airy.[1]

Like many examples of southern upholstered furniture, the Tayloe chair has suffered from the passage of time. During the mid-nineteenth century, the cabriole legs were shortened and fitted with metal casters. Likewise, a late alteration of the armrest members resulted in an ungainly rake to the arms. The accumulation of at least seven nailed-on show textiles also reflects significant changes in the appearance and the function of the chair over time. The uppermost fabric is a Colonial Williamsburg reproduction striped cotton. Beneath it are several nineteenth-century cotton prints, an eighteenth- or early nineteenth-century red wool worsted, and the original blue and cream silk damask and foundation upholstery. A chair with a similarly elegant damask textile is depicted in Matthew Pratt's portrait of Mary Jemima Balfour of Hampton, Virginia (fig. 2), which is about thirty years later than the Tayloe chair.[2]

Although the Tayloe chair could be restored to its original appearance, such an undertaking would compromise a wealth of historic information. Each textile layer speaks to the changing tastes of succeeding generations of owners, and each alteration of the frame tells of the changing function and status of the chair over its 250-year existence. Because so few objects survive with such comprehensive upholstery evidence, the preservation of the chair in its current state takes precedence over restoration to its original appearance.

The Task of the Upholstery Conservator

Apart from the historic information it reveals, the Tayloe easy chair illustrates an indisputable fact—upholstery fares poorly over time. Textiles become brittle and faded, stuffing materials compress and crumble, and webbing stretches and breaks. Whether concerned with function or fashion, owners typically discarded, replaced, or covered up old upholstery when it

267 CONSERVING UPHOLSTERED FURNITURE

began to sag or look outmoded. Usually nothing is left but the upholstery frame, which has been re-stuffed and covered with textiles reflecting more recent tastes. The conservator is often faced with two difficult tasks: preserving extremely fragile upholstery materials when they survive and reconstructing the appearance of the original upholstery when little is left but the bare frame.

In preserving old or original upholstery materials, the conservator is chiefly concerned about arresting deterioration. Many stabilization techniques are drawn from the work of conservators of flat textiles and costumes, though the three-dimensional structure of upholstery often limits the treatment options. The fixed juxtaposition of layers of materials, each having its own properties and each serving a specific purpose, sometimes results in harmful chemical interactions that are difficult to mitigate. Upholstery materials are also constantly under tension, even when not in use, which contributes to their deterioration over time. Dust, dirt, or stains can sometimes be removed, but typically work must be carried out in situ to avoid damaging the upholstery structure. Loose or ripped textiles can be stitched in place using unobtrusive thread, and disintegrating materials may be encapsulated in a stitched-on sheer material. Auxiliary supports are also employed for upholstery that can no longer carry its own weight. Little or nothing can be done about fading, fraying, or extreme sagging. Aesthetic concerns are secondary in the conservation of original upholstery materials, which are valued chiefly as documents of period materials and techniques.

Reconstructing the appearance of historic upholstery from evidence available on a bare seating frame is a very different task. The closest parallel to such efforts is the work of the forensic anthropologist, who attempts to reconstruct the physical features, habits, and health of long-deceased individuals by carefully studying their skeletal remains. In the same way, the upholstery conservator investigates the "skeletal remains" of chairs and sofas, determining from the available evidence information about their history, appearance, and function. The conservator's work is typically complicated by the overlapping evidence of numerous upholstery schemes. Distinguishing individual schemes can be time consuming and in some instances virtually impossible. To produce a credible reconstruction of historic upholstery, one needs to develop a thorough understanding of the techniques, materials, and tastes of the period and place of production. Information might be gathered from various sources. Pictorial references appear in cabinetmakers' guides, paintings, and prints, and documentary evidence exists in inventories, advertisements, letters, and literature of the era. More tangible information comes from the rare examples of upholstered furniture retaining original materials; however, the most important source of information in *any* conservation treatment is the object itself. As bare as an upholstery frame may seem, significant evidence of the original upholstery remains on its surface.

Once the frame has been thoroughly examined and a plan formulated for reupholstery, the conservator then reapplies materials in a manner that maintains the integrity of the bare frame and preserves any evidence of the history of upholstery schemes. The goal of treatment may be to re-create the appearance of one of the early schemes, but this task must be accomplished using unconventional, nonintrusive techniques. Traditional nailing methods are avoided because of the damage they cause, and the upholstery conservator typically engineers a system that clads the frame using auxiliary frame inserts, straps, and custom-formed fittings.

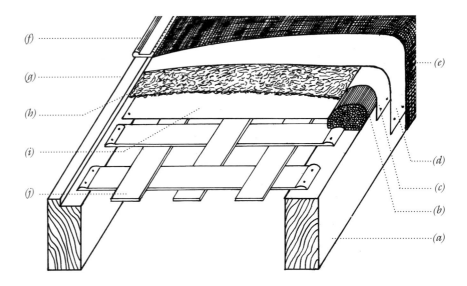

Figure 3 Illustration of a standard eighteenth-century approach to over-the-rail upholstery: *(a)* front seat rail, *(b)* straw or grass roll, *(c)* linen casing for roll, *(d)* top linen, *(e)* show textile, *(f)* removable shoe molding, *(g)* rear seat rail, *(h)* horse hair stuffing, *(i)* foundation linen, *(j)* webbing strips. (Drawing, Leroy Graves; artwork, Wynne Patterson.)

Reading the Evidence

The most important part of any historic upholstery treatment is the examination of the object, since the information derived from that study should guide all decisions about the preservation of early materials and/or the plan for reupholstery. To interpret such evidence correctly, a basic knowledge of traditional upholstery techniques and materials is imperative (fig. 3). Important factors to consider during an examination include the structure and shaping of the frame, evidence left by original nails or other hardware, shadow marks and other clues to the original upholstery profile, fibers or threads relating to the original show material, and evidence of the original decorative trim.

The form, construction, shaping, and tool marks on upholstery frames can reveal a great deal about the original upholstery. For instance, the edge shaping of the board forming the wing of an easy chair provides clues to the original upholstery treatment (fig. 4). If the inner edge of the board was originally rounded with a wood rasp or other hand tool, then the wing may have had tapered, rounded upholstery with, perhaps, a single line of trim outlining the outermost edge (fig. 5). Alternatively, a square-edged board in conjunction with other evidence may indicate that the wing had boxed-edge upholstery (the wing is outlined by a thin panel of show fabric flanked on either side by a line of trim to give it a fuller appearance).

Similarly, a close examination of chair legs can often provide information about the height of the seat upholstery. An eighteenth- or early nineteenth-century British or American chair leg, for example, may retain an original upholstery peak—a triangular projection extending from the top of a front

Figure 4 Easy chair attributed to the Anthony Hay shop, Williamsburg, Virginia, 1750–1770. Mahogany with ash, tulip poplar, and yellow pine. H. 44¹/₈", D. 28¹/₂", W. 31³/₄". (Courtesy, Colonial Williamsburg Foundation; photo, Hans Lorenz.)

Figure 5 Detail of a rasp-shaped wing on the easy chair illustrated in fig. 4, showing clusters of nail holes related to the original webbing on the lower edge of the back and wing.

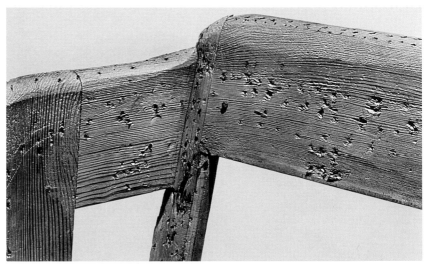

leg post (figs. 6, 7). Such a feature provides practical information about the height of the upholstery on the outer corners of the seat, since upholsterers traditionally pulled the top linen and show fabric tightly over the lightly padded peak.

Figure 7 Detail of an upholstery peak on the side chair illustrated in fig. 6. (Photo, L. Graves and F. C. Howlett.)

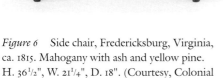

Figure 6 Side chair, Fredericksburg, Virginia, ca. 1815. Mahogany with ash and yellow pine. H. 36½", W. 21¼", D. 18". (Courtesy, Colonial Williamsburg Foundation; photo, Hans Lorenz.)

The application of upholstery is a step-by-step process, and a thorough examination for nail evidence consists of retracing each step in that process. When studying an eighteenth- or early nineteenth-century chair, one first looks for evidence of the original webbing (the support material) in the form of clustered nail holes of relatively large dimension, typically spaced along the upper surfaces of seat rails and the inner edges of frame members (see fig. 5). Evidence will then be sought for each additional nailed layer. The foundation linen, edge rolls, top linen, show fabric, and decorative trim all leave characteristic nail patterns on a chair frame, and their presence or absence, concentration, and location provide useful information about the original upholstery.

By contrast, evidence of the original loft or profile of the upholstery is often minimal. On side chairs that have not been heavily restored or refinished, differences in the color and gloss of the wood just above the back stile/seat rail joints may provide clues. Because the upholstery protected the wood from light and air-borne pollutants, the height and curvature of such "shadows" may indicate whether the seat was lightly or heavily stuffed (figs. 8, 9). Likewise, traces of early finishes or other surface treatments may denote original upholstery boundaries, which were often extended during later upholstery schemes.

The presence of edge rolls on seats, backs, and wings also influenced upholstery profiles (figs. 10, 11). Although the exact diameter of a missing edge roll is difficult to determine, nail evidence can be used to extrapolate dimensions. Closely spaced nailing, for example, suggests a tightly stitched roll and a slim upholstery profile, whereas wider-spaced nailing suggests a looser roll and a rounder profile. A more exact determination is possible if upholstery peaks are present. Edge rolls traditionally abutted upholstery

Figure 8 Armchair, probably Norfolk, Virginia, ca. 1790. Mahogany with ash. H. 38³/4", W. 20³/4", D. 17³/4". (Courtesy, Colonial Williamsburg Foundation; photo, Hans Lorenz.)

Figure 9 Detail of shadow marks indicating early or original upholstery profiles on the chair illustrated in fig. 8.

peaks, so the diameter of a roll was usually equal to the height of the peak above the seat rail.

The stuffing materials used in seventeenth-century Virginia upholstered furniture are unknown because no examples survive. It is logical to assume, however, that the turkeywork and leather chairs listed in early inventories were stuffed with grass or straw, much like their British and New England

Figure 10 Easy chair, England, 1750–1760. Mahogany with beech and deal; remnants of original upholstery. H. 47", W. 32³/₄", D. 25¹/₂". (Courtesy, Colonial Williamsburg Foundation; photo, Hans Lorenz.)

Figure 11 Detail of an original edge roll on the wing of the easy chair illustrated in fig. 10.

counterparts. Curled horsehair became the most common filler during the eighteenth century, and its use in Virginia is documented both in extant upholstery and in documents. Cheaper materials such as grass, tow (flax fibers), and Spanish moss were also common, even in the most expensive Virginia furniture (figs. 12, 13).

Although surviving examples suggest that there is little correlation between the type of stuffing material and the general amount of loft in an early upholstery scheme, the location of the surviving material may still be revealing. Fibers of curled horsehair trapped beneath early nails on the curved arm support of a sofa, for example, might suggest the presence of padding on an area typically covered only by textiles. Likewise, imprints of a straw edge roll on a framing member may indicate the roll's termination points and rough dimensions, extremely helpful information for determining an early upholstery profile.[3]

The discovery of fibers, textile fragments, or leather scraps related to the original show material greatly influences decisions on the final appearance of any upholstery reinterpretation (fig. 14). Though large scraps are ideal sources of information, the conservator must often examine a frame under

Figure 12 Armchair attributed to Edmund Dickinson, Williamsburg, Virginia, ca. 1775. Cherry; oak slipseat. H. 38¹/₄", W. 26¹/₂", D. 18¹/₂". (Courtesy, Colonial Williamsburg Foundation; photo, Hans Lorenz.)

Figure 13 Detail of the slipseat from the armchair illustrated in fig. 12. (Photo, F. C. Howlett.) The seat has its original curled hair and grass stuffing.

Figure 14 Detail of a leather fragment trapped beneath a forged nail on the seat frame of the chair illustrated in fig. 12. (Photo, L. Graves.)

magnification. With persistence and luck, fibers may be discovered beneath the heads of original nails still embedded in the frame. A single fiber can yield valuable information about the color and type of textile (silk, cotton, wool, linen), and bits of thread can provide clues about the texture and weight of a fabric. Similarly, woven fragments can provide insight into the weave or pattern of the original material.[4]

Even if no fibers are found, there may be clues to the original material on the upholstery frame. The weave structure of textiles such as silk, haircloth, or lightweight wool may have been imprinted on the wood by the nail heads that applied the show material or decorative trim (figs. 15, 16). Conversely, the lack of a textile imprint may signify a heavier material, such as needlepoint or leather, or the presence of a thick tape.

Three types of decorative trim were prevalent on eighteenth- and early nineteenth-century American upholstered furniture: brass nails, gimp or tape (known as "lace" during the eighteenth century), and cord. Of the

Figure 15 Side chair, New England, 1790–1800. Mahogany with cherry and yellow pine; original upholstery foundation with remnants of haircloth cover. H. 40³/₈", W. 20³/₄", D. 18¹/₄". (Private collection; photo, Hans Lorenz.)

Figure 16 Detail of textile imprints on the seat rail of the chair illustrated in fig. 15.

three, only brass nails leave evidence that is easily distinguishable on a bare upholstery frame (see fig. 17). This evidence consists of rows of small, regularly spaced nail holes, usually outlining the frame but, during the federal period, occasionally appearing in the form of decorative swags, S curves, or other patterns on the faces of seat rails. Ring-shaped imprints left by the nail heads are often visible around the holes. The holes themselves may be either square (evidence of seventeenth-, eighteenth- or early nineteenth-century cast brass nails) or round (evidence of more recent nails with wire shanks). If no evidence of brass nails is present, then it is likely that the upholsterer

Figure 17 Detail of modern brass nails used to point out the original nail pattern on the chair illustrated in fig. 8.

used gimp, cord, or a combination of the two. Gimp was usually applied with an adhesive or small brads, whereas cord was stitched into the upholstery. In both cases, the evidence remaining on the frame is usually minimal or nonexistent. Here the conservator must look to historic prototypes rather than rely on physical evidence alone.

Although examining upholstery frames is a straightforward, systematic process, evidence of the original upholstery is often fragmentary or obscured. Frames were often upholstered several times, and distinguishing early schemes can be difficult. Unusual deviations from standard period upholstery practices may also be difficult to interpret. Fortunately, however, upholstery was a relatively conservative trade requiring a limited number of techniques and materials. The conservator can thus often determine the original upholstery process from the physical evidence found on an upholstery frame. Where physical evidence is incomplete or difficult to understand, supplementary information gleaned from documents, paintings, and related upholstered forms can shed light on the object's original upholstery scheme.

Five Virginia seating forms illustrate the principles discussed above. A Masonic master's chair made by Williamsburg cabinetmaker Benjamin

Bucktrout (fig. 18) and a Richmond easy chair (fig. 32) retain significant portions of their original upholstery. Accordingly, their treatment involved research into their historic context and examination and preservation of their textile components. By contrast, the Norfolk side chair illustrated in figure 38 and the Winchester sofas illustrated in figures 44 and 45 were almost devoid of original upholstery materials. The replication of period upholstery for the example shown in figure 44 thus drew upon evidence on their frames and information from pictorial and documentary sources.

Bucktrout Masonic Master's Chair
Bucktrout's imposing ceremonial chair may have been commissioned for Peyton Randolph, who served as provincial grand master of Virginia Freemasonry during the early 1770s and as president of the first Continental Congress in 1774. The chair's seat consists of black-grained leather trimmed with brass nails above elaborate, relief-carved rails. Although no other

Figure 18 Masonic master's chair signed by Benjamin Bucktrout, Williamsburg, Virginia, 1769–1775. Mahogany with walnut; original black-grained leather upholstery with brass nail trim. H. 65½", W. 31¼", D. 29½". (Courtesy, Colonial Williamsburg Foundation; photo, Hans Lorenz.)

brass-nailed leather upholstery from Williamsburg survives, Bucktrout obviously used the technique for other work. In October 1772, he sold Robert Carter of Nomini Hall eight "Mahogy Chares Stufed over the Rails with Brass nails."[5]

In Virginia, leather was a common covering for chairs throughout the seventeenth and eighteenth centuries. A 1698 Accomack County will lists "1 Virginia Chooch the bottom Leather," and a 1718 York County estate inventory lists "1/2 doz of Rushia leather Chairs." In 1745, John Walker of Middlesex County owned "12 Mahogany Chairs leather Bottoms" and "2 Elbow do." Williamsburg cabinetmaker Peter Scott used leather seats for a settee and several side chairs that may have been among the standing furniture in the Governor's Palace during the early 1770s (fig. 19). An armchair attributed to Edmund Dickinson, master of the Anthony Hay shop during the mid-1770s, retains fragments of its original leather upholstery (figs. 12, 14), as does a seat frame fragment excavated from the Hay shop site. Furniture makers elsewhere in southeastern Virginia also employed leather, as confirmed by the original slipseats on a pair of smoking chairs from Southampton County (fig. 20). Leather's superior durability may partially account for its prevalence in Virginia chairs retaining original upholstery; nonetheless, evidence suggests that it remained a popular material for chair seats throughout the eighteenth century.[6]

A possible explanation for the frequent use of leather in the Williamsburg vicinity was its availability. Alexander Craig, a Williamsburg tanner and harnessmaker, sold leather and leather-related products to a variety of plantation owners, tradesmen, and cabinetmakers throughout the Tidewater

Figure 19 Settee attributed to the shop of Peter Scott, Williamsburg, Virginia, 1771–1776. Cherry with tulip poplar and white oak. H. 36$\frac{1}{2}$", W. 73", D. 21$\frac{1}{2}$". (Courtesy, Colonial Williamsburg Foundation; photo, Hans Lorenz.)

Figure 20 Smoking chairs, Southampton County, Virginia, ca. 1775. Walnut with yellow pine. H. 32¹/₄", W. 26³/₄", D. 25". (Courtesy, Colonial Williamsburg Foundation; photo, Hans Lorenz.)

region. In 1751, he advertised the "Best Sole and Neats Leather, wax'd Calve Skins and Hides, suitable for Coaches, Chaises, Couches, Portmantuas and Chair Bottoms, in any Quantity." Although saddlemaking and harnessmaking accounted for most of his labor, Craig also provided finish work for carriages and riding chairs. On May 8, 1761, Craig charged Colonel Robert Burwell for "400 Brass nails and Lining a [riding] Chair, the Cushion and wings wt Leather Lace," and on May 2, 1762, he billed Colonel Philip Lee for "100 Brass nails and covering a step of a Charriot." No upholstered riding chairs from Virginia survive, but the fanciful child's phaeton depicted in a mid-eighteenth-century portrait of the Grymes children of Brandon in Middlesex County ties the practice of coach lining to the upholstery of seating furniture (fig. 21). Similar links are also evident in Craig's account book. In addition to selling "black grain," "calfskin," and other leather products to Williamsburg cabinetmaker Anthony Hay, Fredericksburg cabinetmaker James Allen, and Hampton cabinetmaker John Selden, Craig made mattresses, bolsters, and cushions for furniture. Over a five-year period during the mid-1750s, Craig recorded thirteen transactions regarding such work for the couches and easy chairs of Anthony Hay.[7]

The proximity of leatherworkers like Craig was not the sole reason for

Figure 21 *The Grymes Children* attributed to John Hesselius, Brandon, Middlesex County, Virginia, ca. 1750. Oil on canvas. 56" × 66¹/₄". (Courtesy, Virginia Historical Society.)

Figure 22 Easy chair, piedmont region of Virginia, ca. 1790. Black walnut with yellow pine; original leather upholstery. H. 44¹/₄", W. 28¹/₂", D. 22¹/₂". (Courtesy, Colonial Williamsburg Foundation; photo, Hans Lorenz.)

the material's popularity in Virginia upholstery. The fact that Virginians continued to cover their chairs with leather during the late eighteenth century, as demonstrated by a piedmont easy chair (fig. 22) and an Albemarle County armchair attributed to Jefferson's joinery at Monticello (fig. 23), suggests an ingrained stylistic impulse. Like many of their British counterparts, Virginians frequently used the phrase "neat and plain" to describe their predilection for sparsely ornamented, well-made case furniture and other goods. The phrase also applied to rich, durable, monochromatic leather upholstery. On the Bucktrout chair, the "black-grained" leather seat suggests simplicity and permanence, and the line of end-grain leather that defines and reinforces the stitched seams (fig. 24) represents the work of a skilled upholsterer or leatherworker.

The seat frame and upholstery foundation of the Bucktrout chair are characteristic of other British-influenced chairs. Like many British and American chairs with over-the-rail upholstery, the Bucktrout example has diagonal corner braces set into notches in the rails to help the frame resist the force of tightly stretched textiles (fig. 25). The outlines of the upholstery peaks at the top of the front legs are clearly visible beneath the leather (fig. 26).

Figure 23 Armchair, probably Albemarle County, Virginia, ca. 1800. Cherry; original black leather upholstery. H. 34⁷/₈", W. 23¹/₄", D. 19¹/₄". (Courtesy, Colonial Williamsburg Foundation; photo, Hans Lorenz.)

Figure 24 Detail of the black-grained leather and a stitched seam on the chair illustrated in fig. 18.

Figure 25 Preconservation view of the bottom of the chair illustrated in fig. 18. (Photo, L. Graves.)

Although the height of the peaks in relation to the overall rounded loft of the seat led to speculation that the chair received supplemental stuffing in the nineteenth century, X-radiography and careful "exploratory surgery" proved that the seat profile was essentially original (figs. 27, 28).

An attempt to shore up the sagging seat during the early twentieth century resulted in damaged materials and a somewhat elevated profile. This

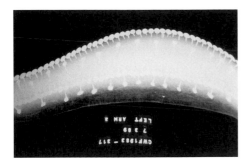

Figure 26 Preconservation detail of the chair illustrated in fig. 18, showing the seat with upholstery peaks visible beneath leather.

Figure 27 X-radiograph of an armrest on the chair illustrated in fig. 18, showing undisturbed original nails. (Courtesy, Robert Berry, Fabrication Division, Nondestructive Evaluation Section, NASA—Langley Research Center.)

Figure 28 X-radiograph taken above the front seat rail of the chair illustrated in fig. 18, showing one strip of webbing, webbing nails, and the front edge roll. (Courtesy, Robert Berry, Fabrication Division, Nondestructive Evaluation Section, NASA—Langley Research Center.)

new support consisted of two pine boards inserted above the diagonal corner braces (fig. 25). Regrettably, the leather was slit along the rear edge to relieve the tension and permit the rear corner braces to be pushed up and out of their notches. This provided sufficient clearance to slide the boards into place and to return the corner braces to their proper positions. Once in place, the new boards elevated the upholstery by approximately three-fourths of an inch. The raised profile and unsightly slit at the rear of the seat convinced us to remove the pine boards in order to repair the damage and develop a better support system for the seat.

Removal of the boards permitted a thorough inspection of the foundation upholstery. To support the deep, wide seat, the upholsterer used only six strips of herringbone webbing (fig. 28). After attaching them to the seat rails (three front-to-back and three side-to-side), he nailed an oversized piece of very coarse foundation linen to the rails above the webbing, allowing it to overhang about four to five inches on each side. Then he created soft, round edge rolls by doubling back the edges of the linen, stuffing it loosely with curled horsehair, and stitching it along the top, inner edges of the rails. After filling the cavity created by the edge rolls with curled horsehair, he covered the seat with a piece of finer-textured linen. Apparently the upholsterer chose to create more loft before nailing on the leather since he added a skimmer of Spanish moss between it and the top linen. Over time, the acidic moss caused holes to form in the top linen.

Before creating a new support, we stabilized the old materials. We gently steamed the webbing and foundation linen to relax the sharp folds caused by the forced installation of the pine boards. Then we enclosed the torn, frayed ends of the webbing and linen with stitched-on Stabiltex fabric. Since the original support materials no longer contained all of the stuffing, we stitched Stabiltex over both sides of the damaged areas of the top linen and

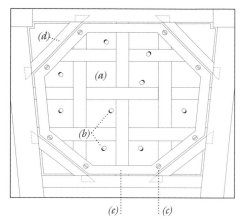

Figure 29 Auxiliary support for the seat of the chair illustrated in fig. 18: *(a)* ¼" acrylic support plate beneath the original upholstery, *(b)* ventilation holes in acrylic support plate, *(c)* bolt and T-nut, *(d)* diagonal brace, *(e)* 4-ply laminated acid-free ragboard. (Drawing, L. Graves; artwork, Wynne Patterson.)

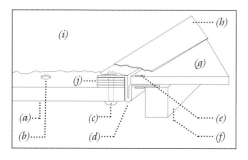

Figure 30 Detail of the corner bracket associated with the auxiliary support for the chair illustrated in fig. 18: *(a)* ¼" acrylic support plate beneath the original upholstery, *(b)* ventilation hole in acrylic support plate, *(c)* bolt and T-nut, *(d)* 24-gauge copper Z-shaped bracket, *(e)* copper rivet, *(f)* diagonal brace, *(g)* triangular-shaped ⅛" acrylic support, *(h)* self-adhesive moleskin, *(i)* silk Crepeline fabric, *(j)* 4-ply laminated acid-free ragboard. (Drawing, L. Graves; artwork, Wynne Patterson.)

encapsulated the curled hair in a case of the same sheer material. At this point, we repositioned the materials in their original locations in preparation for a new auxiliary support.

Several criteria determined the design for the new support. We needed to support all the materials in an approximation of the original loft without intruding on the original frame or upholstery. The system also had to protect the fragile upholstery and be made of materials that would not contribute to further deterioration. Finally, we wanted the system to be removable and not conceal the original materials when in place. The system shown in figures 29–31 satisfied all these criteria. It was easily installed by sliding a corner bracket into place above each of the diagonal braces, then screwing the transparent support plate to the brackets. The support plate is a one-fourth-inch acrylic sheet surmounted by a built-up stretcher of acid-free ragboard spanned by taut silk Crepeline. The silk bears against the original upholstery and creates a one-fourth-inch air space between the original webbing and the acrylic sheet.

With the support in place, we turned our attention to the treatment of the leather. The portion of leather originally attached to the rear seat rail was missing, having been removed when the seat was slashed along the rear edge. To compensate for the loss, we first attached a tab of acid-free cotton fabric to the underside of the slit edge using a polyvinyl acetate adhesive. We then cut a new piece of matching leather, laid it above the tab, and secured it with the same adhesive. To attach the new leather to the back rail, we glued a lightweight aluminum angle to the back edge of the leather with hot-melt adhesive (ethylene vinyl acetate) and riveted a row of closely spaced brass nails to the leather/aluminum strip to simulate the lost decorative trim. We left full-length shanks on three of the nails and tapped them into original holes (plugged) in the rear rail. Having conserved the seat, we completed the treatment of the leather by consolidating areas of minor flaking with a solution of ethulose in water and by patching a one-inch-diameter hole near the center of the seat with a paper fill colored to match the aged leather. Although the completed treatment provides support and inhibits further deterioration, we minimized cosmetic enhancements to maintain the integrity of the leather.

Richmond Easy Chair

The early nineteenth-century easy chair illustrated in figure 32 descended in the Gwathmey family of Burlington, in King William County, Virginia. The chair exhibits features typical of Richmond and Petersburg work, most notably the double ring and cove turning of the legs. As was often the case with easy chairs, this example doubled as a close stool. Resting within the rails is a three-board yellow pine seat with a hole cut for a chamber pot. Although the chair suffered losses to the feet and damage to the joints of the wings, it retained nearly all of its under-upholstery and an early, down-filled, ticking-covered cushion.

The chair had no evidence of a nailed-on show textile, which suggests that it originally had a slipcover. A few features of the upholstery also support

Figure 31   Detail of the underside of the chair illustrated in fig. 18, showing the new auxiliary support. (Photo, L. Graves.)

Figure 32   Easy chair, Richmond, Virginia, ca. 1820. Walnut and maple with white pine, yellow pine, and tulip poplar; original upholstery. H. 45³/₄", W. 30¹/₄", D. 30¹/₂". (Courtesy, Colonial Williamsburg Foundation; photo, Hans Lorenz.)

that conclusion. Top linen encases both the inner and outer surfaces of the wings and back of the chair, giving it a finished appearance. Upholsterers generally applied top linen only to the padded surfaces of chairs intended to receive nailed-on show textiles. In addition, deep clefts in the upholstery at the juncture of the wings and back appear calculated to serve as tuck points for a loosely fitted slipcover.

Slipcovers became common in Virginia during the latter half of the eighteenth century. Most often, they were used to protect expensive or delicate nailed-on fabrics. In 1771, Robert Beverley of Blandfield in Essex County, Virginia, ordered "12 neat plain mahogany Chairs, with yellow worstit Stuff Damask Bottoms . . . & spare loose Cases of yellow & white Check to tie over them." Later references and chairs similar to the Gwathmey example suggest a trend toward using slipcovers as the primary show material. An 1807 Alexandria County suit mentioned the sale of property including two "settees with double covers . . . one large Settee with double Covers . . . [and] fourteen mahogany Chairs, with double slips." Similarly, the 1822 will of Peter Copeland of Richmond listed an "Easy Chair with 4 Covers." The

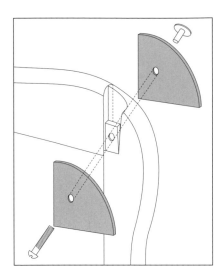

Figure 33 Design for plates used to secure and realign the damaged wing joint of the chair illustrated in fig. 32. (Drawing, L. Graves; artwork, Wynne Patterson.)

Figure 34 Preconservation detail of exposed Spanish moss stuffing from the chair illustrated in fig. 32. (Photo, L. Graves.)

Figure 35 Postconservation view of the easy chair illustrated in fig. 32, showing the stabilized original upholstery.

possession of multiple covers for chairs and sofas suggests their year-round usage, either to vary the covers seasonally or to substitute covers during cleaning.[8]

In conjunction with the curators of furniture and textiles, we decided to incorporate an appropriate slipcover into the treatment plan for the Gwathmey easy chair. The conservation of the frame and surviving upholstery preceded the fabrication of the cover. We lengthened the shortened feet and added casters, using the corresponding details on a virtually identical easy chair as our guide. The loose, fragmented joinery of one of the wings presented a more difficult problem—stabilizing the joint without damaging the adjacent upholstery materials. To realign and strengthen the joint, we sandwiched the adjoining wing members between two small plates of textile-covered copper (fig. 33). We only had to remove a few stitches in the linen cover to position the plates, then we drew them together using an empty three-sixteenth-inch hole formerly occupied by a wooden pin.

The original profile of the easy chair's upholstery had lost definition, in part because of the stretched, frayed, and torn linen. The stuffing had also sagged, despite the upholsterer's attempt to hold it in place with waxed cord

(run through small holes in the framing members and secured with nails). Some of the sagging resulted from deterioration of the unprocessed Spanish moss, or "Spanish Beard," used to stuff the chair (fig. 34). The outer skin of the moss, normally removed during processing, had crumbled to a coarse powder and sifted down to the bottom linen. Although little could be done to correct this problem, we improved the profile by manipulating the stuffing with a long upholstery needle (regulator). Using two-ply linen thread, we then stitched patches of Stabiltex to all areas of worn-through or frayed linen (fig. 35). The final treatment of the under-upholstery involved replicating the missing linen on the front seat rail. Rather than nailing it in place, we glued it to a U-shaped copper plate and friction-fit it to the rail.[9]

No fragment of the original slipcover textile survived, and no Virginia covers from the early nineteenth century are known. As a result, we used a circa 1840 roller-printed, chintz slipcover on an eighteenth-century Boston chair (fig. 36) as the prototype for a new one (fig. 37).[10]

Figure 36 Easy chair, Boston, Massachusetts, 1759. Walnut with white pine and maple; roller-printed chintz slipcover, ca. 1840. H. 46^{1}/$_{8}$", W. 33^{7}/$_{8}$", D. 21^{3}/$_{4}$". (Courtesy, Society for the Preservation of New England Antiquities.)

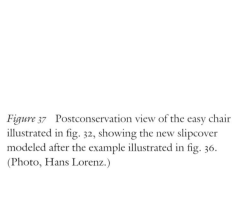

Figure 37 Postconservation view of the easy chair illustrated in fig. 32, showing the new slipcover modeled after the example illustrated in fig. 36. (Photo, Hans Lorenz.)

Norfolk Side Chair

In 1800, Norfolk had eight thousand inhabitants and was the eighth largest city in the United States. The city supported a growing community of cabinetmakers, chairmakers, and upholsterers who provided furniture for consumers in Norfolk and the surrounding towns and plantations of southeastern Virginia and northeastern North Carolina. Urban British styles and construction practices had a profound influence on Norfolk furniture made before and immediately after the Revolution. Although British influences persisted, tradesmen from New England and New York introduced a variety of northern furniture styles during the late eighteenth and early nineteenth centuries. The side chair illustrated in figure 38 may be the product of a cabinetmaker trained in a northern city. No exact prototype for this chair is known; however, examples with heart-shaped backs were made in several northern cities. Elements distinctly associated with Norfolk include the blade-shaped panels on the front legs, the bellflowers with concave outer petals, and the incised shading cuts filled with a black resinous material.[11]

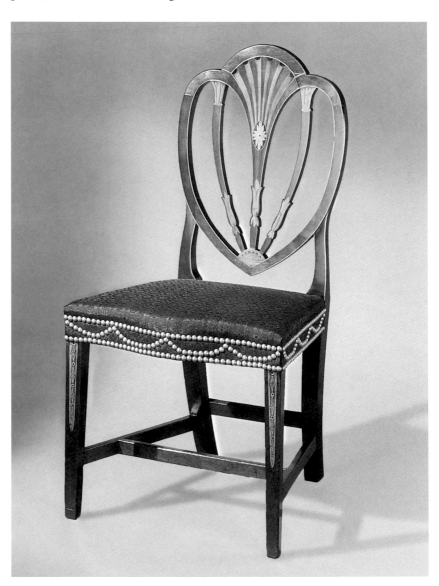

Figure 38 Side chair, probably Norfolk, Virginia, 1790–1810. Walnut and holly inlay with yellow pine. H. 34$^{1}/_{2}$", W. 18$^{3}/_{8}$", D. 17$^{1}/_{2}$". (Courtesy, Colonial Williamsburg Foundation; photo, Hans Lorenz.)

Figure 39 Detail showing evidence of the original brass nail trim on the front seat rail of the chair illustrated in fig. 38. (Photo, L. Graves and F. C. Howlett.)

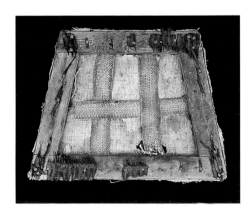

Figure 40 Slipseat frame, Virginia or Britain, ca. 1755. Beech; remnants of original linen and striped, black haircloth. (Courtesy, Colonial Williamsburg Foundation; photo, Hans Lorenz.)

The chair came into the Colonial Williamsburg collection with twentieth-century upholstery that in many respects represented a plausible replication of late eighteenth-century taste and techniques. The loft of the seat was relatively low, the show textile was a medallion-patterned black horsehair, and the decorative trim consisted of a double row of brass nails sandwiching a typical, if somewhat flattened, swag pattern. Upon lifting the nails to expose a portion of the seat rail, clear evidence of square-shanked, cast brass nail trim indicated that the chair had received three over-the-rail treatments early in its history. One consisted of pronounced swags above a single line of brass nails running along the bottom edges of the rails (no upper boundary line of nails was present) (fig. 39). Another consisted of two parallel lines—about two inches apart—of close-set brass nails. The uppermost line of nails in the latter treatment intersected the swags of the first, indicating that the two nail patterns were produced at different times. A third nail pattern differed only slightly from the second, with the upper line of nails sloping downward toward the rear of the side rails. This treatment appeared incomplete and may have been aborted by the upholsterer because of the sloping nail lines.

The twentieth-century upholsterer responsible for the most recent scheme attempted to recreate a nail pattern based on the early evidence. Unfortunately, his design combined two of the early schemes, resulting in a hybrid, flattened swag-pattern between two parallel rows of nails. For our interpretation of the upholstery, we followed the outline of the early swags, which were accompanied by only a single row of nails at the bottom.

No evidence of the show material survived on the frame, so we consulted pictorial sources, documentary references, and other seating furniture to select an appropriate textile. Manufactured in the colonies by 1736 and esteemed for its durability and satinlike appearance, haircloth was one of the most common textiles used on late eighteenth- and early nineteenth-century Virginia chairs. The 1789 estate inventory of Gabriel Galt of Henrico County listed "11 Mahogany chairs hair bottoms." Remnants of a black-striped haircloth survive on a slipseat frame found at Blandfield (fig. 40). This textile may resemble the "22 and 19 Inch narrow Satin Stripe Hair-Seating" mentioned in a 1790 advertisement by Baltimore cabinetmakers Bankson and Lawson. More importantly, an 1811 Norfolk sofa (fig. 41) with remnants of its original haircloth confirms the use of that material in the city and justifies its use on the side chair.[12]

In recent years, upholstery conservators have developed new methods of applying materials to bare frames to avoid the damage caused by traditional nailing techniques. The seat of the chair illustrated in figure 38 has the appearance of nailed-on upholstery, but it is completely nonintrusive. We accomplished this look by creating a "cap" consisting of several components selected for their ease of workmanship, their harmless effect, and their ability to contribute to the illusion of nailed-on upholstery (fig. 42). We used sheet copper for the foundation, because it conforms closely to the chair frame even when overlaid with other materials such as Ethafoam—a rigid polyethylene foam that is lightweight, inert, and easily shaped to simulate an

Figure 41 Sofa labeled by Chester Sully, Norfolk, Virginia, 1811. Mahogany with yellow pine, tulip poplar, and ash. H. 37 7/8", W. 72 5/8", D. 23". (Courtesy, Colonial Williamsburg Foundation; photo, Hans Lorenz.)

upholstery profile. Since Ethafoam can be sculpted to the intended profile, show materials do not need to be stretched tightly over its surface to produce a taut appearance. If sat upon, however, Ethafoam does not fully recover its shape, so we limit its use to exhibition upholstery (functional seats are possible using minimally intrusive techinques, but their design is complicated by the need to compress the stuffing to attain the proper profile and create a comfortable seat). After sculpting the Ethafoam, we applied a layer of polyester batting to soften its appearance and to provide a slightly compressible surface for the application of the textile layers. Because of the open weave of modern haircloth, we first applied a black cotton fabric to prevent the white batting from showing. We lightly stretched the black lining over the surface, folded it over the edges of the copper plates, and glued it to the copper with hot-melt adhesive. We applied the haircloth in a similar manner, with the front corners cut and handstitched to give the appearance of a traditional cover. Finally, we applied the modern brass nails by inserting the wire shanks through holes in the copper plate, trimming the points, and peening over the projecting shanks to rivet them in place. The completed upholstery cap exists as a unit attached to the chair solely by a light friction fit, and we can safely remove it in a matter of seconds to study the chair frame (fig. 43).[13]

Two Winchester Sofas
After visiting with the Tidbald family of Winchester in 1799, Susanna Knox

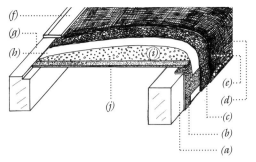

Figure 42 Components of the nonintrusive upholstery system devised for the side chair illustrated in fig. 38: *(a)* front seat rail, *(b)* 24-gauge copper face plate, *(c)* black cotton fabric, *(d)* haircloth show textile, *(e)* brass nails, *(f)* removable shoe molding, *(g)* rear seat rail, *(h)* polyester batting, *(i)* Ethafoam, *(j)* 32-gauge copper foundation. (Drawing, L. Graves; artwork, Wynne Patterson.)

Figure 43 Postconservation view of the side chair illustrated in fig. 38.

wrote: "They live in a large stone house, I was only in the drawing room— that was a very handsome one, elegantly furnished with mahogany—a settee covered with copperplate calico, red and white, the window curtains the same, with white muslin falls, drawn up in festoons, with large tassels as big as my two fists." Situated on the Great Wagon Road at the northern end of the Shenandoah Valley, Winchester was one of the largest towns in the backcountry. It was also an important commercial center and a staging point for migration to the frontier. Like many other travelers from the east, Susanna Knox was impressed by the sophistication of the town and the furnishings and other material goods available there.[14]

Two late eighteenth-century Winchester sofas rival the finest examples from the East Coast. One of these sofas was recently reupholstered following an intensive study of its frame (fig. 44) and the frame of a nearly identical sofa (fig. 45). This side-by-side examination proved beneficial to the

Figure 44 Sofa, Winchester, Virginia, 1790–1800. Black walnut and maple inlay with yellow pine and tulip poplar. H. 37", W. 89", D. 27½". (Courtesy, Colonial Williamsburg Foundation; photo, Hans Lorenz.)

Figure 45 Sofa, Winchester, Virginia, 1790–1800. Black walnut and maple inlay with yellow pine and tulip poplar. H. 37", W. 86½", D. 27¼". (Private collection; photo, Hans Lorenz.)

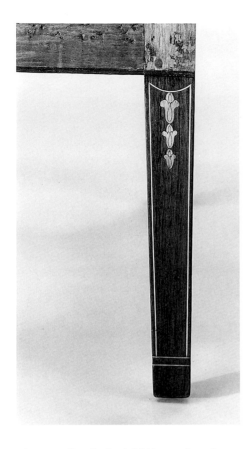

Figure 46 Detail of an inlaid leg on the sofa illustrated in fig. 44.

Figure 47 Detail of the arm assembly and seat rails of the sofa illustrated in fig. 44.

interpretation of missing elements on both examples and enabled us to confirm the authenticity of some unexpected features of the original upholstery on both objects.

The sofas are highly developed examples of early neoclassical seating furniture. Each has a serpentine back, scrolled and sculpted armrests that sweep upward and outward with graceful S curves, and square-tapered legs with inlaid stringing and incised bellflowers (fig. 46). The unconventional form of the bellflowers, which are inverted and have rounded lobes, is the most obvious detail associating them with backcountry production. Other features typical of Winchester work include the use of walnut rather than mahogany as the primary wood, the use of yellow pine and tulip poplar as secondary woods, and the presence of a molded bead along the lower edges of the front and side seat rails. The sofas are part of a group of furniture including a wine cooler, several sideboards, and a pair of card tables, all of which appear to be from the same Winchester shop.[15]

Although varying slightly in form (the example shown in fig. 45 has more pronounced curves on its arms and back), the sofas share many structural features. Both have ribbed structures in the arm assemblies that help define the complex shapes of the arms (fig. 47), inner front legs that are secured with sliding dovetail saddle joints, and evidence of original casters. The sofas also have two curved medial stretchers spanning the front and rear seat rails and nearly identical supports and attachment points for their removable backs. Because their structures are so similar, the unaltered crest rail of the sofa illustrated in figure 45 proved helpful in redesigning the lost upper edge of the other example (fig. 44), which was apparently planed down prior to a twentieth-century reupholstery. By studying the form of the unaltered crest and by measuring the planed-down depths of original brass nail holes found on the altered crest (unaltered areas had nail depths averaging one-half of an inch, whereas those in planed areas were as shallow as one-sixteenth of an inch), we were able to reconstruct an accurate profile that raised the central portion of the altered crest rail as much as three-eights of an inch in height.

Figure 48 Detail of the sofa illustrated in fig. 45, with modern nails pointing out original brass nail locations.

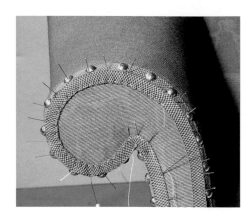

Figure 49 Detail of the sofa illustrated in fig. 44, with new upholstery and trim applied according to evidence found on the frame. (Photo, L. Graves and F. C. Howlett.)

Other shared features of the frames gave insight into the original fabrication and appearance of the upholstery. To augment the nailing surface for the seat webbing, the upholsterer nailed wooden strips to the inner surfaces of the side rails (see fig. 47). His practice of nailing the webbing into shallow dadoes on the upper surfaces of the rails (perpendicular to their length) suggested that he intended to maintain a low upholstery profile on the seats. Molded beads running along the bottom edges of the front and side rails indicate that the lower rail faces were exposed. This seat configuration, referred to as "half over-the-rail upholstery," is rare on sofas of this form. Although obscured by nail damage, remnants of an early finish on the rails of the sofa illustrated in figure 45 provided further evidence that both pieces had half over-the-rail upholstery. (The rails of the other sofa were abraded and veneered during the twentieth century, thus no finish remnants remained.)

The sofas have only a few remnants of original upholstery material. The one shown in figure 44 retains strips of webbing nailed across the ribs of the arm assemblies, and the other sofa (fig. 45) has its original back webbing and foundation linen. Fibers of deer or cow hair adhering to the linen indicate the nature of the original stuffing material. The webbing arrangement and size and spacing of the nails on the sofas is remarkably similar, indicating that both sofas were upholstered by the same hand.[16]

Although no fibers relating to the original show materials of the sofas survived, both pieces have evidence of their earliest decorative trim. On both sofas, square-shaped holes, broken shanks, and head imprints from the original brass nails revealed the same pattern. The nail heads were one-half inch in diameter and spaced an inch and a half on centers. Unlike other neoclassical sofas with similar nailing, the trim on the Winchester examples outlined the inside corners formed by the juncture of the arms and backs and the seat and bottom edge of the lower back rail (fig. 48), in addition to the usual structural components—arm supports, armrests, seat rails, and crest rails. If such features had been discovered on only one sofa, they may have been dismissed as implausible aberrations. As a general rule, upholsterers did not apply expensive brass nails in locations typically covered by cushions or mattresses. Because both Winchester sofas had this unconventional treatment, the reconstructed upholstery features the same profligate use of brass nails.

The trim evidence suggested that the original upholstery on both sofas could have been leather. The brass nails left very few circular imprints on the frame, as they would have if the original covers had been a thin, woven textile. Although a woven tape or gimp beneath the nails could also have prevented the heads from scarring the frame, the very close proximity of the nail holes to the edges of the wooden elements also suggested that the sofas had leather covers. Since leather adds thickness to the surfaces of an upholstery frame, the brass nail trim runs closer to the edges of the frame and occasionally runs off the wood altogether in order to keep the nail trim flush with the corners produced by adjoining leather edges. Another clue in support of leather is the presence of knife cuts, possibly from a tool used to trim the edges, on the left seat rail of the sofa shown in figure 45. Since there were no knife cuts on the other sofa and neither example had conclusive proof that leather was the original show material, the sofa illustrated in figure 44 was reupholstered in a green moreen using a nonintrusive system.

Reupholstery of a sofa frame invariably results in questions regarding the presence or absence of a loose mattress and cushions. One cannot generalize about period upholstery since physical and documentary evidence supports various approaches to mattresses and cushions; however, dimensional studies often provide indications of their presence or absence. For the sofa illustrated in figure 44, a dimensional study provided sound indications of loose back cushions and a seat mattress. Evidence for a mattress grew from a determination of the intended height of the applied seat upholstery. The height from the floor to the upper edge of the seat rails, including an allowance of 2" for original casters, was 16$^{1}/_{2}$". We also found nail evidence for an original edge roll approximately 1" in diameter; thus, the height from the floor to the upper surface of the seat upholstery was approximately 17$^{1}/_{2}$", lower than most eighteenth- and nineteenth-century sofa seats. Since the top edges of the outer legs are 20$^{1}/_{4}$" high, it is logical to assume that the sofa had a 3"-thick mattress. Similarly, loose back cushions are implied by the 25" front-to-back dimension of the seat, as well as by evidence of thinly applied back upholstery. The loose cushions were probably 3 inches thick to coordinate with the seat mattress and to comfortably reduce the depth of the seat.

Most of the features of the replicated upholstery on this sofa were drawn directly from evidence found during the study of the two Winchester examples. As in the case of the show material, however, there were some gaps

Figure 50 Postconservation view of the sofa illustrated in fig. 44, with cushions fabricated according to a dimensional study of the frame. (Photo, Hans Lorenz.)

regarding the original appearance of a few details. The tufting of the back and seat cushions and the tape-covered cord that outlines their edges (figs. 49, 50) are somewhat conjectural, since these features cannot be determined from a bare frame. Both details, however, are based upon sound historic precedent and contribute to the final appearance of the sofa. Much like the upholstery cap for the Norfolk chair (fig. 43), the new upholstery system devised for the sofa minimizes intrusion into the frame.[17]

The preceding case studies document some of the materials and techniques used by upholsterers working in Virginia during the eighteenth and early nineteenth centuries. In addition, these studies document the steps taken by current scholars and conservators to understand and preserve original upholstery, to study and conserve seating furniture that survives in skeletal form, and to replicate the early upholstery schemes determined from such studies.

ACKNOWLEDGMENTS   For assistance with this article, the authors thank Luke Beckerdite, Wallace Gusler, Ronald Hurst, Jonathan Prown, David Peebles, Byron Wenger, Sally Gant, and Martha Rowe. We are especially grateful to Albert Skutans for his contributions to upholstery conservation at Colonial Williamsburg.

1. Object files, acc. 1988–433, Colonial Williamsburg Foundation. Luke Beckerdite, "Architect-Designed Furniture in Eighteenth-Century Virginia: The Work of William Buckland and William Bernard Sears," in *American Furniture,* edited by Luke Beckerdite (Hanover, N.H.: University Press of New England for the Chipstone Foundation, 1994), pp. 28–48. Inventory of the estate of John Tayloe, Richmond County, Virginia, Will bk. 5, 1725–1753, pp. 547–53. The authors thank Wallace Gusler for this reference.

2. V. C. Hall, Jr., *Portraits in the Collection of the Virginia Historical Society* (Charlottesville: University Press of Virginia, 1981), pp. 20–21.

3. F. Carey Howlett, "The Identification of Grasses and Other Plant Materials Used in Historic Upholstery," in *Upholstery Conservation,* edited by Marc A. Williams (East Kingston, N.H.: American Conservation Consortium, Ltd., 1990), pp. 66–91.

4. Kathy Francis, "Fiber and Fabric Remains on Upholstery Tacks and Frames: Identification, Interpretation, and Preservation of Textile Evidence," in Williams, ed., *Upholstery Conservation,* pp. 63–65.

5. F. Carey Howlett, "Admitted into the Mysteries: The Benjamin Bucktrout Masonic Master's Chair," in *American Furniture,* edited by Luke Beckerdite (Hanover, N.H.: University Press of New England for the Chipstone Foundation, 1996), pp. 195–232. Robert Carter Papers, M-82-8, Virginia Historical Society, Richmond, Virginia.

6. Will of Francis Roberts, December 13, 1698, Accomack County, Virginia, Wills, etc., 1692–1715, p. 398a. Estate inventory of Anthony Butts, March 16, 1718, York County, Virginia, Orders, Wills, 8c. No. 15, Part 2, 1716–1720, p. 415. Estate inventory of John Walker, April 19, 1745, Middlesex County, Virginia, Will Book C, 1740–1748, p. 240.

7. *Virginia Gazette,* October 17, 1751. Alexander Craig Account Book, pp. 10, 63, Special Collections, Earl Gregg Swem Library, College of William and Mary, Williamsburg, Virginia. Alexander Craig Ledger, 1749–1756, Special Collections, Swem Library.

8. Robert Beverley to Samuel Athawes, July 16, 1771, Robert Beverley Letterbook, 1761–1775, Library of Congress, as quoted in Linda Baumgarten, "Protective Covers for Furniture and Its Contents," in *American Furniture,* edited by Luke Beckerdite (Hanover, N.H.: University Press of New England for the Chipstone Foundation, 1993), p. 4. Suit referring to the mortgage and sale of the property of William Wilson, July 7, 1807, Alexandria County, Virginia, Complete Records F, 1804–1811, p. 104. Inventory of Peter Copeland, April 20, 1822, Richmond Hustings Wills No. 3, 1820–1824, p. 305.

9. Spanish moss *(Tillandsia usneoides)* is an epiphyte common to the coast of North Amer-

ica. Because it was shipped north beginning in the eighteenth century for use as a stuffing material, its presence in a piece of upholstered furniture offers little indication of the object's place of manufacture. Typically the moss was processed by rotting away the impermanent outer skin, leaving only the tough black fibers that are similar in appearance to curled hair (except for the nodes and branches). The term "Spanish beard" appears in Duke de la Rochenfouchault Liancourt, *Travels through the United States of North America in the Years, 1795, 1796, and 1797* (London, 1800), p. 441.

10. Textile curator Linda Baumgarten and furniture curator Ronald Hurst selected the prototype, and Natalie Larson fabricated the cover.

11. Ronald L. Hurst and Sumpter Priddy III, "The Neoclassical Furniture of Norfolk, Virginia, 1770–1820," *Antiques* 137, no. 5 (May 1990): 1140–53. For more on Norfolk furniture, see Ronald L. Hurst, "Cabinetmakers and Related Tradesmen in Norfolk, Virginia, 1770–1820" (master's thesis, College of William and Mary, 1989).

12. *Pennsylvania Gazette*, December 16, 1736. Inventory of Gabriel Galt, Henrico County, Virginia Will Book No. 2, 1787–1802, p. 65.

13. Susan Adler and Joanna Ruth Harris assisted with the treatment of the Norfolk side chair.

14. Letter from Susanna Knox to her daughters in Fredericksburg, Virginia, April 20, 1799, in *Genealogy of the Fitzhugh, Knox, Gordon, Selden, Horner, Brown, Baylor, (King) Carter, Edmonds, Digges, Page, Tayloe, and Allied Families* (Atlanta, Ga., 1932), p. 20. The authors thank Wendy Cooper and Liza and Wallace Gusler for this reference.

15. The sideboard, wine cooler, and card table are illustrated in Ronald L. Hurst and Jonathan Prown, *Southern Furniture, 1680–1830: The Colonial Williamsburg Collection* (New York: Harry Abrams, 1997), pp. 147–52.

16. The seat of the sofa illustrated in figure 44 was supported by sixteen strips of $1^7/8''$ webbing running front-to-back and five strips running side-to-side. The back of the sofa was supported by twelve vertical strips of $1^7/8''$ webbing and a single strip running side-to-side. The seat of the sofa shown in figure 45 had thirteen strips of $2^1/2''$ webbing running front-to-back and four strips running side-to-side. Its back is supported by eleven vertical strips of $2^1/2''$ webbing and a single horizontal strip. Both seats and back were covered with foundation linen secured with nails, spaced approximately $1^1/2''$ apart. Along with other features, the differences in webbing width and the upholsterer's decision to strengthen the support of the narrower webbing by using a greater number of strips suggest that the sofas were not made concurrently.

17. Debbie Juchem, Ann Battram, Gene Mitchell, and Lucy Binceguerra assisted with the treatment of the Winchester sofa.

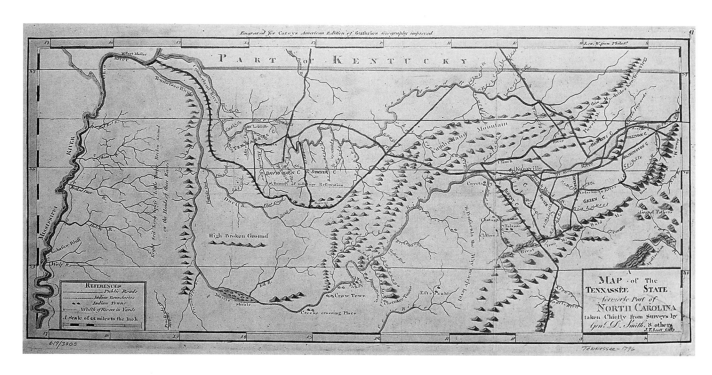

Figure 1 Daniel Smith, map of Tennessee, Philadelphia, 1795. Engraving on paper. 10 ¹/₄" × 21¹/₂".
(Private collection; photo, John Bivins.)

Anne S. McPherson

Adaptation and
Reinterpretation:
The Transfer of
Furniture Styles
from Philadelphia
to Winchester to
Tennessee

▼ DURING THE LATE 1760s, the availability of inexpensive land attracted settlers to the northeastern corner of Tennessee. Although historians David Hackett Fischer and James C. Kelly have noted that the "sweep of settlement through the Valley of Virginia led inexorably into the valley of East Tennessee," settlers also came from other areas, including the coastal and piedmont regions of Virginia and North Carolina. While the earliest settlements were being established, parties of hunters passed through the Cumberland Gap and over the Cumberland Plateau into Middle Tennessee (fig. 1). In 1779 and 1780, three permanent settlements, including Nashville, were established in the Cumberland River Valley in northern Middle Tennessee. Although some of the earliest settlers in Middle Tennessee stopped briefly in the eastern part of the state, the two regions were separated by mountains and "three hundred miles of wilderness." Because of this geographic barrier, East Tennessee and Middle Tennessee developed simultaneously yet independently of each other.[1]

The population in both regions continued to grow throughout the 1780s, particularly after the Revolution when the state of North Carolina sold land to generate revenue and granted land to soldiers. In Middle Tennessee, the earliest settlements centered around Davidson County, where Nashville is located, and Sumner County, the site of settlement in 1779. In upper East Tennessee, Jonesboro, Rogersville, and Greeneville predate Knoxville, which was not settled until 1786. Knoxville, however, became the largest town and the political and economic center of the region soon after William Blount, the newly appointed governor of the Territory South of the River Ohio, chose it as the site of his capital in 1791. The 1795 census of the territory lists 77,272 inhabitants, indicating that settlement grew rapidly in less than thirty years.[2]

As cabinetmakers, journeymen, and apprentices moved from southeastern Pennsylvania into the Valley of Virginia and then into Tennessee, they adapted their designs and construction methods to suit the demands of their new clientele, who often had preconceived notions about what was fashionable. As the largest town and most important style center in the Valley of Virginia, Winchester exerted a powerful influence on objects produced in the Valley and westward. As makers and patrons moved further from the original design source, however, forms were adapted and regionalized. The furniture discussed in this article shows how Delaware Valley styles were interpreted by artisans in Winchester and outlying areas of Frederick County (see Wallace Gusler article in this volume, p. 228, fig. 1) and how

Figure 2 Desk-and-bookcase, Winchester area, Virginia, 1795. Cherry with yellow pine. H. 103³/₄", W. 42¹/₄", D. 24¹/₂". (Courtesy, Colonial Williamsburg Foundation; photo, Hans Lorenz.)

they were further developed and regionalized by cabinetmakers and their patrons in Middle Tennessee and East Tennessee.[3]

Like many Winchester case pieces, the desk-and-bookcase illustrated in figure 2 has several details commonly found on Delaware Valley furniture. The shape of its pediment bears a close relationship to examples from Philadelphia and its hinterlands, but the swagged astragal molding on the tympanum contrasts with the elaborate carving found on some Delaware

Figure 3 Detail of the pediment of the desk-and-bookcase illustrated in fig. 2.

Figure 4 Detail of the writing compartment of the desk-and-bookcase illustrated in fig. 2.

Valley pieces (figs. 3, 5). Likewise, the writing compartment of the Winchester desk-and-bookcase follows a typical Philadelphia plan in having a prospect door flanked by document drawers and pigeonholes with double-ogee valances above two tiers of drawers (figs. 2, 4). Although the Philadelphia desk-and-bookcase shown in figure 5 has shaped interior drawers, most desks made there during the last quarter of the eighteenth century have plain drawer fronts like the Winchester example. The Winchester desk also has ogee feet with filleted, spurred responds. Similar feet occur on Philadelphia case pieces by the mid-1740s and on furniture made outside the city during the last half of the eighteenth century.

Figure 5   Desk-and-bookcase, Philadelphia, 1760–1770. Mahogany with tulip poplar and white cedar. H. 109³/₄", W. 45", D. 25". (Courtesy, Philadelphia Museum of Art, gift of George H. Lorimer.)

Figure 6 Detail of a quarter-column on the desk-and-bookcase illustrated in fig. 2.

Figure 7 Armchair, Winchester area, Virginia, 1769. Walnut with walnut and white pine. H. 40", W. 28³/₈", D. 18³/₄". (Collection of the Museum of Early Southern Decorative Arts.)

By contrast, arched stop-fluting on quarter-columns is a distinctive feature of the Winchester school (fig. 6). Fluted quarter-columns are common on Delaware Valley furniture from the colonial period, but arched stop-fluted ones are unknown. Arched stop-fluted quarter-columns in conjunction with the aforementioned Delaware Valley details occur only on Winchester-school furniture made in the Shenandoah Valley and in Tennessee.[4]

It is difficult to determine when Winchester artisans began producing furniture in the Delaware Valley style. The earliest documented example is a chair with carved shells and Philadelphia-style arms and arm supports dated 1769 (fig. 7); however, most Winchester furniture with Delaware Valley features dates from the 1780s and 1790s. The desk-and-bookcase illustrated in figure 2 is part of a large group of furniture purchased by David Lupton for his house, Cherry Row, built near Winchester in 1794. A related desk from nearby Fauquier County is inscribed "Christopher Frye/ Cabinet Maker/ 1797." Although similar seating and case forms remained popular in the Valley of Virginia until at least 1800, they would have been considered old-fashioned in Philadelphia at that time. The cabinetmakers' price list transcribed by Benjamin Lehman of Germantown indicates that rococo forms were being produced in Philadelphia as late as 1786, but during the 1790s an influx of new cabinetmakers and design books from England brought about a stylistic change. In 1795, *The Journeymen Cabinet and Chair-Makers Philadelphia Book of Prices* set prices for furniture in the neoclassical style.[5]

Although Winchester influences are most apparent in furniture from East Tennessee, one cabinet shop in the Nashville area of Middle Tennessee produced furniture that resembles Winchester work. Because a larger number of shops were involved over a longer period of time in Knox County, the furniture made in the Nashville area will be considered first.

Furniture from the Nashville Area of Middle Tennessee
During his visit to the Cumberland area of Tennessee in 1785, Lewis Brantz wrote, "Nashville is a recently founded place and contains only two houses which, in true, merit the name; the rest are only huts that formerly served as a sort of fortification against Indian attacks." Similarly, when François André Michaux visited Nashville in 1802, he commented on the existence of only "seven or eight brick houses, the remainder consisting of about 120 . . . built with planks." Men of substance, however, were building large houses in the surrounding countryside by the mid-1790s. Daniel Smith, a member of the party that founded Nashville in 1779 and for whom Smith County was later named, completed Rock Castle in Sumner County in 1796 (fig. 8). Michaux described Cragfont, the stone house built by General James Winchester in Sumner County between 1798 and 1802, as "very elegant for the country." Lawyer John Overton built Traveller's Rest, a two-story frame house with a side passage plan, outside Nashville in 1799. The houses constructed in both Davidson and Sumner Counties during this period reflected the growing prosperity of this fertile area of Middle Tennessee.[6]

In addition to building elegant and substantial houses, these men pur-

Figure 8 Rock Castle, Hendersonville, Tennessee, 1796. (Photo, John Bivins.)

Figure 9 Desk-and-bookcase, Nashville area, Tennessee, 1795–1805. Walnut with tulip poplar and walnut. H. 106⁹/₁₆", W. 44¹/₂", D. 22¹/₂". (Courtesy, Ladies Hermitage Association; photo, John Bivins.)

chased locally made furniture to outfit them. The desk-and-bookcase illustrated in figure 9 descended in the family of Andrew Jackson who, according to oral tradition, used it in his law office. Although several details differentiate the Jackson desk-and-bookcase from the Lupton example (fig. 2), the influence of Winchester styles on Middle Tennessee furniture is apparent. Both desks have central prospect doors, fluted document drawers, and double-ogee-shaped pigeonhole valances. The valances on the Jackson desk are significantly deeper than those on the Lupton example, and the interior drawers are arranged two over one rather than two over two (figs. 4, 10). The Jackson desk also has ogee feet with filleted, spurred responds and stop-fluted quarter-columns. The level stop-fluting on this desk (fig. 11) represents a significant departure from the Winchester school, where stop-fluting was invariably arched (fig. 6).

Figure 10 Detail of the writing compartment of the desk-and-bookcase illustrated in fig. 9.

Figure 11 Detail of a quarter-column and writing surface lock rail miter on the desk-and-bookcase illustrated in fig. 9.

The Lupton and Jackson desk-and-bookcases are also constructed differently. Like many Philadelphia case pieces, the Lupton example has three-quarter-height, full-bottom dustboards that are dadoed into the case sides and attached to the drawer rails with a tongue-and-groove joint. The Jackson desk-and-bookcase has drawer supports that are dadoed into the case sides and tenoned into the front and rear drawer rails. This framed support system is relatively common on furniture from southeastern Pennsylvania and the southern backcountry. On the Jackson desk, the method of joining the writing surface lock rail to the case sides is somewhat unusual. Typically, the lock rail fits into a blind dado in the case sides and shows on the surface as a vertical joint; however, the maker of the Jackson example mitered the exposed portion of the joint (fig. 11). Like much rural furniture, this desk-and-bookcase is difficult to categorize stylistically. The shape of the cornice, the quarter-columns, and the ogee feet are rococo features, but the extreme verticality of the bookcase is more in keeping with the neoclassical taste. Conversely, the use of dentil molding only on the front of the bookcase reflects a baroque frontal aesthetic.[7]

The chest of drawers illustrated in figure 12 is from the same shop as the Jackson desk-and-bookcase, and it has the same history of descent. Although the profiles of the principal inner curves of the feet on both pieces are identical, those on the chest have slightly different responds and no fillet at the bottom. The chest also has framed drawer supports, a mitered lock rail below the top, and dovetails of the same size and pitch as those on the desk-and-bookcase. The quarter-columns on both pieces have the same base and capital moldings, but the ones on the chest are not stop-fluted. Apparently Jackson was willing to pay extra for stop-fluted quarter-columns on his desk-and-bookcase, which would have been placed in a public area, but not for his chest of drawers, which may have been in a more private space of his house.[8]

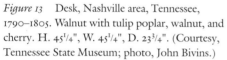

Figure 12   Chest of drawers, Nashville area, Tennessee, 1795–1805. Walnut with tulip poplar. H. 34³/₈", W. 40⁵/₈", D. 20¹¹/₁₆". (Courtesy, Ladies Hermitage Association; photo, John Bivins.)

Figure 13   Desk, Nashville area, Tennessee, 1790–1805. Walnut with tulip poplar, walnut, and cherry. H. 45¹/₄", W. 45¹/₄", D. 23³/₄". (Courtesy, Tennessee State Museum; photo, John Bivins.)

The desk illustrated in figure 13 is a product of the same Tennessee shop. It has all of the distinctive structural features found on the aforementioned pieces, and its writing compartment and stop-fluted quarter-columns are virtually identical to those of the Jackson desk-and-bookcase (figs. 10, 11). The desk interiors, including the layout, the fluted document drawers, and the shape of the valances, are the same. The feet of the desk are much bolder than those on the Jackson examples, and they have different responds and a sharper radius in their principal curve. It is unusual for feet from the same shop to vary as much as in these examples, but there is no doubt that they share a common origin.

Although cherry was the primary wood favored by cabinetmakers in Middle Tennessee, the Jackson pieces and the desk are made of walnut. After his visit to Lexington, Kentucky, between the years 1807 and 1809, Fortescue Cuming noted the "immense expense" of importing mahogany into the southern backcountry and the common use of walnut and cherry in furniture. Michaux considered cherry the "most eligible substitute for mahogany" and noted that the "Wild Cherry Tree is generally preferred to the Black Walnut, whose dun complexion with time becomes nearly black."[9]

The Jackson pieces were probably made between 1796 and 1804. Jackson arrived in Nashville in 1788 and boarded with Rachel Stockley Donelson, the widow of Colonel John Donelson, a co-founder of Nashville. In either 1790 or 1791, Jackson married the Donelsons' daughter, Rachel, and in 1796 they moved to Hunter's Hill, a two-story frame house about thirteen miles north of Nashville. In 1804, debts forced them to sell Hunter's Hill, and they moved to the Hermitage (then a log house). Jackson probably purchased the desk-and-bookcase and chest of drawers while he and his wife were living at Hunter's Hill.[10]

The desk illustrated in figure 13 descended in the family of Colonel John Donelson. In late 1779 and early 1780, he led the flotilla of boats from upper East Tennessee to Nashville as a counterpart to the overland party led by James Robertson. Although family tradition maintains that Donelson brought this desk with him on the flatboat *Adventure,* this history is unlikely for several reasons. First, it is doubtful that a large, expensive case piece would have been transported on a cumbersome flatboat nearly one thousand miles on winding rivers. Second, Donelson died in 1785 (having just returned to Middle Tennessee from Harrodsburg, Kentucky, where he and his family sojourned due to food shortages and Indian troubles in the Nashville area), and the desk is not listed in his estate inventory. Finally, the same cabinetmaker made two pieces of furniture for Andrew Jackson, who came to Middle Tennessee after Donelson's death. It is far more likely that the desk belonged to Donelson's son, John, from whom Jackson purchased Hunter's Hill.[11]

Since both Jackson and Donelson lived ten to fifteen miles outside Nashville in northern Davidson County, the cabinetmaker they commissioned could have lived in either Davidson County or Sumner County (fig. 1). During the late eighteenth and early nineteenth centuries, both counties had comparable numbers of cabinetmakers and joiners. By the 1810s and 1820s, several cabinetmakers worked in northern Middle Tennessee; however, only a few can be documented before 1805. Although the cabinetmaker who worked for Jackson and Donelson remains anonymous, candidates include William A. Crawford, Absalom Davis, John and Thomas Deatherage, Joseph McBride, and Thomas Murray. Unfortunately, no evidence that any of these men trained or worked in the Winchester area has surfaced.[12]

Davidson County cabinetmaker William Crawford owned "One Sett of Tools for Cabinet Work" when he died in 1803. Presumably, this set comprised the "chest of tools" purchased by Absalom Davis for $101.50 at Crawford's estate sale in 1804. Absalom Davis may be the same person who was apprenticed to Stokes County, North Carolina, house joiner Isham Vest in 1798. If so, it is highly unlikely that he made the Jackson and Donelson furniture. John and Thomas Deatherage were cabinetmakers in Nashville by 1802 when they took an apprentice in the cabinet trade. Thomas died in 1812, and shortly thereafter John moved to Kentucky. Joseph McBride of Davidson County took apprentices in 1801 and 1803. The 1815 inventory of his estate lists three work benches and "1 Compleat set of Cabinet Tools." Davidson County Court Minutes record that Thomas Murray took apprentices in the "carpenters and joiners trade" in 1792, 1795, and 1796. Two years later, John Overton sued Murray in the Sumner County Court for failure to complete a bookcase. According to Sumner County historian Walter Durham, a man named Thomas Murray moved from Rowan County, North Carolina, to Middle Tennessee in 1785. If this individual was cabinetmaker Thomas Murray, he is an unlikely candidate for the maker of the Jackson and Donelson furniture. Other individuals recorded in published checklists of Tennessee cabinetmakers have not been included either because they cannot be documented in Middle Tennessee during the late eighteenth century, because they appear to have been house joiners rather than cabinetmakers, or because known examples of their work differ significantly from the Jackson and Donelson furniture.[13]

Furniture from the Knoxville Area of East Tennessee
When John Donelson led his flotilla down the Tennessee River on the way to the Cumberland River Valley in late 1779, he was one of the first white men to pass through the area where Knoxville is situated. After William Blount chose the site as the capital of the Southwest Territory, development of the town proceeded rapidly. By 1792, several houses were under construction, including the dwelling known today as Blount Mansion. Francis A. Ramsey built a "large handsome, two-storied stone house" outside Knoxville about 1798 (fig. 14). Moravian missionaries Abraham Steiner and Frederick de Schweinitz reported that there were about one hundred houses in Knoxville in 1799, compared to about fifty in Nashville. In 1802, Michaux found the lodging in Knoxville to be "very good" but complained that its price was "rather too high" due to the desire of the inhabitants to make money quickly. He also noted the availability of merchandise from Philadelphia, Richmond, and Baltimore but pointed out that every "article

Figure 14 Ramsey House, Knoxville, Tennessee, 1798. (Photo, John Bivins.)

Figure 15 Desk-and-bookcase, Knoxville area, Tennessee, 1790–1800. Walnut with yellow pine and tulip poplar. H. 87¼" (without feet), W. 41⅞", D. 35¼". (Private collection; photo, Museum of Early Southern Decorative Arts.) The brasses, feet, and small strip added to the bottom of the base molding are incorrect replacements.

of English manufacture is sold very dear." Although some consumer goods could be obtained elsewhere, the difficulties and expense of transportation necessitated the purchase of locally made furniture. In 1802, Knoxville had 387 inhabitants, and Knox County had 12,446. This population supported at least four cabinetmakers and a sizable number of house joiners. Four different cabinet shops produced furniture in the Delaware Valley style.[14]

A desk-and-bookcase, four corner cupboards, and a chest of drawers represent the work of one of these shops. Of all the Tennessee desk-and-bookcases known, the example illustrated in figure 15 is most like those produced in southeastern Pennsylvania. It descended in the family of Barclay McGhee who came to East Tennessee from Lancaster County, Pennsylvania, in 1787 and who is listed as a taxpayer in Blount County (located south of Knox County) in 1801. The writing compartment has double-ogee-blocked draw-

Figure 16 Detail of the writing compartment of the desk-and-bookcase illustrated in fig. 15.

Figure 17 Detail of a quarter-column on the desk-and-bookcase illustrated in fig. 15.

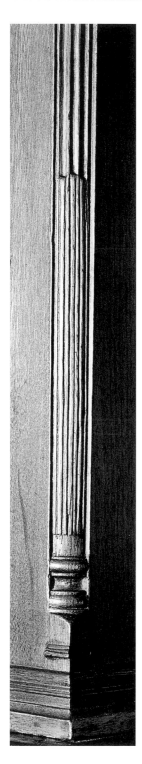

ers that are similar to those of the Philadelphia desk-and-bookcase illustrated in figure 5, although the Tennessee cabinetmaker used a single long drawer in the lower tier (fig. 16). The prospect door on the McGhee desk-and-bookcase is significantly different from those on other Tennessee desks. It has an arched head and a full architrave with a central key block and fluted pilasters with classical base and capital moldings. Much in the high baroque style, the cabinetmaker created a small architectural doorway that provides a "prospect," or view, when open. By contrast, his interpretation of the "skolloped" doors found on many Delaware Valley bookcases is visually disturbing because he used equal-sized panels rather than a single panel or a small panel over a larger one. Drawers that function as fallboard supports are another Delaware Valley detail used by this tradesman. Only one other Tennessee desk with this feature is known.[15]

The relationship of this artisan's work to the Winchester school is apparent in the arched, stop-fluted quarter-columns and chamfers of the McGhee desk-and-bookcase (figs. 17, 18). Although the combination of these corner treatments is unusual, it relates to the superimposition of orders in classical architecture (the higher or more complex the order, the higher the level). The scale of the cornice is also architectural, though it resembles cornices on cupboards made by house joiners. Astragal-scalloped friezes, like the one on the McGhee desk-and-bookcase, are rare in Shenandoah Valley furniture, but they occur frequently on cupboards attributed to the Ralph family of Kent County, Delaware, which typically have astragal-scalloped architraves as well. The Tennessee cabinetmaker used the same astragal scalloping on the applied panel of the fallboard. This panel is reminiscent of those on bookcase doors and tall clock plinths made in rural areas of southeastern Pennsylvania and the southern backcountry.[16]

The corner cupboard illustrated in figure 19 is from the same shop that produced the McGhee desk-and-bookcase. Although the heavy cornice molding and the low scrolled pediment give the cupboard a baroque appearance (figs. 20, 21), it is probably contemporary with the aforementioned piece. In all likelihood, the large size of the cupboard necessitated

Figure 18 Detail of chamfered corner of the desk-and-bookcase illustrated in fig. 15.

Figure 19 Corner cupboard, Knoxville area, Tennessee, 1790–1800. Walnut with yellow pine and tulip poplar. H. 89¼", W. 44" at front face with 5¼" returns. (Private collection; photo, John Bivins.)

Figure 21 Detail of the cornice, rosettes, and plinth of the corner cupboard illustrated in fig. 19.

Figure 20 Detail of the cornice and a quarter-column on the corner cupboard illustrated in fig. 19.

flattening the curve of the scroll to accommodate the breadth without a proportional increase in overall height. Concern with height may also explain why the cupboard never had feet. The shape of the arched doors may be associated with Germanic furniture made in southeastern Pennsylvania and the Shenandoah Valley.[17]

The carving on the corner cupboard (fig. 21) ties it to the Winchester school and, in particular, to the shop that produced the Lupton desk-and-bookcase (fig. 2). Although the rosettes on the Tennessee piece are not as realistic as their Winchester counterparts, both sets have hollowed petals and veining flutes cut with a small, U-shaped gouge (referred to as a veiner). The veining on the corner cupboard most closely resembles that on the leaf appliqués of a high chest that Lupton purchased from the same Winchester shop that made his desk-and-bookcase (figs. 22, 23). The shell pendant below the plinth of the corner cupboard also has fluted gadrooning like the shell on the knee of the high chest (fig. 24), although, again, the carving is more naive on the Tennessee piece.

Several construction and carving details indicate that the McGhee desk-and-bookcase (fig. 15) and the corner cupboards illustrated in figures 19 and 25 are from the same shop and possibly by the same hand. The backs of the cupboard drawers are reverse-pinned to the sides (the dovetail pins are cut in the sides and show at the back rather than at the sides), a distinctive feature that furniture historian Benno Forman ascribed to Germanic cabinet-making traditions. This joinery, which actually weakens the drawer, seems to contradict the overbuilt nature of many German-influenced pieces, however. The cupboards and desk-and-bookcase have cock beading that is pinned to the case around the doors but applied directly to the drawer fronts. The McGhee desk-and-bookcase and the cupboard illustrated in figure 25 have the same cornice moldings and astragal-scalloped frieze, and all three pieces have sawn and applied dentil molding. The corner cupboards and desk-and-

Figure 22 High chest, Winchester area, Virginia, 1795. Walnut with yellow pine and tulip poplar. H. 97", W. 44", D. 24¼". (Courtesy, Colonial Williamsburg Foundation; photo, Hans Lorenz.)

Figure 23   Detail of the pediment of the high chest illustrated in fig. 22.

Figure 24   Detail of the leg of the high chest illustrated in fig. 22.

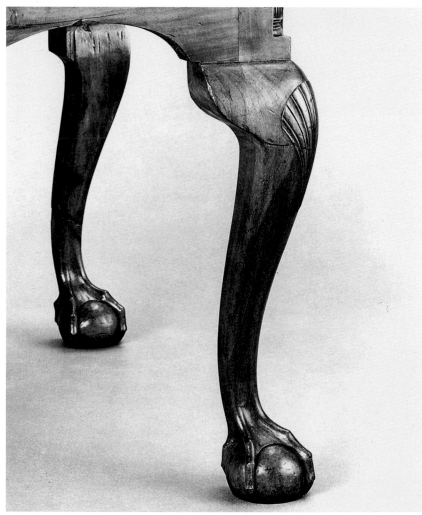

Figure 25 Corner cupboard, Knoxville area, Tennessee, 1795–1810. Walnut with tulip poplar. H. 87³/₄", W. 50³/₄" at front face with 5⁷/₈" returns. (Private collection; photo, Museum of Early Southern Decorative Arts.) The cornice molding rises above the top of the case and consists of separate moldings: the ogee below the dentil course is a single vertical piece that rises to the crown as does the dentil course; the cove is a single vertical piece attached to the dentil course; the crown is a horizontal piece that covers the top edges of the other moldings; the running astragal frieze is glued to the case below.

Figure 26 Detail of a quarter-column on the corner cupboard illustrated in fig. 25. (Photo, John Bivins.)

bookcase also have quarter-columns with the same base and capital moldings, and the pieces illustrated in figures 15 and 25 have arched stop-fluting (figs. 17, 26). Arched stop-fluting differentiates these objects from Nashville-school furniture, which has level stop-fluting. Two other corner cupboards from this same Knox County shop are known, and both are similar in form and decoration to the example illustrated in figure 25.[18]

A chest of drawers from the same shop (fig. 27) shares a number of details with the McGhee desk-and-bookcase and the corner cupboards illustrated in figures 19 and 25: reverse-pinned drawer backs, quarter-column base and

Figure 27 Chest of drawers, Knoxville area, Tennessee, 1795–1810. Walnut with yellow pine and tulip poplar. H. 49⁵/₁₆", W. 39", D. 23¹/₂". (Private collection; photo, Museum of Early Southern Decorative Arts.) The cornice on the chest of drawers is a simpler version of the cornice on the corner cupboard illustrated in fig. 25. The molded board that forms the top of the case and the face-nailed cove molding conceal the dovetails that join the case sides to a board below the top.

capital turnings, applied frieze with astragal-scalloping, and cornice construction (see captions for figs. 25, 27). Like the Jackson and Donelson furniture, the chest and the McGhee desk-and-bookcase have framed drawer supports, but they are pinned into dadoes in the case sides. The front feet on the chest are original and suggest how the original feet of the McGhee desk-and-bookcase and the cupboard shown in figure 25 may have looked.[19]

The furniture from this Knoxville shop is as difficult to date as the Nashville and Winchester work discussed earlier. Stylistically, the McGhee desk-and-bookcase and the corner cupboard illustrated in figure 19 could have been made as early as the 1760s in southeastern Pennsylvania or as early as the mid-1770s in Frederick County, Virginia, but given the late settlement of Knox County, they probably date from the last decade of the eighteenth century. Both pieces show how styles persisted in the backcountry long after they were fashionable in other areas. The cupboard illustrated in figure 25 and the chest of drawers (fig. 27) were made between 1795 and 1810.

Astragal-scalloped friezes appear on two later pieces of East Tennessee furniture. A tall chest (at the East Tennessee Historical Society) with a Greene County provenance, inlaid chamfered corners, and ogee feet with spurred responds is slightly later than the chest illustrated in figure 27 and may represent the work of a cabinetmaker who trained in Knoxville, then moved to Greene County. Another tall chest with French feet and a shaped skirt is the latest example with this frieze design.[20]

Only one piece of furniture survives from each of the three remaining Knoxville shops that produced furniture in the Delaware Valley style. In the past, all three pieces have been attributed to Thomas Hope, who appears to have been a house joiner rather than a cabinetmaker. Hope emigrated from England to Charleston, South Carolina, around 1785 and moved to Knoxville during the mid-1790s. Little is known about his work in Charleston other than his involvement in the construction of Ralph Izard's house. After moving to Knoxville, Hope advertised for an apprentice "to learn the whole art of house carpenter's and joiner's business." In 1797, he offered a reward for house joiner's tools stolen from his "carpenter's work shop" and in 1812 identified himself as a house joiner in a registry of British aliens. Hope is credited with work on a number of houses located in or near Knoxville, including Ramsey House (fig. 14). In 1806, Charles Coffin wrote that he "Stopped for the night at Mr. John Kain's where I conversed with Mr. Hope, his house carpenter, who did work on Colonel McClung's house, built Mr. Izzard's house in Charleston, South Carolina and is accounted one of the best workmen in the country. He showed an excellent book of architecture."[21]

The only references to Hope selling furniture are in the Waste Book of David Henley, an agent of the War Department and the superintendent of Indian Affairs. Henley paid Hope $30.00 "for a double wallnut desk made for Silas Dinsmore," $25.00 "for a desk," and $6.00 "for a table and board to write at." Although the costs of the desks suggest that they were made by a cabinetmaker rather than a house joiner, none of these entries specify that Hope made the furniture. Like Charleston house joiner Richard Moncrieff, he may have simply functioned as a supplier.[22]

The notion that Hope was a cabinetmaker probably originated with the autobiography of J. G. M. Ramsey, whose father built Ramsey House. Ramsey described Hope as an architect, cabinetmaker, and upholsterer and stated that he had made his father's "tall and elegant secretary" and "a massive bureau." His description of the secretary stretches the limits of imagination in relation to the furniture produced in Knoxville during the early nineteenth century:

> In construction he used . . . some American woods he had never seen before (sumac was one of them). As may well be excused in an English mechanic, he put . . . on the top of Colonel Ramsey's secretary the English lions and the unicorn. Colonel Ramsey refused to receive the work till he had placed the American eagles in suitable propinquity to and above the armorials of the British royalty.

Unfortunately, Dr. Ramsey's reminiscences have resulted in the misattribution of much early Knoxville furniture to Hope, including an architectural cupboard, a "compting house desk," a neoclassical secretary-and-bookcase, and the pieces illustrated in figures 28, 30, and 33.[23]

Figure 28 Desk-and-bookcase, Knoxville area, Tennessee, 1795–1810. Cherry with yellow pine. H. 96" (without feet), W. 42¹/₂", D. 22³/₄". (Courtesy, Lawson-McGhee Library; photo, John Bivins.) This example is somewhat unusual in being made of cherry. Walnut is the most common primary wood in East Tennessee furniture.

Figure 29 Detail of the pediment of the desk-and-bookcase illustrated in fig. 28. (Courtesy, Lawson-McGhee Library; photo, Museum of Early Southern Decorative Arts.)

Hope died in 1820 while working on Rotherwood in Boatyard (Kingsport), Tennessee. The meager possessions listed in his inventory included a "box of carpenters tools." Although Hope consistently described himself as a carpenter and joiner, he apparently possessed carving skills. The trusses under the cornice soffits of Ramsey House are attributed to him. In an 1820 letter to his wife, Hope expressed his desire "to set up to carve next Monday."[24]

Oral tradition maintains that Hope made the desk-and-bookcase illustrated in figure 28. Thomas W. Humes, the son of the original owner, left it to the Lawson-McGhee Library at his death in the late nineteenth century. Humes was the half brother of J. G. M. Ramsey, and it is possible that the original attribution was made by him. Even if Hope was a cabinetmaker, it is unlikely that he would have made rococo forms such as this desk-and-bookcase. By the time he immigrated to America, neoclassicism was the rage in both England and Charleston. More importantly, the desk-and-bookcase is clearly associated with the Winchester school.[25]

There are both structural and decorative similarities between the Humes desk-and-bookcase (fig. 28) and the Lupton example (fig. 2). Although the tympanum of the Winchester desk-and-bookcase is taller, both pieces have similar pediment and tympanum profiles (the openings of the tympana merge with the cornice moldings in the same place on both pieces) and flat, two-paneled doors. The doors of the Knoxville piece have flush panels, unpinned joints, and applied cock beading, whereas the doors on the Lupton bookcase have recessed panels, pinned joints, and beaded stiles and rails. Both desk-and-bookcases have full-depth dustboards. The dustboards on the Humes example are one-half the height of the drawer rails, and laths that run the full depth of the case fill the lower halves of the dadoes. The Lupton desk-and-bookcase has three-quarter-height dustboards and wedges rather than lath.

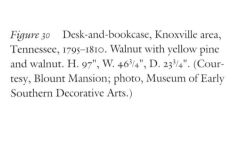

Figure 30 Desk-and-bookcase, Knoxville area, Tennessee, 1795–1810. Walnut with yellow pine and walnut. H. 97", W. 46¾", D. 23¾". (Courtesy, Blount Mansion; photo, Museum of Early Southern Decorative Arts.)

Despite these similarities, the distance separating Winchester and East Tennessee is apparent in the regional adaptations of form, structure, and decoration made by Knoxville cabinetmakers. The rosettes, leaves, and shell on the Humes desk-and-bookcase (figs. 28, 29) are flat and less competently carved than those on the Winchester furniture (see figs. 2, 3, 23). Instead of having quarter-columns with arched stop-fluting on both the upper and lower cases, like the Lupton desk-and-bookcase, the Knoxville example has quarter-columns solely on the lower case, and they are not stop-fluted. The flutes on the Winchester piece return, whereas those on the Humes piece do not. Both desks have fluted document drawers flanking the prospect door, but the door on the Knoxville desk has a cove molding on either side and a small concealed drawer above rather than a full-coved surround like the door on the Winchester example. Philadelphia and Winchester desks typically have pigeonholes above the drawers, but on the Humes desk-and-bookcase this arrangement is reversed.[26]

The desk-and-bookcase illustrated in figure 30 descended in the family of Judge David Campbell, an early Knoxville resident and a contemporary of Governor Blount. Because of its visual similarity to the Humes desk-and-bookcase (fig. 28), the Campbell example has also been attributed to Thomas Hope; however, it clearly represents the work of a second Knoxville cabinetmaker who trained in the Winchester area. The pediment of the Campbell desk-and-bookcase is more closely based on Winchester prototypes than the pediment of the Humes piece (figs. 3, 29, 31). The tympanum of the Campbell bookcase is the same height as that of the Lupton example, and it has a straight astragal molding rather than a swagged one as on the Winchester piece. The point where the tympanum opening merges with the crown molding on the Campbell example is slightly higher than on the Lupton desk-and-bookcase and high chest, although the geometry of

Figure 31 Detail of the pediment of the desk-and-bookcase illustrated in fig. 30.

the tympanum curves is similar. The lunetted astragals on the doors of the Campbell desk-and-bookcase are repeated on another desk-and-bookcase from the same shop that produced the Lupton furniture. The carving on the Campbell piece is also closer to Winchester work than other carving on Knoxville furniture. The leaves on the shell below the plinth is an unusual detail found on furniture from the shop that made the Lupton pieces. The carver of the Campbell desk-and-bookcase used his veiner extensively (even beneath the petals on the rosettes), as did the carver of the Knoxville corner cupboard illustrated in figure 19.[27]

The desk interior and the feet of the Campbell desk-and-bookcase diverge from Delaware Valley and Winchester styles. Rather than having document drawers on either side of the prospect door, the Campbell desk-and-bookcase has carved terms with horizontal flutes, paneled plinths, and Egyptian papyrus-form capitals (fig. 32). The pigeonholes have delicately fluted brackets that spring from gothic clustered columns with leafy capitals. These details, which have no known parallel in Knoxville work, suggest that the maker or owner may have had access to architectural design books. Although the base molding is replaced, the feet are mostly intact. Their long, scrolled responds and ogee elements near the floor lend an earlier but more vernacular appearance to the piece.[28]

The Campbell desk-and-bookcase has several unusual construction details. The bookcase has vertical tongue-and-grooved backboards that are nailed into rabbets in the sides, whereas the desk has a three-panel back. The drawer construction is unlike that of any object illustrated here. Instead of fitting into dadoes in the drawer fronts and sides, all of the drawer bottoms are dadoed into the drawer fronts and nailed into rabbets in the drawer sides. Applied strips fill the voids between the drawer bottoms and sides and serve as runners. The Campbell desk-and-bookcase also differs from the aforementioned Tennessee pieces in having full-depth, full-bottom dustboards.

The tall chest illustrated in figure 33 is a product of the fourth Knoxville cabinetmaker from the Winchester school. Like the Lupton desk-and-bookcase (fig. 2) and several of the case pieces from the Nashville area (see figs. 9, 12, 13), the chest has ogee feet with filleted, spurred responds. Its arched, stop-fluted quarter-columns relate to those on the McGhee desk-and-bookcase (figs. 15, 17) and the corner cupboard illustrated in figure 25, as well as to furniture from the Winchester school (see figs. 2, 6, 22). The chest also has a full-bottom, full-depth dustboard that fits into a half-dovetail dado in the case sides beneath the upper three drawers. The support system for the lower drawers consists solely of the drawer rail, which is half-dovetailed to the case sides, and the drawer supports, which are tenoned to the rail and dadoed to the case sides. The Nashville and other Knoxville examples feature either dustboards or fully framed drawer support systems. Perhaps because this tall chest contains neither of these support systems, the drawer rails are exceptionally deep (five inches). Like the Humes and Campbell desk-and-bookcases (figs. 28, 30), this chest was probably made between 1795 and 1810.[29]

Knoxville records from this period reveal the names of three men who were cabinetmakers and two individuals who may have been. As was the case in Davidson and Sumner Counties, there is no evidence that any of these men trained or worked in Winchester, except, of course, for the furniture itself. Given the existence of four shops producing Winchester style furniture in Knox County, a high percentage of the cabinetmakers mentioned in Knoxville records must have trained or worked near that Virginia town.

Figure 34 Desk-and-bookcase, Greeneville area, Tennessee, 1800–1820. Walnut with tulip poplar. H. 92¼", W. 45¾", D. 20⅜". (Private collection; photo, John Bivins.)

Knoxville cabinetmaker Terrence McAffry immigrated to America from Ireland in 1796. He may have arrived in Philadelphia and traveled down the Shenandoah Valley to Winchester. If so, he may have met his wife, Martha Clopton, there. (A George Clopton was a cabinetmaker in Frederick County, Virginia, during this period.) In Knoxville, McAffry worked as both a cabinetmaker and house joiner. Thomas Hope's copy of *The Builder's Golden Rule* has an 1801 inscription stating that "R. Morrow, Mr. McClure, Mr. McCafry, Mr. Booth, and T. Hope" had agreed on prices to be charged for house joinery work. McAffry took two apprentices in the cabinetmaking trade in 1803. In the April 21, 1810, issue of *Wilson's Knoxville Gazette*, he advertised that his "workmen are equal to any in this state, and his work will be executed in the neatest and most fashionable manner. He will take in exchange for furniture corn, flour, cotton, tow linnen, whiskey and pork." According to the 1820 Manufacturers' Census, three men worked in his shop, producing sideboards, bureaus (including examples with mahogany fronts), tables, and bedsteads. McAffry worked until his death in 1830.[30]

Although the 1820 Manufacturers' Census is the only known document that specifies cabinetmaker James Bray's profession, he appears to have been working in the Knoxville area by 1797, when he married Rachel Smith. In 1802, his name appears on the tax list for Knox County. According to the Manufacturers' Census, he had four workmen who produced secretaries, "charry presses," circular- and straight-front bureaus, tables, and bedsteads.[31]

The 1819 inventory of Moses Crawford included "One set of cabinet makers tools, a few carpenters' tools and some plain stocks . . . several pieces of dry Beach fit for plain stocks, one work bench with a screw and Iron vice, [and] one hundred and ninety one feet of walnut plank." Crawford was in Knoxville by 1806 when his name appears on a Knox County tax list.[32]

Considering the number of Knoxville pieces that have survived from the late eighteenth and early nineteenth centuries, the shop that produced the objects illustrated in figures 15, 19, 25, and 27 must have been a sizable business in operation for several years. Both McAffry and Bray were masters of such shops. Although Crawford may have practiced the cabinetmaking trade for a number of years, he apparently was the only man working in his shop since only one work bench was listed in his estate inventory.

Two other Knoxville men may have been cabinetmakers at the turn of the century. The 1802 inventory and estate sale of Henry Baker listed a turning lathe, a glue pot, mountings for a bureau and a desk, and a number of tools, including a keyhole saw; however, some items normally found in cabinetmakers' inventories are not listed, including a work bench, materials, a dovetail saw, table planes, and other trade-specific tools. On March 27, 1821, the *Knoxville Register* reported that *"An Estate worth notice"* had been left in Feliciana Parish, Louisiana, by John Garrison, a cabinetmaker and carpenter, who about sixteen years before had been a resident of Knoxville. This man could be the same John Garrison whose name appeared on the 1801 tax list for Blount County. Some men who have been included on earlier checklists of Tennessee cabinetmakers have been omitted because their probate inventories indicate that they were house joiners only.[33]

Other Delaware Valley and Shenandoah Valley Influences

Nashville and Knoxville were not the only areas in Tennessee where cabinetmakers made furniture that resembled Shenandoah Valley work. A distinctive variation of the Delaware Valley style developed in Shenandoah County and Rockingham County, Virginia, both located south of Frederick County. Two shops in Greeneville, Tennessee, produced a sizable body of furniture that is more closely related to the styles associated with these two counties than with Frederick County. The range of style and decoration and changing methods of construction demonstrate the versatility and longevity of these Virginia and Tennessee shop traditions.[34]

The desk-and-bookcase illustrated in figure 34 has a Delaware Valley–style interior, with a prospect door flanked by two document drawers and pigeonholes surmounting a two-tier drawer arrangement. The deep valances over the pigeonholes are reminiscent of the valances on the Nashville desk-and-bookcase and desk illustrated in figures 9 and 13. The corner cupboard illustrated in figure 35 is from another Greeneville shop that produced furniture in the Delaware Valley and Shenandoah Valley styles. The cross-pollination of styles and decoration in the small community of Greeneville is evident in the desk-and-bookcase illustrated in figure 36. This desk-and-bookcase is from the same shop and has virtually the same interior as the example illustrated in figure 34; however, its inlaid rope-and-tassel ornament is a distinctive regional variant of the carved rope and tassel on the tympanum of the Greenville corner cupboard (fig. 35). On the desk-and-bookcase shown in figure 36, the inlaid rope and tassel is accompanied by upturned bellflowers, which are a hallmark of later Greene County work.

The furniture produced in Greeneville ranged from relatively plain objects (fig. 34) to more ornamental pieces with idiosyncratic carving or inlay (figs. 35, 36). In part, this variation can be explained by the history of the town. Greeneville played an important role during the early years of settlement in East Tennessee. In 1772, Jacob Brown and one or two families from North Carolina settled on the northern bank of the Nolichucky River in Greene County. Brown's settlement (on lands leased and subsequently purchased from the Cherokee Nation) continued to grow during the 1770s and early 1780s. Frustrated over the lack of government in upper East Tennessee, the residents of the area formed the State of Franklin in 1785. Greeneville was established in 1786 as the capital of the new state. With the formation of the Southwest Territory in 1789, the disestablishment of the State of Franklin, and the choice of Knoxville as the new seat of government, Greeneville's importance waned. According to Michaux, there were no more than forty houses in Greeneville in 1802, all of which were "built of squared beams, arranged like the trunks of trees of which log houses are formed." Some early residents remained, however, and cabinetmakers continued to produce furniture in both plain and distinctively regional styles.[35]

Summary

At least four Knoxville shops produced a sizable body of furniture in the Winchester style; whereas only one Nashville shop worked in this style, and

Figure 35 Corner cupboard, Greeneville area, Tennessee, 1795–1820. Walnut with tulip poplar. H. 95¼", W. 47" at front face with 4" returns. (Private collection; photo, Museum of Early Southern Decorative Arts.)

its surviving output consists of only three pieces. This difference is a reflection of the settlement patterns of the two areas and the cultural background of the cabinetmakers and their patrons. Folklorist Henry Glassie has traced patterns of cultural influence throughout the eastern United States and has noted that the material culture of the southern backcountry is a product of the confluence of English cultural traditions from the Chesa-

Figure 36 Desk-and-bookcase, Greeneville area, Tennessee, 1800–1820. Walnut with tulip poplar. H. 96", W. 44½", D. 22⅜". (Private collection; photo, Helga Studio.)

peake region and Germanic, Scots-Irish, and English traditions from Pennsylvania. According to Glassie, Pennsylvania influences were strongest in the Shenandoah Valley and weakest in the Tennessee Valley and the Bluegrass sections of Tennessee and Kentucky. Although many settlers in East Tennessee came from Pennsylvania and the Shenandoah Valley, Middle Tennessee attracted a larger percentage of settlers from the coastal and piedmont regions of Virginia and the Carolinas. The provenances of the Knoxville and Nashville area furniture discussed in this article confirm these patterns of settlement and cultural influence.[36]

The settlement of northern Middle Tennessee and the histories of the families who owned the furniture discussed in this article suggest that most of the Nashville pieces date from between 1790 and 1805. Some Middle Tennesseans, like their counterparts in Frederick County, Virginia, and East Tennessee, preferred, or at least purchased, furniture that would have been considered old-fashioned along most of the eastern seaboard. Andrew Jackson lived in the piedmont regions of North Carolina and South Carolina before moving to Tennessee. John Donelson, who was born in Brunswick County, Virginia, moved to Middle Tennessee with his wife, parents, and siblings in 1780. Both of these men spent most of their adult lives in the southern backcountry and may have been unaware of, or indifferent to, the prevailing coastal fashions.[37]

Not all of the furniture made in northern Middle Tennessee during this period was as retardataire. James Winchester and Daniel Smith provide striking contrasts to Jackson and Donelson. Winchester came to Middle

Tennessee in 1785 from Westminster, Maryland, about forty miles northwest of Baltimore, after having spent time during the Revolutionary War in Annapolis and Charleston. He brought his nephew William Winchester to Sumner County to assist in the building of his house, Cragfont. William took an apprentice in the cabinetmaking trade in 1802, and according to family tradition made his uncle several pieces of furniture in the neoclassical style—a sideboard, a secretary, a pair of card tables, a pembroke table, and a dining table—before returning to Maryland.[38]

Daniel Smith was born in eastern Virginia and educated at the College of William and Mary, but he spent most of his adult life in the backcountry. In 1783, he moved from southwest Virginia to Tennessee. Unlike Jackson and Donelson, Smith evidently preferred neoclassical furniture. During the 1790s, Smith's nephews, Peter and Smith Hansborough, moved from Philadelphia to Sumner County to assist in the construction of Rock Castle. Like William Winchester, the Hansborough brothers were apparently cabinetmakers and house joiners. A sugar chest and a two-drawer chest (which has been adapted from its original form) attributed to them descended in Daniel Smith's family. Smith also owned a secretary that is markedly similar to the example owned by James Winchester and may be by William Winchester or his apprentice.[39]

In contrast, the Knoxville pieces with provenances descended in families who migrated to East Tennessee from Pennsylvania, the Shenandoah Valley, and Ireland. The McGhees, who owned the desk-and-bookcase illustrated in figure 15, were from Lancaster County, Pennsylvania. The Andersons and McCampbells, who owned the corner cupboard illustrated in figure 19, were from Rockingham County, Virginia. The desk-and-bookcase illustrated in figure 30 descended in the family of Judge David Campbell, who was born in Augusta County, Virginia, and lived in Washington County, Virginia, before moving to East Tennessee. Thomas Humes, the original owner of the desk-and-bookcase illustrated in figure 28, was born in Ireland. Like Jackson and Donelson, these owners may have been unaware of the fashions on the coast and therefore chose furniture made in a style with which they were familiar. The dominant stylistic influences in the Knoxville area emanated from the Delaware Valley and Shenandoah Valley because a majority of the town's cabinetmakers evidently apprenticed or worked as journeymen in the Winchester area.[40]

The convergence of patrons and cabinetmakers with similar cultural backgrounds was particularly strong in Knoxville. In Nashville, however, the cultural composition of the community in general and of the cabinetmakers in particular was different. Although at least one Nashville cabinetmaker produced furniture similar to that made in Knoxville, the broader range of tastes in Nashville was a direct result of settlement patterns in Middle Tennessee. As in the study of most regional furniture, an accurate evaluation of stylistic preferences and characteristics depends heavily upon a significant sample of objects. Recognition of the full extent of Delaware Valley and Winchester influence in Tennessee may bring to light additional furniture that has been misattributed.

ACKNOWLEDGMENTS   The author expresses her gratitude to the following individuals whose assistance has been invaluable: Mary Jo Case, Steve Cotham, Dick Doughty, Jim Hoobler, Ron Hurst, Marsha Mullin, Sumpter Priddy, Jonathan Prown, Susan Shames, and, most of all, John Bivins.

1. Although Tennessee did not become a state until 1796, I refer to the area by its current name. David Hackett Fischer and James C. Kelly, *Away, I'm Bound Away: Virginia and the Westward Movement* (Richmond: Virginia Historical Society, 1993), p. 68. Present-day Tennessee is readily divided into three geographic regions. The Cumberland Mountains separate East Tennessee from Middle Tennessee, and the Tennessee River separates Middle Tennessee from West Tennessee. During the late eighteenth century, however, settlement had not spread west of the Tennessee River, and period references to western Tennessee refer to all the territory west of the mountains. Eastin Morris, *The Tennessee Gazetteer* (1834; reprint, Nashville: Williams Printing Company, 1971), pp. 17–22. J. G. M. Ramsey, *The Annals of Tennessee* (1853; reprint ed., Knoxville: East Tennessee Historical Society, 1967), pp. 205, 275–80.

2. Lucile Deaderick, ed., *Heart of the Valley: A History of Knoxville, Tennessee* (Knoxville: East Tennessee Historical Society, 1976), pp. 2–7. Ramsey, *Annals of Tennessee*, p. 648.

3. The interaction between cabinetmakers and their patrons lies at the heart of the design and production of furniture. According to art historian Edward S. Cooke, Jr. "furniture embodies and manifests the shared values and experiences of its maker and user" (Edward S. Cooke, Jr., "The Study of American Furniture from the Perspective of the Maker," in *Perspectives on American Furniture*, edited by Gerald W. R. Ward [New York: W. W. Norton for the Winterthur Museum, 1988], p. 125). Wallace B. Gusler, "The Arts of Shenandoah County, Virginia, 1770–1825," *Journal of Early Southern Decorative Arts* 5, no. 1 (November 1979): 10. Philip Zea discusses this phenomenon with reference to New England furniture using the model of a wagon wheel. He places the original design source at the hub of the wheel and the regional variations along the spokes. The ends of the spokes obviously connect at the rim, providing another opportunity for exchange of ideas and adaptation of forms (Philip Zea, "Diversity and Regionalism in Rural New England Furniture," in *American Furniture*, edited by Luke Beckerdite and William N. Hosley [Hanover, N.H.: University Press of New England for the Chipstone Foundation, 1995], p. 69).

4. The Colonial Williamsburg Foundation (hereinafter cited as CWF) has four other pieces from the same shop that made the desk-and-bookcase shown in figure 2: two high chests (acc. 1973–206, 1973–325), a card table (acc. 1987–725), and a corner cupboard (acc. 1973–197). One of the high chests is illustrated in figure 22. With the exception of the corner cupboard, all of these pieces were owned by David Lupton, who built Cherry Row on Apple Pie Ridge outside Winchester in 1794. Other furniture from the same shop is recorded in the files at CWF and the Museum of Early Southern Decorative Arts (hereinafter cited as MESDA). See, for example, MESDA research files S-9460, S-11186, and S-13543. Local interpretations of all the Delaware Valley details discussed above occur on furniture from other regions of the southern backcountry. For a discussion of Delaware Valley influences on Piedmont North Carolina furniture, see John Bivins, "A Piedmont North Carolina Cabinetmaker: The Development of Regional Style," *Antiques* 103, no. 5 (May 1973): 968–73; Carolyn Weekley, "James Gheen, Piedmont North Carolina Cabinetmaker," *Antiques* 103, no. 5 (May 1973): 940–44; Luke Beckerdite, "City Meets Country: The Work of Peter Eddleman, Cabinetmaker," *Journal of Early Southern Decorative Arts* 5, no. 2 (November 1979): 59–73; and Beckerdite, "The Development of Regional Style in the Catawba River Valley: A Further Look," *Journal of Early Southern Decorative Arts* 7, no. 2 (November 1981): 31–48. I thank Alan Miller for the information on quarter-columns on Delaware Valley furniture. For more on Philadelphia furniture, see William MacPherson Hornor, *Blue Book of Philadelphia Furniture* (1935; reprint, Alexandria, Va.: Highland House Publishers, 1988). Stop-fluted quarter-columns are common on Newport and Newport-influenced furniture (see Michael Moses, *Master Craftsmen of Newport: The Townsends and Goddards* [Tenafly, N.J.: MMI Americana Press, 1984], passim). John Shearer of Martinsburg, West Virginia, used swagged rather than arched stop-fluting (MESDA research file S-11732).

5. For a discussion of the Winchester armchair, see John Bivins and Forsyth Alexander, *The Regional Arts of the Early South* (Winston-Salem, N.C.: MESDA, 1991), p. 126. For the Frye desk, see Wallace Gusler's article in this volume (p. 233, fig. 22.) Although clearly sharing a

regional aesthetic in the employment of fluted quarter-columns and document drawers and a cove-molded surround to the prospect doors, various details distinguish the Frye desk and the Lupton desk-and-bookcase (fig. 2) and strongly suggest that they are the products of different shops. Not only do the interiors of the two desks have completely different drawer arrangements (the Lupton desk adheres to the typical Philadelphia plan of interior), the proportions of the interiors are different as well. The interior of the signed desk does not have pigeonholes, and it has a wider prospect door and wider document drawers. The desk-and-bookcase has channel molding on the outer side of the document drawers rather than cove molding. The details of the quarter-columns reveal striking differences between the two pieces as well. The Frye desk has generic fluted quarter-columns as compared to the arched, stop-fluted quarter-columns specific to Winchester and Knoxville furniture. Overall, the columns on the desk-and-bookcase are more finely detailed and have capitals and bases that are fully articulated according to classical architecture. The block at the top of the column on the desk-and-bookcase is the same height as the drawer rail, creating linear visual continuity, whereas the block on the Frye desk is greater in height. The signed desk has thicker rails and stiles than the desk-and-bookcase. These characteristics of the Lupton desk-and-bookcase and distinctions between it and the Frye desk are consistent throughout a larger group of furniture that does appear to be the product of the same shop as the Lupton furniture. (See MESDA research files, S-1186, S-10646, S-9460, and 13543). As the drawer bottoms on the Frye desk appear to have been replaced and the feet are replaced, a comparison of certain aspects of drawer construction and foot pattern are not possible. The Frye desk does not appear to be directly related to the Tennessee furniture discussed in this article. Although most of these forms were not rococo in the truest sense of the word, they had details that originated with that style. Harrold E. Gillingham, "Benjamin Lehman, A Germantown Cabinetmaker," *The Pennsylvania Magazine of History and Biography* 54, no. 4 (October 1930), pp. 289–306. Hornor, *Blue Book of Philadelphia Furniture*, pp. 231–70.

6. Lewis Brantz, Memorandum of a Journey (1785), as reproduced in *Early Travels in the Tennessee Country, 1540–1800*, compiled by Samuel Cole Williams (1928; reprint ed., Nashville: Blue and Gray Press, 1972), p. 285. François André Michaux, *Travels to the Westward of the Allegheny Mountains in the States of Ohio, Kentucky, and Tennessee (Undertaken in the Year 1802)* (London, 1805), p. 245. James Patrick, *Architecture in Tennessee, 1768-1897* (Knoxville: University of Tennessee Press, 1981), p. 71. Harriette Simpson Arnow, *Seedtime on the Cumberland* (New York: MacMillan, 1960), p. 234. Michaux, *Travels*, p. 254. James Patrick describes Cragfont as representing "the conquering of the Cumberland by style" (Patrick, *Architecture in Tennessee*, p. 71). Thomas B. Brumbaugh, Martha I. Strayhorn, and Gary G. Gore, eds., *Architecture of Middle Tennessee: The Historic American Buildings Survey* (Nashville, Tenn.: Vanderbilt University Press, 1974), p. 106. In 1800, Davidson County's population was 9,965, and Sumner County's, 4,616. Nashville had a population of 400 in 1804. *History of Tennessee* (Nashville, Tenn.: Goodspeed Publishing, 1887), pp. 360–61. Morris, *Tennessee Gazetteer*, p. 212.

7. The desk-and-bookcase shown in figure 9 was in the Hermitage when the house was acquired by the Ladies Hermitage Association in 1889. The Hermitage had been continuously occupied by members of the Jackson family until the death of Andrew Jackson, Jr.'s, widow in 1888. The desk-and-bookcase and the chest of drawers illustrated in figure 12 were purchased from Colonel Andrew Jackson III (the president's grandson), who reported that they had belonged to his grandfather. The handwritten initials "AJH" on one of the fallboard supports apparently refer to Andrew Jackson Hutchings, a nephew of Rachel Donelson Jackson and a ward of the couple (Files of the Ladies Hermitage Association, and conversations with Marsha Mullin, Curator of Collections, The Hermitage). For other pieces with framed drawer supports, see MESDA research files S-13543 and S-5210 (both from Frederick County) and S-13141, S-14304, and S-11950 (from Piedmont North Carolina). I am grateful to Alan Miller for information on Pennsylvania furniture with similar construction. Although Miller describes the framed supports as Germanic, they also occur on Charleston furniture made by the Scottish immigrant Robert Walker (see MESDA research file S-8045 and S-9038). Such supports may, therefore, be a result of Scottish, Scots-Irish, and Germanic influences.

8. Each additional option added to the cost of a piece. According to Benjamin Lehman, quarter-columns added ten shillings to the cost of a desk (Gillingham, "Benjamin Lehman," p. 290).

9. Fortescue Cuming, *Sketches of a Tour to the Western Country Through the States of Ohio and Kentucky; A Voyage Down the Ohio and Mississippi Rivers; and A Trip Through the Mississippi Territory and Parts of Western Florida* (Pittsburgh, Pa.: Cramer, Spear, & Eichbaum, 1810), p. 164. François André Michaux, *The North American Sylva, or a Description of the Forest Trees of the*

United States, Canada and Nova Scotia, 2 vols. (Paris: J. Mawman, 1819), 2:207.

10. Robert V. Remini, *Andrew Jackson and the Course of American Empire, 1767–1821* (New York: Harper & Row, 1977), pp. 41, 60–68, 131–32. Mary French Caldwell, *Andrew Jackson's Hermitage* (Nashville, Tenn.: Ladies Hermitage Association, 1933), pp. 9–24.

11. James McCague, *The Cumberland* (New York: Holt, Rinehart and Winston, 1973), pp. 58–64. Paul Clements, *A Past Remembered: A Collection of AnteBellum Houses in Davidson County,* 2 vols. (Nashville, Tenn.: Clearview Press, 1987), 1:228. Caldwell, *Andrew Jackson's Hermitage,* p. 7. Arnow, *Seedtime on the Cumberland,* p. 240. Inventory and Division of the Estate of John Donelson, Davidson County Wills and Inventories, July 1790 and April 1791, bk. 1, pp. 166–67, 176, 196–201.

12. There are two published checklists of Tennessee cabinetmakers: Ellen Beasley, "Tennessee Cabinetmakers and Chairmakers Through 1840," *Antiques* 100, no. 4 (October 1971): 612–21; and Derita Coleman Williams and Nathan Harsh, *The Art and Mystery of Tennessee Furniture and its Makers, Through 1850* (Nashville: Tennessee Historical Society and Tennessee State Museum Foundation, 1988), pp. 271–323.

13. Also included in the estate sale were "Desk Mountings" and walnut and poplar plank. Inventory of William Crawford, Davidson County Wills and Inventories, October 1803, bk. 2, p. 338. Estate sale of William Crawford, Davidson County Wills and Inventories, October 1804, bk 2, pp. 397–98. James H. Craig, *The Arts and Crafts in North Carolina, 1699–1840* (Winston-Salem, N.C.: MESDA, 1965), entry 2009. Absalom Davis is listed on Davidson County tax lists in 1805 and 1811. Williams and Harsh, *The Art and Mystery of Tennessee Furniture,* pp. 282, 301. Inventory of Joseph McBride, Davidson County Wills and Inventories, October 1815, bk. 4, p. 376. Walter T. Durham, *Old Sumner: A History of Sumner County, Tennessee From 1805 to 1861* (Gallatin, Tenn.: Sumner County Public Library Board, 1972), p. 62. The inventories of Charles Beasley (Davidson County Wills and Inventories, June 1816, bk. 7, p. 17) and Abram Bledsoe (Sumner County Wills and Inventories, August 1815, bk. 1, p. 225) indicate that they were house joiners. The Jackson and Donelson furniture differs from that made by William Winchester, Smith and Peter Hansborough, Robert Taylor, and John Gillespie (see Williams and Harsh, *The Art and Mystery of Tennessee Furniture,* pp. 29, 73, 79, 100, 109, 110, 131, 132).

14. *Goodspeed's History of Hamilton, Knox, and Shelby Counties of Tennessee* (1887; reprint ed., Nashville, Tenn.: Charles and Randy Elder Booksellers, 1974), pp. 798–99. Despite historian Mary Rothrock's claim, Blount Mansion does not appear to be "the first frame house built west of the mountains." Mary U. Rothrock, ed., *The French Broad–Holston Country: A History of Knox County, Tennessee* (Knoxville: East Tennessee Historical Society, 1946), p. 32. Patrick, *Architecture in Tennessee,* pp. 69–71. Charles Coffin Journal, February 7, 1801, Calvin M. McClung Historical Collection, Lawson-McGhee Library, Knoxville, as quoted in Patrick, *Architecture in Tennessee,* p. 3. "Report of the Journey of the Brethren Abraham Steiner and Frederick C. De Schweinitz to the Cherokees and the Cumberland Settlements," in Williams, comp., *Early Travels in the Tennessee Country,* pp. 454, 508. Michaux, *Travels,* pp. 272–74, 280. Deaderick, ed., *Heart of the Valley,* pp. 70, 74.

15. Pollyanna Creekmore describes McGhee as a merchant and land speculator and states that he is the "progenitor of the McGhee family of Knox, Blount, and Monroe counties" (Pollyanna Creekmore, *Early East Tennessee Taxpayers* [Easley, S.C.: Southern Historical Press, 1980], p. 44). For the history of this object, see MESDA research file S-10416. Rothrock, *French Broad–Holston Country,* p. 448. Hornor, *Blue Book of Philadelphia Furniture,* p. 122. Piedmont North Carolina cabinetmakers James Gheen and Jesse Needham made desks with fallboards supported by the upper drawers (Weekley, "James Gheen," pp. 941, 944; and Bivins, "A Piedmont North Carolina Cabinetmaker," p. 971). The other Tennessee desk with this form of fallboard support is remarkably similar to desks attributed to Gheen. It was made by John Gillespie who came to Tennessee from Rowan County, North Carolina (Williams and Harsh, *The Art and Mystery of Tennessee Furniture,* p. 100).

16. This desk-and-bookcase was formerly attributed to the northern Shenandoah Valley because of its Delaware Valley details and the arched stop-fluting. For an illustration of a "Ralph cupboard," see Bernard L. Herman, *The Stolen House* (Charlottesville: University Press of Virginia, 1992), p. 185, fig. 5.9. A cellaret with a running astragal applied along the bottom edge of its case is illustrated in Gerald W. R. Ward, *American Case Furniture in the Mabel Brady Garvan and Other Collections at Yale University* (New Haven, Conn.: Yale University Press, 1988), pp. 444–45, fig. 230. Although Ward attributes the cellaret to North Carolina, it may be from Knox County. The scalloping on the Yale cellaret has drilled holes in the center of each astragal, a detail not found on the East Tennessee pieces discussed in this article.

17. This cupboard has a well-documented history in northern Knox County. It was originally owned by members of the Anderson and McCampbell families who moved to East Tennessee from Rockbridge County, Virginia, during the late eighteenth century. A member of the Swiss Truan family purchased a tract of land from Robert M. Anderson in 1849. The house and its contents, including the cupboard, were part of the sale (MESDA research file S-11228).

18. Benno M. Forman, "German Influences in Pennsylvania Furniture," in *Arts of the Pennsylvania Germans*, edited by Scott M. Swank (New York: W. W. Norton, 1983), p. 123. One of these cupboards (private collection) was nearly identical in form and decoration to figure 12, although it is slightly smaller and has quarter-column flutes that extend from the capitals to the bases. On all of the pieces with quarter-columns illustrated in this article, the flutes stop approximately 3/4" short of capitals and bases. The other cupboard (private collection) has a wide medial molding and no quarter-columns or drawers. A corner cupboard that may be related to this group is illustrated in Namuni Hale Young, *Art and Furniture of East Tennessee* (Knoxville: East Tennessee Historical Society, 1997), p. 29, fig. 51.

19. This chest was formerly attributed to the North Carolina Piedmont based upon the scalloped frieze (MESDA research file S-11647). This particular form of scalloped frieze is different from that found in North Carolina. The Carolina friezes are generally of an undulating wave form (see MESDA acc. 2023-20).

20. East Tennessee Historical Society, acc. 93.4. MESDA research file S-13024. This chest was purchased in Greene County in the early twentieth century.

21. On June 2, 1788, the *State Gazette of South Carolina* reported that Hope led the city's architects in a procession in Charleston. Although the city directory for 1790 lists Hope as a cabinetmaker at 15 Friend Street, furniture historian Brad Rauschenburg speculates that the description of Hope's trade may be inaccurate since Friend Street was a center for carpenters, and no other cabinetmakers are listed on that street. Evidence of Hope's work for Izard lies solely in the naming of one of his children for Ralph Izard and an entry in the journal of Charles Coffin of Knoxville regarding a conversation he had with Hope. Kenneth Scott, comp., *British Aliens in the United States During the War of 1812* (Baltimore, Md.: Genealogical Publishing Co., 1979). Beatrice St. Julien Ravenal, *Architects of Charleston* (Columbia: University of South Carolina Press, 1992), pp. 88–89. Susan Douglas Tate, "Thomas Hope of Tennessee, c. 1757–1820, House Carpenter and Joiner" (master's thesis, University of Tennessee, 1972), pp. 35–37, 42. Bradford L. Rauschenberg, *Charleston Cabinetmakers, 1680–1820* (Winston-Salem, N.C.: MESDA, forthcoming). *Knoxville Gazette*, November 14, 1796, and March 20, 1797, as cited in Tate, "Thomas Hope," pp. 46–47. Hope's involvement in the construction of Ramsey House is based upon an autobiography written by J. G. M. Ramsey (son of Frances Ramsey of Ramsey House) in the late nineteenth century. Tate, "Thomas Hope," pp. 82–86. The book of architecture referred to by Coffin is probably William Pain's *The Builder's Golden Rule, or the Youth's Sure Guide* (1782). Hope's copy of this book, minus its cover, is in the McClung Historical Collection, Lawson-McGhee Library, Knoxville. Journal of Charles Coffin, 1775–1853, as cited in Tate, "Thomas Hope," pp. 93, 96.

22. Entries for January 18, 1797, February 6, 1797, and February 13, 1797, in the Waste Book of David Henley, as cited in Tate, "Thomas Hope," p. 59. Rauschenberg, *Charleston Cabinetmakers*.

23. W. B. Hesseltine, ed., *Autobiography and Letters of Dr. J. G. M. Ramsey* (Nashville: Tennessee Historical Commission, 1954), p. 9, as cited in Tate, "Thomas Hope," p. 51. The "compting house desk" is in the collection of Blount Mansion (acc. 2-79). The secretary-and-bookcase is recorded in MESDA research file S-11911 and is illustrated in Williams and Harsh, *Art and Mystery of Tennessee Furniture*, p. 74, fig. 74. It descended in the Joseph Strong family and is attributed to Hope because he worked on Strong's house.

24. Tate, "Thomas Hope," pp. 130–33. Inventory of Thomas Hope, Knoxville Wills and Inventories, July 1821, bk. 3, p. 285. Thomas Hope to Elizabeth Hope, January 29, 1820, transcription of letter, McClung Historical Collection.

25. In 1802, Margaret Russell Cowan married Thomas Humes, a Knoxville merchant who had immigrated from Ireland. After Humes's death, she married Francis Ramsey in 1820 (Rothrock, *French Broad–Holston Country*, p. 471). Ramsey's inventory indicates that the desk-and-bookcase belonged to his widow and was property from her former marriage (Inventory of Francis A. Ramsey, Knox County Wills and Inventories, April 1821, bk. 3, pp. 249–56). The oral tradition linking Hope with the Humes desk may stem from the fact that Thomas Hope and Thomas Hope, Jr., received $286.50 from Humes's estate; however, this payment was probably for carpentry work. Humes's inventory lists plank, brick, locks, hinges, screws, glass,

and paint for projects he had commenced "or made contracts for the building of previous to his death" (Inventory of Thomas Humes, Knox County Wills and Inventories, January 1817, bk. 2, pp. 308–10; Report on the Settlement of the Estate of Thomas Humes, Knox County Wills and Inventories, July 1818, bk. 3, pp. 33–34).

26. Apparently, the bookcase originally overhung the back of the desk by about 1½". The bookcase now sits on top of the base molding, which is approximately 1¼" deep. A positioning rail attached to the leading edge of the bottom of the bookcase (behind the doors) is missing. Holes in the top of the desk indicate that this rail was screwed from below to secure the bookcase. The dovetails of the bookcase and those of the drawers of the lower case are similar.

27. Campbell (1750–1812) moved from Virginia to Greene County, North Carolina, in 1782. He was one of three judges that President Washington appointed for the Southwest Territory in 1790 (Rothrock, *French Broad–Holston Country*, pp. 389–90). MESDA research file S-9460. Another desk-and-bookcase from this Winchester shop has lunetted inlay in the panels of its doors (MESDA research file S-13543).

28. With the exception of the fluted brackets (which are a standard architectural design), none of the details of the desk interior are found in *The Builder's Golden Rule*, the only architectural book known to have been owned by Hope. The side facing of the right front foot is replaced, and the front facing of the left front foot has been altered. MESDA research file S-23411 shows an East Tennessee desk that originally had similar feet.

29. This tall chest has been attributed to Hope based on its descent in his family. Although it is now owned by a Hope descendant, the chest was purchased, not inherited.

30. McAffry was twenty-six when he immigrated (Scott, comp., *British Aliens*, as cited in MESDA artisan files). McAffry was commissioned as a lieutenant in the Knox County militia in 1801. Creekmore, *Early East Tennessee Taxpayers*, p. 16. In 1784, Clopton took an apprentice to learn the "art of a carpenter and Joiner" (Frederick County Deed Book 20, October 5, 1784, p. 281). Clopton's 1803 estate inventory included carpenters' tools, "Goiners' tools," and a work bench (Inventory of George Clopton, Frederick County [Virginia] Will Book 7, September 1803, pp. 134–36). *Wilson's Knoxville Gazette*, April 21, 1810. Williams and Harsh, *Art and Mystery of Tennessee Furniture*, pp. 298, 301.

31. Silas Emmett Lucas, Jr., and Ella Lee Sheffield, *35,000 Tennessee Marriage Records and Bonds, 1783–1870*, 3 vols. (Easley, S.C.: Southern Historical Press, 1981), 1:147.

32. Creekmore, *Early East Tennessee Taxpayers*, p. 19. 1820 Manufacturers' Census. The account of the sale of his estate also listed a glue pot (Inventory of Moses Crawford, Knox County Wills and Inventories, April 1820, bk. 1, pp. 178–84). Creekmore, *Early East Tennessee Taxpayers*, p. 75.

33. Inventory of Henry Baker, Knox County Wills and Inventories, October 1802, bk. 1, p. 106. Account of the Sale of the Estate Sale of Henry Baker, Knox County Wills and Inventories, January 1803, bk. 1, pp. 108–12. Williams and Harsh, *Art and Mystery of Tennessee Furniture*, p. 287. Creekmore, *Early East Tennessee Taxpayers*, p. 38. The inventory of William Baker lists chisels, gouges, hammers, files, a rasp, an iron square, and "1 sett of mountains," but does not list a work bench, or a glue pot, or any planes (Knox County Wills and Inventories, July 1804, bk. 1, pp. 150–51). Similarly, the inventory of Jacob Neff includes a variety of planes, some chisels, gouges, and gimlets, irons for a turning bench, and a pair of hinges for a cupboard (Knox County Wills and Inventories, January 1805, bk. 1, p. 164).

34. See Gusler, "Arts of Shenandoah County," pp. 15–35.

35. Ramsey, *Annals of Tennessee*, pp. 110, 334–35, 433, 541–42, 558. Richard Harrison Doughty, *Greeneville: One Hundred Year Portrait, 1775–1875* (Greeneville, Tenn.: by the author, 1975), pp. 4–5, 11–13. Michaux, *Travels*, p. 280.

36. Furniture attributed to John Gillespie of Sumner County, Tennessee, has Delaware Valley details, and it resembles work attributed to North Carolina cabinetmaker James Gheen (see note 15 above). Henry Glassie, *Patterns in the Material Folk Culture of the Eastern United States* (Philadelphia: University of Pennsylvania Press, 1968), pp. 234–35. Glassie underestimates the Pennsylvania influence in North Carolina (see Robert W. Ramsey, *Carolina Cradle: Settlement of the Northwest Carolina Frontier, 1747–1762* [Chapel Hill: University of North Carolina Press, 1964], pp. 23–51, 117–29, 138–51).

37. Remini, *Andrew Jackson and the Course of American Empire*, pp. 1–36. Clements, *A Past Remembered*, pp. 222–28. Richard Carlton Fulcher, comp., *1770–1790 Census of the Cumberland Settlements* (Baltimore, Md.: Genealogical Publishing Co., Inc, 1987), p. 29.

38. Walter T. Durham, *James Winchester, Tennessee Pioneer* (Gallatin, Tenn.: Sumner County Library Board, 1979), pp. 1–12. Michaux stated that carpenters from Baltimore had assisted in

the building of Cragfont (Michaux, *Travels*, p. 254). For Moses Morrish's apprenticeship to Winchester, see Sumner County Court Minutes, bk. 1, p. 346. The furniture attributed to Winchester is illustrated in Williams and Harsh, *Art and Mystery of Tennessee Furniture*, pls. 9 and 15 and figs. 73, 125, and 129.

39. Jay Guy Cisco, *Historic Sumner County, Tennessee* (1909; reprint ed., Nashville, Tenn.: Charles Elder Bookseller, 1971), pp. 296–98. Rather than return to Philadelphia, the Hansborough brothers settled in Logan County, Kentucky, north of Sumner County. The tools purchased by Peter Hansborough at the estate sale of his brother in 1818 indicate that the two continued to do house joinery and possibly make furniture (Account of the Estate Sale of Smith Hansborough, Logan County, Kentucky Wills and Inventories, August 1818, bk. B, pp. 140–41). Patrick, *Architecture in Tennesse,* p. 18. Williams and Harsh, *Art and Mystery of Tennessee Furniture*, p. 109. This secretary is illustrated in ibid., fig. 72.

40. Rothrock, *French Broad–Holston Country,* pp. 389–90.

Elizabeth A. Fleming

Staples for Genteel Living: The Importation of London Household Furnishings into Charleston During the 1780s

▼ IN 1802, JOHN DRAYTON of Charleston candidly characterized his late eighteenth-century contemporaries: "Charlestonians sought in every possible way to emulate the life of London society. They were too much enamoured of British customs, manners and education to imagine that elsewhere anything of advantage could be obtained." The Charleston home was a significant arena in which this parroting of London trends took place. Customs records, commercial account books, correspondence, newspapers, and journals reveal that relatively expensive and fashionable household furnishings were imported into Charleston in considerable quantities throughout the eighteenth century (fig. 1). These goods, neither necessities nor unique manufactures unobtainable from other sources, allowed Charlestonians to enjoy more cultivated, visibly genteel, and leisure-filled lives.[1]

By examining the quality and type of household goods imported into Charleston from London during the decade following the Revolutionary War, this article will show how Charlestonians furnished their interiors and how their imported purchases related to local production and to the London luxury-goods market. The value, appearance, function, and in some cases supplier of these imported goods shed light on the Anglicized nature of late eighteenth-century Charleston, its citizens' preferences and values, and their position within the British Empire.

Figure 1   Thomas Leech, *A View of Charleston,* London, 1774. (Collection of the Museum of Early Southern Decorative Arts.) This view shows the east side of the city, where most of the ships arriving from London would have docked.

The household goods and the English-style interior spaces they filled served as instruments of self-identification for Charlestonians. The supply of and demand for British household goods sprang from Charleston's long-standing economic and cultural connection with London. Since the first yield of export staples—particularly rice and indigo—in the early eighteenth century, Charleston's livelihood had been linked to England's capital city. Charlestonians identified more closely with London than with the Puritan culture of New England or the rural planter society of the Chesapeake Bay region. By the 1780s, the Charleston community was dependent upon international trade and attuned to stylish design. Its citizens' strong interest in material possessions and fashionable interior space encouraged their creation of stylish, London-derived interiors.

This article is separated into two sections according to the means by which Charlestonians created English-style interiors. The first focuses on personal contact, considering individual requests for various household items and orders customized to meet a particular household's needs. The second part examines bulk shipments sold by Charleston merchants. Both sections concentrate on commodities handled by the eighteenth-century upholder, a term used interchangeably with "upholsterer" during the period. Robert Campbell's *The London Tradesman* (1747) describes an upholsterer as the supplier of fashionable furniture for the home. The upholsterers' profession entailed fitting beds, window curtains, and wall hangings, covering chairs with stuffed seats, as well as coordinating a complete domestic environment for a client. Of primary focus within this study are upholstered and unupholstered seating furniture, beds and related equipment, looking glasses, and carpets. Objects such as decorative accessories, wall hangings, and brass accouterments for fireplaces will be examined to a lesser degree. The emphasis on upholsterers' goods offers a window into Charlestonians' living environments, domestic pastimes, and patterns of consumption.[2]

Previous scholarly work on household commodities imported into the North American colonies from Britain has focused principally on ceramics and tea wares. These investigations have shown how imported ceramics and the genteel customs they served bridged social divisions and how colonists used such goods to express political and cultural beliefs. How do more physically imposing household goods—those items that demonstrate a greater degree of sophistication in the execution of genteel customs—augment these assertions? As noted by historian Richard Bushman, many American colonials owned one tea cup and/or one silver spoon. Logic, however, suggests that where there was a mahogany tea table, there was a tea service of relative portent, and, where there was a card table, there was an environment in which leisure activity took place. Examining imported household furnishings will broaden the scope of preceding research and outfit a picture of Charleston in the 1780s as a community invigorated by London interior fashions.[3]

Personal Contact

In 1793, Joseph Lewis of London sued the estate of Thomas Hutchinson of

Charleston for failing to pay for household furnishings shipped to Hutchinson in October 1783. The goods included:

On board the Charleston Packet:	Sterling
2 pier Glasses—gold & varnished Japan borders	46.4.0
2 Girrandoles with dolphins	6.6.6
12 carved mahogany oval back chairs	19.16.0
2 Inlaid card tables, banded, strung & thurm feet	12.14.0
1 2 foot 6 inch inlaid pembroke table	5.10.0
A Sattin Wood Liquor Case	5.3.6
A Lady's dressing table of mahogany, taper feet	4.12.0
1 6 foot Wainscot double screw'd bedstead, sattin wood posts . . . fine white fring'd lace petticoats vallance and bases	69.12.0
On board the Emperor:	
12 Rich Carved Cabriole Mahogany chairs stuffed backs and seats	77.17.6
2 6 foot Cabriole Sopha's	44.0.0

The 1790 Charleston city directory includes two men named Thomas Hutchinson. The first, Thomas Hutchinson, Sr., is listed as a planter living on East Bay. His son, Thomas Hutchinson, Jr., is described as a planter residing at 21 South Bay. Whether to furnish the home of father or son, this order reveals that Charleston planters were eager to acquire fashionable, and often quite expensive, London-made household goods. The furniture in the order also documents leisure entertainments, such as card playing, and the pursuit of such activities within a sophisticated setting featuring gilded pier glasses, dolphin-carved girandoles, richly carved and stuffed chairs and sofas, a pembroke table, and a satinwood liquor case.[4]

According to *The Cabinet-Maker's London Book of Prices* (1788, 1793)—a piece-rate price guide published for masters and artisans—size, materials, structural options, and decorative features determined the price of a piece of furniture. In terms of documented price and quality, several of the items purchased by Hutchinson were comparable to similar objects made by London cabinetmakers such as Gillow and Company and George Seddon, who primarily served an upper middle–class clientele. The girandoles, valued at £3.3.3 individually, cost approximately the same as the very expensive girandoles made by Gillow and Company. In that firm's Estimate Sketchbook, 1784–1787, a girandole with gilding cost £3.1, whereas one "in the plainest way" cost £1.10. The pembroke tables listed in the same book range in value from £1.5.6 to £5.18.8. The latter valuation was for a satinwood pembroke table with a round top and classical inlay. Since this price exceeds that of Hutchinson's pembroke table by a mere eight shillings, it is likely

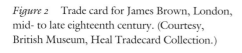

Figure 2 Trade card for James Brown, London, mid- to late eighteenth century. (Courtesy, British Museum, Heal Tradecard Collection.)

that his example had inlay of similar quantity and quality and can thus be associated with the more costly objects produced by Gillow and Company.[5]

The £4.12 price of the lady's mahogany dressing table included in the Hutchinson shipment similarly compares with that of dressing tables made by furniture workshops like Gillow and Company. Such firms were esteemed more for their fine workmanship than for their stylistic originality. A veneered dressing table with a lift top, a concealed mirror, and tulipwood cross-banding was priced at £3.0.4 in Gillow and Company's Estimate Sketchbook. A 1778 bill from London cabinetmaker George Seddon listed a "Veneer'd Dressing table wth glass in ye slides" at £5. An inlaid dressing table produced by Anglo-Swedish cabinetmaker Christopher Furhlogh was priced at £4.6 on a 1786 receipt. Although on par with pieces from these second-tier London workshops, the Hutchinson dressing table cost at least several pounds less than those produced by the city's premier firms. Thomas Chippendale, for example, charged Sir Rowland Winn £7.7 for a japanned dressing table. A more expensive, mahogany-veneered dressing table made in 1763 for Queen Charlotte's apartments cost £9.15. With these comparisons in mind, the Hutchinson dressing table seems to have been a piece of substantial quality, although not of the highest attainable.[6]

When contrasted with similar objects produced by Gillow and Company, the Hutchinson goods with extravagant prices are the card tables, seating furniture, and bedstead. In 1786, Gillow and Company sold Edward Standish a pair of satinwood card tables with broadcloth playing surfaces and tulipwood banding for £3.17.6—a price almost four times less than Hutchinson's two card tables. Although expensive in the second-tier London cabinetmaking market, the value of the tables and some of the seating furniture purchased by Hutchinson corresponds to the price of similarly described objects in the Order Book for the James Brown Upholstery and Cabinet Warehouse, a London firm located near the St. Paul's Churchyard (fig. 2). The January 8, 1784, order for Captain Farley of Antigua includes two oval card tables valued at £12.7, seven shillings less than the Hutchinson pair. On November 4, 1786, James Latouche of Jamaica ordered twelve vase-back mahogany chairs priced at £19.16, exactly the same price as Hutchinson's oval-back chairs.[7]

By comparison, the stuffed mahogany chairs and cabriole sofas sent to Hutchinson cost considerably more than their equivalents in the James Brown Order Book. For her Pall Mall townhouse, a Mrs. Kepple ordered twenty cabriole chairs with stuffed seats and backs, each costing approximately £4—less than half the price of the Hutchinson chairs. Reverend Daniel Williams placed a similar order with Brown's firm for his Hanover Square residence in London on October 26, 1784. It included "14 Vase back Drawing Room Arm Chairs stuft backs, seats & Arms made of good Mah^y & finished in mixt Damask, bass naild, price not to exceed four Guineas each . . . Stripe Cases to d^o of Yellow Cotton at 16/ . . . 2 Cabriole 5 ft. 3 Sophas to match d^o . . . 2 Cases to d^o." The order totaled £104.4, expensive but almost twenty pounds less than the twelve chairs and two sofas shipped to Hutchinson. The cost of Hutchinson's suite pales, however, in comparison to a comparable gilded set made by Chippendale for the State Dressing Room of Harewood House in 1773. Perhaps Hutchinson's upholstered chairs and sofas were difficult to package and handle on a transatlantic voyage, and their price reflects extensive shipping costs.[8]

Unlike other furnishings purchased by Hutchinson, the wainscot bedstead valued at £69.12 was comparable in price to several bedsteads produced by Chippendale and William and John Linnell. In 1766, John Linnell made several five-foot wainscot bedsteads complete with upholstery for William Drake, Esq., charging between £25 and £40 each. A mahogany bedstead from Chippendale's shop cost Sir Rowland Winn £64.4.9 in June 1766. His firm also produced two completely outfitted mahogany bedsteads, costing approximately £78 and £90, for the Earl of Egremont in 1777 and 1778. These bedsteads, although expensive when compared with those produced by Gillow and Company, were far less costly than the grandest of Chippendale's manufactures, such as the state bedstead with a dome canopy made for Harewood House in 1772 and priced at £250. Although Hutchinson's bedstead corresponds in price with comparable examples produced by London's premier cabinetmaking firms, its cost appears high when compared with other furniture in his order. Unlike affluent nobility, who outfitted entire homes with furnishings by tradesmen of Chippendale's stature, Carolina planters like Hutchinson only purchased a few very expensive pieces.[9]

Generally speaking, the prices of Hutchinson's furniture are consistent with those of similarly described objects made by first- and second-tier cabinetmakers in London and by the leading cabinetmakers in smaller British cities. His furnishings likewise relate very closely to those sold by the James Brown Cabinet and Upholstery Warehouse. This firm had a few noble patrons, such as the Countess Dowager of Glasgow, Sir John Trevelyan, and Lord Saltoun Fraserburgh, but the majority of its clientele were from gentry, mercantile, and professional families in London, provincial Britain, and her foreign territories. The purchasers of Gillow and Company's higher-priced products were of corresponding social and economic standing. Hutchinson's purchases are compatible with these consumption patterns. He was able to acquire expensive household objects and enjoy leisurely activities; however, he remained outside the uppermost echelons of British society.[10]

The aforementioned eighteenth-century receipts, account books, and estimate sketchbooks suggest the importance of furnishing a home with objects readily identifiable as expensive and London made. For prominent Charlestonians such as Hutchinson, imported household furnishings represented a material link with genteel British society. Hutchinson's order validates historian Timothy H. Breen's notion of American Anglicization. Breen asserts that, prior to developing a common cultural identity, American colonists first had to integrate themselves fully into the British Empire. Conversely, Hutchinson's order complicates Breen's claim that consumer behavior became increasingly standardized during the second half of the eighteenth century. Hutchinson's purchases suggest a desire to distinguish himself and his home by displaying furnishings different from the majority of those imported or made locally. As historian Cary Carson has observed, "the consumer revolution would make comrades of ladies and gentlemen half a world away while leaving near but unequal neighbors worlds apart."[11]

Additional Charleston evidence substantiates this notion that the desire to diverge from common consumer experiences, to indulge in customized furnishings for a home, was a prevalent practice among prosperous Charlestonians during the late eighteenth century. In October and November of 1786, a Mrs. Robinson of Charleston purchased from James Brown's firm a mahogany commode priced at £16.16, several carpets at £27.7.3, plain pea-green paper at £4.4, and a tea tray at £2.2. The price of the mahogany commode, with its round top, drawers, and plated hardware, exceeded that of a neat satinwood commode with handles and locks made by John Linnell for Sir John Griffin, Baronet, in 1779 by £6.6. Although the cost difference undoubtedly reflects the use of different materials and carriage expenses, the price of Mrs. Robinson's commode is also remarkable when compared with two relatively expensive mahogany commodes, estimated at £7.10.9 and £6.4.7¹/₄ by Gillow and Company.[12]

According to advertisements in the *South Carolina Gazette*, all of Mrs. Robinson's goods could have been acquired from Charleston sources. These sources included either merchants who had recently imported commodes, tea trays, carpets, and other household furnishings or local cabinet-makers who were capable of filling orders for London-style furniture. Even fashionable wallpaper had been imported by Charleston paper-hanger and upholsterer John Blott since the mid-1760s. Under these circumstances, Mrs. Robinson probably purchased London goods in order to individualize her domestic environment and distinguish it as one furnished with commissioned, London-made objects instead of standard imports or locally made pieces. This attempt to differentiate her home from those of her contemporaries demonstrates the role appearances played in maintaining social status. Mrs. Robinson's order suggests that she and her fellow Charlestonians put a premium on authentic, as opposed to imitation, London goods and on personal contact with the London luxury-goods market.[13]

The demand in Charleston society for authentic and customized London household furnishings is further confirmed by a September 5, 1789, receipt for furniture shipped to Nathaniel Heyward of Charleston. The name of the London supplier and the cost of many of the goods are missing; nevertheless, the receipt describes furnishings exported by one London firm and intended for a single room in Heyward's house (fig. 3): £32.2 worth of glass, ten chairs with caned seats at 31 shillings each, a matching suite of two armchairs and one sofa, cushions lined with calico for the seating furniture, and an assortment of textiles including "fine ell wide chintz Cotton for Curtains & Sopha cases . . . Best Cotton lace . . . deep brown silk fringe . . . brown silk Line . . . [and] silk vellum ornamented." Also listed are items for hang-

Figure 3 Photograph showing the Nathaniel Heyward House, Charleston, South Carolina, built ca. 1780–1790. (Courtesy, Historic Charleston Foundation.) The house has been demolished.

ing the window curtains, including "20 wrought brass Cloakpins . . . 1 Sett of Pulley laths and brackets . . . [and] 1 Set of Vallen leaf Cornices for d° Japanned & ornamented to match the Cotton." Unupholstered household goods comprise the last part of the receipt, which includes two japanned firescreens, one thread Wilton carpet of sixty-seven yards, a satinwood pembroke table, two satinwood circular card tables, a satinwood card box, two satinwood tea caddies (one double and the other single), and a set of steel firedogs, tongs, and shovel.[14]

The items described in the bill were probably for Heyward's drawing room or parlor. Judging from the prices and descriptions of the objects, his furniture was of very high quality. The chairs and sofa cost considerably less than the set shipped to Thomas Hutchinson six years earlier, but their price is still comparable to that of similarly described goods in the James Brown Order Book. Similarly, the satinwood tables and japanned firescreens were undoubtedly costly and in keeping with the latest London neoclassical fashion.

More notable than the style and expense of these pieces, however, is their method of purchase. Heyward acquired the furnishings for an entire room at one time at considerable expense rather than assembling the contents piecemeal. His order was larger than either Hutchinson's or Mrs. Robinson's. Although Hutchinson purchased an assortment of fine, expensive goods, his furnishings were probably used throughout his house. Like their counterparts throughout the British Empire, Charlestonians such as Heyward could and did have entire rooms outfitted with fashionable, coordinated London goods. Such spaces epitomized the desire among some Charlestonians to imitate the London style exactly.

Bulk Importation

Direct personal contact was not the only way to acquire London-made household furnishings during the 1780s. Goods for general consumers were exported in bulk from London to Charleston and then sold by general store merchants. How did the price and quality of such goods compare with the items imported by individuals for a particular home or room? To generalize, the furnishings arriving in bulk served Charlestonians who lacked contacts in the London furniture market, the ability to visit London, or the interest in customized work but who still wanted authentic English furnishings.

The household goods listed in the account book of London merchant James Douglas reveal a great deal about the general consumption of London-made furnishings exported to Charleston (fig. 4). Between August 1784 and August 1786, twenty-one different London firms supplied Douglas with household goods for these shipments: eight firms furnished cabinetwares and upholstered goods; two supplied looking glasses; two provided musical instruments, sheet music, and storage cases; two supplied only floor coverings; one furnished ceramic tableware and decorative objects; and six provided small household furnishings as well as other semidurables and durables. Three of the latter firms supplied ironware and brassware for the fireplace; one also equipped Douglas with dressing boxes, lanterns, and candlesticks; and another provided tea chests.[15]

Figure 4   Detail from *Ichnography of Charleston*, published in London in 1790 from a survey taken by Edmund Petrie in 1788. (Courtesy, Library of Congress.) The two Charleston mercantile firms receiving and selling goods shipped by Douglas were (*a*) Cochran and William McClure and (*b*) James Gregorie.

The London suppliers of typical upholsterers' wares, including cabinet-wares, upholstered goods, looking glasses, and small household accessories, operated their businesses in close proximity to one another and generally provided relatively inexpensive goods of similar quality for genteel consumers. Five of these firms—Nicholas Phene, Pitt & Chessey, William Rawlins, William and Thomas Wilkinson, and Wilson & Dawes—were located in Broker's Row, Moorfields, during the 1780s (fig. 5). This district was a primary location for furniture warehouses, auctioneers, and second-hand dealers. Nicholas Phene, an upholsterer and auctioneer who used the

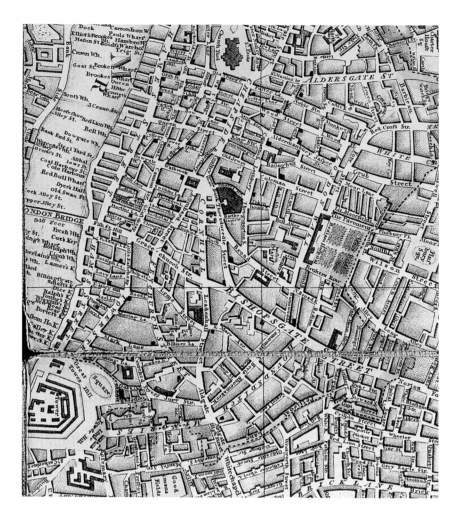

Figure 5 Detail from J. Fairburn, *London and Westminster*, 1800. (Courtesy, Map Collection, Yale University Library.) The map shows Broker's Row just east of Moorfields.

sign of the "Golden Plough" on his trade card, worked at 18–19 Broker's Row after 1780. Pitt & Chessey began trading in London in 1769 and were located at 13 Broker's Row during their business dealings with James Douglas. Their trade card (fig. 6) advertised "Houshold Goods both New & Old at the most Reasonable Rates . . . in the Genteelest Taste" and upholsterer's work in "as Good and Cheap a manner as at any Shop In Town." William Rawlins, another Broker's Row cabinetmaker, upholsterer, appraiser, and undertaker, also sold new and used household goods. All of these Broker's Row firms offered a variety of upholstery services. Their clientele, as inferred by trade card terminology and the all-encompassing nature of their businesses, consisted of individuals for whom gentility and economy were concerns.[16]

The same can be said about the two other suppliers with Broker's Row addresses, William and Thomas Wilkinson and Wilson & Dawes. These firms were warehouses, able to deal with wholesale, bulk, and customized orders. The former advertised as a "Cabinet, Upholstery, Carpet & Looking Glass Warehouse," the latter as an upholsterer, undertaker, and furniture warehouse. The two suppliers of looking glasses, although located away from Broker's Row, were similar, volume-oriented businesses. According to *Kent's London Directory* of 1787, William Ford was a looking glass ware-

Figure 6 Trade card for Pitt & Chessey, London, ca. 1780. (Courtesy, British Museum, Heal Tradecard Collection.)

houseman at 58 Lombard Street. The partnership of Walker & Beck ran a looking glass manufactory, located at 46 Fish Street Hill, London.[17]

In contrast, the William Fleming who provided twenty-six cabinet and upholstery items for Douglas's October 19, 1784, shipment was a relatively upscale cabinetmaker and upholsterer. He is most likely the William Fleming who worked at 4 Chandos Street in Covent Garden from 1775 to 1808 and who supplied two mahogany medicine chests to Hopetoun House, Lothian, in 1775. A William Fleming also subscribed to Sheraton's *The Cabinet-Maker and Upholsterer's Drawing-Book* in 1793.[18]

Other identifiable London suppliers to James Douglas were those offering fireplace accouterments such as firedogs, shovels, and tongs. John Horsley & Son were "Brass Founders" at Haberdashers Walk, Hoxton, in northeast London from 1783 to 1790, and Taylor & Bailey were "Iron-mongers" on Little Tower Street in 1785.[19]

Table 1 presents the quantity and value of the household goods provided by fifteen different suppliers to James Douglas. The warehouse firms, William and Thomas Wilkinson, William Ford, and Walker & Beck, pro-

Table 1.

Suppliers of Specified Household Goods Listed in the James Douglas Account Book, 1784–1792. (Valuations are in pounds decimal, rounded up to the nearest thousandth. N.C. indicates that the figure is incalculable due to group pricing.)

Supplier	Quantity	Minimum price	Maximum price	Average price
Cabinetwares, upholstery, looking glasses				
Fleming, William	26	1.575	4.250	2.761
Phene, Nicholas	50	.175	6.300	1.781
Pitt & Chessey	67	.600	7.600	1.882
Rawlins, William	5	2.363	4.308	3.529
Russell, John	23	N.C.	N.C.	N.C.
Swain(e), T.	2	1.000	1.000	1.000
Wilkinson, Wm. & Th.	72	.642	.900	.715
Wilson & Dawes	44	.200	8.400	.882
Looking glass manufactures				
Ford, William	104	.092	1.800	.477
Walker & Beck	135	.083	4.500	.774
Musical instruments				
Bremner, Robert	2	8.925	8.925	8.925
Longman & Broderip	22	.525	16.800	4.500
Firedogs, shovel & tongs				
Horsley, John & Son	52	.150	4.200	.718
Taylor & Bailey	43	.125	3.675	.718
Walker, William & Alex	7	1.200	3.100	2.300

vided greater quantities of goods than any of the other suppliers. In general, the more goods of a particular type that a firm supplied, the lower the average cost per item. For example, William Fleming and William Rawlins exported a smaller number of goods but at a higher average cost per item than did the other firms in their category. Rawlins's high average cost per item related to the type of object supplied—bureaus and tables, but no chairs. Of the suppliers of both cabinetware and upholstery, William and Thomas Wilkinson provided the greatest quantity of goods at the lowest average cost per item.

Several of Douglas's suppliers, including Pitt & Chessey, Nicholas Phene, and Wilson & Dawes, provided goods that ranged in cost from a couple of shillings to six and eight pounds a piece. Cost variances within the same categories of goods probably reflected Douglas's or his suppliers' attempts to satisfy a wide range of customers. As savvy entrepreneurs, they almost certainly made provisions for varying tastes, needs, and economic concerns.

Table 2 delineates the variety of household goods exported by Douglas to Charleston merchants during the years 1784 to 1786. Large, expensive items such as bedsteads, various cabinetwares, organs, and sofas were exported in small numbers, whereas looking glasses, glassware, inexpensive

| Table 2. | | Price of Household Goods in the James Douglas Account Book. (Includes only a small portion of the various types of goods that Douglas exported to Charleston. Valuations are in pounds decimal, rounded up to the nearest thousandth. Diverse items valued as a group are listed at the end of the table and not incorporated into object-type breakdowns.) | |

Item	Minimum price	Maximum price	Average price
Beds			
Bedstead (6)	1.250	8.400	2.858
Mattress/ Mattress & Pillow (36)	.250	2.100	1.020
Cabinetwares			
Bookcase (1)	5.000	5.000	5.000
Bureau (3)	4.304	4.308	4.307
Chest/Chest of Drawers (4)	2.200	6.300	4.825
Commode (5)	4.200	5.775	4.835
Desk/Writing Desk (5)	.375	5.250	2.650
Sideboard (3)	5.250	7.600	6.383
Floor covering			
Bulk—Scotch: yard price (total valuation: 20.783)	.100	.158	.136
Bulk—Wilton: yard price (total valuation: 54.054)	.225	.225	.225
Rug (45)	.575	.775	.675
Scotch Carpet (5)	1.900	7.361	3.626
Wilton Carpet (5)	7.000	12.250	9.170
Mirrors & glass			
Brass Burnished Glass (23)	.092	.275	.175
Dressing Glass (23)	.083	.167	.124
Glass (83)	.092	4.500	.930
Pier Looking Glass (2)	3.150	3.150	3.150
Sconce (18)	.213	1.675	.678
Swing Glass (48)	.188	.950	.395
Musical instruments			
Guitar (8)	3.150	8.925	5.578
Organ (2)	10.500	16.800	13.650
Violin (12)	.525	4.000	2.096
Spinnet (2)	10.000	10.000	10.000
Seating furniture			
Chair (66)	.600	1.250	.793
Elbow/Arm Chair (72)	.642	1.750	.778
Sofa/Settee (3)	1.575	5.250	2.767
Stool (2)	.200	.200	.200
Tables			
Card (19)	.750	2.900	1.725
Dining (10)	1.600	4.375	3.378

Table 2. continued

Item	Minimum price	Maximum price	Average price
Gaming (3)	.725	.925	.792
Night (5)	.900	3.150	1.570
Pembroke (8)	.900	2.900	2.016
Tea (2)	.800	1.350	1.075
Other (4)	.900	1.500	1.281
Dining accouterments			
Knife Case (9)	.800	1.200	.900
Rum Case (3)	3.675	3.675	3.675
Wine Cooler (5)	1.500	2.625	2.350
Dressing accouterments			
Commode Box w/ Glass (9)	.825	1.400	1.214
Dressing Box (37)	.275	1.800	.857
Bason Stand (1)	.600	.600	.600
Fireplace accouterments			
Dogs—Pair (55)	.175	4.200	1.105
Screen (8)	.900	1.750	1.256
Shovel & Tongs—Pair (40)	.125	.600	.274
Tea accouterments			
Tea Caddy (6)	.200	.325	.271
Tea Chest (16)	.250	.750	.366
Tea Tray (6)	.138	.950	.554
Miscellaneous			
Derby Figures - Pair (6)	.400	1.050	.742
Group pricing			
12 Chairs; 2 Elbow Chairs; 2 Card Tables; 4 Window Curtains			15.000
1 Dining Table; 2 Wine Coolers			3.675

Note: 1.75 = 35 shillings or 1.15.0 pounds sterling; 1.00 = 20 shillings or 1.0.0 pounds sterling; .50 = 10 shillings.

carpets, chairs, and fireplace utensils were shipped in greater quantities. The three categories of goods exported in the greatest quantity were looking glasses and glasswares (197 items), seating furniture (157 items), and fireplace accouterments (103 items). The two classes of goods exported in the lowest quantities were cabinetwares (21 items) and dining accouterments (19 items). Six different types of cabinetwares were supplied, but only three types of dining accessories—knife cases, rum cases, and wine coolers—appear in the shipments destined for Charleston.

The goods exported by Douglas were described in simple, straightforward terms in his account book. The most common adjectives were "mahogany," "neat," "gilt," "fine," "inlaid," and "plain." "Mahogany" differentiated 173 tables, chairs, dressing glasses, and tea chests. "Neat" characterized eighty different items. Sixty-three objects were gilded, including sconces, looking glasses, dressing boxes, guitars, and organs. Only eight swing glasses, commodes, and card tables were described as having inlay or inlaid parts. Fifteen objects, from swing glasses to pembroke tables and commodes, were described as "plain." The frequency with which the terms "mahogany," "gilt," and "neat" were used suggests the fashionable nature of the exported goods. During the eighteenth century, the term "neat" was often used to describe furniture that was simply adorned but well-made and classically correct in proportion and detail.

The most expensive objects exported by Douglas were a fifteen-key organ with four stops, two barrels, a gilded front, and a stand priced at £16.16; a Wilton carpet measuring five feet by seven feet priced at £12.5; and two mahogany spinets priced at £10 each. Only seven other objects in all of the nine shipments to Charleston were valued at over £6. They included a bedstead with curtains at £8.8, two chests of drawers with serpentine fronts at £6.6 each, a sideboard with an inlaid front at £7.12, a Scotch carpet measuring six feet by seven and one-quarter feet at £7.7.2, and two elegant guitars of the "newest construction" with cases and strings, each at £8.18.6. The cheapest objects were twenty-three mahogany dressing glasses with an average value of two shillings six pence. Hardly a necessity, dressing glasses appealed to consumers interested in acquiring London-made amenities at minimal expense.

Of all the household objects included in the Douglas shipments, bedsteads had the greatest range in minimum and maximum price, a difference of £7.3. The most expensive bedstead was supplied by Wilson & Dawes, but its £8.8 price included curtains. As indicated in the account book, the other beds had yet to be dressed. Two field beds with canopy tops and mahogany posts were priced at £2.8 each (fig. 7). This price seems low when compared with Gillow and Company's mahogany beds, which ranged in price from £3 to £6. The Douglas beds are, in fact, more comparable in price to beech beds by Gillow and Company. The value of the Douglas beds is also less

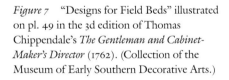

Figure 7 "Designs for Field Beds" illustrated on pl. 49 in the 3d edition of Thomas Chippendale's *The Gentleman and Cabinet-Maker's Director* (1762). (Collection of the Museum of Early Southern Decorative Arts.)

than that of examples made in Charleston during the 1770s. In 1771, cabinetmaker Thomas Elfe charged £40 South Carolina (approximately £5.13.3 sterling) for a mahogany bedstead with "Eagles, Claws & plane knees with castors" and £20 (approximately £2.17.2 sterling) for a poplar bedstead with mahogany posts and castors. The different prices for the Elfe beds undoubtedly relate to their form, size, materials, and workmanship; however, the lower prices for Douglas's mahogany beds may be the result of their having been made in a large shop with a specialized workforce. Such shops could produce standard furniture forms much faster and cheaper than their smaller competitors.[20]

Bed "furniture" was also included in Douglas's shipments. The firm Livesey & Preston supplied five different types of mattresses and/or mattress and pillow combinations. In ascending value, these included common mattresses, linen mattresses, "crankey" mattresses of varying sizes, checked mattresses, and "tick" mattresses with hair stuffing. The presence of mattresses and other bed furniture, which could easily have been made in Charleston, indicates that even the most basic manufactured goods were shipped to the colonies during the 1780s.

High-quality case furniture represented the other end of the export spectrum. Five firms—Longman & Broderip, Nicholas Phene, Pitt & Chessey, William Rawlins, and John Russell—furnished Douglas with six different forms. The Pitt & Chessey bookcase, priced at £5, was comparable to relatively elaborate case pieces produced in London during the late eighteenth

Figure 8   Design for a bookcase illustrated on pl. 1 in *The Cabinet-Makers' London Book of Prices* (1793). (Courtesy, Winterthur Museum Library.)

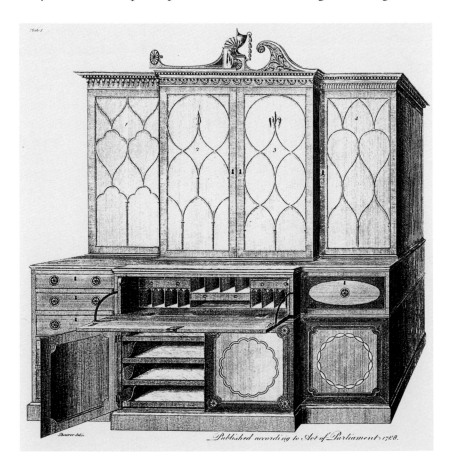

Figure 9 Design for a dressing commode illustrated on pl. 10, fig. 4, in *The Cabinet-Makers' London Book of Prices* (1793). (Courtesy, Winterthur Museum Library.)

century. *The Cabinet-Makers' London Book of Prices* illustrates a library bookcase six-feet long and eight-feet high priced at £5.15 (fig. 8). A satinwood bureau and bookcase made by Gillow and Company cost £5.4. The prices and descriptions of the bureaus and chests in the Douglas shipments suggest that they were more than simple, functional pieces but of lesser value than similar forms by Gillow and Company.[21]

The five commodes exported by Douglas included two mahogany examples valued at £4.4 each and one dressing commode with drawers priced at £5.15.6. The latter piece, although over two pounds more expensive than a dressing commode with a serpentine front pictured in *The Cabinet-Makers' London Book of Prices* (fig. 9), was less expensive than all but one of the commodes listed in the Gillow and Company Estimate Sketchbook. The lesser-priced Gillow and Company commode, estimated at £3.17.5, had French feet. The three sideboards shipped by Douglas follow a similar pattern. The most expensive Douglas sideboard, one with a fine inlaid front, cost four pounds more than the most expensive sideboard described in *The Cabinet-Makers' London Book of Prices*, "a celleret sideboard, with an eliptic middle, and ogee on each side." Sideboards produced by Gillow and Company ranged in cost from £4 to £8.[22]

The furniture forms exported by Douglas were apparently more expensive than their standard-priced counterparts in London but less costly than comparable pieces made by Gillow and Company. Likewise, Douglas's furniture was less expensive than London work commissioned by wealthy Charlestonians. This latter difference suggests a distinction of price and possibly of form and ornament between interiors outfitted through custom orders and those outfitted with general imports.

The values of looking glasses in the Douglas shipments depended upon the size and the amount of carving or gilding on the frame. Brass-burnished glass was the only type of mirror exported without a frame, and it had the lowest average price per unit. The most expensive looking glasses were two large, square, carved and gilded glasses supplied by Walker & Beck. The two "handsome" pier glasses, valued at £3.3 each, also had carved and gilded decoration. The remaining mirrors and glass varied greatly in both embellishment and size. The forty-eight swing glasses, for example, were described as "plain," "stringed," "gilt-edged with shells," "oval-shaped with bent pillars," "neat oval-shaped," and "mahogany." As decorative arts scholar Elisabeth Garrett asserts, looking glasses were an essential domestic ornament, providing supplemental light and evidence of familial wealth through size, abundance, and ornament.[23]

Most of the seating furniture in Douglas's shipments consisted of bulk consignments, often including side chairs and arm or elbow chairs. The quantity of side chairs was generally six times greater than that of corresponding arm or elbow chairs, which may reflect the presence of sets in his shipments. Consumers undoubtedly had the option of purchasing these chairs in almost any combination, from single examples to large sets with multiple side chairs and arm or elbow chairs. Pitt & Chessey supplied two identifiable sets comprised of twelve side chairs and two armchairs. In both sets, the side chairs were valued at 16 shillings each, and the armchairs, at £1.5 each. By comparison, Thomas Elfe's shop produced sets of twelve mahogany scrollback chairs in 1771 and 1772; the chairs in both sets cost just over £7 South Carolina (or just over £1 sterling) a piece—a value midway between the Pitt & Chessey prices for side and armchairs. At 12 shillings each, the thirty mahogany side chairs furnished by Wilson & Dawes were comparable in price to mahogany fan-back chairs produced by Gillow and Company during the 1780s.[24]

The seating furniture in Douglas's shipments incorporated a variety of materials and decorative features. While sixty-four of the chairs were not described, fifty were listed as made of mahogany. William and Thomas Wilkinson supplied twenty-four elbow chairs with double brass nails, and William Fleming provided two mahogany corner night chairs with elbows and stone pans valued at £1.13 a piece. Douglas's shipments also included a small number of settees and sofas, such as the one furnished by Pitt & Chessey and priced at £5.5. By comparison, a Gillow and Company sofa with a mahogany top cost £3.10. For just over £5.15.6, Thomas Chippendale provided Sir William Robinson with "a large mahogany sofa stuff'd in linen & Quilted wt Castors on the feet &c."[25]

The suppliers of the fifty-four tables exported by Douglas included William Fleming, Pitt & Chessey, Nicholas Phene, William Rawlins, John Russell, William and Thomas Wilkinson, and Wilson & Dawes. Card and dining tables were exported in sets and individually. Douglas's shipments included three pairs of card tables and three sets of mahogany dining tables. The dining table sets, the cheapest of which cost £6.6, were more expensive than the most costly individual dining tables. This value exceeded by approximately two pounds the most expensive single dining table supplied by Pitt & Chessey and a mahogany dining table set produced by Thomas Elfe in November 1771. William Fleming provided the two most expensive dining table sets: one was secondhand, and the other, measuring ten feet by four feet six inches, had moveable round ends and spring hinges that permitted the tables to be joined. With the exception of these sets of card and dining tables, all other table forms were individual units.[26]

William Fleming evidently supplied the most ornate tables. He provided four neat, circular mahogany card tables, with inlay, brass borders, and green cloth lining priced at £2.18 a piece; six neat, mahogany pembroke tables, two square in shape and four oval-shaped and inlaid; and a mahogany night table with drawers, a folding top, a stone pan, and flint-glass water bottles. Oddly enough, Fleming supplied goods for only one early shipment, that of October 19, 1784. A lack of general demand for these very fine objects or a change in Douglas's business after 1784 are possible explanations for the termination of the Fleming-Douglas business relationship.

The pattern of table values is consistent with that of other categories of goods. The price of the least expensive card tables, supplied by Wilson & Dawes, equaled that of the most costly card table in *The Cabinet-Makers' London Book of Prices*. The more expensive inlaid card tables exported by Douglas were comparable in price to a Gillow and Company circular card table with banding and stringing estimated at slightly over £2. This price was also comparable with that of card tables made for Eliza Pinckney by Thomas Elfe in March 1768. The price of Fleming's neat, oval, inlaid mahogany pembroke tables at £2.18, however, appears cheap compared to a Gillow and Company inlaid pembroke table with a round top costing over £5.18. Pricing clearly reflected the materials, ornament, and quality of workmanship in each object. As such, these comparisons generally situate the Douglas goods and hence the furnishings in Charleston's Anglo interiors within the fashionable and relatively expensive realm of the London furniture market.[27]

The Douglas furnishings categorized as accouterments offer a final picture of how frequently and in what manner English goods could be sprinkled throughout the Charleston home. Many of these objects were made of wood and used for dining and dressing. The mahogany knife cases, wine coolers, and rum cases were undoubtedly used in dining rooms. Equipped with partitions and glass bottles, the rum cases not only offered elegant storage for spirits but also were portable enough to be carried to secondary residences or on trips. The multitude of commode and dressing boxes with differing sizes, glass shapes, and decorative details suggests that variety was important to Charlestonians interested in setting themselves apart with London-made furnishings. Such goods could be found in all corners of the home.

The mass export of these household accessories to Charleston necessitates a clarification of the relationship between the quantity of goods shipped and their cost. The goods that were generally inexpensive and exported in large numbers can be separated into two categories: objects that were not manufactured in the colonies (plate glass for mirrors and carpets), and objects that were generally less expensive than their locally made counterparts (looking glasses, dressing glasses, glassware, dining and tea accessories, and certain types of ironware). All of these goods enabled consumers to distinguish their homes through the purchase of relatively inexpensive and inconsequential luxuries from London.

Table 3 examines the quantity of minimum- and maximum-priced goods shipped by James Douglas. This summary demonstrates that the least expensive goods in a category were not necessarily exported in substantial quantities nor in larger quantities than the most expensive goods within the same category. What seems more significant, however, was the offering of a wide variety of goods from which a consumer could pick and choose. Walker & Beck exported only twelve of the cheapest looking glasses, which had oval metal frames and were identical in size and shape. The firm also provided thirty-six additional glasses with oval metal frames in different sizes. The suppliers of dining and dressing accessories and firedogs, shovels, and tongs also refrained from exporting large numbers of identical objects. As such, they gave consumers with different tastes, personal requirements, and interiors a wider selection of goods. The objects with low unit prices exported in the largest numbers were chairs. This finding suggests a significant demand for inexpensive London-made seating. Such objects,

Table 3.

Quantity and Supplier of Minimum- and Maximum-Priced Goods in the James Douglas Account Book, 1784–1792. (When only one item is in a category or when minimum and maximum prices are identical, information is only listed in the maximum-price column.)

Item	Quantity at minimum price	Supplier	Quantity at maximum price	Supplier
Beds				
Bedstead (6)	2	Pitt & Chessey	1	Wilson & Dawes
Mattress/Mattress & Pillow (36)	2	Livesey & Preston	6	Livesey & Preston
Cabinetwares				
Bookcase (1)	. . .	. . .	1	Pitt & Chessey
Bureau (3)	1	Rawlins, Wm.	2	Rawlins, Wm.
Chest/Chest of Drawers (4)	1	Pitt & Chessey	2	Pitt & Chessey
Commode (5)	2	Phene, N.; Pitt & Chessey	1	Phene, N.
Desk/Writing Desk (5)	2	Longman & Broderip	1	Pitt & Chessey
Sideboard (3)	1	Phene, N.	1	Pitt & Chessey
Floor covering				
Bulk—Scotch: yard price (total valuation: 20.783)	59 yds.	Jones & Wakeman	96 yds.	Jones & Wakeman
Bulk—Wilton: yard price (total valuation: 54.054)	. . .	. . .	240 1/4 yds.	Jones & Wakeman
Rug (45)	15	Hill, Jm.	15	Hill, Jm.
Scotch Carpet (5)	1	Jones & Wakeman	1	Jones & Wakeman
Wilton Carpet (5)	1	Jones & Wakeman	1	Jones & Wakeman
Mirrors & glass				
Brass Burnished Glass (23)	6	Ford, Wm.	6	Ford, Wm.
Dressing Glass (23)	6	Walker & Beck	4	Walker & Beck
Glass (83)	12	Walker & Beck	2	Walker & Beck
Pier Looking Glass (2)	. . .	. . .	2	Walker & Beck
Sconce (18)	3	Ford, Wm.	1	Ford, Wm.
Swing Glass (48)	8	Ford, Wm.; Walker & Beck	1	Ford, Wm.
Musical instruments				
Guitar (8)	3	Longman & Broderip	2	Bremner, Rt.
Organ (2)	1	Longman & Broderip	1	Longman & Broderip
Violin (12)	2	Longman & Broderip	2	Longman & Broderip
Spinnet (2)	. . .	. . .	2	Longman & Broderip
Seating furniture				
Chair (66)	30	Wilson & Dawes	12	Pitt & Chessey
Elbow/Arm Chair (72)	36	Wilkinson, Wm. & Th.	2	Pitt & Chessey
Sofa/Settee (3)	2	Pitt & Chessey	1	Pitt & Chessey
Stool (2)	. . .	. . .	2	Wilson & Dawes
Tables				
Card (19)	4	Wilson & Dawes	4	Fleming, Wm.
Dining (10)	1	Pitt & Chessey	2	Pitt & Chessey

Table 3 continued.

Item	Quantity at minimum price	Supplier	Quantity at maximum price	Supplier
Gaming (3)	2	Phene, N.	1	Phene, N.
Night (5)	3	Wilkinson, Wm. & Th.	1	Fleming, Wm.
Pembroke (8)	2	Wilkinson, Wm. & Th.	2	Fleming, Wm.
Tea (2)	1	Pitt & Chessey	1	Pitt & Chessey
Other (4)	1	Phene, N.	1	Pitt & Chessey
Dining accouterments				
Knife Case (9)	4	Wilkinson, Wm.& Th.	2	Phene, N.
Rum Case (3)	. . .	. . .	3	Fleming, Wm.
Wine Cooler (5)	1	Phene, N.	2	Phene, N.; Pitt & Chessey
Dressing accouterments				
Commode Box w/ Glass (9)	1	Walker & Beck	2	Walker & Beck
Dressing Box (37)	2	Howard, Rt.	2	Ford, Wm.
Bason Stand (1)	. . .	. . .	1	Pitt & Chessey
Fireplace accouterments				
Dogs—Pair (55)	6	Taylor & Bailey; Horsley, Jn.	1	Horsley, Jn.
Screen (8)	1	Phene, N.	2	Phene, N.
Shovel & Tongs—Pair (40)	3	Taylor & Bailey	1	Horsley, Jn.
Tea accouterments				
Tea Caddy (6)	1	Walker & Beck	2	Walker & Beck
Tea Chest (16)	2	Trimbey & Bell	1	Trimbey & Bell
Tea Tray (6)	1	Walker, Wm. & Al.	1	Walker, Wm. & Al.
Miscellaneous				
Derby Figures—Pair (6)	1	Akerman & Shaw	1	Akerman & Shaw
Group pricing				
12 Chairs; 2 Elbow Chairs; 2 Card Tables; 4 Window Curtains				Russell, Jn.
1 Dining Table; 2 Wine Coolers				Phene, N.

most likely used in multiple numbers, could be customized for individual households by means of upholstery.

Goods exported from London to Charleston for the general consumer were certainly less expensive than those custom-ordered by individuals; however, the household furnishings listed in Douglas's account book were still of reasonable quality. They were more expensive than their standard counterparts in *The Cabinet-Makers' London Book of Prices* but cheaper than similar goods produced by Gillow and Company, presumably because they were less elaborate, made of less expensive materials, or required less labor.

Figure 10 Thomas Watson, teapot and stand from a service shipped by James Douglas to James Gregorie on March 17, 1785. (Private collection; photo, Gavin Ashworth.)

The household furnishings exported by Douglas appealed to clients interested in acquiring fashionable London items but incapable of or uninterested in placing custom orders. Although these consumers may have been from a lower socioeconomic level than those who custom-ordered London goods, wealthy Charlestonians may also have purchased generic imports for secondary locations in their homes or to fill out sets or replace damaged objects. These imports allowed Charlestonians to follow London fashion and to exercise some degree of personal choice. They resembled genteel consumers in Britain, some of whom no doubt patronized the same firms that supplied Douglas.

The household goods, both custom and speculative, imported for Charleston consumers during the 1780s were typically those that made everyday life more commodious and pleasurable: looking glasses to adorn and illuminate living spaces; tables and accessories for gaming, dining, and serving tea (fig. 10); specialized case forms for dressing, writing, and storing clothing and books; and musical instruments. This pattern, which relates to what J. H. Plumb has called the "commercialization of leisure," corresponds to an increased interest by affluent, genteel residents of colonial British America in pursuing private, leisurely activities. According to Plumb, culture and leisure in the public sphere ceased to be elitist in the eighteenth century. The goods serving private leisure activities thus became the means by which individuals of a certain social and economic class could distinguish themselves from others and articulate their status within the genteel society of the British Empire.[28]

If the importance of material possessions lies in what they say about an owner and his position within a complex social system, then what exactly do these imported household furnishings say about residents of Charleston in the 1780s? By furnishing their homes with London imports, Charlestonians were driven neither by low cost, necessity, nor inability to acquire similar, locally made objects. There must have been some intrinsic, singular value to owning these London goods. If "to have is to be," then Charlestonians' demand for imported, London-made luxuries was ultimately an act of conspicuous consumption with the end result being self-definition. Charleston citizens used such furnishings as a means of visually establishing their place in genteel British society as well as achieving more subtle distinctions within their own community.[29]

1. John Drayton, *A View of South Carolina, as Respects Her Natural and Civil Concerns* (1802; reprint ed., Spartanburg, S.C.: Reprint Company, 1972), pp. 217–18. In the introduction to *The Refinement of America: Persons, Houses, Cities* (New York: Alfred A. Knopf, 1992), p. xv, Richard Bushman characterizes gentility as "the visible expression of gentry status, the most sharply defined social class in the colonies. . . . Gentility simply gave expression to a universally acknowledged division, and actually had the comforting effect of reinforcing the established social order." Bushman then proceeds to discuss how such things as homes, furnishings, tea apparatus, manners, apparel, and speech visibly defined one as genteel and part of polite society.

2. Robert Campbell, *The London Tradesman* (1747; reprint ed., Devon, Eng.: David & Charles Reprints, 1969), pp. 169–70.

3. Timothy H. Breen, "'Baubles of Britain': The American and Consumer Revolutions of the Eighteenth Century," *Past and Present* 119 (May 1988): 75. See also George Miller, Ann Smart Martin, and Nancy Dickinson, "Changing Consumption Patterns, English Ceramics and the American Market from 1770 to 1840," unpublished lecture, 1989, Winterthur Museum Library, Winterthur, Delaware. Bushman, *Refinement of America*, pp. 184–85.

4. Joseph Lewis vs. Estate of Thomas Hutchinson, Judgment Rolls, 1793, Roll 253A, District of Charleston, Court of Common Pleas, Charleston, S.C., as cited in M. Allison Carll, "An Assessment of English Furniture Imports into Charleston, South Carolina, 1760–1800," *Journal of Early Southern Decorative Arts* 11, no. 2 (November 1985): 4. James W. Hagy, *People and Professions of Charleston, South Carolina, 1782–1802* (Baltimore, Md.: Clearfield Company by Genealogical Publishing Co., 1992), p. 15.

5. "Reprint of the Cabinet-Maker's London Book of Prices, 1793," *Furniture History* 18 (1982): 23. All of my references to the *Cabinet-Makers' London Book of Prices* refer to the 1793 edition. Sarah Nichols, "Gillow and Company of Lancaster, England: An Eighteenth-Century Business History" (master's thesis, University of Delaware, 1982), p. 7, categorizes Gillow and Company as a "one-rung-down-the-ladder establishment" within the English furniture industry. Estimate Sketchbook, 1784–1787, vol. 93, Gillow and Company Archive, Westminster Public Library, London.

6. Nichols, "Gillow and Company," p. 15. Estimate Sketchbook, 1784–1787. Robert Smith, "A Bill from George Seddon," *Antiques* 78, no. 4 (October 1960): 362. John Hayward, "A Further Note on Christopher Fuhrlogh," *Burlington* 119, no. 7 (July 1977): 490. Christopher Gilbert, *The Life and Work of Thomas Chippendale*, 2 vols. (London: Studio Vista, 1978), 1:191. Ralph Edwards and Margaret Jourdain, *Georgian Cabinet-makers c. 1700–1800* (London: Country Life, Ltd., 1955), p. 154.

7. Estimate Sketchbook, 1784–1787. James Brown Order Book, vol. 1, January 4, 1782–October 11, 1784, C107/109, Public Record Office, London. James Brown Order Book, vol. 2, October 13, 1784–May 27, 1788.

8. James Brown Order Book, vol. 2, October 13, 1784–May 27, 1788. According to Gilbert, *Thomas Chippendale*, 1:207, these items cost £120 and £64, respectively.

9. Helena Hayward and Pat Kirkham, *William and John Linnell: Eighteenth Century London Furniture Makers*, 2 vols. (London: Studio Vista, 1980), 1:160–61. Gilbert, *Thomas Chippendale*, 1:183, 285, 206–20.

10. James Brown Order Book, vol. 1, January 4, 1782–October 11, 1784; vol. 2, October 13, 1784–May 27, 1788. Estimate Sketchbook, 1784–1787.

11. Timothy H. Breen, "An Empire of Goods: The Anglicization of Colonial America, 1690–1776," *The Journal of British Studies* 25, no. 4 (October 1986): 499. Breen, "Baubles of

Britain," p. 79. Cary Carson, "The Consumer Revolution in Colonial British America. Why Demand?" in *Of Consuming Interests: The Style of Life in the Eighteenth Century*, edited by Ronald Hoffman, Cary Carson, and Peter J. Albert (Charlottesville: University of Virginia Press, 1994), p. 502.

12. James Brown Order Book, vol. 2, October 13, 1784–May 27, 1788. Hayward and Kirkham, *William and John Linnell*, 1: 165. Estimate Sketchbook, 1784–1787.

13. See, for example, advertisements in the *South Carolina Gazette*, October 24, 1781, February 27, 1784, and July 7, 1784. For Blott, see artisan files, Museum of Early Southern Decorative Arts, Winston-Salem, North Carolina.

14. Nathaniel Heyward Receipt, September 5, 1789, box 2, folder 14, Manigault Family Papers, South Caroliniana Library, University of South Carolina, Columbia.

15. James Douglas Account Book, 1784–1792, William L. Clements Library, University of Michigan, Ann Arbor. The recording format in the James Douglas Account Book, listing separately the objects' prices and the packaging and wharfage costs, insures a reliable comparison between Douglas's unit prices and retail prices in London. The tables and related analysis concerning Douglas's suppliers, valuations, and descriptions in the following pages derive from a database compiled by the author from records in the James Douglas Account Book. The two Charleston mercantile firms receiving and selling goods shipped by Douglas were Cochran and William McClure and James Gregorie.

16. Geoffrey Beard and Christopher Gilbert, *Dictionary of English Furniture Makers 1660–1840* (London: W. S. Maney & Son, Ltd., 1986), pp. 693, 700, 730, 976, 986. Pitt & Chessey trade card and William Rawlins trade card, Tradecard Collection, Print Room, British Museum, London.

17. Beard and Gilbert, *Dictionary of English Furniture Makers*, pp. 976–77, 986. Guildhall London Directories, 1781–1790, microfilm, Archive Department, Westminster Public Library, London. Beard and Gilbert, *Dictionary of English Furniture Makers*, p. 934.

18. Beard and Gilbert, *Dictionary of English Furniture Makers*, p. 364; Craftsman card catalogue, Department of Furniture & Woodwork, Victoria and Albert Museum, London.

19. For John Horsley & Son, see Bradford L. Rauschenberg, "Reconsidering Charleston Brass Andirons, Types II and III: An Essay on the Use of Theory Replacement in Material Culture," *Journal of Early Southern Decorative Arts* 17, no. 2 (November 1992): 47. For Taylor & Bailey, see *Kent's London Directory* (1785), Guildhall London Directories, 1781–1790, microfilm, Archive Department.

20. Estimate Sketchbook, 1784–1787. Mabel L. Webber, ed., "The Thomas Elfe Account Book, 1768–1775," *South Carolina Historical and Genealogical Magazine* (hereinafter cited *SCHGM*) 36, no. 1 (January 1935): 9; and 36, no. 2 (April 1935): 63. The prices given for pieces listed in the Thomas Elfe Account Book are approximate pounds sterling conversion of prices in South Carolina pounds. Between 1768 and 1775, seven pounds in South Carolina currency equaled about one pound sterling.

21. "Reprint of the Cabinet-Maker's London Book of Prices," p. 49. Estimate Sketchbook, 1784–1787.

22. "Reprint of the Cabinet-Maker's London Book of Prices," p. 139. Estimate Sketchbook, 1784–1787.

23. Elisabeth Donaghy Garrett, *At Home: The American Family 1750–1870* (New York: Harry N. Abrams, 1990), p. 46.

24. Webber, ed., "Thomas Elfe Account Book," *SCHGM* 36, no. 2 (April 1935): 63; and 37, no. 1 (January 1936): 25. The set ordered in November 1771 cost Thomas Waring a total of £90 South Carolina. The other set ordered in August 1772 cost Elias Ball £85 South Carolina. Estimate Sketchbook, 1784–1787.

25. Estimate Sketchbook, 1784–1787. Gilbert, *Thomas Chippendale*, 1:142.

26. Webber, "Thomas Elfe Account Book," *SCHGM* 36, no. 2 (April 1935): 63.

27. "Reprint of the Cabinet-Maker's London Book of Prices," p. 101. Estimate Sketchbook, 1784–1787. Webber, "Thomas Elfe Account Book," *SCHGM* 35, no. 2 (April 1934): 58.

28. For more on the professionalization and commercialization of leisure activities from sport to cultural events throughout the eighteenth century, see J. H. Plumb, "The Commercialization of Leisure in Eighteenth-century England," in Neil McKendrick, John Brewer, and J. H. Plumb, *The Birth of Consumer Society: The Commercialization of Eighteenth-Century England* (London: Europa Publications Limited, 1982), p. 284.

29. Helga Dittmar, *The Social Psychology of Material Possessions: To Have is To Be* (Hertfordshire, Eng.: Harvester Wheatheaf, 1992), p. 5.

Nancy Goyne Evans. *American Windsor Chairs*. New York: Hudson Hills Press in association with the Henry Francis du Pont Winterthur Museum, 1996. 744 pp.; 25 color and 1,000+ bw illus., 24 maps, checklist of American Windsor craftsmen, 1745–1850, glossary, bibliography, index. $125.00.

One of the more common clichés in the world of American decorative arts scholarship is the greeting of a new publication as "long awaited" or "eagerly anticipated." Rarely, however, has a work been so deserving of either description as is *American Windsor Chairs* by Nancy Goyne Evans. This epic study—the first of three related volumes—brings to fruition nearly thirty years of research that has been tantalizingly revealed to the public over the last several decades in formative lectures and articles. As befits a multidecade research project, the finished book is monumental in scale, measuring more than seven hundred pages in length and weighing in at eight-and-a-half pounds. More importantly, however, *American Windsor Chairs* is weighty in content, skillfully merging traditional decorative arts analysis with doses of history, socioeconomic evaluation, demography, ethnography, and quantification in the form of remarkable physical and documentary evidence.

Book reviews frequently provide a detailed synopsis of the work's story-line or contents; however, in the case of *American Windsor Chairs,* I probably would obfuscate in a few short pages what Evans deftly coordinates in seven hundred. Instead, some generalizations about key ordering concepts and themes will have to suffice. Unlike many earlier Windsor studies, this book is not guided by the conventions of formal analysis; rather, *American Windsor Chairs* is a regional study that seeks to identify local traditions as a means of bringing order to the complex story of Windsor chairmaking in the eastern United States. Interpretive unity is further enhanced by two essential Windsor themes that weave in and out of the text. The first argues that early (pre-1800) American Windsor chair traditions are largely indebted to British craft traditions—an idea suggested by past Windsor historians but never before so clearly presented. Beginning with a consideration of the evolution of the ancient stick stool into the recognizable British turned chair, Evans then usefully builds upon Benno Forman's theories about the development of turnery and joinery customs in seventeenth-century England.

The introductory material not only provides decorative arts readers with a solid foundation upon which to interpret the form but also helps clear up many of the unsubstantiated folk tales and cultural myths that have long colored the Windsor story. The elusive source of the term "Windsor," for instance, is conclusively tied to outdoor garden seating furniture created in the 1720s for Windsor Castle, which should put an end to any speculation that the term reflects an origin in the namesake English town. Similarly strong evidence in the form of copious illustrated examples, documented references, and period paintings and prints charts the development and "refinement" of the design from the decades after 1720—although Evans's dichotomous use of "refined" and "crude" to describe early Windsor designs betrays her stated goal to avoid speculative aesthetic analysis.

In short, the introductory material is highly original and greatly advances current understanding of the Windsor form. Certain ideas are sure to spark constructive debate among Windsor enthusiasts, particularly the implication that the form not only originated but also subsequently evolved in London and the surrounding Thames Valley. British folk or vernacular enthusiasts, notably those who work with the massive body of West Country material, may well be disconcerted by this rather circumscribed notion of urban diffusion. Part of this debate may be fueled by the fact that many American subgroups appear less tied to London customs than to rural British traditions. Complicating Evans's perspective is the sketchy chapter on "Diffusion of the Form Beyond London," which glosses over the myriad British regional traditions identified by recent vernacular furniture historians. In any event, Evans's work stands as a highly useful counterbalance to the recent British work of Bernard D. Cotton, Christopher Gilbert, Claudia Kinmonth, and Thomas Crispin and should inspire an international gathering of the minds—perhaps a symposium—on Anglo-American Windsor traditions.

The main body of the text presents a massive and unparalleled level of regional Windsor analysis. As might be expected, the starting point is the early traditions of Philadelphia, beginning with a splendid overview of the early Philadelphia high-back chair and followed by an exploration of the subsequent developments of the form. Immediately apparent are Evans's boldly dated Windsor chronologies, a major advancement in a field prone to rather haphazard date attributions. After Philadelphia, the study moves into strong explorations of New York and Rhode Island and then into the rest of New England, including an insightful comparison of Connecticut Windsors that links local forms to the hearts-and-crowns turned chair tradition. Each regional section reiterates the primary theme regarding the dependence of early American designs on established British prototypes.

Along the way, readers gain privileged access to the remarkable Windsor literacy that allows Evans to move well beyond formal description and into thoughtful analyses of even the most intricate stylistic and structural developments, such as the progression of individual turned leg elements, seat shapes, and carving, along with parallel developments in construction. The obscure fact is revealed that the diagonal grain orientation of many Windsor seats reflects the most economical way to lay out seat blanks on an uncut board. Similar diagnostic significance is applied to subtle design changes, for instance to the rearward movement of medial braces behind the midpoint of the stretchers on Philadelphia chairs, as well as the curious evolution of arm spurs, which reflect changing ideas about visual weighting and structural integrity. To assist the reader, Evans lays bare her own mental process by comparing and contrasting new concepts with previously illustrated examples.

The second major thesis in *American Windsor Chairs* appears in the latter part of each regional section. It centers around the pronounced American break with British Windsor chairmaking traditions after 1790 and the subsequent emergence of increasingly idiosyncratic Windsor forms. The author tracks the movement away from British Windsor customs, which largely continued to emulate earlier forms, and toward highly innovative designs that sometimes borrowed stylistic details from European classical furniture forms. Here, at last, is a sound argument in favor of the "Americanness" of American Windsor chairs. The analysis of post-revolutionary forms helps put to rest the common but historically inaccurate categorization of Windsor chairs as "stick" furniture. Presented instead is a broader and more sensible inclusion of all sorts of turned, plank-seated chairs, including "fancy" chairs, which are excluded from most Windsor studies but which typically represent the product of Windsor shops. Readers thus are not only given insightful reinterpretations of early American Windsor makers, such as Joseph Henzey and Francis Trumble in Philadelphia and the Ash brothers in New York, but are also introduced to later, unrecognized makers such as John Murdick of Strasburg, Pennsylvania, Elijah Stanton of Conway, New Hampshire, and William Coles of Springfield, Ohio.

The massive body of material in *American Windsor Chairs* is made more user friendly by Evans's formulaic—and I use this word in a positive light—arrangement of each section. Beginning with a brief regional description, often with a socioeconomic focus, the material then generally leads into a chronological exploration of Windsor chairs, with each progressive stage further subdivided into particular examinations of forms and even singular elements or ideas. Especially helpful along the way are the repeated cross-references to earlier illustrations and ideas, which emphasize the organic nature of the American Windsor tradition. Evans repeatedly alludes to the widespread influence of Philadelphia traditions on other areas, and she reveals the curious evolution of Rhode Island Windsors from highly idiosyncratic designs produced during the culturally unstable 1780s and 1790s to more familiar and emulative designs made during the more stable early decades of the nineteenth century.

As with any study, there are areas of concern in *American Windsor Chairs*. Although perhaps not meant to be read narratively, the material does reveal unmistakable ebbs and flows. For example, the explorations of late Windsor chairmaking traditions in New York are surprisingly brief, as is the consideration of the extensive fancy chair legacy of early nineteenth-century Baltimore. Another minor criticism surrounds Evans's confusing and, arguably, oxymoronic term "vernacular-chair industry" in the section on Providence, Rhode Island. More problematic is the description of the Windsor customs west of Philadelphia: "Chairmakers working within the Pennsylvania German craft tradition produced most Windsor furniture in Pennsylvania during the second half of the eighteenth century" (p. 107). In fact, the chairs illustrated differ only marginally from earlier, British-inspired Philadelphia examples. The accompanying text likewise fails to substantiate the use of cultural modifiers such as "Pennsylvania-German" and "Germanic." Lacking further evidence, these southern Pennsylvania Windsors are perhaps better understood as Anglo-Philadelphia expressions with a slight German accent.

Most troublesome is the final section of the book. After more than five hundred pages on the Windsor chairs of the mid-Atlantic and New England states, only one hundred pages are devoted to chair production in "other" regions, including the South (which not only consists of the coastal or "Old" South but also the Gulf Coast and lower Mississippi Valley) and the massive Midwest. Also grouped into this regionally confused last section is an examination of the influence of American Windsors on Upper and Lower Canada. Geographically and demographically, all of these places deserve a more thorough analysis; moreover, the relegation of regions outside of the Northeast to the "back of the book" represents a tired and highly questionable American decorative arts practice. Even a cursory examination of the Windsor customs of these regions suggests the potential for the same intensive analysis, including the identification of intra- and interregional practices, afforded to northeastern traditions. Readers are given a county-by-county overview of the Windsor traditions in Connecticut, whereas the non-northeastern sections in general are superficially treated. Admittedly, the mere mention of the South, the Midwest, and Canada puts Evans light years ahead of earlier scholars, but the unbalanced attention only prolongs stale decorative arts stereotypes about these cultural centers.

Do not, however, let that criticism detract from the overall significance of this publication. In the fall of 1997, Windsor enthusiasts will have the further pleasure of reading Evans's second volume in the trilogy, *American Windsor Furniture: Specialized Forms*. A concluding volume tentatively entitled *American Windsor Furniture: From Craft Shop to Consumer* will follow, a work that ultimately places the greatest interpretive burden on Evans's shoulders. Despite brief forays into other historical methodologies, volumes 1 and 2 are primarily quantified, diagnostic analyses of regional Windsor customs. The last book, on the other hand, aims to provide the cultural synthesis lacking in the first two. In particular, volume 3 will provide much-needed interpretive and contextual theorizing on makers, patrons, shop organization, and craft practices. Also to be tackled, I hope, is a detailed consideration of the Windsor trade's complex role in America's emerging national industrial framework and related analysis in the areas of competition, partnerships, and artisan movement. Until the arrival of this concluding statement, however, readers have plenty to dazzle their eyes and challenge their brains in *American Windsor Chairs*.

Jonathan Prown
Colonial Williamsburg Foundation

Jeffrey P. Greene. *American Furniture of the 18th Century: History, Technique, Structure.* Newtown, Conn.: Taunton Press, 1996. 311 pp.; 274 color and bw illus., 96 line drawings, appendixes, glossary, bibliography, index. $45.00.

In his introduction, Jeffrey Greene says that *American Furniture of the 18th Century* "is intended to present the craftsman's art to the connoisseur and connoisseurship to the craftsman" (p. 2). This statement describes just the book I needed and could not find thirty years ago, the one I wanted for students two decades ago, and one I would still enjoy reading. Because I assume that the readers of this journal are often asked for book suggestions and courses of study about American furniture, I read Greene with two audiences in mind: the scholar as well as the student.

I would have welcomed the inclusive survey Greene presents in the first part of this book thirty years ago; now much is redundant. Then, only Albert Sack aesthetically sorted and evaluated objects in *Fine Points of Furniture: Early American* (1950). Since 1970 and the publication of John Kirk's *Early American Furniture,* however, furniture aesthetics has been well taught in print. In the last quarter century, thorough studies have been published that present connoisseurship and furniture history to all, including craftsmen. Many, however, are specific to a collection or a region, and thus a general work is welcome. Greene promises even more, however—a craftsman's view. This perspective has only been attempted a few times in the past. For connoisseurs interested in craft, Frances Gruber Safford assembled a fine seventeenth-century joinery show accompanied by a catalogue at the Metropolitan Museum of Art in 1972. Robert F. Trent did the job very well for upholstery through a symposium, his writings, and with a show in 1983 at the Connecticut Historical Society. Philip Zea's essay, "Construction Methods and Materials," in Brock Jobe and this author's *New England Furniture, the Colonial Era* (1984), provides a craftsman's view but is limited to New England.

Greene divides his book into three parts, dealing discretely with style, methods and materials, and sample objects. He sees the study of American furniture as encompassing the views of antiquarians, furniture historians, and craftsmen, or as he also says, connoisseurs and craftsmen. I usually characterize the several approaches similarly: that of the antiquarian (homage-history), the historian (furniture-history), material culturist (culture-talk), eye-oriented connoisseur (exemplified for me by Kirk, thus Kirk-speak), and the artisan-centered view (epitomized by the late Benno Forman, hence Forman-focus). Greene's idea of treating the views of the connoisseur, historian, and artisan hints at a welcome integration of Kirk-speak and Forman-focus.

Greene usually avoids homage-history. He neither promises nor usually presents culture-talk. He recognizes that furniture history is more than style-sorting and handles styles fairly but not always accurately. I would choose Oscar P. Fitzgerald's *Four Centuries of American Furniture* (1995) over part one of Greene, although Greene's is a prettier book.

When Greene attempts Kirk-speak, it comes out as dealerese. He says furniture built by traditional methods is "furniture that has a soul," objects are "refined" and "well-proportioned," Peter Blin is a "consummate craftsman," and, of a Hadley chest, "its carving was remarkable." A global search for the word "refined" while the manuscript was in the computer would have helped to delete some of this tone. I fault the editor.

Sometimes Greene's approach is parochial. "American craftsmen, inspired by English styles, infused a purity of line and a refined sense of proportion into their designs." He sees European work as "plagued" by ornament while enthusing that American furniture "had a spirit and clarity that was missing from the English pieces on which it was based" (p. 5). Not long ago, all vernacular furniture, American and British, brought yawns from British furniture historians, so we might overlook Greene's American bias.

I become disconcerted when seventeenth-century stools are called "practical" and when "more conventional" modifies chairs of the era. I am further discomforted when Greene presents cane chairs as a "subset" of banister backs, or when he saddles art history with such phrases as "low, solid and horizontal format" and "the observer cannot help but wonder how their creators were inspired." When speaking of stain and paint, he confuses homage-history with history: "Historians all too often attempt to find serious reasons for every aspect of early American life, as if these [Puritans] were dour souls who needed a solid reason for every action." He continues: "the long New England winters called for something to brighten them up. To deny these people their spontaneity robs their surviving work of some of the creativity and individualism that is inherent in any handcraft" (p. 15). What historian speaks of "dour souls"? Greene writes, "New Englanders found themselves . . . struggling to hold onto Puritan ideals while becoming increasingly prosperous" (p. 19). (And I thought "becoming increasingly prosperous" was their ideal. Well, we disagree.) Unlike Greene, I think regionalism was still strong as the nineteenth century began. And so on. China tables are not, as Greene defines them, "tea tables in the Chinese manner" (p. 70). He should have known, before undertaking a book like this, that though there was furniture "in the Chinese manner," the "china" in china table refers to porcelain, as in the cups, teapots, and other wares displayed on the table. Greene undertook a huge task—his book is very inclusive—but he bit off more than he can chew or I can swallow.

He does well including various design terms, something not easily done, though he may be too inclusive in defining "Brewster" and "Carver" as terms for chairs. I wish he had dated the nonperiod terms he defines so that the reader would know when the term originated or when it was used. He felicitously describes a William and Mary case piece as an "orderly display of drama" but continues: "In subtle ways, the vertical mass of these pieces was made apparent. Feet and bases were designed to show that they carried weight. It was as if Enlightenment logic sought to make it evident that designers went to great lengths to achieve Baroque drama" (p. 17).

The important element of Greene's approach is in "explaining the techniques of the period furniture maker"—Forman-focus in print. Not until 1981 did Forman's "The Origins of the Joined Chest of Drawers" appear in the *Nederlands Kunsthistorisch Jaarboek*. Much of his work waited for his spiritual heir and scholarly descendant, Robert Trent, who, with Robert St. George, put together Forman's research in *American Seating Furniture, 1690–1730* (1988). In lieu of craft-oriented reading, my peculiar road to furniture research was to dust the American furniture at the Museum of Fine Arts, Boston, in return for being allowed to examine objects to see how they were made. As I dusted, I asked myself, "Why did he (the craftsman) do it like that?"

I read Greene while asking the same question. I looked for Forman-focus. The summary on the back of the book jacket says: "In the second part, he explains and illustrates the techniques of the period furniture maker, including joinery and authentic construction; carving, turning and inlay. . . ." As I read part two, I kept in mind the question I had asked while dusting. Greene, billed as "a self-taught furniture maker," could be expected to speak to this self-taught furniture historian in craftsman's terms. I listened for the craftsman's voice that I hear from Allan Breed of York, Maine. Breed and I occasionally disagree about period methods, but he gives me a craftsman's view.

Greene's discussion of the dovetail shows a limited view of period craft. This criticism may be picky, but I don't think the dovetail enabled, as Greene says, "drawers to be built of very thin wood, because they no longer needed to be nailed together" (p. 18). I think the craftsman's material drove the craftsman's joint. The change from joinery to cabinetry was not "*brought about* by the use of the dovetail joint" (p. 19; my italics); rather, cabinetry was *brought about* by broad timbers. Dovetailing was the craftsman's response to a material then new to the English woodworker—wide boards from wood shipped from the Americas.

Englishmen had complained about their joined furniture and the lack of furniture woods. Then pine from New England, black walnut from southern colonies, and mahogany from the Caribbean—all in unprecedented widths—arrived in woodworkers' shops in London and America. I think Greene fails to identify with the period craftsman who finally was able to make furniture with wide boards. We know that craftsmen found the raw material amazing. Joiners, almost upon landing in America, changed their technique of forming the tops for lift-lid chests, eschewing the familiar joined lids for board lids. Greene addresses American native hardwoods as being less easily riven but readily sawn. He misses the point entirely. He refers to the adoption of native hardwoods, saying it "coincided with the emerging tastes in furniture aesthetics" (p. 116). I would suggest it more than coincided.

Greene contrasts enclosing a joined house frame with enclosing a joined chest. Evidently unaware of historic building practices in timber-poor Britain, he mentions that English timber frame houses were "covered by a sheathing that became the walls and roof" (p. 7). Actually, house frames, like joined chests, were filled in—with wattle and daub, lath and plaster, or brick. Sheathing was rare in Britain but common in New England, where the weather was colder and wood was plentiful.[1]

Occasionally, Greene ignores history. Stating "it is not known for certain what kind of stains (if any) were used in 17th-century America," he then imagines the use of stain "to impart at least an even tone if not darken the wood" (p. 15). He rejects the idea of any furniture being left by the maker without a finish, because "finish would have protected and enhanced their work" (p. 15). I hear the voice of a modern craftsman who cannot believe that earlier craftsmen would do anything he would not. I want their voices, however, not his.

He omits Windsor chairs from the book and does not address stick construction; yet, stick construction has relevance for round mortises and tenons, as on the turned legs of high chests. Greene features a veneered high chest on turned legs from the Museum of Fine Arts, Boston, but misses the opportunity to discuss the cabinetmaker's problem (pp. 218–19). He speaks of the legs as design elements, with words like "drama" and "spectacular," but not as structural elements. He notes a "rare combination of construction methods," saying that the rear legs are set into glue blocks, and the front legs into corner posts (the front legs into the skirt go unmentioned) but, alas, makes no other comment. He seems unaware of the structural challenge posed by such a high chest base. He comments that the contour of the stretchers imparts a "unifying effect . . . needed to put these legs in context and have them make sense in relation to the whole" (p. 30) but says nothing about the stretchers holding the base together. Could such turned legs endure without stretchers tying them together at their ankles?

He actually avoids talking craft and craftsmen. Choosing to illustrate a Joseph Hosmer-made high chest from Concord, Massachusetts, he does not note its square feet (p. 55). Those feet probably indicate that Hosmer had no lathe upon which to turn them; therefore, Hosmer had to obtain the turned drops for the skirt from a turner. That's Forman-focus.

To whom, then, is Greene talking? In part two—"The Methods and Materials of the 18th-Century Cabinetmaker"—phrases like "can be used to" or "it is easier to" read like a manual for woodworkers. His five appendixes are: wood and wood movement, a list of period publications, resins, colorants, and finishes. He advocates (p. 178) leaving the turner's pattern uncut, and transferring the design to the turning blank from a drawing on wood. But was that period practice? I doubt an eighteenth-century turner transferred the pattern as depicted in the illustrations. I suspect the turner cut out his flat pattern and then worked the wood largely by eye. Greene's illustrated caliper-check would strike him as strange, wasteful, and superfluous. Part two does not explain the product or period crafts to the connoisseur.

If not part two, then perhaps part three—"Examples of Style and Structure"—with its text, color illustrations, and exploded drawings might explain the craftsman's point of view. Alas, the first piece, a chest with drawers, appears in blurred color, its maple surface reworked and, as Greene says, "probably painted originally." Then why choose it for color reproduction? The one-inch square drawing above the text is so tiny and light that it offers no assistance to the reader of the text below. The reader must turn the page to find its full-page drawing—opposite text on a dressing table. The dressing table's structural notes also share the page with a one-inch drawing, leaving its full-sized drawing opposite another fuzzy photo on the next two pages. Part three is thus poorly designed and, at least in my copy, includes some poor color reproductions. The drawings in their large manifestations, however, are wonderful.

Many of the illustrations are very good; most drawings are clear and have excellent graphic explanations. (A Henry Sargent painting on p. 102 is printed in reverse.) The time-line endpapers are a fine idea, but the

American line (the others are English and French) could use more than six illustrations for two hundred years.

The book makes good use of sidebars, some of which are clear and concise. One has important design points of furniture styles, another clarifies style names, and one lists the time required to build furniture (unfortunately restricted to the federal era). One drawn sidebar depicts ball-and-claw foot variations; another, federal card table shapes. Some sidebars, however, seem superfluous: for example, Chippendale and the law (the Englishman and English customs law), and French polishing, which Greene notes was first described in print in 1825, well after the eighteenth century. Chapter six of part one is entitled "Revisiting Ancient Splendor: American Empire (1810–1830)," going well beyond the parameters of the book's title. This publication just attempts too many things.

Greene is not for the reader of *American Furniture*. If I belabor its problems, I do so to make clear why I do not recommend it for students. We need an exhibition and catalogue on eighteenth-century cabinetmaking for museum-goers curious about how objects were made and to show the relationship of aesthetics to craft. By comparing similar objects (for example, glue-blocked case bottoms and facades), viewers could discover the same hand at work on two objects and a variety of shops at work on lookalikes. We also need more exploded models, such as those Allan Breed made for the "Portsmouth Furniture: Masterworks from the New Hampshire Seacoast" exhibition in 1993. The exploded drawings in Greene's book are its strongest asset.

I am giving this book to a friend (who will enjoy it) who repairs antique furniture and will love the drawings, and who can readily find connoisseurship elsewhere in his library. We still need the book Greene promised.

Myrna Kaye
Lexington, Massachusetts

1. If I seem unfair in mentioning lids on joined chests and framed house construction in a review of a book on eighteenth-century furniture, note that Greene's first chapter covers 1607–1690 under the rubric "Prelude to Change."

Pat Kirkham. *Charles and Ray Eames: Designers of the Twentieth Century.* Cambridge, Mass.: The MIT Press, 1995. x + 486 pp.; numerous color and bw illus., chronology, bibliography, index. $55.00.

If you live in America, it's a safe bet that you've sat on a piece of Eames furniture. Most decorative arts scholars know the designs of Charles and Ray Eames intimately, and their status as landmark individuals in furniture history is taken for granted. The most renowned pieces, however, have also become the most commonplace examples of institutional furnishing—the 1946 DCW or "potato chip" chair in bent plywood and its metal-legged counterpart, the DCM; the 1955 stackable plastic side chair; the 1956 lounge chair and ottoman, a unique blend of the progressive and the luxurious; and the Tandem Sling airport seating of 1962. All pervade the American landscape, and we are all conscious of them to a greater or lesser degree as characteristic furniture of the postwar period. Most of us don't realize, however, that we have also seen Eames films and perhaps visited an Eames exhibition. In her recent study, Pat Kirkham (formerly of DeMontfort University, Leicester, and currently at the Bard Graduate Center for Studies in the Decorative Arts in New York City) addresses the whole panorama of Eames design in an even-handed treatment that emphasizes diversity and biographical backdrop and focuses more on process than on product.

Kirkham construes process broadly, and in many ways her book is a biography that focuses on Charles and Ray as a married couple as well as a design team. The book begins by comparing the respective childhoods of the two artists, in spite of the relative dearth of biographical information on Ray's early life. Kirkham's narrative assumes an almost affectionate tone, partially because she gleaned a good amount of her information from discussions with Ray herself. As a result, the Eameses as a couple undergo a metamorphosis in Kirkham's book. Gone is the traditional vision of Charles as the mathematically inclined architect of design whose keen sense of corporate demand ensured his success in the financial, as well as aesthetic, domain. In its stead we get a personal picture of a fun-loving couple, whose creative energy could just as easily be expressed in the impromptu invention of Halloween masks as in the design of storage units. One never loses sight of the Eames collaboration as an interaction between soul mates of the most intimate and mutually encouraging variety. The Eameses' "sense of fun" to which Kirkham repeatedly refers comes across in playful descriptions of studio debates, game playing, and Christmas cards designed by the couple. This image of a frolicsome, dynamic design duo palliates the Eameses' reputation as the crafters of a design aesthetic for American big businesses. At times a bit too much confetti is thrown, and the "sense of fun," for all its recreational ease, becomes an urgent mantra drowning out a less flattering story about Charles as the corporate design king. No matter how many times we read about his nice black Ford, chosen "only for beauty and good design, never for ostentation" (p. 61), it's hard to forget the aura of wealth and good, old-fashioned capitalistic zeal that surrounded Eames production.

Kirkham's study of "functioning decoration," a phrase invented by the Eameses to describe their own novel use of imported and improvised knick-knackery, is also marked by an overgenerous handling of her subjects' taste. Just what is meant by this seeming oxymoron is unclear, and in interpreting it Kirkham is ambitious rather than precise. For the Eameses, functioning decoration was a design strategy in which "objects were taken out of their usual contexts for visual effect" (p. 143). Their home was a pastiche of elements drawn from the realm of modern design and art, "the repertoire of white bourgeois taste" (p. 183), and a variety of traditional and touristic crafts idioms. They might juxtapose a Kandinsky painting, a run-of-the-mill glass candelabrum, and Native American basketwork, each element in the ensemble adding to the visual impact of the others.

Kirkham's goal is to use the concept of "functioning decoration" to tie together the Eameses' wide-ranging and often kitschy personal taste with their more high-minded design projects. To some extent, the connection is convincingly drawn, but the very flexibility of the idea inhibits its interpretive power. For instance, Kirkham's account of the antecedents of the Eames house interior is very broad, touching upon nineteenth-century parlors, Victoriana, the arts and crafts movement, *and* "Mexicana" revivalism. Doubtless some or all of these historical moments may have influenced the Eameses, who apparently cared little for historical and geographical specificity. The vagaries of their decorating taste, however, are transported directly and uncritically into the book, duplicating their inconsistencies rather than dispelling them. In the process, Kirkham assumes a coherence that simply isn't there. What exactly is the relationship between the Eameses' obsession with masks, their insertion of whimsical elements into Herman Miller advertisements (like a ghostly image of Charles, sitting on the floor and proudly holding a fish up for inspection), their collection of Kachina dolls, and their commercial line of toys and children's furniture? Despite Kirkham's suggestion that "objects can and do carry and take on myriad meanings" (p. 175), such seemingly trivial manifestations of design are not rigorously analyzed. The inclusion of such diversity under the broad rubric of "functioning decoration" does little beyond emphasizing the diversity itself, without giving us insight into the underlying cultural assumptions behind the Eameses' ideas about the decorative.

Kirkham's biographical method is more effective when it is put at the service of one of the central projects of the book—the recuperation of Ray as an active participant in the Eames collaboration. There are a number of strategies Kirkham employs to this end. One of the most imaginative is an analysis of Ray's characteristic style of dress. Her trademark A-line dresses and jumpers are read here as social texts. This outfit, which she wore into old age, becomes in Kirkham's reading a site of negotiation where a woman in a male work environment could play with the signifiers of femininity to her own advantage. The denim and gingham fabrics favored by Ray connoted work, and the skirts were not so frilly or confining as to inhibit her movements or to impeach her authority in the workplace. At the same time, they were not so masculine as to raise questions about her sexuality. This section is remarkable for its methodological novelty in the wake of more conservative readings of the Eames design.

Much more traditional is Kirkham's hirstory of Ray's life in the pre-Charles era, when she emerged as a fully formed modernist acquainted with contemporary fine art idioms. As a member of the American Abstract Artists group, a student of Hans Hoffman, a friend of Lee Krasner, and an accomplished, published graphic design artist, Ray takes her place among the members of the New York avant-garde. Indeed, in Kirkham's analysis, her constant grappling with modern forms is largely responsible for the characteristic, undulating shapes of Eames furniture. We see, for instance, that when Charles was pushing the envelope on plywood technology and demonstrating its uses to the military in the form of leg splints, Ray was investigating the formal possibilities of the medium in sculpture.

At times Kirkham's efforts to establish Ray's prowess as an artist in command of "modern structure" stretch farther than they have to. Trying to work the New York avant-garde connection to Ray's benefit, Kirkham overemphasizes the affinity between her work and that of her teacher, Hans Hoffman. With the paradigmatic DCW, Kirkham sees the undulating forms of the seat and back in terms of Hoffman's "push and pull" painting techniques. Although the push and pull effect may be there, anyone familiar with Hoffman's work will pause at the comparison, wondering how its keyed-up colors and rectilinear patches actually bear any similarity to the biomorphism of the DCW. The argument is well made, nevertheless, that Ray was an accomplished and respected designer in her own right and that she was greatly responsible for the look of much of what has been attributed to Charles alone.

Kirkham's personal approach, typified by this concentrated analysis of Ray's early years, is justified by the fact that she is covering well-traveled ground. In addition to their appearance in virtually every survey of postwar design, the Eameses have been the subject of monographic texts since an issue of *Architectural Design* was devoted to them in 1966. Most significant among these historical accounts is *Eames Design* (1989) by one-time Eames office staff members John and Marilyn Neuhart in consultation with Ray. Kirkham's book offers itself as a complement to this more encyclopedic treatment. Overall, the book steers clear of specific historical detail, instead emphasizing the designers' personal outlook. Unlike the chronological *Eames Design*, the book is organized according to the Eameses' various enterprises—architecture, furniture, exhibitions, and films. Within each of these categories, Kirkham tries to fill the gaps left by earlier, more focused studies. For example, the intensive scrutiny of the Case Study House #8 available in James Steele's recent book, *Eames House* (1994), is not repeated here. Instead, Kirkham compares it with early architectural designs by Charles and the contemporary but less well-known Entenza house (Case Study House #9), designed in collaboration with Eliel Saarinen.

Readers interested primarily in furniture may be disappointed by the relatively light coverage (sixty of the book's nearly four hundred pages) of it. In her rapid overview, however, Kirkham provides an important corrective to previously authoritative texts, such as Arthur Drexler's catalogue for the Museum of Modern Art (1977). She places projects in their immediate context with brief histories of salient institutions and movements, such as the Cranbrook Academy of Art, California modern architecture, and the Herman Miller Furniture Company. Similarly, she compares significant Eames pieces to immediate precedents and contemporary works by designers like Marcel Breuer, Harry Bertoia, and Isamu Noguchi. She departs from the pure stylistic analysis of Drexler's text and emphasizes the external dialogue that fed into Charles and Ray's collaborations.

In some cases, though, Kirkham could do more in the way of analysis. While discussing the 1951 DCM, she remarks on the paradoxical reception of the side chair, which rapidly became "visible in design conscious circles and invisible in the ordinary world" (p. 236). Despite (or perhaps because of) its ubiquity, the DCM ceased to register as progressive design and instead became a fully normalized part of the American institutional landscape. The reader, however, is left to wonder whether this invisibility was intentional. Was this trait particular to the Eames design project? Or was it a larger phenomenon, symptomatic of the design climate of the 1950s?

In another tantalizing passage, Kirkham mentions a path-not-taken in table design. Although the famous elliptical coffee table of 1951—a landmark of postwar modernist design—is always seen in basic black, it was originally intended to have optional silver, gold, and patterned laminates. These planned surface treatments, she claims, "illustrate that there were more varied tendencies within modernist design than is often supposed" (p. 244). This claim is challenging and important, but Kirkham does not pursue it as far as she could. She refrains from extended speculation on the marketing potential of laminated pieces, closing the discussion abruptly. She argues that such decorative treatments were considered "vulgar" at the time and so would probably not have been viable. Possibly, but if so, then aren't the laminates simply an aberration from modernism rather than an alternative strand of it? Kirkham identifies the most interesting aspects of the Eameses' interaction with the broader world of design, but her intense concentration on Charles and Ray prevents her from capitalizing on her ideas.

More satisfying is the discussion of the critical reaction to the Eames collaboration. For example, one of the first applications of their new plywood technology resulted in the design of stackable children's chairs, stools, and tables in 1945. Made of inexpensive material and stained in bright colors, this "modern design" had a slight wrinkle—a hand hole in the back of the chairs in the shape of a heart. Although critics admired the chairs for their demonstration of pure plastic form, the heart was called an "absurdly romantic symbol" (p. 216) and was attributed to Ray's sentimental disposition. The assumption was that Ray, as a woman, had a greater proclivity for romanticism than did her more restrained husband. Kirkham impeaches this line of reasoning, demonstrating not only that hearts have long ornamented the backs of chairs but that *both* Charles and Ray used the motif throughout their careers. At this point her argument shines. The heart chairs exposed certain rules governing modern design and the inflexibility of those rules. Onto the Eames collaboration, critics grafted dichotomies of the scientific and the sentimental, the modern and the nostalgic, that were gendered at their base. By showing that both Charles and Ray shared responsibility for their designs, Kirkham exposes the binary categorizations of modernist criticism, which have placed Ray in the background.

The most successful sections of the book, and those that will ensure its importance as a reference text for scholars of design, deal with Eames films and exhibitions. Here Kirkham is in largely uncharted territory, and she adroitly communicates the designers' development of these media for the presentation of information in a persuasive and appealing manner. Some examples will be surprisingly familiar to readers who only know Charles and Ray for their chairs. Many will have seen the exhibition *Mathematica*, still on exhibit at the California Museum of Science and Industry and the Boston Museum of Science, in which a random cascade of plastic balls forms a predicted bell curve; or the charming film *Powers of Ten*, in which the "camera" zooms in and out at exponential speed on a photo of a sleeping man, showing him at galactic and molecular scale. The inclusion of this material is instructive, particularly in that it sheds light on the ideas underlying Eames furniture design. For example, many of their films take a "how-to" approach to their subjects, reinforcing the Eameses' consistent fascination with process. Similarly, their 1964 exhibition *Think*, shown at the IBM pavilion at the New York World's Fair, entertainingly packaged science for mass consumption. In the same way, technology was foregrounded in Eames furniture as an attractive means to a more comfortable public environment.

With the inclusion of such material, Kirkham does justice to the diversity and scope of Eames production, finding new resonances within their work. By recovering the couple's film and exhibition work, *Charles and Ray Eames: Designers of the Twentieth Century* shows that new methodologies can cast even the most canonical figures in a fresh, new light. Kirkham effectively combines personal anecdote and historical analysis, breathing new life into the biographical mode. In addition, the recounting of Ray's prowess and experience with modern design introduces gender dynamics into furniture history. New avenues of inquiry into Eames design might move forward from this point, investigating not only the personalities behind the objects but the social function of the objects themselves. This book proffers valuable, new strategies of looking at modernism and its favored designers.

Glenn Adamson and Sarah Rich
Yale University

Donald L. Fennimore. *Metalwork in Early America: Copper and Its Alloys from the Winterthur Collection*. Winterthur, Del.: Winterthur Museum, 1996. 472 pp.; numerous color and bw illus., glossary, bibliography, index. Distributed by Antique Collectors' Club. $69.50.

The literature on base metals in America is, like the noblest metal, where you find it. A great deal of information on copper, brass, pewter, and pewter-like alloys, for example, can be found in the publications of the Rushlight Club, because those metals were used to fashion lighting devices; similarly, much of interest about brass is found in the bulletins of the National Association of Watch and Clock Collectors. There are also any number of monographs on fireplace equipment, firefighting equipment, kitchenalia, bells, and so on, in many of which the interested student is compelled to reconstruct the absent source references. Conversely, the subject is sometimes organized by material, as by the Schiffers in *The Brass Book* (Exton, Pa.: Schiffer Publishing, 1978) or by the engaging Henry Kauffman in *American Copper and Brass* (New York: Bonanza Books, 1979). Authoritative articles on the subject are distributed in the pages of *Connoisseur*, *Apollo*, and *Antiques*, and frequently the last word on a particular facet was written more than half a century ago.

Donald L. Fennimore has done us all a tremendous service in producing *Metalwork in Early America: Copper and Its Alloys*. As curator of a history museum with a varied collection, my first reaction to this handsome volume was relief at finally having a reliable crib sheet with which to write labels. It is perhaps more fitting to say that the work is a distinguished resource filling a long-vacant niche. Furniture historians and collectors will find in the "Hardware" section a most extensive and authoritative review of cabinet handles (drawer pulls) and casters, hinges, tacks, keyhole escutcheons, and finials. These items once contributed a great deal to the presentation and cost of furniture and are still acknowledged to be significant (how important are original brasses?), but they are rarely understood. Seventeen entries document cabinet handles and escutcheons found on American furniture from 1680 to 1830; in addition to presenting a chronological series of authentic examples, the entries expand on the makers, middlemen, and consumers who made use of these essential ornaments. The fireplace equipment and lighting entries will also interest furniture collectors who have encountered related examples, usually grouped under the rubric of "smalls" and accorded little attention other than as complements. In *Metalwork in Early America* the reader will also find lucid descriptions of technological change, shop structure, and trade practice, processes that parallel or intercept furniture manufacture in a variety of ways and are thus of great interest to the furniture scholar.

Although not, as the author points out in his introduction, a comprehensive history of the subject, *Metalwork in Early America* provides informed access to the encyclopedic Winterthur collection, which means it very nearly amounts to the same thing. Fennimore begins his introduction with a brief description of the nature of the collection. The truly extraordinary depth of the museum's holdings is further suggested in the catalogue entries with references to, for example, the twenty-three examples in the collection related to the seventeenth-century European candlestick described in entry 101. The next three chapters provide some of the context within which the author has interpreted the collection. The first, "Mining and Manufacture," describes alloying, the mining and smelting of ore, and the casting and finishing of brass and copper objects. The second, "Marketing," describes the kind and quantity of goods (particularly English) available in America, shipping, the relationship between English manufactures and American retailers, and the use of pattern books. The third, "Marking and Metallurgy," addresses the use of manufacturers' marks on English and American goods and the alloys of copper.

There are 322 individual entries on objects from the Winterthur collection. In addition to the name, place of origin, date range, dimensions, and material, each header also lists the proportions of metals present in the alloy—the result of testing in the Winterthur laboratory. The entries are for the most part about three hundred words in length and are laid out with admirable clarity—one per page with accompanying illustration(s). Within this disciplined format, the author set himself the task of integrating information on "function, use, technology, economics, trade, and history," then met this ambitious goal using to a considerable degree the words of "makers, users, and social historians first connected with the objects" (p. 10). In large part, the tasks both of description and appreciation are assumed by the photographs of George J. Fistrovich. Sumptuous, sensuous, and dignified, Fistrovich's photographs, in addition to recording the visual "facts" about each object, capture the fashionability and smartness these objects once conveyed to their owners. The photographs are accorded ample space on the page (see, for example, the full-page illustration of a furniture hinge on page 411), and the 300-line printing yields an admirable clarity and resolution to the images. I would fault only the reversed contrast of the engraving on the tobacco boxes in entries 208 and 209 and the rotation of the images of the medals in entries 222, 224, and 225, minor quibbles that perhaps stand out only in contrast to the uniformly excellent integration of images and words on the page.

The author divided the objects into six groups according to function: food and drink, heating, lighting, measurement, personal, and hardware. Within the entries, Fennimore has included dozens of narratives on such topics as the rules of the Worshipful Company of Founders for its members, the development of burning fluids for use in lamps, and the exotic alloy paktong. The author has carefully avoided redundancy in the catalogue entries while relating these accounts, at the same time eschewing tedious cross-referencing; the entries stand alone, and they function together. On occasion the particulars of one of these narratives appear out of order (for instance, the statement on the real significance of the Argand lamp occurs in entry 167, the seventh in a series of spirit lamps), but the entries are so engaging that few readers will resist reading all that relate to a particular form anyway.

Among the many narratives woven into the catalogue is the account of the trade in copper and brass by William Cooper Hunneman (1769–1856) of Boston. William Hunneman is best known for the andirons and occasional tea kettle marked with his surname, which appear occasionally on the market; his surviving account books document an extensive and varied manufactory located first in Boston's industrial North End and later in Roxbury.[1] There were several aspects to Hunneman's business. He advertised in 1812 that he intended to "keep on hand a general assortment of Copper and Brass articles, commonly wanted for house, ship or mechanical uses."[2] Among the household goods noted in his account books were andirons, tea kettles, and warming pans, marked examples of which are included in the Winterthur collection.[3] Hunneman sold these goods to retail customers, to Boston hardware dealers like John Odin, and to other Boston founders, including William Holmes. To Holmes, Hunneman also sold "andiron work" (unfinished castings) by the pound. The foundry floor must have been dominated by sleigh bells during the winter months, since Hunneman was selling them, to Odin and others, by the dozen and gross. Hunneman provided goods to some of Boston's ship chandlers and also manufactured specialized products for the Navy Yard in Charlestown and for the young American fleet, particularly during the War of 1812. He outfitted the gun decks of the legendary ships of that conflict—the *Hornet*, the *Wasp*, the *Frolic*, the *Constitution*—with tools and fasteners made necessarily of brass and copper to avoid sparks and provided them, as well, with lightning rods and fire engines. The fire engines Hunneman supplied the navy, at a cost of $500 to $700 each, he produced under a patent originally held by Jacob Perkins and Allan Pollock; Pollock's share of the first two engines sold, Hunneman noted in 1803, was $100 each.[4] Hunneman advertised in 1812 that he had already sold twenty-five engines, mostly to Massachusetts, Maine, and New Hampshire communities, though one went to Petersburg, Virginia.[5] By his own and other accounts, Hunneman made a superior product; when Concord, Massachusetts, bought one of his engines around 1817, its stiff action so puzzled the members of the fire company, who were used to a small and weak pump, that they asked the maker to come out and examine it. Satisfied by Hunneman's explanation, the fire company found that, used properly, the new pump threw a stream as high as the belfry of the meetinghouse.[6]

The "articles . . . for mechanical uses" Hunneman advertised included a number of stills for Boston's busy distillers, machine work for the Franklin Cotton Manufacturing Company, and, of special interest to readers of this journal, clock and timepiece work for the Roxbury clockmakers. Hunneman sold unfinished gear castings and plates by the pound to Simon Willard, William Cummens, Aaron Willard, Aaron Willard, Jr., Elnathan Taber, and John Willard, as well as circles (bezels for the dial cover) and side ornaments (side arms) for patent timepieces, although he did not seem to provide clock balls (finials), hinges, keyhole escutcheons, or pendulum bobs.

Before the famous textile mills in Lowell and Lawrence transformed the nature of production and labor in America, the base metal trade pioneered many of the production and marketing strategies commonly thought of as artifacts of the Industrial Revolution. Several current research projects into New England base metal workers promise to shed further light on the methods, motivations, and products of American preindustrial manufacturers and, by comparison, may shed light on the development of furniture making. John Hamilton is researching a specialized and complex manufactory that was developed by gunsmith Edwin Wesson (1811–1849) of Grafton, Massachusetts, between 1837 and 1849. Philip Zea (one of Fennimore's students) is working on pewterer, brazier, and whitesmith Samuel Pierce of Greenfield, Massachusetts, whose evolving, contingent career denies the common notion of the life of a craftsman. Research presently being conducted by Robert Cheney on painted-iron dial clocks suggests some remarkable connections between the Roxbury clockmakers and the related trades in provincial England. Cheney and Zea have already published a fine account of the Willards' innovations in the batch making of tall case and wall-hanging clocks in *Clockmaking in New England, 1725–1825: An Interpretation of the Old Sturbridge Village Collection* ([Sturbridge, Mass.: Old Sturbridge Village, 1992]; see the review by David Jaffee in *Winterthur Portfolio* 30, nos. 2/3 [summer/autumn 1995]: 182–84). These activities were going on at the same time and place that cabinetmakers John and Thomas Seymour of Boston were helping to change the business of furniture manufacture and the marketing of decorative arts (along with the Willards and William Hunneman, among others), a subject currently being investigated by Robert Mussey, Anne Rogers Haley, and others. All these studies promise to enhance the appreciation and understanding of the material that has been admired and collected for more than a century and continues to reward earnest connoisseurship, material exemplified by the collections at Winterthur.

Fennimore thus has accomplished a great deal with *Metalwork in Early America*. It is a reliable source book for collectors and an integrated assemblage of studies useful to anyone interested in preindustrial manufacture. It provides as well a model of research and presentation that will inform the "future author of a definitive history on the subject," whose advent Fennimore predicts in his introduction.

David F. Wood
Concord Museum

1. The account books are in the U.S.S. *Constitution* Museum, Charlestown, Massachusetts, acc. no. 831.1 and 831.2.

2. *Independent Chronicle*, Boston, Massachusetts, January 6, 1812.

3. See catalogue entries 17, 68, and 95; see also entry 41, a fender footman by Hunneman, and entry 5, a posnet by Hunneman and Martin Gay.

4. Hunneman's ad in the *Independent Chronicle*, January 27, 1812, cites the inventor as James Perkins, although in his day book Hunneman records on May 26, 1802, a debit to Jacob Perkins "for publishing pumps in two papers." Also in the day book is an entry dated March 26, 1803, noting that Pollock's share of the first two engines sold was $100 each.

5. *Independent Chronicle*, Boston, Massachusetts, January 27, 1812.

6. Edward Jarvis, *Traditions and Reminiscences of Concord, Massachusetts, 1779–1878*, edited by Sarah Chapin (Amherst, Mass.: University of Massachusetts Press, 1993), pp. 27, 135.

Cary Carson, Ronald Hoffman, and Peter J. Albert, eds. *Of Consuming Interests: The Style of Life in the Eighteenth Century*. Charlottesville: University Press of Virginia, for the United States Capitol Historical Society, 1994. 721 pp.; bw illus., tables, line drawings, index. $79.50.

Here is an extensive, representative selection of commissioned articles about late seventeenth- and eighteenth-century consumerism that will prove extremely useful to those (like the reviewer) who are not consumed by this hyper-aggressive scholarly literature. The essayists are all major authorities in their respective fields: Kevin M. Sweeney, Lois Green Carr, Lorena S. Walsh, Edward A. Chappell, Richard L. Bushman, Karin Calvert, Margaretta M. Lovell, Cynthia Adams Hoover, David D. Hall, Barbara G. Carson, Nancy L. Struna, Timothy H. Breen, and the principal editor for the volume, Cary Carson.

Two major foci are much in evidence: the strong literature on vernacular architecture and the equally powerful, computerized statistical analysis for which historians of the Chesapeake are noted. Looming over all is Cary Carson's essay, "The Consumer Revolution in Colonial British America: Why Demand?" which is, in a somewhat coy manner, placed last when it ought to have been the lead essay; by sheer bulk (214 pages!) it reduces all the other contributions to the status of grace notes. Carson's essay does, however, rehearse the pertinent bibliography in a useful, if somewhat quixotic way, and it poses a fundamental series of questions that simplify matters without distorting them.

Industrialism was caused by consumerism. In other words, we must invert the catch phrase "supply and demand" to read "demand then supply." Carson, following the lead of art historians who have investigated seventeenth-century interiors, concludes that this demand did not start in the Georgian period (after 1714) but, rather, in the 1650s when Louis XIII's and Louis XIV's courts prompted imitation by royal, noble, and urban bourgeois sectors of society all over Europe. London merchants were perhaps the first to abstract from Versailles and the Louvre the concept of an articulated suite of rooms furnished with coordinated textiles, sets of chairs and tables, and ceremonial groupings of gaming equipment, portraits, ceramics, glass, and other objects. In other words, they were the first in the English-speaking world to translate what had been exclusively courtly values into a middle-class or professional standard of genteel comportment. The French prototype upon which these merchants drew, in turn, represented an important northern European conceptual transition from the royal court as a mobile hunting party to a fixed administrative and artistic center, more on the order of the court of Rudolph II at Prague.

The prototypes for this sort of royal activity were in Italy, at the papal court in Rome and the more stable city-states like Florence. Carson does not investigate the meaning of this grand level of cultural transfer for his emerging English consumerism and gentility of the 1650s, but it seems logical to theorize that genteel comportment in ritualized activities, like sampling wine, gaming, tea drinking, and so forth, was based not simply in paying court to a royal figure but in evincing sufficient humanistic training. After all, even the bitterness surrounding the Reformation and the eclipse of Italy's economic power by the Atlantic states did not relieve northern Europeans of a servile deference toward the Italian wellsprings of humanistic learning. Just as surely, the paradigm for the genteel manner resided in classical sources. There is some grounds for seeking part of the English variant of the genteel in the virtuosos of Charles I's court, many of whom paid extended visits to Italy and displayed a profound command of Renaissance literature and the arts. Charles I himself was a powerful, if not particularly endearing, prototype for the rigid posture, impassive features, clipped diction, lack of emotional involvement, exquisite costume, and artistic accomplishments that came to be recognized as traits of the English gentleman by the eighteenth century.

Another title for this anthology, thus, might have been "American Historians and Partisans of the Vernacular Discover Elemental Truths of Art History." For all the exquisitely attuned discussions of how assorted English role models and marketing strategies were mediated by strong vernacular or regional impulses in the colonies, the fact remains that courtly behavior and the accoutrements that articulate it *are* courtly and largely artistic in origin.

Carson greatly emphasizes the idea that genteel comportment and rituals were made necessary by the mobility of the middling sort (what we might today term businessmen, professionals, and civil servants), both within England and out of England to the colonies. This idea is intriguing and useful, at least for the 1650–1700 period. A view of genteel comportment as having utility value goes a long way toward explaining why consumerism could evade radical Protestant injunctions against materialism and display. It would be wise, however, to remember how Puritan commentators such as Richard Baxter failed to reconcile weaned affections with the need to express and reinforce hierarchy through display. What drove Independents in England back into the Anglican church in some numbers after 1660 was not fear of the restored monarchy and church but doctrinal loathing for the disregard of property among Diggers, Levellers, and Quakers.

All the essays deal with ramifications of the introduction and marketing of various media and their impact on behavior. One formulation that needs to be questioned is the presumed priority of architectural space in reinforcing genteel behavior and new standards of formality, privacy, and individuation. Discussions of the interface between "Georgian" and vernacular architectural plans often give the impression that the plans engendered the organization of ritual behavior and the disposition of objects. At the risk of seeming a partisan of the decorative arts, this reviewer would like to assert that, even as consumerism engendered industrialism (to some degree), so genteel rituals and objects engendered architectural form. This assertion flies in the face of Herbert Read's classic 1955 essay, *Icon and Idea*, as well as the basic thrust of art historical formalism in general, but it is more consistent with historical practice.

A useful caution in all this talk of rampant consumerism is provided by Edward A. Chappell's essay, which notes that fully three-quarters of the population were excluded from genteel consumerism by poverty and structured inequality until well into the nineteenth century. This point is apt and refreshing. One more observation that might strongly qualify the eighteenth-century bias of this anthology is that the value systems of all modern observers of pre-1800 American culture are irretrievably influenced by a deep-seated, modern ambivalence toward industrialism. Is this not what is so alluring yet so annoying about walking the streets of Colonial Williamsburg? Not only is the presentation almost entirely based on elite architecture and decorative arts but the purported romance of the exercise relies on the contrast between the restored area and, say, Secaucus, New Jersey. In particular, our middle-class instinct that there is such a thing as redemption through study of preindustrial crafts is a distinctly nineteenth-century fiction that this anthology fails to explicate and refute.

Robert F. Trent
Wilmington, Delaware

Patrick Sheary. *American Case Furniture, 1680–1840: Selections from the DAR Museum Collection*. Washington, D.C.: DAR Museum, 1997. Unpaged; bw illus., line drawings, checklist. $9.50.

This catalogue of about 112 pages accompanied an exhibition at the DAR

Museum in Washington, D.C., held between June 6 and October 31, 1997. The exhibition included twenty-five pieces of case furniture from the museum's collection of approximately one thousand examples of American furniture gathered since 1912. Of those twenty-five, fifteen are illustrated and catalogued in depth in this inexpensive, spiral-bound publication of the "desk-top" type.

Although the book was produced in a modest, economical format that exhibits some typographic evidence of being hastily produced, the text is a solid, serious look at furniture ranging from a seventeenth-century Wethersfield chest to a mahogany Empire desk and bookcase. The objects catalogued include a variety of forms, including chests and chests of drawers, desks, a sideboard, a high chest, a dressing table, and the somewhat unusual forms of a china press and clothespress. New England, Middle Atlantic, and North Carolina formal cabinetmaking traditions are represented, along with two Pennsylvania German painted chests. The entries are arranged roughly chronologically by style, from late baroque through late neoclassical, and each new style is introduced with a short general statement. About half of the objects fall into the mid-eighteenth-century "late baroque/ rococo" category, with a few earlier and later examples rounding out the presentation. An overall image of each piece (occasionally a little murky due to the inexpensive production process) is provided, and introductory line drawings offer a guide to terminology.

Although it is technically the catalogue of a temporary exhibition, Patrick Sheary's extensive entries make *American Case Furniture* more closely resemble a collection catalogue. Each entry begins with a heading of basic "tombstone" information—form, accession number, materials (apparently identified by eye), place of manufacture, date, style (using art history terminology), maker (if known), inscriptions, credit line, and dimensions— followed by a lengthy interpretive essay that discusses the function of the object and sets forth the reasoning behind the regional attribution offered in the heading. These narratives are well done and reflect current scholarship on each of the individual pieces. There seems to be some confusion regarding the use of the terms "early baroque" and "mannerist," which here are discussed virtually as synonyms when applied to Wethersfield and Hadley chests, and "Georgian" might have been a simpler term to use for the 1730–1790 period instead of "late baroque / rococo"; but the analysis of each piece is informative and helpful.

The strength of this work, however, lies in its very detailed observations concerning the design, construction, and condition of each object. After reading these extensive notes, one feels secure that these objects have been thoroughly and carefully analyzed and the results set forth in an unvarnished fashion. This is a great service to the serious researcher and collector. Each will treasure the detailed construction notes, for as scholarship has evolved, the identification of diagnostic features has become ever more esoteric. Sheary's detailed descriptions and construction notes will save other researchers a good deal of fieldwork and allow for a greater understanding of individual DAR pieces within a wide context. Furniture historians will also be grateful for the equally minute observations concerning condition. Many of the objects catalogued have had more than their share of repairs and restoration—the Wethersfield chest was "revived" extensively at the turn of the century, several objects have had their feet replaced, and so forth. It is important to have this information on the record so that the image of the piece is not necessarily taken at face value. Those who are less interested in such facts can simply ignore these passages. The history (or provenance) of each piece is also provided, although not in as much depth as with the other categories. There are, for some pieces, tantalizing family histories that might have been followed up with probate or genealogical research (as with the early history of a Boston desk owned by Christopher Marshall) or inscriptions (as with "W.H. Edwards, 1872" on the North Carolina china press) that might have been pursued more assiduously. Taking care of the time-consuming task of provenance research is one of the greatest services the author of a collection catalogue can perform for other scholars.

Most of the objects catalogued here are perhaps best seen as representative of their kind rather than as aesthetic masterpieces. The "Mary Burt" Hadley chest is one of the highlights of the collection, being in good condition and one of the few such chests with a full name inscription. Other notable objects are a fine Baltimore sideboard with elegant inlaid ovals, owned originally by the Gist family, and a Rhode Island shell-carved high chest owned by the Child family.

The DAR Museum's holdings have been published before—most notably by Elisabeth Donaghy Garrett in a collection-wide survey entitled *The Arts of Independence: The DAR Museum Collection* (1985) and in a number of publications devoted to their outstanding textile collection—but it is probably fair to say that the furniture collection is not widely known. Patrick Sheary's catalogue admirably corrects that situation for these fifteen examples of case furniture.

Gerald W. R. Ward
Museum of Fine Arts, Boston

Edward S. Cooke, Jr. *Making Furniture in Preindustrial America: The Social Economy of Newtown and Woodbury, Connecticut,* vol. 10 of Studies in Industry and Society, ed. Philip Scranton. Baltimore: Johns Hopkins University Press, 1996. Xiii + 295 pp.; 53 bw illus., 21 tables, 3 charts, appendixes, glossary, bibliography, index. $45.00.

Edward S. Cooke's *Making Furniture in Preindustrial America: The Social Economy of Newtown and Woodbury, Connecticut* is an important volume that stands at a crossroads. It embodies the fruits of nearly two decades of study devoted to the eighteenth-century furniture of southwestern Connecticut. Students of American furniture familiar with Cooke's catalogue *Fiddlebacks and Crooked-backs: Elijah Booth and Other Joiners in Newtown and Woodbury, 1750–1820* (Waterbury, Conn.: Mattatuck Historical Society, 1982) and his articles in *Antiques* (1984) and *American Furniture* (1995) will recognize the chairs, tables, and case pieces analyzed in this new book. And like his important essay "The Study of American Furniture from the Perspective of the Maker" (1988), this book brings to bear the insights gained from the analysis of furniture in understanding the roles that social, economic, and cultural factors played in shaping furniture production. In this field of study Cooke's work on eighteenth-century furniture production continues to lead the way, building upon the pioneering approaches of Charles F. Montgomery, Charles Hummel, and Benno Forman, and the specific research of Robert F. Trent on the turned chairs of coastal Connecticut.

In this book, Cooke goes further, seeking to explore and map the intersection between New England social history and furniture making. Here he draws upon and contributes to the academic study of colonial New England towns that during the past three decades has produced a plethora of community studies. His exploration of the communities of woodworkers in Newtown and Woodbury is, for good and ill, firmly situated in this tried and true if somewhat tired approach to New England social history. His book does demonstrate once again that the parochial focus of the community study provides an unusually rich and textured portrait that can deepen if not always broaden our understanding of New England social history.

Finally, and most promising, is the book's apparent effort to situate local craft production within the burgeoning study of what has been called the eighteenth-century consumer revolution. Focusing generally on such imported, factory-produced goods as ceramics, metalwares, textiles, and the like, these largely documentary and quantitatively based studies have sought to delineate and explain the proliferation of things and their expanding social role. Cooke attempts to refine our understanding of the process by using locally produced furniture as a gauge of the pace and degree to which rural Connecticut consumers embraced new forms, new social fashions, and ultimately new mores. His findings here are suggestive and his interpretations challenging, but not always convincing. His work does make clear that the production and consumption of locally manufactured furniture has a place in the emerging story of the dramatic growth of domestic artifacts during the eighteenth century.

The opening three chapters of the book lay out the material, social, and economic environment in which the furniture makers of Newtown and Woodbury worked. Chapter 1 outlines the "spectrum" or varieties of woodworkers and describes the variation in techniques, tools, and task-difficulty to be found in these towns. The author broadly sketches the emergence of the eighteenth-century shop joiner, the primary producer of furniture, from the seventeenth-century joiner and the "ambidextrous" or unspecialized woodworkers of the late seventeenth and early eighteenth centuries who often combined carpentry work, housewrighting, and joinery. His discussion makes clear two important points often slighted in overdrawn contrasts between the seventeenth-century joiner and the eighteenth-century cabinetmaker: eighteenth-century cabinetmakers were truly joiners who owed much to the techniques of the previous century, and they were usually proficient turners. The same woodworkers who made cherry, scroll-top chests often produced painted, flag-seated, turned chairs to go with them.

The second and third chapters describe the patterns and variations in work that shaped craft careers from training to production to eventual retirement. Here the analysis makes very effective use of such documentary evidence as account books, probate inventories, tax lists, and a collective biography of ninety-five Newtown and eighty-one Woodbury woodworkers. (Two lengthy appendixes, on pages 201 to 231 contain the individual biographical sketches of these woodworkers.) Like most recent studies, this book emphasizes the importance of the social context in which the artisan worked. From his beginnings as an apprentice, a shop joiner functioned in a context defined as much by social obligations and expectations as by an economic relationship with the market. Seasonal agricultural rhythms and local economies affected the timing of production—turned chairs were made during the winter months and case furniture throughout the year, with work concentrated in February to April and August to November— and the types of furniture produced. Despite the emphasis placed on the interdependence between agricultural and craft economy, Cooke takes pains to demonstrate that these rural artisans made sophisticated use of available labor sources, employed such labor saving devices as templates and patterns, and drew upon English and urban colonial design sources. Controlling the "nature of work"—knowledge, materials, and applications—workers responded to the "context of work"—the reactions and demands of local clientele (p. 41). For Cooke, the finished product must be viewed as a result of this dialogue between craftsman and consumer.

Over the course of the eighteenth century, the balance between by-employment as woodworkers and agricultural activity shifted for shop joiners in rural communities toward a greater concentration on craft activity. Within this broad trend, however, differences existed in the pace of change and the balance maintained between tradition and innovation. In Newtown, native-born woodworkers combined significant agricultural activity with furniture production. These economic choices produced greater stability in craft personnel throughout the eighteenth century, resulting in less diversity in the community's furniture production. In neighboring Woodbury, economic choices produced an elite who desired more genteel consumer goods but fewer native-born, locally trained craftsmen to satisfy these demands. This situation attracted a large number of outsiders who did not establish long-lived shop traditions, and it encouraged "competitive performance," which introduced local consumers and other woodworkers to a variety of new forms and techniques (p. 183).

In two later chapters, 6 and 7, Cooke expands upon these distinctions resulting from different socioeconomic contexts of production. While acknowledging that the furniture of the two towns had much in common, he focuses his analysis on the "subtle constructional and decorative differences" distinguishing their shops' production (p. 120). In Newtown, existing chair forms indebted to coastal Connecticut shops influenced the adoption of stylistic elements and construction techniques associated with the "Queen Anne" or Georgian style and the Chippendale style. Production rhythms shaped by turning, though quickening in response to increased demand, assured the continued domination of painted, flag-bottomed, turned chairs. Case pieces remained distinguished by technical proficiency and understated ornamentation (p. 143). More labor-intensive techniques—for instance, sawing and paring tight-fitting dovetails, rabbeting drawer bottoms, and dovetailing tops—continued to characterize the "overengineered" case furniture produced by late-eighteenth-century Newtown shops.

Woodbury furniture makers, working in an environment characterized by competition and *greater mobility among craftsmen,* produced chairs and case pieces that bespoke more diverse sources of design—coastal Connecticut; the Connecticut Valley; New London County, Connecticut; Boston; New York; and possibly Pennsylvania—and revealed choices in technique intended to speed production. The author is at his best dissecting a Woodbury Windsor—"The tapered column, crisp urn, and large-bellied baluster of each leg resemble New York examples, and the triple-bead molding on the bow is seen most frequently on Windsors from the Connecticut River Valley" (p. 158)—or explaining why "long, deep kerf marks on the inside corner of the drawer fronts indicate that the joiner cut out his dovetails in the fastest way possible" (p. 161). These woodworkers, often new to the environment, had to respond to the changing taste of local consumers who had "stronger ties to the external market" of imported household goods and had "greater awareness of fashion's short swings" (p. 188).

Convincing as an analysis of furniture production, the book pushes further to deepen our understanding of the two communities' entire social economies. At the physical center of the book and at the core of the analysis lie two chapters, 4 and 5, which are devoted to delineating the socioeconomic structures of the two towns and uncovering the different sources of consumer demand. This bold effort is unfortunately constrained by its community-study approach and straightjacketed by an interpretation that turns this intersection of furniture study and social history into one of those traffic rotaries in which the unwary driver feels trapped.

As in many of the earlier studies of colonial New England communities, much emphasis is placed on such population dynamics as overall population growth and persistence rates, which measure the relative mobility or stability of the population. From these quantitative indices of social actions, cultural patterns and attitudes have often been inferred in a rather functionalist manner. Cooke makes much of the apparent difference between the two communities' overall persistence rates (not just that of woodworkers): more stable, traditional Newtown is contrasted with more mobile, less stable, almost urban Woodbury. I say apparent difference because the evidence provided in table 5 on page 71 of the book does not really support the weight placed on this factor. For five of the six decades analyzed, the gross persistence rate in Newtown exceeds that in Woodbury by an average of 0 percentage points; in the 1790s the difference was a more noticeable 9 percentage points. Still, the underlying difference for the entire period from 1770 to 1820 is actually 1.5 percentage points, which is meaningless. More striking is the basic similarity of the declining patterns of residential persistence found in both towns as land reserves decreased, forcing sons of local farmers to migrate while at the same time opportunities in trade attracted the land-poor sons of farmers from elsewhere. But for Cooke the presumed difference in persistence rates preserved in Newtown "the inherently conservative consumer and producer values of a yeoman town" (p. 109), whereas in neighboring, less stable Woodbury, "many townspeople lacked a common value system achieved through longevity or continuity in Woodbury" (p. 151), a rather sweeping assessment that appears to overlook such presumably shared Yankee values as hard work, reformed Protestantism, and republicanism.

The resulting comparative interpretation of traditional Newtown and more cosmopolitan or less traditional Woodbury that emerges from the numbers is overdetermined—gray in Newtown is interpreted as a shade of white, while gray in Woodbury is viewed as a shade of black. In Newtown, the 33 percent of the land left as woodlands and unimproved land is evidence of the town's conservatism, but the 29 percent of the land remaining as woodlot and unimproved land in Woodbury is evidence of the town's degree of agricultural development (pp. 78, 87). There really is not much difference here statistically. People in Newtown were supposedly slower to adopt the Windsor chair, which either "achieved moderate popularity" (p. 98) or remained "rare" (p. 158) when compared to its reception in Woodbury, though the actual number of references to the ownership of these chairs in both towns between 1790 and 1824 is again rather similar when viewed as numbers rather than percentages: in the 1790s, two in Newtown and one in Woodbury; in the 1800s, four in Newtown and six in Woodbury; in the 1810s, seven in Newtown and thirteen in Woodbury; and in the 1820s, thirteen in Newtown and fifteen in Woodbury (computed from table 14, p. 97). Again, there is not much difference. Still, Cooke argues that the presumed difference goes even deeper, for in traditional Newtown the "customer preference for painted turned chairs permitted the easy accommodation of the new Windsor chair" (p. 98), whereas in more cosmopolitan Woodbury the Windsor's "desirability . . . may have been due less to the familiarity of its turned construction and painted decoration than to its symbolic connections with the world beyond Woodbury's boundaries" (p. 110). Perhaps, but couldn't the opposite be just as true, or at least true for some customers in each town?

The analysis of society and economy does a more convincing job of delineating and describing the emergence of a self-conscious gentry elite in Woodbury. These were the holders of money at interest, the possessors of large herds, and the more obvious participants in the external market economy, though I feel that Cooke, like some other scholars, overdraws the distinction between local economy and an external economy. Members of these gentry families and those who began to emulate them were the first purchasers of imported consumer goods, of new furniture forms, and of the more highly ornamented, though not necessarily better-made, Woodbury furniture. Rather than being a "gentry town" contrasting sharply with a traditional Newtown, Woodbury was a basically traditional rural town with a gentry. This Woodbury gentry, much like its counterparts to the East, the River Gods of the Connecticut Valley, participated to a greater degree in *both* the more parochial, traditional world of the town and its producers *and* the larger, more cosmopolitan Anglo-American world of books, fashions, and the consumer revolution. As historian Peter Burke has observed, changes in popular culture were not so much "substitutive" as "additive."[1]

The furniture of Woodbury as well as the probate evidence discussed by Cooke suggest that such a layering of stylistic and cultural influences and allegiances instead of sharp dichotomies is the best way to view this gentry class and those who began to emulate them and their possessions in Woodbury, as well as the residents of "traditional" Newtown. "Painted, turned, flag-seated chairs represented the bulk of common seating forms in eighteenth-century Woodbury" as well as Newtown (pp. 152, 97). In Woodbury, more expensive, possibly more cosmopolitan, crooked-back chairs only "encroached" during this period (pp. 155, 97). Even some of these crooked-back chairs "remained rooted in the turned chair tradition" (p. 156). Similarly, a particular Woodbury chest of drawers "demonstrates an indebtedness to local ornamental features and more distant regional constructional traditions" (p. 162). In neighboring Newtown, not just greater quantities of turned chairs and plain chests but such relatively rare furniture forms as desks, dressing tables, expensive cases of drawers, and possibly stands distinguished the household inventories of wealthier residents (pp. 105, 108–9). Interestingly, the overall frequency of ownership of such ornamental furnishings as clocks and looking glasses in both communities appears to be very similar (p. 105).

When viewed from a greater distance, as historian Bruce Daniels did in his book on the Connecticut town, both Newtown and Woodbury appear to be lightly populated, agricultural country towns with little mercantile activity.[2] Yet even here a sizeable and growing segment of the population desired increased quantities of furniture regardless of the particular modes of expression and finish, a fact documented by the growing quantities found in the probate inventories of the residents of both towns. In a number of places Cooke speaks of customer demand to explain such production, making a notable contribution to the interpretation of the consumer revolution as a demand-driven phenomenon (pp. 30, 38, 199). Still, Cooke appears reluctant to admit this is really the case in traditional Newtown, arguing at times that the increased quantities of furniture resulted from "natural accumulation," that is, gradual intergenerational accumulation, an unlikely possibility given the New England practice of partible inheritance and the well-documented role of this practice in diminishing the overall size of landholdings from one generation to the next (pp. 93–94, 150). Elsewhere in the text he does back away from this dubious assumption (p. 99).

Even the more traditionally produced furniture forms in Newtown bespoke a new world of material culture shaped by popular culture and commerce. When they are viewed from the perspective of rural material culture of the late seventeenth and even early eighteenth century, it is hard to regard mid- or even later-eighteenth-century desks, dressing tables, expensive cases of drawers, crooked-back chairs, and stands as traditional furniture (pp. 43, 108–9, 149). The small, relatively inexpensive stand—basically eighteenth-century accent furniture—was not a traditional form even if its turned production may have been very traditional. Regardless of the mode of production or the exact stylistic mode, producers and certain consumers in Newtown as well as those of Woodbury created during the later eighteenth century a world in which household things played more important roles in society and the economy. Again the observations of Peter Burke are suggestive: "the commercial revolution led to a golden age of traditional popular culture (material culture, at least), before the combined commercial and industrial revolutions destroyed it."[3] Artifacts such as Newtown furniture and New England's "folk" gravestones were all products of popular culture and the commercial market revolution; they, their makers, and their consumers were *of* the market as well as being *in* it, probably from some time in the late seventeenth century or the early eighteenth century.

Kevin M. Sweeney
Amherst College

1. Peter Burke, *Popular Culture in Early Modern Europe* (New York: Harper & Row, 1978), p. 257.

2. Bruce C. Daniels, *The Connecticut Town: Growth and Development, 1635–1790* (Middletown, Conn.: Wesleyan University Press, 1979), pp. 58, 60, 141, 164.

3. Burke, *Popular Culture in Early Modern Europe,* pp. 245–46.

Compiled by
Gerald W. R. Ward

Recent Writing on American Furniture: A Bibliography

▼ THIS YEAR'S list includes primarily works published in 1996 and through June of 1997; a few earlier publications that had previously escaped notice are also cited. The short title *American Furniture 1996* is used in citations for articles and reviews published in last year's issue of this journal, which is also cited in full under Luke Beckerdite's name.

I am grateful to Milo Naeve, Steve Stenstrom, Jonathan Fairbanks, and especially Neville Thompson of Winterthur for their assistance, and to the staffs of the library of the Museum of Fine Arts, Boston; the Portsmouth Athenaeum; and the Winterthur Museum. As always, I would be grateful to receive suggestions for material that should be included in these annual lists. Review copies of significant works would also be appreciated. Copies and citations may be sent to:

Gerald W. R. Ward
Carolyn and Peter Lynch Associate Curator of
American Decorative Arts & Sculpture
Museum of Fine Arts, Boston
465 Huntington Avenue
Boston, Massachusetts 02115

Adair, William. "Stanford White's Frames." *Antiques* 151, no. 3 (March 1997): 448–57. 17 color and 9 bw illus.

Albertson, Karla Klein. "The Cadwalader Family: Art and Style in Early Philadelphia." *Antiques and the Arts Weekly* (January 17, 1997): 1, 68–69. 11 bw illus.

Albertson, Karla Klein. "Charles Rennie Mackintosh" (exhibition and book review). *Antiques and the Arts Weekly* (January 31, 1997): 1, 68–69. 10 bw illus.

Ames, Kenneth L. "Surface Charm." *Art & Antiques* 20, no. 1 (January 1997): 46–53. 13 color illus. (Re inlay.)

Artful Interiors: Rooms with a View: The Transition from Decoration to Design, 1750–1950. New York: New York Public Library, 1996. Unpaged; bw illus., checklist, bibliography. (A small pamphlet, with an introduction entitled "Documenting Domestic Interiors Through Key Literature" by Paula A. Baxter and Heidi Martin Winston, accompanying an exhibition held from November 16, 1996, through March 29, 1997.)

"Autumn Americana." *Christie's International Magazine* 13, no. 8 (October 1996): 69. 3 bw illus. (Re eighteenth-century Boston and Philadelphia furniture at auction.)

Aynsley, Jeremy. *Nationalism and Internationalism*, vol. 1 of *Design in the 20th Century*. London: Victoria and Albert Museum, 1993. 72 pp.; 66 bw illus., bibliography, index.

Bacot, H. Parrott. "Chêne Vert in East Baton Rouge Parish, Louisiana." *Antiques* 151, no. 3 (March 1997): 438–47. 16 color illus.

[Baker Furniture]. *Fine Furniture Reproductions: 18th Century Revivals of the 1930s and 1940s from Baker Furniture*. Atglen, Pa.: Schiffer Publishing, 1996. 188 pp.; 600+ illus. (Reprint of 1940 Baker Furniture catalogue.)

Ball, Robert W. D. *Nautical Antiques with Value Guide*. Atglen, Pa.: Schiffer Publishing, 1994. 240 pp.; numerous bw illus., price guide. (See "Nautical Furnishings and Accessories," pp. 165–86.)

Bartlett, Margo. "Pie Safes and Candle Molds: Garth's Auction." *Antiques and the Arts Weekly* (December 27, 1996): 56–57. 9 bw illus. (Re auction of pie safe collection of Dennis and Louise Paustenbach of Woodside, California.)

Baumeister, Mechtild, and Wolfram Koeppe. Exhibition review of Ulrich Leben, *Bernard Molitor, 1755–1833: Ébéniste parisien d'origine luxembourgeoise* / Pariser Kunsttischler Luxemburger Herkunft. In *Studies in the Decorative Arts* 4, no. 1 (fall/winter 1996–97): 138–40. 1 bw illus.

Beach, Laura. "American Decorative Arts from the Concord Museum." *Antiques and the Arts Weekly* (December 6, 1996): 1, 68–70. 11 bw illus.

Beach, Laura. "Sleepless Near Seattle: Word of a Newport Desk Sends Experts on Puget Sound Fishing Expedition." *Antiques and the Arts Weekly* (May 2, 1997): 1, 66B–66E. 20 bw illus.

Beckerdite, Luke. "Immigrant Carvers and the Development of the Rococo Style in New York, 1750–1770." In *American Furniture 1996*, pp. 233–65. 57 color and bw illus.

Beckerdite, Luke, ed. *American Furniture 1996*. Milwaukee, Wis.: The Chipstone Foundation, 1996. xii + 344 pp.; numerous color and bw illus., bibliography, index. Distributed by University Press of New England, Hanover and London.

Berliner, Nancy. "Furniture of the Late Ming Dynasty." *Antiques* 150, no. 2 (August 1996): 178–87. 15 color and 1 bw illus.

Billcliffe, Roger. "Charles Rennie Mackintosh's Furniture." *Antiques* 150, no. 4 (October 1996): 494–505. 12 color and 4 bw illus.

Binzen, Jonathan. "James Krenov, Master of the Handmade." *Home Furniture*, no. 7 (summer 1996): 32–39. 13 color and 3 bw illus., bibliography.

Bivins, John, Jr. "Furniture of the North Carolina Roanoke River Basin in the Collection of Historic Hope Foundation." *Journal of Early Southern Decorative Arts* 22, no. 1 (summer 1996): 42–90. 35 bw illus.

Blakemore, Robbie G. *History of Interior Design and Furniture from Ancient Egypt to Nineteenth-Century Europe*. New York: Van Nostrand Reinhold, 1997. viii + 392 pp.; numerous color and bw illus., line drawings, bibliography, index.

Boggs, Brian. "Evolution of a Chair." *Home Furniture*, no. 8 (October 1996): 26–31. 5 color illus., 2 line drawings.

Boston University Art Gallery. *Pilgrims and Progressives: The Colonial Revival in Massachusetts*. Boston: by the Gallery, 1996. 23 pp. typescript.

Bristow, Ian. *Architectural Colour in British Interiors, 1615–1840*. New Haven: Yale University Press, 1996. 320 pp.; 166 color and 54 bw illus.

Bristow, Ian. *Interior House-Painting, Colours and Technology, 1615–1840*. New Haven: Yale University Press, 1996. 320 pp.; 49 color and 37 bw illus., 48 paint chips.

Bronner, Simon J. *The Carver's Art: Crafting Meaning from Wood*. Rev. ed. Lexington: University Press of Kentucky, 1996. xiii + 210 pp.; illus., map.

Brown, Michael K. "A Boston Tambour Desk." *Antiques* 151, no. 1 (January 1997): 202–5. 3 color and 1 bw illus.

Brunk, Robert S., ed. *May We All Remember Well: A Journal of the History and Cultures of Western North Carolina*. Vol. 1. Asheville, N.C.: Robert S. Brunk Services, 1997. 287 pp.; illus. (The first issue of this new journal includes articles on furniture by Jerry Israel, Jack E. Lindsey, and others.)

Budis, Erin M. *Making His Mark: The Work of Shaker Craftsman Orren Haskins*. Old Chatham, N.Y.: Shaker Museum and Library, 1997. 32 pp.; 16 bw illus., bibliography.

Carruthers, Annette. *Good Citizen's Furniture: Arts and Crafts Collections at Cheltenham*. London: Cheltenham Art Gallery and Museum in association with Lund Humphries, 1994. 168 pp.; 12 color and 205 bw illus., bibliography, index.

The Chair Show: A National Juried Exhibition of Chairs from throughout the U.S. Organized by the Southern Highland Craft Guild. Asheville, N.C.: Folk

Art Center, 1995. Unpaged; 47 bw illus., checklist. (Introduction by Katherine Duncan; comments by Rosanne Somerson.)

[Christie's]. *The Collection of Kay and Richard Barrett*. Sale 8704. New York: Christie's, June 17, 1997. 145 pp.; color and bw illus. (Includes some furniture.)

Churchill, Edwin A. Review of Kenneth Joel Zogry, *"The Best the Country Affords": Vermont Furniture, 1765–1850*, and Charles A. Robinson, with an introduction by Philip Zea, *Vermont Cabinetmakers and Chairmakers Before 1855: A Checklist*. In *American Furniture 1996*, pp. 318–21.

Coleridge, Anthony. "The Hope-Weir Cabinet." *Antiques* 151, no. 6 (June 1997): 852–59. 7 color and 2 bw illus. (Re cabinet, probably Scottish, late 1750s, with *pietre dure* panels.)

Condon, Lorna. "Inside SPNEA: Daguerreotypes of Plymouth." *Old-Time New England* 74, no. 261 (spring 1996): 32–47. 13 bw illus. (Includes images taken ca. 1853 of William Brewster's chair, Peregrine White's cabinet, and Edward Winslow's easy chair.)

Cooke, Edward S., Jr. "The Aesthetics of Craftsmanship and the Presence of the Past: Boston Furniture-Making and Wood-Carving." In *Inspiring Reform: Boston's Arts and Crafts Movement*, ed. Marilee Boyd Meyer, pp. 58–69. Wellesley, Mass.: Davis Museum and Cultural Center, 1997. Color and bw illus. Distributed by Harry N. Abrams, New York. (See also the checklist of the exhibition and craftsmen biographies.)

Cooke, Edward S., Jr. *Making Furniture in Preindustrial America: The Social Economy of Newtown and Woodbury, Connecticut*, vol. 10 of *Studies in Industry and Society*, ed. Philip Scranton. Baltimore: Johns Hopkins University Press, 1996. xiii + 295 pp.; 53 bw illus., 21 tables, 3 charts, appendixes, glossary, bibliography, index.

Cooke, Edward S., Jr. "Turning Wood in America: New Perspectives on the Lathe." In *Expressions in Wood: Masterworks from the Wornick Collection*, ed. Tran Turner, pp. 39–47. Oakland,

Cal.: Oakland Museum of California, 1996. 7 bw illus.

Cornforth, John. "Cotehele, A Property of the National Trust in Cornwall." *Antiques* 151, no. 6 (June 1997): 860–69. 17 color illus. (Includes seventeenth- and eighteenth-century English furniture.)

Cotton, Bernard D. Review of Nancy Goyne Evans, *American Windsor Chairs*. In *Regional Furniture Society Newsletter*, no. 25 (winter 1996): 5–6.

Craig, Theresa. *Edith Wharton: A House Full of Rooms: Architecture, Interiors, and Gardens*. New York: Monacelli Press, 1996. 240 pp.; 100 color and 100 bw illus., bibliography, index.

Crom, Theodore R. "The Bagnall Family of Boston, 1712 to 1782: Benjamin, Benjamin, Jr., and Samuel." *NAWCC Bulletin* 38, no. 6 (December 1996): 765–72. 11 bw illus., bibliography.

[Dallas Museum of Art]. "Vanderbilt Console Acquired." *Friends of the Decorative Arts Newsletter* 7, no. 1 (winter 1997): 1. 1 bw illus. (Re console by Herter Brothers, 1881–1882.)

Davis, John. "Children in the Parlor: Eastman Johnson's *Brown Family* and the Post-Civil War Luxury Interior." *American Art* 10, no. 2 (summer 1996): 50–77. 16 color and bw illus.

"Deerfield Acquires Hadley Chest." *Maine Antique Digest* 24, no. 8 (August 1996): 6A–6B. 1 bw illus. (Re two-drawer chest ca. 1715 with initials HD for Hepzibah Dickinson [1696–1761] of Hatfield, Massachusetts. See also *Antiques and the Arts Weekly* [July 19, 1996]: 16.)

Denker, Bert. Review of William C. Ketchum, Jr., and the Museum of American Folk Art, *American Cabinetmakers: Marked American Furniture, 1640–1940*. In *American Furniture 1996*, pp. 307–9.

Deutsch, Carole. "Nakashima Goes On." *Maine Antique Digest* 24, no. 9 (September 1996): 10A. 3 bw illus.

Duncan, Alastair. *Art Deco Furniture: The French Designers*. Rev. ed. New York: Thames and Hudson, 1997. 192 pp.; 68 color and 244 bw illus., appendix, bibliography, index.

Dunlop, Hank. "Fernside: The Estate of

Alfred Andrew Cohen and Emilie Gibbons Cohen." *Nineteenth Century* 16, no. 2 (fall 1996): 28–37. 12 bw illus.

[Dunnigan, John]. "New Work by . . . John Dunnigan . . . at Peter Joseph Gallery." *Antiques and the Arts Weekly* (August 23, 1996): 16.

Du Pasquier, Jacqueline. *Mobilier bordelais et parisien*. Paris: Editions de la Réunion des musée nationaux, 1997. 187 pp.; color and bw illus., bibliography.

"Early Washing Machine in Deerfield." *Antiques and the Arts Weekly* (December 27, 1996): 26. 1 bw illus. (Re ca. 1810 example recently acquired by Historic Deerfield; see also Eleanor H. Gustafson, "Museum Accessions," *Antiques* 151, no. 3 [March 1997] 390.)

Eidelberg, Martin, ed., with essays by Steven C. Dubin, Martin Filler, Lenore Newman, Witold Rybczynski, and Jan L. Spak. *Designed for Delight: Alternative Aspects of Twentieth-Century Decorative Arts*. Paris and New York: Montreal Museum of Decorative Arts/Flammarion, 1997. 320 pp.; numerous color illus., index.

Erlandson, Robert A. "A Peter Stretch Lantern Clock." *NAWCC Bulletin* 39, no. 3 (June 1997): 320–22. 3 bw illus.

Edwin, Charles. "These Clocks All Look Alike . . .". *Antiques and the Arts Weekly* (November 1, 1996): S16–S17. 6 bw illus.

Evans, Nancy Goyne. "Frog Back and Turkey Legs: The Nomenclature of Vernacular Seating Furniture, 1740–1850." In *American Furniture 1996*, pp. 17–56. 34 bw illus.

Evans, Nancy Goyne. "When the Top Came Off: A Connecticut Chest Identified." *Maine Antique Digest* 25, no. 4 (April 1997): 26B–27B. 5 bw illus. (Re chest of drawers in Winterthur Museum collection dated 1789 and signed by James Higgins of Middle Haddam.)

"Exhibition Highlights Designs of Edward J. Wormley." *Antiques and the Arts Weekly* (February 14, 1997): 16. 1 bw illus. (Re exhibition at Lin/Weinberg Gallery, New York City.)

Failey, Dean. "The Collector's Dream." *Christie's International Magazine* 14, no. 5 (June 1997): 50–51. 3 color illus. (Re collection of Kay and Richard Barrett.)

Faxon, Susan, et al. *Addison Gallery of American Art, 65 Years: A Selective Catalogue.* Andover, Mass.: Addison Gallery of American Art, Phillips Academy, 1996. 511 pp.; numerous color and bw illus., index. (Includes Boston chest of drawers, ca. 1680–1700, and Philadelphia chest-on-chest, ca. 1760.)

Fenichell, Stephen. *Plastic: The Making of a Synthetic Century.* New York: HarperBusiness, 1996. xi + 356 pp.; bw illus., index. (Journalistic account with some references to plastic furniture and upholstery.)

Fennimore, Donald L. *Metalwork in Early America: Copper and Its Alloys from the Winterthur Collection.* Winterthur, Del.: Winterthur Museum, 1996. 472 pp.; numerous color and bw illus., glossary, bibliography, index. Distributed by Antique Collectors' Club.

[*Fine Woodworking*]. *Design Book Seven: 360 Photographs of the Best Work in Wood.* Newtown, Conn.: Taunton Press, 1996. 185 pp.; 360 color illus., index.

Fish, Marilyn. *The New Craftsman Index: An Annotated Chronology, Subject, and Author Index of Gustav Stickley's the Craftsman, 1901–1916. With an Essay on the History of the Craftsman Magazine and Instructions on the Use of the New Craftsman Index.* Lambertville, N.J.: Arts and Crafts Quarterly Press, 1997. 219 pp.; bw illus.

Fitzgerald, Oscar P. "Furniture." In *The Dictionary of Art,* ed. Jane Turner, 31:623–34. London: Grove, 1996. bw illus., bibliography. (There are many other articles on all aspects of American, English, European, and other regional types of furniture scattered throughout this new thirty-four volume reference work.)

Follansbee, Peter, and John D. Alexander. "Seventeenth-Century Joinery from Braintree, Massachusetts: The Savell Shop Tradition." In *American Furniture 1996,* pp. 81–104. 1 color and 25 bw illus., appendix, chart.

Forman, Bruce R. "The American White Painted Dial: A Pictorial Essay." *NAWCC Bulletin* 38, no. 1 (February 1996): 3–14. 26 bw illus., bibliography.

Forrest, Tim. *The Bulfinch Anatomy of Antique Furniture: An Illustrated Guide to Identifying Period, Detail, and Design.* A Bulfinch Press Book. Boston: Little, Brown and Co., 1996. 160 pp.; 500+ color and bw illus., index.

The Frame in America, 1860–1960. Foreword by Mary Ann Goley; essay by William B. Adair. Washington, D.C.: Fine Arts Advisory Panel, Federal Reserve Board, 1995. 20 pp.; bw illus., line drawings, bibliography, exhibition checklist.

Friary, Donald R. "The Jonathan Smith, Jr., Chest on Chest on Frame." *Antiques* 151, no. 1 (January 1997): 222–23. 1 color and 1 bw illus.

Furniture History 32 (1996): 1–204. Numerous bw illus. (Nine articles on English revival furniture.)

"Furniture Maker Database." *Maine Antique Digest* 24, no. 9 (September 1996): 8A. (Re computer database list of cabinetmakers being prepared by David Hewett.)

The Furniture Society [Newsletter] 1, no. 1 (May 1997): 1–8. bw illus. (First publication of new organization designed "to advance the art of furniture making by inspiring creativity, promoting excellence, and fostering understanding of this art and its place in society.")

Gaffney, John. "The Pratt Family of Clockmakers." *NAWCC Bulletin* 38, no. 3 (June 1996): 320–23. 8 bw illus., 1 table.

Garner, Phillipe. *Sixties Design.* Köln: Taschen, 1996. 176 pp.; numerous color and bw illus. (Includes some furniture.)

Garrett, Wendell. "The Quest for Early American Furniture: A Choir of Six Collectors." *At Sotheby's* 2, no. 1 (January/February 1997): 4–5. 6 bw illus.

Gaulkin, Zachary. "Is It Ruhlmann, or Is It Pollaro?" *Home Furniture,* no. 8 (October 1996): 84–89. 13 color illus.

Gilbert, Christopher. *Pictorial Dictionary of Marked London Furniture, 1700–1840.* Leeds, England: Furniture History Society in association with W.S.

Maney and Son, 1997. 480 pp.; 1,050+ bw illus., index.

Gonzales, Roger, and Daniel Putnam Brown, Jr. "Boston and New York Leather Chairs: A Reappraisal." In *American Furniture 1996,* pp. 175–94. 31 color and bw illus.

Good, Richard. *Victorian Clocks.* London: British Museum Press, 1996. 208 pp.; 15 color and 175 bw illus. (Re English clocks.)

Gordon, Lynn. *ABC of Design.* San Francisco: Chronicle Books, 1996. Unpaged; line drawings of chairs.

Greene, Jeffrey P. *American Furniture of the Eighteenth Century: History, Technique, Structure.* Newtown, Conn.: Taunton Press, 1996. 311 pp.; 274 color and bw illus., 96 line drawings, appendixes, glossary, bibliography, index.

Grier, Katherine C., ed. "Gendered Space and Aesthetics: A Special Issue." *Winterthur Portfolio* 31, no. 4 (winter 1996): 199–301. Numerous bw illus. (Contains five articles, some of interest to furniture historians.)

Gruber, Alain, et al. *The History of the Decorative Arts.* Vol. 2, *Classicism and the Baroque in Europe.* New York: Abbeville Press, 1996. 496 pp.; 472 color and 336 bw illus., glossary, bibliography, index. Vol. 3, *Neoclassicism to Art Deco.* New York: Abbeville Press, 1997. 496 pp.; 550 color and 214 bw illus., glossary, bibliography, index.

Guild, The. *Art for the Wall, Furniture, and Accessories,* vol. 11 of *The Designer's Sourcebook.* Madison, Wis.: Kraus Sikes, 1996. 256 pp.; numerous color and bw illus., index.

Gura, Judith B. "Edward Wormley's Modernism Gets a Revival." *Antiques and the Arts Weekly* (March 7, 1997): 42–43. 9 bw illus.

Gusler, Wallace B. "Anthony Hay, A Williamsburg Tradesman." In *Common People and Their Material World: Free Men and Women in the Chesapeake, 1700–1830: Proceedings of the March 13, 1992, Conference Sponsored by the Research Division, Colonial Williamsburg Foundation,* ed. David Harvey and Gregory Brown, pp. 23–32. Williamsburg, Va.: Colonial

Williamsburg Foundation, 1996. 4 bw illus.

Gustafson, Eleanor H. "Museum Accessions." *Antiques* 150, no. 3 (September 1996): 252. 1 color illus. (Re gilt Philadelphia armchair, 1785–1815, acquired by Bayou Bend.)

Gustafson, Eleanor H. "Museum Accessions." *Antiques* 151, no. 5 (May 1997): 656. 3 bw illus. (Re console table, 1881–1882, made by Herter Brothers, acquired by Dallas Museum of Art; wainscot chair, Essex County, Massachusetts, 1640–1685, acquired by Bayou Bend; and joined chest with two drawers, Hatfield, Massachusetts, ca. 1715, acquired by Historic Deerfield.)

Habegger, Jerryll, and Joseph H. Osman. *Sourcebook of Modern Furniture.* 2d ed. New York: W.W. Norton, 1996. 576 pp.; 1,200+ bw illus., bibliography, indexes.

Hafertepe, Kenneth. Review of Charles A. Robinson, *Vermont Cabinetmakers and Chairmakers before 1855: A Checklist,* and Kenneth Joel Zogry, *The Best the Country Affords: Vermont Furniture, 1765–1850.* In *Winterthur Portfolio* 31, no. 1 (spring 1996): 84–88.

Harrison, Stephen G. "The Nineteenth-Century Furniture Trade in New Orleans." *Antiques* 151, no. 5 (May 1997): 748–59. 18 color and 5 bw illus.

Haslam, Malcolm, comp. *Marks and Monograms: The Decorative Arts, 1880–1960.* Rev. ed. London: Collins and Brown, 1995. 448 pp.; 2,000+ line drawings, index. (See "American Furniture and Textiles," pp. 388–92.)

Hauffe, Thomas. *Design.* Hauppauge, N.Y.: Barron's Educational Series, 1996. 192 pp.; numerous color and bw illus., glossary, chronology, bibliography, index.

Hays, John. "Out of America." *Christie's International Magazine* 14, no. 1 (January/February 1997): 39–40. 2 color illus. (Re Bliss family Boston, Massachusetts, chest-on-chest, ca. 1770.)

Heckscher, Morrison H. "Duncan Phyfe, *revisitus.*" *Antiques* 151, no. 1 (January 1997): 236–39. 3 color illus.

Hewett, David. "Repro 'Townsend'

Kneehole Creates a Stir." *Maine Antique Digest* 25, no. 6 (June 1997): 28A–31A. 17 bw illus.

Hewitt, Mark Alan. "Words, Deeds, and Artifice: Gustav Stickley's Club House at Craftsman Farms." *Winterthur Portfolio* 31, no. 1 (spring 1996): 23–51. 17 bw illus.

Himmelheber, Georg. *Cast-Iron Furniture and All Other Forms of Iron Furniture.* London: Philip Wilson Publishers, 1996. 240 pp.; color and bw illus., bibliography, index. Distributed by Antique Collectors' Club, Wappingers Falls, New York. (Also published as *Mobel aus Eisen: Geschichte, Formen, Techniken* [Munich: C. H. Beck, 1996].)

Hines, Tommy. "Shaker Furniture from South Union, Kentucky." *Antiques* 151, no. 5 (May 1997): 724–31. 12 color and 1 bw illus.

Hohenlohische Möbelkunst in Dorf, Stadt, und Schloss: Eine Ausstellung in der Hirschwirtscheuer Künzelsau. Sigmaringen: Jan Thorbecke Verlag, 1996. 136 pp.; illus.

Home Furniture, no. 7 (summer 1996) through no. 11 (June/July 1997). (In addition to articles cited individually, this magazine contains short profiles and illustrations of work by contemporary woodworkers.)

Hornung, Clarence P. *Treasury of American Design and Antiques.* Reprint. New York: Abradale Books, Harry N. Abrams, 1997. xxvii + 846 pp.; 2,901+ color and bw illus., index.

Horton, Frank L., and Sally Gant. "An Eighteenth-Century Sideboard Table." *Antiques* 151, no. 1 (January 1997): 214–15. 2 color and 1 bw illus.

Hosley, William. *Colt: The Making of an American Legend.* Amherst: University of Massachusetts Press, 1996. 256 pp.; 50 color and 125 bw illus., bibliography.

Hosley, William. "The Romance of a Relic: Sam Colt's Charter Oak Relic Furniture." *Folk Art* 21, no. 3 (fall 1996): 49–55. 5 color and 3 bw illus.

Hosley, William. "Vermont's Finest: Vermont Furniture of the 18th and 19th Centuries and Its Makers." *Art & Antiques* 18 (October 1995): 68–73. Illus.

Howe, Katherine S. "The French Connection: The Herter Brothers, the Second Empire and Elm Park." *Nineteenth Century* 16, no. 2 (fFall 1996): 21–27. 10 bw illus.

Howlett, F. Carey. "Admitted into the Mysteries: The Benjamin Bucktrout Masonic Master's Chair." In *American Furniture 1996,* pp. 195–232. 45 color and bw illus.

Hughcs, Peter. *The Wallace Collection Catalogue of Furniture.* Vol. 1, *Gothic and Renaissance Style, Carved Furniture, Lacquer Furniture, Barometers, and Clocks.* Vol. 2, *Boulle Furniture, Veneered Furniture.* Vol. 3, *Gilt Bronze, Miscellaneous Pieces, Appendices, Index.* London: Wallace Collection and Antique Collectors' Club, 1996. 1700 pp.; 1150 color and bw illus.

Hughes, Robert. *American Visions: The Epic History of Art in America.* New York: Alfred A. Knopf, 1997. ix + 635 pp.; 365 color and bw illus., index. (Contains some furniture.)

Hummel, Charles F. Review of Johanna Miller Lewis, *Artisans in the North Carolina Backcountry.* In *Winterthur Portfolio* 31, no. 1 (spring 1996): 67–70.

[Hurwitz, Michael]. "Japanese-Inspired Furniture of Michael Hurwitz . . . at Peter Joseph to Nov. 30." *Antiques and the Arts Weekly* (October 18, 1996): 118.

[Ingersoll, Ian]. "Traditionalist Furniture." *Antiques and the Arts Weekly* (March 21, 1997): 19. 1 bw illus. (Re exhibition of contemporary woodwork at Brookfield [Conn.] Craft Center.)

Ioannou, Noris. *The Barossa Folk: Germanic Furniture and Other Craft Traditions in Australia.* Roseville East, New South Wales, Australia: Craftsman House, 1995. 368 pp.; color and bw illus., maps, bibliography, index.

Jaffee, David. Review of Philip Zea and Robert C. Cheney, *Clock Making in New England, 1725–1825: An Interpretation of the Old Sturbridge Village Collection.* In *Winterthur Portfolio* 30, nos. 2/3 (summer/autumn 1995): 182–84.

James, David. *The Upholsterer's Pocket*

Reference Book: Materials, Measurements, Calculations. Lewes, England: Guild of Master Craftsmen Publications Ltd., 1995. 167 pp.; color illus., 200+ line drawings, glossary, index. (Includes some references to old English furniture.)

Jenkins, Emyl. "The Chippendale Style." *Home Furniture*, no. 8 (October 1996): 78–83. 14 color and bw illus.

Jiaqing, Tian. *Classic Chinese Furniture of the Qing Dynasty*. Trans. Lark E. Mason, Jr., and Juliet Yung-Yi Chou. London: Philip Wilson, Joint Publishing, Antique Collectors' Club, 1996. 308 pp.; 350+ color and bw illus.

Jobe, Brock. "A Portsmouth Settee at Winterthur." *Antiques* 151, no. 1 (January 1997): 184–87. 4 color and 1 bw illus.

"John Widdicomb Furniture Exhibition Through September 12, [1996], in Grand Rapids." *Antiques and the Arts Weekly* (September 6, 1996): 67.

Johnson, Don. "Garth's Sells Paustenbach Collection of Pie Safes and Americana." *Maine Antique Digest* 25, no. 1 (January 1997): 12D–14D. 21 bw illus.

Johnson, Don. "Possessed Possessions: A Book Review." *Maine Antique Digest* 24, no. 10 (October 1996): 32D–33D. 2 bw illus.

Jones, David. *The Vernacular Chair in Fife*. Fife, Scotland: Kirk Wynd Press Cupar, 1996. Unpaged; illus., entries.

Kangas, Matthew. "Ries Niemi." *Metalsmith* 17, no. 2 (spring 1997): 38–39. 2 bw illus. (Exhibition review of contemporary metal furniture.)

Kaplan, Wendy, ed. *Charles Rennie Mackintosh*. New York: Abbeville Press and Glasgow Museums, 1996. 383 pp.; 114 color and 135 bw illus., chronology, bibliography, checklist, index.

Kelly, Caitlin. "Art Meets Craft." *Art and Antiques* 19 (summer 1996): 62–67. Illus. (Re contemporary studio furniture.)

Kennedy, Chris, Andy Lin, and Larry Weinberg. *Edward Wormley: The Other Face of Modernism: An Exhibition of Mid-Century Furniture Designs*. Ed. Judith Gura, Chris Kennedy, and Larry Weinberg. New York: DESIGNbase®/ Lin-Weinberg Gallery, 1997. 76 pp.; numerous bw illus., appendix, bibliography.

Keno, Leigh, Joan Barzilay Freund, and Alan Miller. "The Very Pink of the Mode: Boston Georgian Chairs, Their Export, and Their Influence." In *American Furniture 1996*, pp. 267–306. 47 color and bw illus.

Ketchum, William C., Jr. *Simple Beauty: The Shakers in America*. New York: Smithmark, 1996. 128 pp.; 130 color illus., index.

Kingery, W. David, ed. *Learning from Things: Method and Theory of Material Culture Studies*. Washington and London: Smithsonian Institution Press, 1996. x + 262 pp.; bw illus., bibliographical references.

Klimaszewski, Nicolai, with an essay by Peter Joseph. *New Furniture: Beyond Form and Function*. Ithaca, N.Y.: Herbert F. Johnson Museum of Art, Cornell University, 1996. n.p.; bw illus., checklist.

Knowles, Eric. *Discovering Antiques: A Guide to the World of Antiques and Collectibles*. New York: DeAgostini Editions, 1996. 224 pp.; 500+ color illus., bibliography, index.

Kolle, Jefferson. "Period Furniture in an Authentic Setting." *Home Furniture*, no. 11 (June/July 1997): 10, 12. 4 color illus. (Re Strawbery Banke Museum, Portsmouth, New Hampshire.)

Kolle, Jefferson. "A Shaker and a Mover." *Home Furniture*, no. 10 (April 1997): 20–23. 8 color illus. (Re contemporary woodworker Ian Ingersoll of West Cornwall, Connecticut.)

Kotula, Nickolas. "The Faking of Antique Furniture." *Maine Antique Digest* 25, no. 3 (March 1997): 44C–45C. 1 line drawing.

Kotula, Nickolas. "Historical Cabinet-making Construction." *Maine Antique Digest* 25, no. 3 (March 1997): 8C–9C. 6 bw illus.

Kramer, Miriam. "Report from Europe: Frames." *Antiques* 151, no. 1 (January 1997): 40. 3 color illus. (Re two London exhibitions of British picture frames.)

Lambert, Susan. *Form Follows Function*, vol. 2 of *Design in the 20th Century*. London: Victoria and Albert Museum, 1993. 72 pp.; 70 bw illus., bibliography, index.

Lambourne, Lionel. *The Aesthetic Movement*. London: Phaidon Press, 1996. 240 pp.; 140 color and 80 bw illus., bibliography, index.

Landsmark, Ted. "Sankofa: Honoring African-American Craft." *Antiques and the Arts Weekly* (October 15, 1996): 1, 68–70. 17 bw illus.

Landsmark, Ted. Review of Mary E. Lyons, *Master of Mahogany: Tom Day, Free Black Cabinetmaker*. In *American Furniture 1996*, pp. 309–11.

Leben, Ulrich. "Iron and Steel Furniture in France." *Antiques* 150, no. 3 (September 1996): 346–55. 17 color illus.

Lindsey, Jack L., and Darrel Sewell. *The Cadwalader Family: Art and Style in Early Philadelphia*. *Philadelphia Museum of Art Bulletin* 91, nos. 384–85 (fall 1996): 1–48. Color and bw illus., appendix, checklist, bibliography. (An issue containing four articles; see especially Lindsey's article, "The Cadwalader Town House and Its Furnishings," pp. 10–23.)

Linley, David. *Extraordinary Furniture*. New York: Harry N. Abrams, 1996. 192 pp.; 200 color and 30 bw illus., glossary, bibliography, index.

Locklair, Paula. "New in the Collection." *The Luminary* (Newsletter of the Museum of Early Southern Decorative Arts) 17, no. 2 (fall 1996): 6–7. 5 bw illus. (Includes references to pattern and price books; Virginia shaving stand, 1805–1815; and West Virginia cylinder desk, ca. 1805, acquired by the museum.)

Locklair, Paula. "New in the Collection." *The Luminary* (Newsletter of the Museum of Early Southern Decorative Arts) 18, no. 1 (spring 1997): 6–7. 7 bw illus. (Includes cherry armchair, South Carolina, 1640–1660, on loan to MESDA.)

Lovelace, Joyce. "Recalling Asilomar." *American Craft* 57, no. 3 (June/July 1997): 66–68. 9 bw illus.

Lucie-Smith, Edward. *The Art of Albert Paley: Iron, Bronze, Steel*. New York:

Harry N. Abrams, 1996. 231 pp.; numerous color and bw illus., catalogue, chronology, bibliography, index.

McCallum, Kent. *Old Sturbridge Village*. New York: Harry N. Abrams, 1996. 224 pp.; 80 color and 115 bw illus., index. (Includes a few references to furniture collection.)

McInnis, Maurie D., and Robert A. Leath. "Beautiful Specimens, Elegant Patterns: New York Furniture for the Charleston Market." In *American Furniture 1996*, pp. 137–74. 41 color and bw illus.

McPhee, John. "Furniture Stories: Horns." *Home Furniture*, no. 11 (June/July 1997): 86. 1 color illus.

Maher, Thomas K. *The Kaufmann Collection: The Early Furniture of Gustav Stickley*. Cincinnati, Ohio: Treadway Gallery, 1996. 106 pp.; color illus., bibliography.

Marling, Karal Ann. *Graceland: Going Home with Elvis*. Cambridge: Harvard University Press, 1996. 258 pp.; line drawings, sources. (Re a certain type of twentieth-century furniture and interior decoration.)

Marquette, Rona. "The Mysterious Case of the Himmelbergerin Chest." *Winterthur Magazine* 43, no. 2 (summer 1997): 31. 1 color illus.

Marsh, Madeleine. *Miller's Collecting the 1950s*. New York: Miller Publishing, 1997. 144 pp.; 300+ color and bw illus. Distributed by Antique Collectors' Club, Wappingers Falls, New York.

Mason, Lark E., Jr., and Hugo K. Weihe. "The Ultimate Folding Chair." *Sotheby's Preview* (October 1996): 37. 1 color illus. (Re Ming Dynasty Chinese chair to be offered at auction.)

Mayer, Roberta A. "The Aesthetics of Lockwood de Forest: India, Craft, and Preservation." *Winterthur Portfolio* 31, no. 1 (spring 1996): 1–22.

Mayor, Alfred. Review of Edward S. Cooke, Jr., *Making Furniture in Preindustrial America: The Social Economy of Newtown and Woodbury, Connecticut*. In *Antiques* 151, no. 1 (January 1997): 50. 1 color illus.

Mayor, Alfred. Review of Alexander von Vegesack, Peter Dunas, and Mathias

Schwartz-Clauss, eds., *100 Masterpieces from the Vitra Design Museum Collection*. In *Antiques* 151, no. 5 (May 1997): 662. 1 color illus.

Meikle, Jeffrey L. *American Plastic: A Cultural History*. New Brunswick, N.J.: Rutgers University Press, 1995. 403 pp.; 15 color and 55 bw illus., bibliography, index.

Menz, Christopher. *Australian Decorative Arts, 1820s–1990s: Art Gallery of South Australia*. Adelaide, Australia: Art Gallery Board of South Australia, 1996. 176 pp.; numerous color illus., checklist, bibliography, index. Distributed by Thames and Hudson. (Includes some furniture of comparative interest.)

Metcalf, Bruce. "Howard Werner." *American Craft* 57, no. 1 (February/March 1997): 92. 1 color illus.

[Metropolitan Museum of Art]. "Recent Acquisitions: A Selection, 1995–1996." *Metropolitan Museum of Art Bulletin* 54, no. 2 (fall 1996): 51. 1 bw illus. (Notation by Catherine Hoover Voorsanger on Herter Brothers side chair, ca. 1865–1870.)

Meyer, Marilee Boyd, and Barbara Rhines. "Boston: A City's Contribution to American Arts and Crafts." *Antiques and the Arts Weekly* (February 28, 1997): 1, 68–71. 12 bw illus.

Miller, J. Abbott. Review of Pat Kirkham, *Charles and Ray Eames: Designers of the Twentieth Century*. *Studies in the Decorative Arts* 4, no. 1 (fall/winter 1996–1997): 118–20.

Miller, Judith, and Martin Miller, eds.; John Bly, chief consultant ed.; Lita Solis-Cohen and Kelvyn Grant Lilley, American consultants *The Antiques Directory: Furniture*. Rev. ed. New York: Crescent Books, 1995. 639 pp.; 7,000 color and bw illus., glossary, index. Distributed by Random House Value Publishing.

Mitchell, Paul, and Lynn Roberts. *Frameworks: Form, Function, and Ornament in European Portrait Frames*. London: Paul Mitchell in association with Merrell Holberton, 1997. 480 pp.; 300 color, 70+ bw illus., bibliography, index. Distributed by University of Washington Press.

Mitchell, Paul, and Lynn Roberts. *A History of European Picture Frames*. London: Paul Mitchell in association with Merrell Holberton, 1996. 136 pp.; 36 bw illus., 56 line drawings, bibliography, index. Distributed by University of Washington Press.

Montgomery, Liza. "An Unlikely Trilogy" (book review). *Antiques and the Arts Weekly* (March 21, 1997): 110. 3 bw illus.

Mooberry, Doug. "A Cabinetmaker's Dream." *Home Furniture*, no. 8 (October 1996): 36–40. 9 color and 1 bw illus. (Includes note on "The Holmes Bookcase: A Colonial Treasure," by J. Thomas Savage.)

Moore, William D. "Masonic Lodge Rooms and Their Furnishings, 1870–1930." *Heredom: The Transactions of the Scottish Rite Research Society* 2 (1993): 99–136. Illus.

Moore, William D. "M.C. Lilley & Company: Manufacturers of Masonic Furniture." *The Scottish Rite Journal* 100, no. 9 (September 1992): 59–64. Illus.

Moore, William D. Review of John D. Hamilton, *Material Culture of the American Freemasons*. In *American Furniture 1996*, pp. 311–14.

Naeve, Milo M. "Louis Comfort Tiffany and the Reform Movement in Furniture Design: The J. Matthew Meier and Ernest Hagen Commission of 1882–1885." In *American Furniture 1996*, pp. 3–16. 16 bw illus.

Nelson, Marion John, ed. *Material Culture and People's Art among the Norwegians in America*. Northfield, Minn.: Norwegian-American Historical Association, 1994. xii + 228 pp.; 125 illus., bibliography.

Newell, Helen B., and Bruce R. Forman. "The Account Book of Jacob Hertz." *NAWCC Bulletin* 39, no. 3 (June 1997): 303–6. 3 bw illus.

Nylander, Richard C. "Inside SPNEA: Of Pointed Arches." *Old-Time New England* 74, no. 262 (fall 1996): 47–57. 12 bw illus.

"Of Angels and Insects in Remote Pennsylvania." *Christie's International Magazine* 14, no. 5 (June 1997): 84. 1 color illus. (Re chest of drawers,

1835–1840, from Mahantango Valley, Pennsylvania.)

Okonowicz, Ed. *Possessed Possessions: Haunted Antiques, Furniture, and Collectibles*. Elkton, Md.: Myst and Lace Publishers, 1996. 112 pp.; illus.

"Opulence and Distinction: Two Exhibits at MCNY Highlight N.Y. Craft." *Antiques and the Arts Weekly* (December 20, 1996): 50–51. 7 bw illus. (Re long-term installation of New York furniture entitled "Furniture of Distinction.')

Orlin, Lena Cowen. *Elizabethan Households: An Anthology*. Washington, D.C.: Folger Shakespeare Library, 1995. viii + 164 pp.; bw illus., index. (Re seventeenth-century English furniture.)

Ostergard, Derek E. "My Favorite Chair." In *[Catalogue of] The 42nd Annual Winter Antiques Show: A Benefit for East Side House Settlement*, pp. 14–17. New York, 1996. 4 color illus.

Palmer, Arlene. "Gustave Herter's Interiors and Furniture for the Ruggles S. Morse Mansion." *Nineteenth Century* 16, no. 2 (fall 1996): 3–13. 9 bw illus.

"A Parisian in New York." *Christie's International Magazine* 14, no. 5 (June 1997): 26. 1 color illus. (Re card table, ca. 1815, labeled by Charles-Honoré Lannuier.)

Parry, Linda. "William Morris and the Green Dining Room." *Antiques* 150, no. 2 (August 1996): 198–205. 10 color and 2 bw illus.

Parry, Linda, ed. *William Morris*. New York: Harry N. Abrams, 1996. 384 pp.; 394 color and 165 bw illus., checklist, bibliography, index.

Payne, Christopher. *Miller's Collecting Furniture: The Facts at Your Fingertips*. Woodbridge, England: Antique Collectors' Club, 1996. 192 pp.; illus.

Peck, Amelia, James Parker, et al. *Period Rooms in the Metropolitan Museum of Art*. New York: Harry N. Abrams in association with the Metropolitan Museum of Art, 1996. 304 pp.; 200 color and 25 bw illus.

Pierce, Donna, and Marta Weigle, eds. *Spanish New Mexico: The Spanish Colonial Arts Society Collection*. Sante Fe: Museum of New Mexico Press,

1996. Vol. 1, *The Arts of Spanish New Mexico*. xi + 171 pp.; 574 color illus., index. Vol. 2, *Hispanic Arts in the Twentieth Century*. xi + 111 pp.; numerous color and bw illus., appendixes, index.

Piña, Leslie. *Fifties Furniture*. Atglen, Pa.: Schiffer Publishing, 1996. 256 pp.; 426 color and bw illus., bibliography, index.

Podmaniczky, Michael. "A Thomas Crow Labeled Tall Clock." *Winterthur Magazine* 43, no. 2 (summer 1997): 20. 2 color illus.

Poesch, Jessie. Review of E. Bryding Adams, ed., *Made in Alabama: A State Legacy*. In *Winterthur Portfolio* 31, no. 1 (spring 1996): 73–77.

Pressler, Rudolf, and Robin Straub. *Biedermeier Furniture*. Atglen, Pa.: Schiffer Publishing, 1996. 230 pp.; 500+ illus.

Prown, Jonathan, and Richard Miller. "The Rococo, the Grotto, and the Philadelphia High Chest." In *American Furniture 1996*, pp. 105–36. 41 color and bw illus.

Puig, Francis J. Review of John A. Fleming, *The Painted Furniture of French Canada, 1700–1840*. In *American Furniture 1996*, pp. 314–18.

Randall, Richard H., Jr. "Designs for Philadelphia Carvers." In *American Furniture 1996*, pp. 57–62. 8 bw illus.

Rauschenberg, Bradford L. "An American Eighteenth-Century Garden Seat in the 'Chinese Taste.'" *The Luminary* (Newsletter of the Museum of Early Southern Decorative Arts)18, no. 1 (spring 1997): 1, 4–5, 8. 6 bw illus. (Re garden seat, Somerset County, Maryland, 1760–70, recently acquired by MESDA.)

Rauschenberg, Bradford L. "From Cupar, North Britain, to MESDA: A Unique Copy of Thomas Sheraton's 1793 *Cabinetmaker and Upholsterer's Drawing Book*." *The Luminary* (Newsletter of the Museum of Early Southern Decorative Arts) 17, no. 2 (fall 1996): 4. 1 bw illus. (Re English pattern book, acquired by MESDA, owned originally by cabinetmaker Robert Walker [1772–1833] of Charleston, S.C.)

Reed, Cleota. "Gustav Stickley and Irene Sargent: United Crafts and the Craftsman." *Syracuse University Library Associates Courier* 30 (1995): 35–50. Illus.

Regional Furniture 10 (1996): 1–129. 2 color and numerous bw illus. (Contains ten articles on a variety of topics pertaining to Irish, Australian, English, and other furniture.)

Regional Furniture Society Newsletter, no. 24 (summer 1996); no. 25 (winter 1996). Each 16 pp.; bw illus. (News, notes, reviews, pictures, and other useful information, primarily about English vernacular furniture.)

Roberts, Derek. *Skeleton Clocks: Britain, 1800–1914*. Woodbridge, England: Antique Collectors' Club, 1996. 272 pp.; 45 color and 358 bw illus.

Robinson, Mary E. G., and Charles A. Robinson. "The Ingalls and the Hoyts: 19th Century Windsor Chairmakers of Danville, Vermont." In *Village in the Hills,* ed. Susannah Clifford, pp. 237–48. West Kennebunk, Me.: Phoenix Publishing, 1994. Illus.

Robinson, Roger W., and Herschel B. Burt. *The Willard House and Clock Museum and the Willard Family Clockmakers*. Ed. Robert S. Edwards. [Columbia, Pa.]: [National Association of Watch and Clock Collectors], 1996. vii + 262 pp.; 370+ color and bw illus., appendix.

Rogers Historical Museum. *The Sagers: Pioneer Cabinetmakers*. Rogers, Ark.: by the Museum, 1996. 35 pp.; bw illus., bibliography.

Rogers, Malcolm, and Gilian Wohlauer. *Treasures of the Museum of Fine Arts, Boston*. New York: Abbeville Press, 1996. 320 pp.; 282 color illus., index. (Picture book with some illustrations of furniture.)

Rush, Michael. "James Schriber: Links to the Past." *American Craft* 56, no. 5 (October-November 1996): 68–71. 5 color illus.

Rush, Michael. "Michael Hurwitz." *American Craft* 57, no. 2 (April/May 1997): 62–66. 5 color illus.

[Sack, Israel, Inc.]. *Opportunities in American Antiques*. New York: Israel Sack, Inc., [1997]. 57 pp.; color and bw illus.

Sargentson, Carolyn. *Merchants and Luxury Markets: The Marchands Merciers of Eighteenth- Century Paris*. Malibu, Cal.: Victoria and Albert Museum in association with the J. Paul Getty Museum, 1996. 240 pp.; 30 color and 80 bw illus., bibliography, index. Distributed by Oxford University Press.

Sheary, Patrick. *American Case Furniture, 1680–1840: Selections from the DAR Museum Collection*. Washington, D.C.: DAR Museum, 1997. Unpaged; bw illus., checklist.

"Shelf Clock Brings $61,600 at Pook." *Antiques and the Arts Weekly* (December 27, 1996): 29. 3 bw illus. (Re Boston-style clock made by Lemist and Tappan of Philadelphia, ca. 1810.)

Sherman, Stuart. *Telling Time: Clocks, Diairies, and English Diurnal Form, 1660–1785*. Chicago: University of Chicago Press, 1996. xv + 323 pp.; illus., bibliography, index.

[Simpson, Tommy]. *Tommy Simpson*. New York: Leo Kaplan Modern, 1996. 24 pp.; color and bw illus.

Simon, Jacob. *The Art of the Picture Frame: Artists, Patrons, and the Framing of Portraits in Britain*. London: National Portrait Gallery, Antique Collectors' Club, 1997.

Smith, Thomas Gordon. "Living with Antiques: Millford Plantation in South Carolina." *Antiques* 151, no. 5 (May 1997): 732–41. 15 color and 2 bw illus.

Solis-Cohen, Lita. "Exhibition of What's Going on Around the Painting." *Maine Antique Digest* 24, no. 9 (September 1996): 44B–45B. 14 bw illus. (Re picture frame exhibition at Lowy Company, New York.)

Solis-Cohen, Lita. "Making a Market for Wharton Esherick's Work." *Maine Antique Digest* 24, no. 7 (July 1996): 44D–46D. 21 bw illus.

Solis-Cohen, Lita. "Shearer Desk Sells for $110,000." *Maine Antique Digest* 24, no. 7 (July 1996): 10A. 2 bw illus.

[Sotheby's]. "American Decorative Arts." In *Sotheby's Art at Auction: The Year in Review, 1995–96*, pp. 184–87. London: Conrad Octopus Limited, 1996. 6 color illus. (Includes some furniture.)

[Sotheby's]. *Important Americana: American Furniture, Clocks, Decorations, American Folk Art, Folk Paintings and 20th Century Self-Taught Art*. Sale 6957. New York: Sotheby's, January 17 and 19, 1997. Unpaged; numerous color and bw illus. (Includes biographies by Wendell Garrett and others of, and furniture from, the collections of Sadie Weiss Stauffer, Easton, Pennsylvania; Mr. and Mrs. Charles F. Schilling of Meadowbrook, Pennsylvania; Mr. and Mrs. James Eric Butt; Mr. and Mrs. S. Chesley Anderson, Alameda, California; and Frances Ingalls, Cleveland, Ohio. See also Sotheby's, *Arcade Auction: Property from the Collection of Mrs. Sadie W. Stauffer, Easton Pennsylvania*, sale 1561 [New York: Sotheby's, January 23, 1997].)

[Sotheby's]. *Important Americana from the Collection of Mr. and Mrs. James O. Keene*. Sale 6954. New York: Sotheby's, January 16, 1997. Unpaged; numerous color and bw illus. (Includes "James Keene, A Personal Reminiscence" by Graham Hood and other biographical material; contributions to catalogue entries by Joan Barzilay Freund.)

Southern Arts and Crafts, 1890–1940. Charlotte, N.C.: Mint Museum of Art, 1996. 136 pp.; numerous color and bw illus., biographies, bibliography. (Includes some furniture.)

"Southern Arts and Crafts: Birmingham Exhibits a Regional Phenomenon." *Antiques and the Arts Weekly* (March 15, 1997): 1, 68–69. 5 bw illus. (Includes some furniture.)

Sprigg, June. Review of Timothy D. Rieman and Jean M. Burks, *The Complete Book of Shaker Furniture*. In *Studies in the Decorative Arts* 4, no. 2 (spring/summer 1997): 123–25.

Swank, Scott T. Review of Marion Nelson, ed., *Norwegian Folk Art: The Migration of a Tradition*. In *Studies in the Decorative Arts* 4, no. 1 (fall/winter 1996–1997): 126–29.

Tacha, Athena. "Furnishings and Landscaping: Weltzheimer/Johnson House, Oberlin, Ohio." *Allen Memorial Art Museum Bulletin* 49, no. 1 (1995): 22–26. Illus., bibliography. (Included in a special issue of this journal devoted to a house designed by Frank Lloyd Wright.)

Tambini, Michael. *The Look of the Century*. New York: DK Publishing, 1996. 288 pp.; numerous color and bw illus., glossary, index.

Tenner, Edward. "The Life of Chairs." *Harvard Magazine* 99, no. 3 (January-February 1997): 46–53. 10 color and bw illus.

Thiel, P. J. J. van, and C. J. de Bruyn Kops. *Framing in the Golden Age: Picture and Frame in 17th-Century Holland*. Trans. Andrew P. McCormick. Amsterdam: Rijksmuseum; Zwolle: Waanders, 1995. 375 pp.; 33 color, numerous bw illus., line drawings, bibliography, indexes.

Three Centuries of New Hampshire Furniture Making. Concord: New Hampshire Historical Society; Canterbury, N.H.: New Hampshire Furniture Masters Association, 1996. Unpaged; color and bw illus. (Auction catalogue of contemporary furniture with essay by James L. Garvin on "New Hampshire as a Cabinetmaking State.")

"Treasure: Remains of the Day." *Harvard Magazine* 99, no. 5 (May/June 1997): 88. 1 color and 2 bw illus. (Re three chairs, ca. 1913–1914, made by A. K. Jones with wood from Harvard's Class Day Elm, and now in Harvard Archives collection.)

Varnum, William Harrison. *Arts and Crafts Design: A Selected Reprint of Industrial Arts Design*. Foreword by Timothy L. Hansen. 1916. Reprint. Salt Lake City, Utah: Gibbs Smith, 1995. 248 pp.; 2 color and 128 bw illus., 65 line drawings, index.

Vilinsky, Beth. "James Mont: The Bad-Boy of Mid-Century Modernism." *Christie's International Magazine* 14, no. 5 (June 1997): 22. 1 color illus.

von Vegesack, Alexander, Peter Dunas, and Mathias Schwartz-Clauss, eds. *100 Masterpieces from the Vitra Design Museum Collection*. Weil am Rhein, Germany: Vitra Design Museum, 1996. 270 pp.; 137 color and 285 bw illus., biographies.

Ward, Gerald W. R., comp. "Recent Writing on American Furniture: A Bibliography." In *American Furniture 1996*, pp. 323–34.

Waters, Deborah Dependahl. "Is It Phyfe?" In *American Furniture 1996*, pp. 63–80. 27 bw illus.

Weston, Richard. *Modernism*. London: Phaidon, 1996. 240 pp.; numerous color and bw illus., bibliography, biographies, index. (Includes some furniture.)

Wharton, Edith, and Ogden Codman, Jr. *The Decoration of Houses*. 1897. Reprint. New York: Classical America, The Arthur Ross Foundation, and W.W. Norton, 1996. 294 pp.; 16 color and numerous bw illus., index. (Includes modern essays by Henry Hope Reed, John Barrington Bayley, William A. Coles, and Alvin Holm, and other interpretive material.)

Wilk, Christopher, ed. *Western Furniture: 1350 to the Present Day in the Victoria and Albert Museum, London*. New York: Cross River Press, 1996. 231 pp.; 50 color and 250 bw illus., index.

William Morris Revisited: Questioning the Legacy. Essays by Jennifer Harris. [London]: [Crafts Council], [1996]. 95 pp.; color and bw illus.

[Winterthur Museum]. "Winterthur's Tall Clocks: Chimes of Earlier Times." *Winterthur Magazine* 43, no. 2 (summer 1997): 16–17. 4 color illus.

Wissing, Douglas A. "Forms of the Fatherland: Indiana Germans and Their Handmade Furniture, 1835–1860." *Traces of Indiana and Midwestern History, A Publication of the Indiana Historical Society* 8, no. 3 (summer 1996): 28–33. 5 color illus., bibliography.

"Women's Work." *Christie's International Magazine* 14, no. 1 (January-February 1997): 41. 2 color illus. (Re Sargent family Boston worktable, ca. 1800, and Corlis-Brown family Providence desk and bookcase, ca. 1769.)

Wood, David F. "A Group of Concord, Massachusetts, Furniture." *Antiques* 151, no. 5 (May 1997): 742–47. 12 color illus.

Wood, David F., ed. *The Concord Museum: Decorative Arts from a New England Collection*. Concord, Mass.: Concord Museum, 1996. xvii + 160 pp.; 29 color and numerous bw illus., appendix, index. (Includes furniture entries by David L. Barquist, Nancy Goyne Evans, Brock Jobe, Robert F. Trent, Gerald W.R. Ward, David F. Wood, and Philip Zea.)

Woodham, Jonathan M. *Twentieth-Century Design*. Oxford and New York: Oxford University Press, 1997. 287 pp.; 148 color and bw illus., bibliography, timeline, index.

Wright, Elizabeth, and James Broadbent. *Soft Furnishings, 1830–1930*. Glebe, Australia: Historic Houses Trust of New South Wales, 1995. 164 pp.; 235 illus. Distributed by Acanthus Books, New York. (Guide to "curtains, drapery, case-covers, blinds and trimmings.")

Zimmerman, Philip D. "The Art and Science of Furniture Connoisseurship." *Antiques* 152, no. 1 (July 1997): 96–103. 17 color illus., line drawing.

Zimmerman, Philip D. "The Livingstons' Best New York City Federal Furniture." *Antiques* 151, no. 5 (May 1997): 716–23. 16 color and 1 bw illus.

Index

Virginia, 177, 188–90; and neoclassical furniture, 54–55, 58, 62, 67, 77, 84, 91, 93, 102(n14); sgraffito, 135–36; trim on upholstered furniture, 274–76, 289, 294; and Winchester school, 255–57, 261–62. *See also* Carving; Inlay

de Hooch, Pieter, 30, 31(fig.)

Delaware Valley influences, 299–303, 309–10, 312, 317, 325, 327–28

de Longemare, Nicholas, 219–20

Dend hydrinade Astrea (Terkelsen), 203, 204(fig. 6)

Derby, Anstis, 104(n42)

Derby, Elias Haskett, 104(n38)

Derby family, 71

de Rochefort, Charles, 199, 222(n8)

Derrickson, Derrick, 22–23

de Schweinitz, Frederick, 308

Desel, Charles Lewis, 49, 51, 58, 59, 101(n5), 110

Deserne, Joseph, 29

Design: British/German influences in Charleston, 107–8, 115–24, 125(n15); Charleston and neoclassical, 47–48, 49–100; diffusion and, 329(n3); Dutch influence in Chesapeake, 21; and Eames furniture, 367–69; and French Huguenots in South Carolina, 197, 203–18; and furniture from western Maryland, 140–42, 143–49, 151–65; German-British exchanges of, 49, 113–15, 144; Irish influence in Virginia, 171, 172–93; neat-and-plain style, 17, 281, 349; Tennessee adaptations, 299–300, 304–28; Winchester school and furniture, 232–62, 300–303; and Windsor chairs, 361. *See also* Decoration; *specific designs*

Design books: and diffusion of new designs, 68, 303; furniture designs in, 17(fig.), 143, 349(fig.), 350(fig.), 351(fig.); in Tennessee, 322

Designs of Chinese Buildings, Furniture, Dresses, Machines, and Utensils (Chambers), 143

Desk-and-bookcases: Charleston neoclassical, 65, 79–81, 86(fig.), 87–88, 87(fig. 32); German, 102(n14); Philadelphia, 301, 302(fig.); Tennessee, 250, 259(fig.), 260(fig.), 265(n27), 304–5, 304(fig. 9), 305(figs.), 309–10, 309(fig.), 310(figs.), 311(fig. 18), 316, 318(fig.), 319–22(& figs.), 320(fig.), 321(fig.), 322(fig.), 324(fig.), 325, 327(fig.), 329(n5), 330(n7),

331(n16), 332(n25), 333(nn 26, 28); from western Maryland, 145–49, 146(figs.), 147(fig.), 151; West Virginia, 160–61; and Winchester school, 234(figs.), 235–37, 235(figs.), 240–41, 300–303, 300(fig.), 301(figs.), 303(fig. 6), 304–5. *See also* Secretary-and-bookcases

Desks: Tennessee, 306(fig. 13), 307, 329(n5); from western Maryland, 135(& figs.); and Winchester school, 161(figs.), 232, 233(figs.), 237, 238, 256, 257(figs. 47, 48), 261–62, 262(fig.), 263(n12)

DeVries, David Peterson, 22

Dickinson, Edmund, 274(fig. 12), 278

Dielenschrank, 112(fig.), 113

Dining tables: from eastern Virginia, 180–81, 184(fig. 27), 185(figs.), 192; imported from London, 352

"Diversity and Innovation in American Regional Furniture," xi

Doggett, Henry, 73

Doll, Anna Maria Schisler, 138

Doll, Catharina (Hartmann), 136

Doll, Charlotte Storm, 138

Doll, Conrad (grandson), 137(& fig.)

Doll, Conrad (son), 137, 138

Doll, Johannes (father), 136–37

Doll, Johannes (son), 137

Doll, Joseph, 136, 137, 138–39, 151, 167(nn 22, 23, 24, 25)

Donelson, John, 307, 308, 327

Donelson, John (son), 307

Donelson, Rachel Stockley, 307

Dorchester Mills, 104(n38)

Dorff, Tille, 132–33

Douglas, James, 342–56, 356(fig.)

Dovetail construction, 32, 39(n15), 365

Dowglas, Edward, 25

Downs, Joseph, xii, 4

Drake, William, 339

Drayton, John, 335

Dressing tables: from Boston, 15(fig.); design books and, 351(fig.); from eastern Virginia, 178, 179(fig. 17); and South Carolina Huguenots, 217(& fig. 38), 221(fig.)

Drexler, Arthur, 370

du Brevill, Jean, 212

Dulany, Daniel, 128

Dunston, William, 204

Durham, Walter, 308

Dutch immigrants, 21, 22–26, 198

Dutch influences, 21, 25–37, 44–45

Eames, Charles and Ray, 367–72

Eames Design (Neuhart and Neuhart), 370

Eames House (Steele), 370

Earl of Egremont, 339

Earl of Leicester, 21

Early American Furniture (Kirk), 363

Eastely, John, 258–60

Economy: Charleston, 47, 48, 72; of early western Maryland, 127–28; of Rappahannock River basin, 171, 192–93; in western Virginia, 230–31, 263(n7)

Eddis, William, 128, 129, 130

Edge rolls, 271–72, 273(& fig. 11), 283(fig. 28), 295

Edwards, John, 107

Edwards (John) House, 108(fig. 2)

Elder, William Voss III, xiii

Elfe, Thomas, 50, 111–12, 350, 352, 353

Elizabeth I, Queen, 21

Emmett, Dan, 9

Endicott family, 71

End of the Rebellion in the United States, The (Kimmel), 2(fig.)

England: exports to Charleston from, 336–57; furniture from, 67(fig. 19), 273(figs.); and the Netherlands, 21–22, 23. *See also* British influences

Entenza house, 370

Ethafoam, 289–90

Evans, Elijah, 143, 144(fig.)

Evans, Nancy Goyne, 359–62

Exhibitions, Eames, 371–72

Fairbanks, Jonathan, 20(n12)

Farley, Captain, 339

Fashion, Charleston, 335–57

Faulkner, William, 10, 11

Fawsett, John, 25

Fennimore, Donald L., 372–76

Fessler, John, Jr., 149, 168(n36)

Fessler, John, Sr., 138(fig.), 139, 149(& fig. 32), 151, 156(fig. 44), 157, 167(n26), 168(n39)

Fiddlebacks and Crooked-backs: Elijah Booth and the Other Joiners in Newtown and Woodbury, 1750–1820 (Cooke), 380

Fillson, John, 145, 168(n35)

Films, Eames, 371–72

Finch family, 177

Fine Points of Furniture: Early American (Sack), 363

Finlayson, Mungo, 50